PROMOTING AGRICULTURAL EXPORT CROPS & CO-OPERATIVE SOCIETIES
IN TANZANIA DURING THE BRITISH & POST COLONIAL ERA, C 1914 - 2014

Somo M.L. Seimu

TSL Publications

First published in Great Britain in 2022
By GWAA / TSL Publications, Rickmansworth

Copyright © 2022 Somo M.L. Seimu

ISBN / 978-1-914245-41-1

The right of Somo M.L. Seimu to be identified as the author of this work has been asserted by the author in accordance with the UK Copyright, Designs and Patents Act 1988.

All rights reserved. No part of this publication may be reproduced, stored in a retrieval system or transmitted, in any form or by any means without the prior written permission of the publisher, nor be otherwise circulated in any form of binding or cover other than that in which it is published and without a similar condition being imposed on the subsequent buyer.

Cover by Moses Liheta Seimu

Dedication

This book is dedicated to my wife and friend Severa and our sons Moses, Jordan and Fabian, who all along have been a source of inspiration to me. My sisters Graciana, Dominica, Devota and Pulkeria, also my brothers Festo and Basili, who have always and proudly given me the confidence. It is also dedicated to beloved father, Athanas Makanyaga Liheta, my beloved mother Apolonia Basili Liheta (*Binti Basili*), brothers, Borgias (*Jazz*), Veremundi (*Boss*) and Teofano (*Liheta*), Deo and my sisters Katarina and Veneranda (*Mama Sikujua*) who sadly are not around today to see this achievement.

Contents

Abbreviations	8
Preface	**11**
1. From the Berlin Conference to World War 1	**16**
Table 1: European powers' colonies by 1920	17
1.1: WWI in Europe and the German African colonies	21
1.2: Development in the African colonies	21
1.3: The colonial military and police forces	24
1.4: Paris Peace Conference	26
Table 2: Tanganyika Provinces and Districts, 1959	29
1.5: Poll and Hut Taxes	31
1.6: African Associations and involvement in political space	32
Table 3: Election Results 1960	41
1.7: Consolidation of TANU political power	42
2. Promotion of Cash Crop Farming	**47**
Table 4: Number of tax payers in all provinces, 1931	48
2.1: Characteristics of the agricultural sector	51
2.2: The Agricultural Department	56
Table 5: Staff of the Agricultural Department 1950-1960	57
2.3: Agricultural Research	58
3 Cash Crop Farming Among Smallholders	**60**
3.1: Cotton farming in the Western Cotton Growing Area	60
Table 6: Cotton seed distribution to growers in 1922-1927	63
3.2: Coffee farming in Kilimanjaro Region	67
Table 7: Coffee growers and farm size from 1928/29-1939/40	67
Table 8: Cotton Bales sold by Ginners 1935-1946	68
Table 9: Names of outstanding small scale coffee growers 1920s- 1930s	69
3.2.1: Role of the Colonial Authority	70
Table 10: Coffee producers and acreage	71
3.2.2: Settler reaction	71
3.2.3: Grower reaction against settler agitation	72
3.2.4: Colonial Authority reaction to settler agitation	75
Table 11: Coffee trees owned by KNPA members, 1930	76
3.3: Coffee farming in Kagera Region	76
3.3.1: Coffee industry under British rule, 1916-1961	77
Table 12: Coffee production and value for 1928-1929	78
3.3.2: Response from growers and chiefs	78
Table 13: Tons of coffee exports and revenue in GBP (Bukoba & Tanganyika)	80

Table 14: Number of coffee trees in Kagera Region by 1937	83
3.4. Coffee production in the Southern Highlands	85
Table 15: Coffee seedlings distributed to growers	86
Table 16: Coffee production zones in Rungwe and Mbozi	87
Table 17: Coffee production in tons	87
3.4.1. Coffee producing areas Rungwe and Mbozi Districts	87
Table 18: Coffee production in Mbeya and Rungwe Districts	87
Table 19: Coffee production groups in Rungwe Clusters	88
3.5. Rice production in Mbeya and Songwe Regions	88
Table 20: Rice varieties	88
4. Post-WW2 Agricultural Colonial Policy	**90**
5. Post-Independence Agriculture Policy	**94**
5.1: Agricultural development schemes	94
5.2: Socialism and self-reliance	95
6. Cash Crop Marketing	**98**
6.1: Coffee marketing by the KNPA	98
6.2: Coffee marketing in Bukoba	99
Table 21: Licensed and *abalanguzi* traders, 1930-1936	99
6.3: Statutory Marketing Boards	100
Table 22: Zomes and appointed agents	105
6.4: Cotton marketing in the WCGA	108
6.4.1: Cotton transportation in the WCGA	111
Table 23: Road funding in some districts in the WCGA	112
6.5: Tobacco marketing in Western Province	112
7. Emergence of Co-operatives	**114**
7.1. The Co-operative Societies' Ordinance	127
Table 24: Societies affiliated to the TCGA	130
7.2: Merchant opposition to the Co-operative Ordinance	130
8. Strangulation of the KNPA & Emergence of the KNCU	**132**
8.1: Imposition of the KNCU on coffee growers	138
8.2.1 Section 36 of the co-operative legislation	141
8.2.2: The Chagga Rule	142
Table 25: Coffee Production (in tons) and payment, 1932-1946	143
8.2.3: Riots against poor coffee price	144
8.2.4: The Native Agriculture Control Bill	150
8.2.5: Statutory marketing boards	152
9. Bugufi and NGOMAT	**156**
9.1: Bugufi	156
Table 26: Coffee production (tons) in Ngara, 1936/37 to 1950/51 seasons	157
Table 27: Coffee Buying Posts and Production (tons) in Bugufi	158
9.2: NGOMAT	158
Table 28: Tobacco production in Songea District	159

Table 29: Co-operatives, members, Tobacco produce and payments	160
10. Failed Attempts	**162**
10.1: Western Cotton Growing Area (WCGA)	162
10.2: Southern Highlands	164
10.3: Kagera Region	166
11. Post-World War Two Crop Marketing	**173**
11.1: Repeal of the Agricultural Control & Marketing Ordinance, 1937	175
11.2: Relaxation of Agricultural Marketing Emergency Orders	176
12. Agricultural Marketing Co-operatives (AMCOs)	**178**
12.1: The UNO	181
12.2: The 1945 Fabian Colonial Bureau Report	183
12.3: Colonial Office intervention	184
12.4: Amendments to the Co-operative Ordinance	186
Table 30: Co-operative Unions during the Colonial Era	192
Table 31: Number of Co-ioerative Societies in 1959 and 1960	192
12.4: Reaction to the Recommendations	192
13. Post World War II Co-operative Development	**194**
13.1: Southern Highlands Province	194
Table 32: Co-operative societies in Kyela, Rungwe and Mbozi	196
13.2: The Bukoba Co-operative Union	198
Table 33: Licensed Coffee Dealers in Bukoba District Chiefdoms	199
13.2.1: Political Decisions	202
13.2.2: Development in Bukoba after WWII	205
13.2.3: Development in the WCGA	217
Table 34: Secondary Societies (Unions) Affiliated to the VFCU	221
14. Post-colonial Era	**222**
14.1: Co-operative Movement Expansion Policy	222
Table 35: Number of Co-operative Societies, 1961-1971	225
Table 36: Regional/area Distribution of Co-operatives, 1965	226
Table 37: Co-operative Unions Registered after Independence	228
14.2. The Presidential Commission	230
14.3. Dismantling agricultural marketing secondary societies	234
Table 38: Regional Co-operative Unions	235
14.3 Ideological orientation and National Development Plans	240
14.4. Illegitimacy of primary marketing co-operatives	240
14.5. The disbandment of co-operative unions	242
Table 39: Co-operative Societies in Tanzania as at June 2011	252
15. Conclusion	**253**
References	**262**

Abbreviations

AMNUT	All Muslim National Union of Tanganyika
ANC	African National Congress
ASP	Afro-Shirazi Party
BNCB	Bukoba Native Coffee Board
CCM	Chama Cha Mapinduzi
CO	Colonial Office
CS	Chief Secretary
CUT	Co-operative Union of Tanganyika
DA	Director of Agriculture
DC	District Commissioner
DO	District Officer
GAPEX	General Agricultural Export Company
ICA	International Co-operative Alliance
JUWATA	Jumuiya ya Wafanyakazi Tanzania
KNCS	Kilimanjaro Native Co-operative Society
KNCU	Kilimanjaro Native Co-operative Union
KNPA	Kilimanjaro Native Planters Association
LEGCO	Legislative Council
LSMB	Lint and Seed Marketing Board
MNCB	Moshi Native Coffee Board
NA	Native Authority
NAPB	National Agricultural Products Marketing Board
NCU	Nyanza Co-operative Union
NDL	National Distributors Limited
NEC	National Executive Council
NGA	Native Growers Association
NGOMAT	Ngoni and Matengo Co-operative Union
NMC	National Milling Corporation
NUTA	National Union of Tanganyika Workers
OTTU	Organisation of Tanzania Trade Unions
PC	Provincial Commissioner
PDP	People's Democratic Party
RTC	Regional Trading Companies
SILABU	Sisal Labour Bureau
SNA	Secretary for the Native Affairs
TAA	Tanganyika African Association
TANU	Tanganyika African National Union
TFL	Tanganyika Federation of Labour
TFTU	Tanzania Federation of Free Trade Unions

TNA	Tanzania National Archive
TRAU	Tanganyika Railway African Union
UCS	Union of Co-operative Societies
UNO	United Nations Organisation
URT	United Republic of Tanzania
UTP	United Tanganyika Party
VFCU	Victoria Federation of Co-operative Union
WCGA	Western Cotton Growing Area

Preface

This book begins by examining political and historical developments in mainland Tanzania with specific focus on the agricultural export crops such as coffee, cotton and tobacco produced by the African small-scale growers in various districts which from the 1930s were marketed through agricultural marketing co-operatives. The book first traces the colonization of the territory by two European powers which were fundamental in promoting agricultural export crops by small-scale growers and eventually the emergence of co-operatives.

The first colonial power in the territory was Germany which colonised the country then called German East Africa (GEA) that comprised Tanganyika, Rwanda and Burundi from 1885 to 1919. The British followed from 1919 to 1961. During its rule in GEA, the Germans invested in transport infrastructure, installed communication lines, built a military force (*Schutztruppe*) and developed tropical agricultural research stations. In collaboration with missionaries they promoted export crops among African small-scale producers. Importantly, they promoted two parallel competing agricultural sectors split between European plantation/settlers and African small-scale growers.

They subdivided the territory into districts, headed by district Commissioners, to facilitate colonial administration. At village levels *Akida* and *Jumbe* were deployed from coastal villages and townships to help in administration, collection of taxes, judge criminal and other cases and recruit labourers for colonial projects. Political differences between Germans and Arabs, also religious misunderstandings, that is Muslims and Christian Missionaries as well as the colonial officials, marked the beginning of the replacement of *Akida* and *Jumbe* who were Muslim by the missionary-educated local personnel.

The book analyses the preparations and strategies associated with the longest battle which ever took place in Sub-Sahara Africa, First World War, 1914–1919 that saw the Germans ousted by the British King's African Rifles (KAR) and Belgian *Force Publique*. This was the longest war fought in the country owing to resistance from GEA's military force, the *Schutztruppe* that was under command of Paul Emil von Lettow-Vorbeck. The Germans were defeated and all German colonies were placed under the League of Nations Mandate System which was instituted in 1919. The administration of then GEA was handed to the British under Article 119 of the 1919 Versailles Peace Treaty supervised by the League of Nations. The Peace Treaty marked the beginning of British rule in the country that it renamed

Tanganyika; a name that was maintained until 1964 when the country (Tanganyika) and Zanzibar formed a Union, becoming Tanzania.

The British adopted most of the German colonial policies, rebuilt damaged transport infrastructure, and facilitated the revival of abandoned plantations. The British divided the territory into three administrative levels: the provinces, districts and Native Authorities (NA). The German's 11 districts were redivided into 24 and placed under 8 provinces, headed by district and provincial commissioners respectively. The creation of the NAs were provided for under the Indirect Rule policy. Under the NA villages came under chiefs and headmen all with birth roots originating from within the local ethnic groups. The NAs collected taxes, judged cases based on customary law, recruited labourers for colonial projects and for plantations, and bought crops from growers under the Native Treasury No. 2 and Suspension Accounts.

The British perpetuated a land policy that restricted land alienation to limit the number of landless populations, brought in land legislation that provided Africans access to land ownership based on customary law that they used to produce both food and cash crops. The genesis of land policy in Tanzania is the Land Ordinance (Cap.68) of 1923, which was based on the Northern Nigerian ordinance of 1907. The two competing agricultural sectors split between European plantation/settlers and African small-scale growers that originated in the German colonial era were maintained. Thus, African small-scale growers were favourably accommodated and encouraged to produce economic crops such as coffee, cotton and tobacco alongside the settlers. The European plantation and settlers depended on African labourers who were recruited from various parts within the country of which the NA played a part. Some labourers were recruited from neighbouring countries. Further impetus for labour recruitment to work in sisal plantations was evident from the mid-1940s due to increased sisal fiber demand in the world market.

The colonial authority ensured African small-scale growers produced cash crops facilitated by enforcement of compulsory measures. The growers were supplied with seeds and provision of farming and post-harvest guidelines. A series of African-produced crops legislation and policies as well as markets for the produce were put oin place. Encouragement to produce these crops was sustained regardless of the situation, whether economic stability and prosperity or economic depression and the Second World War. The main crop buyers were farmer-based organisations, private traders (merchants mostly of Indian background), and the Native Administration under the Native Treasury No. 2 and Suspension Accounts.

From the 1920s the welfare of the people in the territory was a priority as required by the League of Nations and maintained under the United

Nations Organisation (UNO). This enabled the colonised to form associations and organisations to protect and serve their interests. This marked an era when tens of organizations were established that drew membership from various nationalities such as Africans, Asians (Indians in particular) and Europeans. These ranged from workers in industrial, transport (railway, habour), domestic and plantation sectors. The African workers in these sectors organised themselves under the Tanganyika African Association (TAA) which became pivotal in the rise of the labour movement and eventually the political struggle for independence. TAA for example was transformed into a political organisation, the Tanganyika African National Union (TANU) in 1954 and became so popular that it galvanised trade unions, traders and co-operatives, successfully leading them in pressing for independence from the British, who granted it in December 1961.

The small-scale growers too formed farmer-based organisations. The most popular and 'troublesome' was the Kilimanjaro Native Planters Association (KNPA) formed in 1922 and registered in 1925. The plantation owners as well as settlers had their associations that served and protected their interests. The KNPA had support from colonial officials, but lost its credibility due to opposition against some colonial policies. As the KNPA became unpopular among colonial officials it was labeled a subversive organization which required replacing as a matter of urgency. Hence, promulgation of the Co-operative Ordinance in 1932 that provided for the formation and registration of agricultural marketing co-operatives first in Kilimanjaro where in 1933 the Kilimanjaro Native Co-operative Union (KNCU) and its affiliated societies were registered. This development was followed by Bugufi in Biharamulo district (now Ngara district) and in Ruvuma region then Songea district in 1936. The Indian community, Ismailia sect in particular traders, exploited this opportunity to form and register savings and credit co-operative societies from 1938. Thereafter, the colonial authority obstructed all initiatives emanating from growers in the territory to form and register co-operatives.

Moreover, the protests, Coffee Riots in Moshi districe, poor produce prices and attempts to hold up cocoa produce in West Africa prompted the creation of producer marketing boards. In Tanzania, the first was the Moshi Native Coffee Board (MNCB) and several other localised crop-specific boards like the Bukoba Native Coffee Board set up to control agricultural produce of which co-operatives were appointed agents of the boards as per the legislation that provided for their formation.

The 1940s and 1950s were decades that saw growing interest and pressure from international organisations for agricultural marketing co-operatives in the colonies. The Colonial Office, Fabian Colonial Bureau, UNO and International Labour Organization (ILO) were all involved and fruitfully engaged colonial authorities across colonies to form co-operatives to serve the interests of the colonised. The move was partly to engage the colonised to be part of the economic restructuring after Second World War devastation and to improve co-operative members' livelihood. These were decades when agricultural crop prices in the world market were favourable so that encouragement of co-operatives was viewed by the colonial power as facilitating the extraction of agricultural resources to generate colonial government revenues and were therefore exploited to provide in the expansion of crop farming, deliver extension services to growers and provide reliable markets across villages.

Consolidation of powers under the ruling party, TANU became a common feature soon after independence. For example, the trade unions were brought under government control owing to a number of strikes. The local government created under the auspices of indirect rule by British colonial power was brought to an end. The political scenario witnessed adoption of a one-party state enriched under the interim constitution. Such political development has a premise anchored on majority votes TANU won during the late 1950 and early 1960s' elections. Thus, all opposition political parties in the country were declared illegal.

The book shows that attainment of independence was characterised by continuity of the colonial agricultural policies and encouragement of agricultural marketing co-operatives. At this stage, the co-operatives were 'temporarily' spared government's control. Thus, they retained their business status and position in handling crops but as the crop marketing boards' agents. Moreover, the co-operatives' position was reinforced as they were required to handle and monopolise marketing of all crops (both cash and food) largely to circumvent private traders.

This was further reinforced through nationalization of major means of production and services under *Azimio la Arusha* (ArD) that shaped and marked a stepping stone for a socialist ideological (*Ujamaa*) orientation in the country. Agricultural marketing co-operatives from the onset of independence were considered key partners in the development of the country's economy. Against this backdrop, it was an obligation for the co-operatives to comply with the 1960's government policies on rural development, propagating *Ujamaa* ideology and formation of the apex organization, the Co-operative Union of Tanganyika (CUT) with its formation engineered by the government. At the same time, the government embarked upon promotion of co-operatives in villages across the country.

By the mid-1960s agricultural marketing co-operatives faced a business crisis; several were terminated and some became bankrupt due to poor management. Several restructurings followed, especially when the President appointed a Commission to investigate the challenges facing agricultural marketing co-operatives. One of the recommendations adopted by the government was the formation of regional co-operatives that ended decades of the colonial created structure. The 1970s saw implementation of most of the Presidential recommendations, for example, replacement of the marketing boards by crop authorities. Strangulation of agricultural marketing co-operatives following a declaration of preference for villages as a new type of co-operative that culminated in abolishing regional co-operative unions at a time when the country was crippled by economic crisis. Towards the end of 1970s, the ruling party was renamed *Chama cha Mapinduzi* (CCM) that provided a platform for having a new constitution in 1977 that recognised the ruling party as not only a political party but also supreme. CCM's supremacy provided a basis for bringing all organizations under the ruling party. At this juncture, co-operatives were not spared, hence, CUT renamed *Jumuiya ya Washirika* as per the *Jumuiya ya Washirika* Act of 1979, 9 of 23 May, made *Washirika* the sole representative of the co-operative movement in Tanzania and a political wing for control of the entire movement's members.

The abolition of the agricultural marketing co-operatives lasted for less than six years. New legislation was passed in 1982 to restore the agricultural marketing co-operatives. All in all, most could not recover from the damage caused. The restoration coincided with a free market economy. Most could not compete with traders in terms of price paid to growers and most had lost their foreign markets. Thus recovery became a challenge throughout the 1990s and 2000s. The very law that restored agricultural marketing co-operatives maintained perpetuation of ruling party influence and control over the co-operatives. The 1992 and 2003 co-operatives legislation made little difference. The 2013 legislation was a significant departure as it restricted politicians from being co-operative society office bearers.

1. From the Berlin Conference to World War 1

By the nineteenth century Germany was an industrial power-house in Europe fostering imperial expansion in search and control of raw materials and markets for its manufactured commodities. Other European countries like Belgium, Britain, France and Portugal had for centuries been pre-occupied with commercial activities across continents that culminated in the scramble for commercial control in Africa, at its height, when Germany joined in. By the last quarter of the nineteenth century the Belgian King was well established in the Congo Basin, Britain had an influence along the West Africa coast, the Nile River, Southern and Central Africa, while France was well established in West Africa, and Portugal was established in Angola, Guinea-Bissau, São Tomé and Príncipe, Cape Verde and today's Mozambique.

Germany was a newcomer to empire-building following its unification. From the early 1870s, the Germans had a well-established interest in German East Africa, German West Africa, Cameroon and Togo. Despite the European countries having established interests in the various African territories, boundaries were not in existence which presented room for potential conflict. Moreover, none officially recognised the interests of another so that in 1884/85 the European powers convened in Berlin for a conference at the invitation of the German Chancellor, Otto von Bismarck, to regulate activities linked to colonisation. The Berlin Conference not only partitioned the African continent among European powers but also ensured the Congo Basin was free for trade that extended east to the Indian Ocean which the Sultan of Zanzibar agreed.[1] It opened the Niger and Congo rivers for international navigation and declared them neutral in case of war. At the time of colonisation, Tanzania mainland was landlocked as 10 kilometres along the coastline was under control of Zanzibar's Sultan. The barrier was removed upon Germany's purchase of the strip.[2]

The Berlin Conference participants were Germany, Austria-Hungary, Belgium, Denmark, France, Britain, Italy, the Netherlands, United States of America (USA), Portugal, Russia, Spain, Sweden, Norway, and the Ottoman Empire. The conference was called to discuss inter-alia:

a. Solving European rivalries especially in strategic areas, for instance France and Britain in Egypt over the Suez Canal.

---

[1] Heinz Schneppen, *Why Tanzania is where it is: Tanzania's Colonial Boundaries from Berlin Conference 1984-1885 until its independence* (Dar es Salaam: National Museums of Tanzania Occasional paper no. 11, 1998) pp. 1-3

[2] Heinz Schneppen, *Why Tanzania is where it is*, p. 1

b. Making peaceful agreements in partitioning the African continent.

Sweden had an interest in the conference which was to ensure its missionaries operating in Congo were protected.[1] However, none of the African ethnic groups or chiefdoms were invited to the conference. The European powers agreed the 'right to conquest' and brought to an end the existing chiefdoms, as all African ethnic groups were brought under control of a specific European colonial power. The 1884/5 Berlin conference concluded the scramble for Africa and confirmed the colonisation of African countries by European nations.[2] Two African countries, Ethiopia and Liberia, remained under indigenous control until the outbreak of WWI.

Table 1: European powers' colonies by 1920

Colonial powers	Colonies in Africa	Colonies outside Africa
Britain	33	50
France	8	33
Germany	4	13
Portugal	5	2
Belgium	1	1

Source: John Atkinson Hobson, *Imperialist parallels then and now Part I New Imperialism 1884-1913*, 1902

The Berlin Agreement of 1885 included a provision which implied that countries holding territory in the central strip of Africa running between the Atlantic and Indian Oceans could proclaim the area neutral in the event of a European war. The agreement also provided for free trade, freedom of religion and worship, and special protection for missionaries and explorers across the continent. The agreement (the Berlin Act) spelt out that:

a. To gain public acceptance, the primary purpose of the conference was to end slavery by Black and Islamic powers and to prohibit the slave trade in their respective spheres.
b. The Congo Free State was confirmed as private property of the Congo Society ensuring this was the private property of King of the Belgians, Leopold II.
c. 14 signatory powers were entitled to free trade in the Congo basin and Lake Nyasa (Lake Malawi).
d. Niger and Congo rivers were declared free for shipping traffic to export raw materials.
e. The Principle of Effective Occupation to stop powers setting up colonies in name only was limited to the African irregular coast but colonial

---

[1] David Nilsson, Sweden-Norway at Berlin Conference, 1884-85: History, National Identity-Making and Sweden's Relations with Africa, *Current African Issues* 53 (Nordica Africa Institute Uppsala, 2013)

[2] Archibald Church, *East Africa: A New Dominion A Crucial Experiment in Tropical Development and its Significance to the British Empire* (London: H.F. & G. Witherby, 1927) p. 32

powers claimed rights over lands in the interior by establishing a base on the coast.
f. Any new acts of possession of any portion of the African coast had to be notified to all signatory powers.
g. In marking regions or 'spheres of influence', each European power had an exclusive right to 'pursue' the legal ownership of land in the eyes of the other European powers.

Between 1885 and 1890, the German Empire annexed the two independent African kingdoms of Rwanda and Burundi, forming the north-western portion of what became the colony of German East Africa (the *Deutsche Ostafrikanische Eisenbahngesellschaft*; DOAEG/GEA).[1] This area was not effectively occupied or controlled by the colonial power, however. For the Belgians, the German presence in East Africa was a threat to the security of Congo. Germany thus had four colonies in Africa which were Togoland, Cameroon, Namibia (then South West Africa) and German East Africa (later Tanganyika and now Tanzania, Rwanda and Burundi).[2]

Prior to World War One (WWI), none of the European powers envisaged their African colonies becoming involved in a European war as the Berlin Act of 1885 included neutrality clauses for the various colonies in sub-Saharan Africa.[3] Against this backdrop, the governors of German East Africa and British East Africa (modern-day Kenya) signed the 1885 Congo Act that stated that African colonies would remain neutral in the event of an European war.

Dr Heinrich Schnee, a civilian governor of GEA took office in 1912. This was after some years of native resistance against colonial imposition, for example the Arabs' resistance along the coast led by Bushiri ibn Salim al Harth that lasted for two years, 1888 to 1889,[4] and resistance from the WaHehe of Iringa under Chief Mkwawa against some of the cotton farming policies along the coast and as far as Mahenge which led to the conflict popularly referred to as *maji maji*. By the outbreak of WWI, the *schutztruppe* (armed force) had accumulated extensive combat experience and knowledge of the terrain from quelling several uprisings in GEA. The appointment of Schnee was an indication that stability as well as law and order were achieved and martial law was no longer necessary with the exception of Iringa and Mahenge. Moreover, his appointment as governor marked the

---

[1] Robert M. Mambo, Mittleafrika: The German Dream of An Empire Across Africa in the Late 19th and Early 20th Centuries: An Overview, *Transafrican Journal of History* vol. 20 (1991) pp. 161-180. Charles Horden & H. Fitz M. Stack (eds) *Military Operations in East Africa Volume 1, August 1914 – September 1916* (London: HMSO, 1941) p. 525

[2] Mambo, Mittleafrika, pp. 161-180

[3] Horden & Stack (eds) p. 525

[4] Valerie J. Hoffman, East Africa from: The Islamic World Routledge, In Andrew Rippin (ed), *The Islamic World* (London: Routledge, 2008) pp. 39-52

beginning of the civilian administration in GEA. Against this backdrop, it was unnecessary and costly to keep a large *schutztruppe* and the army was placed under a civilian commander, the governor.

After establishing peace and order in the country, the Germans proceeded to install a railway system and to build harbours necessary for the economic development of the territory. The Central Railway extended from Dar es Salaam through Tabora to Kigoma – a distance of 1,250 kilometres built by Greek contractors.[1] The railway infrastructure consumed large sums of money, mostly a loan amounting to about 156,000,000 marks.[2] The Germans also built the Usambara Railway which ran from Tanga on the coast to Moshi, covering a distance of 354 kilometres, and planned to build a railway from Tabora on the Central Railway to Shinyanga, Lake Victoria Nyanza and eventually to Ruanda and Urundi, and to extend the Usambara Railway to Arusha and – plans which the war brought to an untimely end.[3]

The British saw Germany's improvement of the transport infrastructure as well as the wireless communication network designed for German shipping lines and which provided telegraph services to various administrative stations in its colonies as nothing other than preparing for domination of the continent and thus a threat to British economic interests. Telegraphic stations were erected by the Germans along major Central Railway line stations such as Dar es Salaam, Morogoro, Kilimatinde, Ujiji (Kigoma) and Mpwapwa. There were also some stations along the Tanga line (Usambara Railway), namely Korogwe, Mombo, Moshi and Arusha, and in the northwest at Mwanza. Along the coast, stations were erected in such towns as Bagamoyo, Pangani and Tanga.[4]

The Central Railway in GEA posed serious commercial competition to the Mombasa–Uganda Railway for imports and exports from Great Lake countries such as Belgian Congo.[5] The German intention behind investing in railway infrastructure was to exploit business opportunities in the Belgian Congo as provided for under the Berlin Act which stipulated that the country was free for anyone to further commercial interests.[6] The planters and settlers in the Eastern Congo felt it was an opportunity for an alternative export route for their agricultural goods. Central Railway construction began in 1905, reached Morogoro in 1907, then Tabora in 1912 and was completed when it reached Kigoma town on the Lake Tanganyika shore in 1914. The British viewed construction of the railway as a preparatory attempt for rapid deployment of military forces in case of war and a step

[1] Raymond Leslie Buell, *The Native Problem in Africa* (New York: Macmillan, 1928) p. 425
[2] Buell, *The Native Problem in Africa*, p. 426
[3] Ibid.
[4] Mambo, *Mittleafrika*, pp. 161-180
[5] Albert F. Calvert, *German East Africa* (London: T. Werner Laurie, 1917) p. 111
[6] Calvert, *German East Africa*, pp. 29-30

towards an invasion of neighbouring Congo.

Additionally, Cameroon, a German colony, was a threat to British interests in West Africa as both the German territory and Nigeria, a British colony, fell outside the Congo Neutrality Act. Thus, the outbreak of WWI was an opportunity to address such a threat on Britain's West Africa doorstep.

In the 1890s, Portugal had financial difficulties that prompted laying off civil servants, cutting salaries for those not affected and terminating various development projects.[1] Yet, it could still not pay its external debts and thus political turmoil was evident in its colonies.[2] Portugal approached Britain for a loan. The circumstances appeared clear that Portuguese colonies would be used as mortgage either as collateral for a loan or as means for loan repayment. Upon leakage of this information, Germany showed an interest in collaborating with Britain in providing a loan to Portugal. This was interpreted by Germany as an opportunity for acquiring new colonies in Africa, particularly Angola, Canaries/Cape Verde, Walvis Bay, northern Mozambique, southern Malawi which was British, Zanzibar and East Timor in Asia.[3]

However, the German ambition did not materialise as Britain had signed treaties with both Portugal and Zanzibar which Britain was not prepared to betray.[4] Moreover, Britain rejected the German idea because it was unhappy seeing Germany's interest in Zanzibar where it had political and commercial interests. Similarly, on learning of Germany's interest in its colonies, Portugal became suspicious and refused to co-operate with Germany. Against this backdrop, the Portuguese believed Britain would be a reliable ally against Germany's ambition to expand into Portuguese colonies.

Despite these difficulties, the acquisition of new colonies that would supply raw materials for Germany's expanding industrial sector was a priority. However, this did not materialise until the outbreak of WWI when the invasion and occupation of Belgium by the Germans in 1914 was employed as a carrot and stick to demand Belgium hand over the Belgian Congo as a condition to withdraw its forces.[5] This move annoyed other powers, especially Britain and the United States of America (USA).

---

[1] Robert Dennis Fiala, The Anglo-German agreement over Portugal's African colonies, 1898 (Master of Arts Dissertation, University of Nebraska at Omaha, 1963, Student Work. 437. https://digitalcommons.unomaha.edu/studentwork/437)

[2] P. White, *A Century of Spain and Portugal. 1788-1898* (London: Methuen & Co., 1909) pp. 350-351

[3] Mambo, Mittleafrika, pp. 161-180

[4] Ibid.

[5] Editorial Notes, *Journal of African Affairs*, vol. 16 (1916-1917) p. 337

1.1: WWI in Europe and the German African colonies

The First World War began in eastern Europe following the assassination by Bosnian-Serb student Gavrilo Pricip of Archduke Franz Ferdinand, the heir to the Austrian throne, and his wife on 28 June 1914 at Sarajevo. This set off a series of events which led to the outbreak of war,[1] as Austria responded militarily against Serbia with the approval of its ally, Germany. Since Serbia had Slavic ties with Russia more countries were brought into action.

Other alliances came into play.[2] For example, Russia began to mobilise its armed forces to protect Serbia, which brought Germany into the war in defence of its ally Austria-Hungary. France had a diplomatic treaty with Russia; and Britain had a similar treaty with France. Since France was obliged by treaty to support Russia, Germany saw the two as a threat and declared war against both Russia and France.[3] In attacking France, Germany invaded Belgium on 4 August 1914. Belgium then requested support from Britain, the latter responding positively by declaring war against Germany the same day (4 August 1914).[4]

By then several British territories such as India, Australia, South Africa and Canada had offered their support to the colonial power. Portugal entered the war in March 1916, while the USA was drafted into the war against Germany in April 1917 to protect its interests.[5] Japan joined the war in support Britain, as did Italy in 1915.

1.2: Development in the African colonies

Germany, however, had been making war preparations for years under the Schlieffen Plan. The Belgian authority saw this as a threat to its European soil as well as its colony in Africa, today's Democratic Republic of Congo, then the Belgian Congo.

Such a threat changed the Belgian government's commitment to uphold the Congo Neutrality Act because it became a matter of urgency to defend its territory. Hence, Belgium went to war against Germany not only in Europe, but also in Africa where its colony shared its eastern border with GEA.

At the outbreak of WWI in Europe, Dr Heinrich Schnee did not

---

[1] Samuel R. Williamson, Jr, The Origins of World War I, *The Journal of Interdisciplinary History*, vol. 18, no. 4, The Origin and Prevention of Major Wars (Spring, 1988) pp. 795-818, doi.org/10.2307/204825

[2] Anne Samson, *World War I in Africa: The Forgotten Conflict among the European Powers* (London: IB Tauris, 2013) pp. 167-185

[3] Steven E. Miller (ed), *Military Strategy and the Origins of the First World War: An international Security Reader* (Princeton, 1980)

[4] Bernadotte E. Schmitt, The First World War, 1914-1918, *Proceedings of the American Philosophical Society*, vol. 103, no. 3 (15 June 1959) pp. 321-331

[5] Schmitt, The First World War, pp. 321-331

envisage that GEA would be a theatre of war. As it turned out it was the only colonial theatre where the German force managed to evade capitulation until the armistice was signed in Europe.[1] Schnee's standpoint was based on his thinking that the European powers would uphold the neutrality of colonies in case of hostility in Europe as provided for by the Berlin Act. However, he was worried that the colonised would exploit the war against his administration if incited by the British.[2] Generally, Schnee did not support the idea of drafting the country into war as he was well aware of the consequences. Instead, Schnee's priority was infrastructure development and improvement of the colonised througheconomic projects.

In January 1914 Lieutenant Colonel Paul Emil von Lettow-Vorbeck was deployed to GEA as military commander.[3] Understandably, von Lettow-Vorbeck's view was not the same as the governor's. The governor was civilian personnel whose thinking was political, looking to adhere to the Berlin Act on neutrality whereas von Lettow-Vorbeck had military solutions for resolving conflicts. Von Lettow-Vorbeck arrived when political and military tension was building in Europe.[4] To showcase his military command and that he was in charge, von Lettow-Vorbeck advised his subordinates to ignore the governor's orders.[5] In familiarising himself with the land, von Lettow-Vorbeck travelled across the country meeting with *shutztruppe* commanders at the military stations. By then GEA had sixty military stations and posts, some of the which were Madibira, Ukwega, Umero, Kiberege, Kwamtoro, Mbulu, Fort Ikoma, Mkalama, Sanjo, Chibitoke, Gisenyi, and Gifumbiro. Others were located at Kasanga (then Bismarckburg), Mahenge, Dar es Salaam, Ujiji, Lindi, Kilimatinde, Arusha, Kondoa, Liwale, Songea, Bujumbura, Tabora and Iringa. Through his visits von Lettow-Vorbeck established the country's military strategies in the event of invasion given that GEA was surrounded by British colonies which implied the country would have several war fronts. The visits provided him with good knowledge of the country's terrain to prepare for and conduct guerrilla or mobile warfare in later years.

He noted that GEA was vulnerable due to the number of soldiers available to secure the vast country, about 995,000 km^2 (384,172 square miles) with 2,700 mile long frontiers,[6] using outdated military hardware especially guns and poorly trained native askari who required immediate attention to modernise.[7] Also, the territory was surrounded by colonies that

---

[1] Samson, *World War I in Africa*, pp. 3-4; F.S. Joelson, *The Tanganyika Territory (Formerly German East Africa): Characteristics and Potentialities* (New York D. Appleton & Co., 1921) p. 237
[2] Hew Strachan, *The First World War* (Oxford: University Press, 2001) p. 575
[3] Joelson, *The Tanganyika Territory*, p. 231
[4] Ibid.
[5] Joelson, *The Tanganyika Territory*, p. 232
[6] David French, *British Strategy & War Aims 1914-1916* (London: Allen & Unwin, 1986) p. 27

were under other European powers who were suspicious of German ambitions and hostile to each other.¹ Upon the outbreak of war, fighting occurred on all fronts.² Kilimanjaro in the north faced Kenya, Victoria Nyanza faced Kenya and Uganda in the north-west, Kivu and Tanganyika in the west faced the Belgians, Portuguese East Africa (Mozambique) in the south, Rhodesia (Zambia) and Nyasaland (Malawi) in the south-west, and also the British on the Indian Ocean in the east.

GEA was undoubtedly the most valuable colony the Germans had in Africa. The country's location was strategic: it was the eastern link in the transcontinental line of steam communication, by rail and water, from the Indian to the Atlantic Ocean. The country had strategic importance for political and economic interests in East and Central Africa bordering the Indian Ocean.³ The British government viewed the German African colonies, and German East Africa in particular, as a strategic threat and a springboard for ground attacks against British, and friendly powers, that could disrupt the flow of resources needed by the British Empire. The most dangerous threat were the ports of German East Africa,⁴ havens for the German cruisers designed to raid British controlled sea-lanes.

Having analysed GEA vulnerability, von Lettow-Vorbeck embarked upon preparatory measures such as mobilising the *schutztruppe* and integrating the police force into the army under his command. Additionally, he mobilised resources, streamlined war supplies and the *Königsberg* kept its 16 companies on standby in case of war. At this juncture, von Lettow-Vorbeck was well prepared in the event of an attack by its neighbours.

Von Lettow-Vorbeck conducted military reconnaissance over significant strategic bases to facilitate subduing the enemy, for example, the Uganda railway in order to create supply difficulties in Kenya and Uganda.⁵ To achieve this, he presented a plan to deploy the military on Kilimanjaro. The idea was rejected by Governor Schnee on the grounds of creating a vacuum in other places that could be exploited by natives against the colonial authority.⁶ But the two were in agreement over securing Dar es Salaam which by and large was the colonial administrative town that had a large concentration of Germans who deserved protection and to secure the

---

[7] Paul von Lettow-Vorbeck, *My Reminiscences of East Africa* (Nashville: Battery Classics, 1989) p. 5

[1] Frank R. Cana, Frontiers of German East Africa. *The Geographical Journal* vol. 47, no. 4 (Apr., 1916) pp. 297-303, https://doi.org/10.2307/1779697

[2] Cana, Frontiers of German East Africa, pp. 297-303

[3] Michelle Moyd, Ordeal and Opportunity: Ending the First World War in Africa, *The Fletcher Forum of World Affairs*, vol. 43, no. 1, Global Transformations: A Century Since The Great War (Winter 2019) pp. 145-153

[4] von Lettow-Vorbeck, *Reminiscences of East Africa*, p. 25

[5] von Lettow-Vorbeck, *Reminiscences of East Africa,*, p. 21

[6] Ibid.

Königsberg to help in attacking enemy ships.¹ The *Königsberg* was conducting operations in the Indian Ocean when war was declared. In one of its operations it sank HMS *Pegasus* and bombed the *Helmut* in Zanzibar harbour before sailing to Rufiji delta where it was destroyed in December 1915 by British cruisers, aircraft and monitors brought in from Britain.

1.3: The colonial military and police forces

The colonial powers in African countries formed small size military and police forces that consisted of officers recruited from Europe and the local population. The military police and police forces were created primarily to facilitate peace and order in the colonies. The created military forces within the African territories had no serious strategic importance hence their small size, until the outbreak of WWI.²

GEA had well trained soldiers for any combat who served in the regular and reserve army.³ The regular army referred to as the Protective Force, or *schutztruppe*, which before the outbreak of the war consisted of 216 Europeans and 2,540 soldiers (*askari*)⁴ from over half-a-dozen ethnic backgrounds,⁵ such as Wanyamwezi, Wasukuma and some Arabs recruited from Egypt. Some Somalians had been used to quell rebellions against German colonial rule across the country.⁶ The British military force in East Africa called the King's African Rifles (KAR),⁷ was organised similarly to the German East African Protective Force.⁸ But prior to the outbreak of war, units of the KAR were disbanded for economic reasons.⁹ Essentially, by August 1914, the British East Africa troops in Uganda, and Malawi (then Nyasaland) were small in number and poorly trained compared with the German *schutztruppe*.¹⁰

The Kenyan settler communities made themselves available to serve the army and attack Germans in Tanganyika.¹¹ The British mobilised soldiers

---

1 von Lettow-Vorbeck, *Reminiscences of East Africa,*, p. 21

2 Ross Anderson, *World War I in East Africa 1916-1918* (University of Glasgow, 2001) pp. 21-40, https://www.academia.edu/17269264/ World_War_I_in_East_Africa_1916-1918

3 Michelle Moyd, Making the Household, Making the State: Colonial Military Communities and Labor in German East Africa, *International Labor and Working-Class History*, no. 80 (Fall 2011) pp. 53-76, doi:10.1017/S014754791100007X

4 Byron Farwell, *The Great War in Africa (1914-1918)* (New York: W.W. Norton & Co, 1986) p. 109; Calvert, *German East Africa*, p. 11

5 Calvert, *German East Africa*, p. 10

6 Moyd, Making the Household, pp. 53-76

7 Ross Anderson, Norforce: Major General Edward Northey and the Nyasaland and North Eastern Rhodesia Frontier Force, January 1916 to June 1918, *Scientia Militaria* vol. 44, no. 1, 2016, pp. 47-80. doi:10.5787/44-1-1162

8 Horden & Stack, p. 15

9 W.D. Downes, *With the Nigerians in German East Africa* (London: Methuen & Co, 1919) p. 16

10 Downes, *With the Nigerians*, p. 16

in West Africa as well as India for the war against Tanzania.¹ This coincided with activating military co-operation with France in West Africa where they overran Togo and Cameroon. Similar cooperation was forged with South Africa.²

Upon the outbreak of war in Europe and escalation of conflict in other German African colonies, Dr Schnee approached the British to consider neutrality. The British disregard of a diplomatic solution was demonstrated by the bombing of the wireless station at Dar es Salaam on 14 August without resistance from the Germans.³ At this juncture, it was obvious that the 1885 Congo Act agreeing the African colonies would remain neutral in the event of a European war was dishonoured. While the governor maintained neutrality, Lt. Col. Paul Emil von Lettow-Vorbeck, commander of GEA's *schutztruppe*, was outraged when two German boats were attacked off the coast of Dar es Salaam.

As the war escalated, Schnee reluctantly supported von Lettow-Vorbeck's plans agreeing to deploy the *schutztruppe* along the northern border with Kilimanjaro, and recalling the reserve army and retired soldiers. Resources were further mobilised. For example, women skilled in tailoring were mobilised to sew army uniforms and native growers to supply food.⁴ The *schutztruppe* uniform, long sleeved shirts and trousers with boots, was important for bush combat and protecting soldiers from insect (mosquitoes, tsetse flies, bees and wasps) bites. Women treated injured soldiers and supplied water to military camps.⁵

Driven from the north, the German forces took refuge in the lower Rufiji valley and then Mahenge. Close pursuit, however, did not leave them long in possession of the Rufiji, and Mahenge similarly fell to the Belgians. Consequently by 1 December 1917, most GEA territory fell under the allies, Belgium and Britain.⁶

In September 1918 von Lettow-Vorbeck marched north from Mozambique on his way back to GEA. On his arrival in Ruvuma region he encountered the KAR prompting him to change his plan by evading a trap set up by the British by crossing into Zambia.⁷ As in Mozambique, von

---

11 Anderson, Norforce

1 Timothy H. Parsons, Mobilising Britain's African Empire for War: Pragmatism vs Trusteeship, *Journal of Modern European History/Zeitschrift für moderne europäische Geschichte/Revue d'histoire européenne contemporaine*, vol. 13, no. 2, The Crisis of Empire after 1918 (2015) pp. 183-202

2 Farwell, *The Great War in Africa*, pp. 25-26

3 Downes, *With the Nigerians*, p. 16

4 von Lettow-Vorbeck, *Reminiscences of East Africa*, pp. 69-70

5 Farwell, *The Great War in Africa*, p. 228

6 G.M. Wrigley, The Military Campaigns against Germany's African Colonies, *Geographical Review*, Jan., 1918, vol. 5, no. 1 (Jan., 1918) pp. 44-65, doi. 41.204.146.190, 9/2/2021

Lettow-Vorbeck exploited battles to replenish medical supplies and have access to food supplies from the local population.[1] When he reached the Chambeshi River on the morning of 14 November 1918, the British Magistrate Hector Croad appeared under a white flag informing him of the armistice. Von Lettow-Vorbeck marched his force to Mbala (Abercorn) in Zambia about 155 miles from the GEA border two weeks after the armistice in Europe.[2] On his surrender at Abercorn, on 25 November, von Lettow-Vorbeck still had with him one 155 German officers and NCOs, nearly 1,200 askari, one field gun, 37 machine-guns, 200,000 rounds of ammunition and a quantity of other war material.[3]

After some days, General von Lettow-Vorbeck was granted a safe passage to travel from Mbala to Mpulungu, a port on Lake Tanganyika where he boarded the SS *Goetzen* (today MV *Liemba*) to GEA. On his return to Germany as a national hero, he was promoted to army general.

The first 'liberated' areas north of central railway line came under British civil administration with effect from March 1916, but this did not imply the country was under British control. The country remained under martial law (military rule) until 1919 during which time Horace Byatt was the country's first administrator assisted by General Smuts. Following the signing of the peace treaty, Germany was compelled to renounce its overseas possessions including GEA. This was followed by the decision by the allied powers to confer administration of GEA to Britain based on the principles set out by the League of Nations. The Belgians continued to administer the GEA areas that they liberated, namely Tabora, Kigoma and Bukoba.[4]

1.4: Paris Peace Conference

At the end of the war, a peace conference was held in Paris in early 1919 where British, French and Belgian powers reiterated their desire to keep control of Germany's African territories. This led to, among other peace conference results, the formation of the League of Nations' mandate system. The 1919 Paris peace conference provided, under Article 119 of the Treaty of Versailles, for the allied powers to acquire the German territories as mandates rather than colonies. Hence, the war resulted in a restructuring of the colonial map of Africa.[5]

---

[7] Harry Fecitt, The Fighting in Northern Rhodesia in November 1918, *The Society of Malawi Journal*, vol. 71, no. 2 (2018) pp. 15-23

[1] Fecitt, Fighting in Northern Rhodesia, pp. 15-23; Samson, *World War I in Africa*, p. 89

[2] Fecitt, Fighting in Northern Rhodesia, pp. 15-23

[3] Joelson, *The Tanganyika Territory*, p. 237

[4] Edward Humphrey Manisty Leggett, The Tanganyika Territory, *Journal of the Royal Society of Arts*, vol. 70, no. 3643 (September 15, 1922) pp. 737-752

[5] Timothy Stapleton, *Africa: War and Conflict in the Twentieth Century* (New York: 2018) pp. 36-37; Pitman B. Potter, Origin of the System of Mandates under the League of Nations,

The Paris peace conference reconfigured the map of Africa as Britain got a lion's share of GEA, Belgium was handed part of GEA, the territory split into two countries, Rwanda and Burundi. Kionga was handed back to Portugal.[1] France got Togo and Cameroon, while South Africa annexed South West Africa (Namibia).

Specifically, Article 22 of the Treaty specified that (1) Colonial territories taken from the enemy were not to be annexed by the victorious powers; (2) These colonial territories were to be put under the joint sovereignty of the allied and associated powers; (3) They were entrusted to the tutelage of certain individual advanced nations; (4) This tutelage was to be exercised by the mandatories under the supervision of the League of Nations; (5) The open door was to be maintained in colonial territories so far as the mandatory had any power over them as such; (6) Natives could be used in a military capacity only for local defence and police; (7) The people of the mandated territories were to have a voice in the choice of the mandatories.

GEA was therefore neither a colony nor protectorate. But Britain administered Tanganyika just like any other British territory.[2] In this regard, the British created an administrative system similar to one applied in Northern Nigeria, which was indirect rule following handover of the military rule by General Jan Smuts to the civilian administration headed by Horace Archer Byatt.

The terms of the mandate stated that 'until such time as the native peoples is able to stand by themselves under the strenuous conditions of the modern world ... the material and moral well-being and the social progress of the inhabitants forms a sacred trust of civilisation'. Nothing was said about how soon the inhabitants might expect to be able to stand on their own feet. The principle of eventual withdrawal had been established, but the timing was not yet on the agenda. The League doctrine, largely drafted by Britain, effectively became the basis of future British colonial policy, with the colonies seen as embryo self-governing dominions within the British Commonwealth.

In accordance with the mandate terms, Byatt's priorities included ensuring the resumption of commerce, agricultural production mainly of cash crops such as cotton, coffee and tobacco, as well as restoring the destroyed transport infrastructure.[3] Initially, Byatt's administrative initiatives faced

---

The American Political Science Review, Nov, 1922, vol. 16, no. 4 (Nov 1922) pp. 563-583, doi. 197.221.218.100 on 12/2/2021; Buell, *The Native Problem in Africa*, p. 428

[1] The German conquest of Kionga, in Mozambican territory was officially recognised on 10 September 1894.

[2] W.R. Louis, *Germany's Lost Colonies 1914-1918* (Oxford: University Press, 1967)

[3] Michael D. Callahan, Nomansland: The British Colonial Office and the League of Nations Mandate for German East Africa, 1916-1920, *Albion: A Quarterly Journal Concerned with British Studies* vol. 25, no. 3 (Autumn, 1993) pp. 443-464; David L. Schoenbrun, A Past

opposition from the military elements who considered themselves having ultimate authority. However, the end of the war and the award of the mandate brought the friction to a close.[1]

This provided room to rename the country. Some fanciful suggestions were made for the new acquisition such as Azania, Bantuland, New Maryland, Windsorland, Eburnea, and Lululand.[2] Evidently, this was an attempt to avoid referring the country as either a colony or a protectorate. In 1920 Byatt managed to convince the East Africa Department in the CO to rename it Tanganyika based on the inspiration of Lake Tanganyika. Fortunately the then Colonial Secretary agreed on an unambiguously native name; initially designated the Tanganyika Protectorate, this was soon changed to Tanganyika Territory.[3]

By 1914, the GEA territory had been divided into 24 administrative areas of which 19 were civil districts administered by district commissioners. The district commissioners were assisted, at the beginning of British rule, by *akida* and *jumbe*, all responsible for among other things collection of taxes. *Akida* were also responsible for judging cases in the local courts. During the German period, two districts, Mahenge and Iringa, were under military control and three others, Bukoba, Burundi and Rwanda, were granted residence status.[4] This was basically designed to facilitate administrative purposes.

The British created eight provinces, each of which was under a provincial commissioner who was responsible to the governor for the administration of the province. The provinces were units headed by a Provincial Commissioner (PC) as chief representative of the governor responsible for political and administrative matters. A number of specialised departments such as health, education, agriculture and veterinary in the province were responsible to the PC.

Each province, in turn, was divided into a number of districts that were placed under district Commissioners or Officers who were responsible to the Provincial Commissioner. The Provincial Commissioner and his district Commissioners or Officers had to see that the laws of the territory were applied and observed. And that the interests and well-being of the inhabitants were safeguarded.

In 1924 the districts were brought under the Provinces as shown in Table 2. Initially eleven provinces were created but the number was reduced due

---

Whose Time Has Come: Historical Context and History in Eastern Africa's Great Lakes, *History and Theory*, vol. 32, no. 4, Beiheft 32: History Making in Africa (Dec 1993) pp. 32-56
[1] Callahan, Nomansland
[2] TNA (UK) CO 691/29 29530: Horace A. Byatt Memorandum to CO, New Names for German East Africa, 21 January 1919
[3] John Iliffe, *A Modern History of Tanganyika* (Cambridge: University Press, 1979) p. 247
[4] Leggett, The Tanganyika Territory, pp. 737-752

to financial difficulties between 1930 and 1934, for example, Bukoba and Lake Provinces were amalgamated in 1931.¹ Three more provinces were formed after WWII in which Bukoba was elevated to a province.²

Table 2: Tanganyika Provinces and Districts, 1959

Province	Districts
Central	Dodoma, Kondoa, Mpwapwa, Singida, Iramba,
Eastern	Bagamoyo, Kilosa, Kisarawe, Mafia, Morogoro, Rufiji, Ulanga
Lake	Geita, Kwimba, Maswa, Mwanza (Urban), Mwanza (Rural), Musoma, North Mara, Shinyanga, and Ukerewe
Northern	Arusha, Masai, Mbulu and Moshi
Southern	Kilwa, Lindi, Masasi, Mtwara, Nachingwea, Newala, Songea and Tunduru
S'thern Highlands	Chunya, Iringa, Mbeya, Njombe and Rungwe
Tanga	Handeni, Lushoto, Pangani, Tanga (Urban) and Tanga (Rural)
Western	Kahama, Kasulu, Kibondo, Kigoma, Mpanda, Nzega, Tabora and Ufipa
West Lake	Biharamulo, Bukoba and Karagwe

Source: Tanganyika Annual Reports, 1924-1930 (London: HMSO)

The provinces shown in Table 2 were restructured into administrative regions and districts following independence in 1961, and further subdivided. Until 2010 there were 21 regions in the Tanzanian mainland, with 24 in 2014.

Upon the British assuming control of GEA, the German district commissioners were replaced while *jumbe* and *akida* of Arab and Swahili background from the coast appointed by Germans were accommodated by the new colonial authority to assist given their rich knowledge of the people and the country.³ The *jumbe* was usually the head of a single village, while the *akida* was the head of a group of villages. Importantly, the immediate replacement of *akida* could have been an administrative disaster for the British who were new in the country. Chiefs headed the Native Authority (NA).

The Native Authorities were created and a new administration installed which included some administrators who had served under German rule, that is *akida* and *jumbe*. By 1912 the German colonial authority had begun abandoning recruitment of Swahili and Arabs due to some religious suspicions and protests by missionaries who thought the scheme facilitated the spread of Islam in the territory.⁴ Understandably, *akida* and *jumbe* governed

---

¹ Bukoba District Book
² Ibid.
³ Leggett, The Tanganyika Territory, pp. 737-752
⁴ John Iliffe, *Tanganyika under German Rule, 1905-1912* (Cambridge: University Press, 1969) p. 182; Karim F. Hirji, Colonial Ideological Apparatuses in Tanganyika under the Germans, in

under protection of the colonial authority. Some of their functions included monitoring peace and order, acting as court of law based in most instances on Islamic Law, executing punishment for the offenders, arranging compulsory labour to serve in colonial projects, and collecting taxes from the colonised. The British effectively adopted the German policy, but emphasised abandoning the *akida* and *jumbe* as local administrators as this would imply continuity of German rule. Local tribal chiefs and headmen were preferred by the British primarily to reinforce the Native Authority or local administration.

The *jumbe* and *akida* were gradually replaced with the introduction of tribal rule provided for under Indirect Rule which had been in force with effect from 1925 when the German administrative system was abandoned. This was a move to resuscitate the original indigenous native administration, hence, the Native Authority (NA). The Wasukuma had local titles such as *Mtemi* or chief, *Bambilija* or *Balamji* who were sub-chiefs and *Banangwa* or village headmen. Among the WaChagga of Kilimanjaro and Meru of Arusha a chief is titled *Mangi* and *Mukama* among the WaHaya of Kagera region. They were referred to as *Nkosi* among the Wangoni of Songea and *Umalafyale* among the Nyakyusa of Mbeya. The use of local terms for chiefs and village headmen signified a departure from the German administrative system and the beginning of a new era. This provided ethnic groups with some degree of recognition and a revival of the pre-German colonial era indigenous administrative system but modified for local administration under Indirect Rule.

Under British Indirect Rule, the Native Administration was responsible for the collection of native taxes; they approved and supervised native treasury expenditure; directed famine relief and other emergency measures and supervised development activities. They had judicial authority, not only in the official sense but as advisers and guides to the native people.

Sir Donald Cameron, adopted indirect rule in Tanzania which he brought from Northern Nigeria. Here the Native Authority (NA) were headed by hereditary or selected chiefs and the village headmen at village level under supervision of British colonial officers. Their role was primarily to foster peace and order as well as ensure the socio-economic development of the colonised.[1] In this regard, the central government retained its powers (authority) and exercised supervision and control, responsibility and authority for the well-being of the natives. Supervision in this context was regarded as the provision of advice and guidance in discharging their

---

M.H.Y. Kaniki (ed),*Tanzania Under German Rule* (London: Longman, 1979) pp. 201-2; Frieder Ludwig, *Church and State in Tanzania: Aspects of Changing Relationship*, 1961-1964 (Leiden: Brill, 1999) p. 66

[1] Tanganyika Territory: Annual Report for the Year 1931, Colonial No. 71 (London: HMSO, 1932) p. 11

administrative functions and assisting with greater responsibilities in local administration.[1]

Indirect rule was employed and exploited to serve the interests of the colonial authority. This was facilitated by the appointment of chiefs. The appointee was expected to be a good collaborator with the colonial authority. Under indirect rule the colonial authority had powers to dismiss unwanted chiefs. Their appointment was not expected to be a nuisance to the Colonial authority. Chiefs were basically figureheads and tools to rubber stamp colonial policies.

The NA was made responsible for enacting bye-laws, supervision of agriculture development and marketing. It was also responsible for revenue collection which was provided for under Native Authority Ordinance, 1923. The NA treasuries were created and placed under the chiefs, and as per the legislation, taxes were collected by the local chiefs. This was formerly a responsibility of European district officers whose responsibility was to supervise the NAs.

1.5: Poll and Hut Taxes

The most important established revenue source for the Native Authorities was the native hut or poll tax imposed by colonial authorities on Africans. The Native Authorities established in 1925, included overseeing local chiefs who were responsible for collecting taxes on behalf of the government. Taxation of natives was also a means to force them to grow cash crops for foreign markets especially in Britain and European countries.[2]

The NA treasuries were created which also fell under the chiefs. The treasuries raised revenues from various sources including taxes (poll and hut). Part of the collected revenues were kept and the other disbursed to the central government. Revenue collected by the chiefs was spent on aspects such as salaries, development of infrastructure and provision of social services (health and education).[3]

Taxes paid in colonial currency rather than in-kind was essential to produce the desired outcome as well as monetise the African communities.[2] The governor had power to reduce the tax in less developed districts, and there was no reason why the tax had to be uniform throughout any given territory. Taxation facilitated the primitive accumulation of capital and creation of markets among Africans for imported goods to generate further revenue for the colonial administration.

At the grassroots level, administration was under the local tribal chiefs

---

[1] Annual Report to Trusteeship Council for 1947

[2] Walter Rodney, *How Europe underdeveloped Africa* (Dar es Salaam: Tanzania Publishing House, 1973)

[3] Göran Hydén, *Beyond Ujamaa in Tanzania: Underdevelopment and an Uncaptured Peasantry* (Berkeley: University of California Press, 1980) p. 84

whose power and functions were defined under the NA Ordinance that included tax collection. The chiefs were assisted at village level by a headman who was utilised for local administration and collection of taxes, recruitment of labourers and enforcing law and order in their respective areas of jurisdiction.[1] This endowed them with vast control over their subjects and they used their influence to enforce recommended colonial agriculture practices and marketing legislation as well as policies. The enforcement of agriculture policies by the chiefs was facilitated through the Native Authority Ordinance which gave local authorities power to issue orders to growers that enforced proper standards of cotton cultivation.[2] In this respect, the whole administrative structure was central in facilitating the colonial economy and in realising the self-sufficiency policy[3] largely aimed at ensuring that Britain was less involved with the day to day administrative costs in running colonial governments.[4] However, from the beginning of the 1930s there was some change of policy under the Colonial Development Act of 1929 that made provision for some financial aid to the British colonies.

1.6: African Associations and involvement in political space

Under Cameron's governorship, reforms in Tanganyika were implemented by creating administrative areas to provide for effective expedient control over the territory and preservation of the indigenous political institutions that were exposed to modernisation and democratisation processes. Cameron in justification of indirect rule pointed out that:

> it is impossible for us to administer the country directly through British officers, even if we quadrupled the number we now employ, and I cannot foresee any future political state in which it would be possible to do so except under a completely Europeanised system of government in which the native would express himself through a ballot box.[5]

Under the mandate agreement Britain allowed both the indigenous cash crop farming sector and European plantation economy to co-exist. As a result, in 1925 Tanganyika was exporting twice as many agricultural crops as exported before the war, and from 1923, the country no longer needed grant-in-aid from the Imperial Government.[6]

---

[1] Mwanza District Book

[2] Ibid.

[3] British Aid – 5 Colonial Development: a factual survey of the origins and history of British aid to developing countries (London: The Overseas Development Institute) p. 6

[4] A Report from a Special Committee to the Fabian Colonial Bureau on Co-operation in the Colonies (London: George Allen & Unwin) p. 21

[5] Tanganyika Government Circular No. 50, 1925

[6] Zoe Marsh & K.W. Kingsnorth, *An introduction to the History of East Africa* (Cambridge: University Press, 1957) pp. 231-232

The mandatory power for administering Tanganyika was guided by Article 3 of the Mandate Agreement which stipulated that Britain was responsible for peace, order, and good government of the territory, 'and for the promotion of the material and moral well being and the social progress of its inhabitants.' Article 5 stressed that Britain had a responsibility for 'the emancipation of all slaves and for as speedy an elimination of domestic and other slavery as social conditions will allow', and compulsory or forced labour among natives was unacceptable.[1] However, the Article provided an exception for essential public works and services only in return for adequate remuneration.

Britain was also charged by the League of Nations to ensure 'the well-being of people not yet able to stand by themselves'.[2] This was demonstrated by the formation of several African voluntary farmer-based organisations in rural areas, workers associations in urban areas as well as ethnic (tribal) organisations in urban areas with branches in rural areas during the 1920s and 1940s. One of the tribal organisations was the Bukoba-Buhaya Union established in 1924 and led by Clemens Kiiza. A growers' organisation was the Kilimanjaro Native Planters Associations formed in 1922 and registered in 1925. One workers' association was the Tanganyika Territory African Civil Service Association (TTACSA) formed in Tanga in 1922 by Martin Mdudumi Kayamba. The objectives of the TTACSA were:

a. Protect its members' interest,
b. Representation for the interests of Africans,
c. To maintain close fellowship,
d. Maintain sportsmanship,
e. Free reading and social advancement,
f. Represent African views in debates over government issues.

In 1929, TTACSA was transformed into the Tanganyika African Association (TAA). Some of the TAA founding members were: Kleist Sykes, Elder bin Sudi, Ibrahim Hamis, Zibe Kidasi, Ali Said Mpima, Suleiman Majisu, Raikes Kusi, Rawson Watts and Cecil Matola. Kleist Sykes, was the first Secretary of the TAA. TAA soon embarked upon opening branches across the country, and by 1939 there were nine in the country and 39 in 1948. Its expansion was evident in the Lake Province villages and districts where it had branches in Ukerewe, Tarime, Musoma, Bukoba, and Nasa. By the 1940s and early 1950s, TAA was vibrant in the Lake Province where individuals like A.S. Kandoro, Bokhe Munanka, Paul Bomani and Joseph Kaselabantu were key players. TAA held its annual conferences regularly which facilitated in galvanising the organisation.

---

[1] League of Nations, Reports of Mandatory Powers, on the Administration under Mandate of Tanganyika Territory, 1925
[2] Article 22 of the Covenant of the League of Nations

The 1920s had been a busy decade during which the colonial authority formed the Legislative Council (LEGCO) in 1926 in response to recommendations by the Ormsby-Gore Commission. However, during the period of the mandate system (1920-1945) there was no Tanganyikan who was a LEGCO member. This was under the pretext that none was qualified, mainly due to an inability to communicate in the English language thereby preventing them from participating fully and following debates held in the LEGCO's sessions.[2] But the governor, Chief Secretary (CS) and Secretary of Native Affairs (SNA) promised Tanganyikans that their interests would be protected.[3] Conon Gibbons, the British headmaster of Minaki Secondary School near Dar es Salaam, represented Tanganyikans in the LEGCO for 25 years.

Finally, in 1945 the first Africans and Tanganyikans, Abdiel Shangali[1] a chief of Hai from 1926 to 1946 and Makwai from Usiha-Samuye chiefdom in Shinyanga district, were appointed members of LEGCO. Ten years later, in 1955 there were 10 Tanganyikan LEGCO members, 10 Asian and 10 European. An Executive Council was also set up in Tanganyika responsible for guiding the work of the government led by the Chief Secretary. Other members were Attorney General, Treasurer, and Principal Medical Officer as well as heads of departments, renamed Ministries in 1952.

Post-World War II saw the League of Nations succeeded by the United Nations (UNO) on 18 April 1946,[2] and the Permanent Mandate Commission was replaced by The Trusteeship Council. With that the former mandated territories were placed under the Trusteeship System which was provided for under Article 77. The Charter of the UNO and the Trusteeship Agreements were more specific concerning political advancement than the Covenant of the League and the mandate agreements. The Charter proclaimed 'self-government or independence' as the aim of the Trust Territories.[3] The Trusteeship Council was more directly concerned with the problems of the trustee territories[4] and despatched Visiting Missions to Tanganyika every three years to evaluate social, economic and political developments.[5] Mission visits provided a closer international watch on the manner in which Britain governed Tanganyika. The Trusteeship System brought about some changes under which Britain was required to promote the development of free and suitable political institutions in the territory; an

---

[1] He collaborated with the colonial government in 1937 against coffee rioters which led to his promotion as Paramount chief.
[2] Chapters XII and XIII of the U.N. Charter, Articles 75 to 91
[3] Article 76 (b) of the UNO Charter
[4] B.G. Chidzero, *Tanganyika and the International Trusteeship* (Oxford: University Press, 1961)
[5] The United Nations Trusteeship Council, *United Nations Visiting Mission to the Trust Territories in East Africa, Report on Tanganyika Together with Related Documents,* 4 Volumes for 1948, 1951, 1954 and 1960

increasing share in the administration and other services; also participation of Tanganyikans in advisory groups and the LEGCO. These reforms did not allow for Tanganyikans to engage in political parties. Nevertheless, two important factors brought change.

The development associated with land alienation prompted TAA to venture into politics and redefine its orientation on welfare of the colonised. The political element was adopted during its 1945 Dodoma conference and shaped its political direction to mobilise the masses for political action. As a result, a political unit was set up in 1951 that comprised the following members: Abdulwahid Sykes, Sheikh Hassan bin Amir, Hamza Master Mwapachu, Said Chaurembo, John Rupia and Stephen Mhando. Abdulwahid Sykes was Acting President until he was defeated by Julius Nyerere in the 1953 election.[1]

In April 1954, Edward Twining introduced the Registration of Societies Ordinance which made compulsory the registration of all organizations. Under the Ordinance, each organisation applying for registration had to outline their objectives, rules, the organisers' names, occupations as well as their addresses. Under this Ordinance, political organisations, too, had to apply for registration. Until early 1954 there was no political organization in the territory.

A second pressing factor was the Visiting Mission's report that recommended a timeframe for the British to consider granting independence to the country. The report established lack of political enthusiasm among the African people for independence. This was demonstrated by lack of political parties and political immaturity among the colonised people that undermined opportunity to demand independence. The Visiting Mission report concluded that owing to such political gaps the country could attain independence within 20 to 25 years.[2] It was forecast that such independence could perhaps be somewhat before 1975 but not later than 1985.

The recommended timeframe was a political challenge and an impetus to transform TAA into a political party that could fill the gap identified by the Visiting Mission. This opportunity was grasped by TAA. At its 7 July 1954 annual conference it transformed into a political party, renamed Tanganyika African National Union (TANU), with Julius Kambarage Nyerere as its President.[3] TANU took over the branches which had been established by TAA, and had the following objectives:

a. Prepare the people of Tanganyika for self-rule and to fight tirelessly for national freedom — *Uhuru*

---

[1] Mohamed Said, *The Life and Times of Abdulwahid Sykes (1925-1968): The untold story of the Muslim struggle against British colonialism in Tanganyika* (London: Minerva Press, 1998)

[2] Editorial, *The Tanganyika Standard*, 26 January 1955

[3] George Dunheved, *Julius Nyerere: A biography* (Dar es Salaam: Government Printer, 1961) p. 5

b. Fight tribalism and any other factor which would hinder the development of unity among Africans
c. Abolish all segregation
d. Encourage and help workers to establish trade unions
e. Cooperate with other organizations whose aims and objectives were not contrary to those of TANU.

With that, TANU became the sole voice for all sufferers and championed the grievances and aspirations of the masses. One of the issues that TANU protested was the Visiting Mission timeframe for independence. It also strongly exerted pressure on the colonial authority for adult universal suffrage.[1] These arguments were presented in New York at the UNO General Assembly.[2] It was argued by Julius Nyerere that criteria for granting independence to Tanganyika should not be 'judged on the basis of the least progressive elements of its population'. As Nyerere strongly argued the case for independence, he received significant support from the members of the Assembly. This prompted a visit to the country by the UNO Visiting Mission that endorsed Tanganyika being capable of reaching self-government very much earlier than the 20 to 25 years.[3]

The revised timeframe for granting independence signified a new political development in favour of TANU and the colonised in particular which angered the British. The British therefore embarked upon frustrating the political opportunities that were emerging in favour of the colonised. They restricted political activities, closed TANU branches and denied new ones being registered. Nyerere was restricted from engaging in politics.

The spread of TANU across the country sent an alarm to the colonial authority that had to craft mechanisms to split the Tanganyika population by weakening TANU's popularity. As a result, the colonial authority spearheaded the formation of a new political party, the United Tanganyika Party (UTP) in 1956, to stand against TANU.

The timing in the formation of the UTP was not only to mitigate against TANU which was gaining political momentum day-by-day and creating political hysteria for the colonial authority which feared losing the territory. It was also designed to promote multiracial politics, unlike TANU, that appeared to engage in propagating African interests. Against this backdrop, UTP managed to obtain backing from the Aga Khan Ismaili, white settlers and wealthy businessmen who financed the party.[4] This might have been orchestrated by the colonial authority to ensure TANU did not win a

---

[1] Editorial, *The Tanganyika Standard*, 5 April 1956

[2] Dunheved, *Julius Nyerere*, p. 5

[3] Ibid.

[4] R.G. Gregory, *Quest for Equality. Asian Politics in East Africa, 1900-1967* (New Delhi: Orient Longman, 1993) p. 109

majority of LEGCO seats. However, TANU's popularity and acceptance among the colonised could not be blocked. This was demonstrated by the 1958 election results which saw all TANU nominated candidates win seats irrespective of their racial background. A.H. Jamal, K.L. Jhaveri and M.N. Rattansey were Indian.[1] A.Y.A. Karimjee became the Speaker of Parliament; M.M. Devani became Mayor of Dar es Salaam with D.K. Patel as Deputy Mayor.[2] This challenged the widely held notion by the UTP that TANU was a racist political party.

However, some TANU members were dissatisfied with TANU. They thought the party was too moderate against the colonial authority and accommodation of other races.[3] They were of the opinion that a radical position was most suitable in challenging the colonial authority. In February 1958, Zuberi M. Mtemvu, a former provincial secretary of TANU declared the formation of the African National Congress (ANC). This decision to split from TANU was taken during the 1958 Tabora election.[4] Presumably, Zuberi Mtemvu expected to exploit the TANU annual conference to his advantage by gaining support from TANU members at the conference.

In rural areas, the co-operative movement, especially the agricultural marketing co-operatives (AMCOs) were supportive of the spread and growth of TANU that partly fuelled the struggle for independence in the country. In the Lake Province, particularly in the WCGA where TANU was banned, AMCOs clandestinely provided venues for TANU to run political activities. In a number of incidences, TANU appealed to workers to strike. Importantly, they asked their members to vote for TANU candidates during elections. TANU maintained close association with the co-operative movement after independence when it facilitated the formation of the national federation, the Co-operative Union of Tanganyika (CUT) in 1963.

In the mid-1950s more trade unions were registered in Tanganyika. For example, 16 new unions registered, hence there were 23 in the territory with 13,000 members.[5] Of these, 17 trade unions decided to merge in 1957 to form the Tanganyika Federation of Labour (TFL). The total trade union membership was claimed to be 205,000, practically all of whom were under the TFL. Some of the trade unions affiliated to TFL were Tanganyika African Custom Union, Dockworkers and Stevedore's Union, Tanganyika

---

[1] Marie-Aude Fouéré. Indians are exploiters and Africans idlers! The production of racial categories and socio-economic issues in *Tanzania. Indian Africa: Minorities of Indian-Pakistani Origin in Eastern Africa*, 2013, p. 20

[2] Ibid.

[3] Henry Bienien, *Tanzania: Party Transformation and Economic Development* (Princeton: University Press, 1970) p. 51

[4] Ibid., p. 54

[5] Kenneth Sanders, Commissioner of Labour, Hansard. Tanganyika Legislative Council Debates (Dar es Salaam), 31st Session, vol. 2, 13, 12, 1956, p. 793

Domestic and Hotel Workers Union, Tanganyika African Local Government Workers Union, Tanganyika Mine Workers' Union, Tanganyika Plantation Workers' Union. National Union of Post Office and Telecommunications' Employees, Tanganyika Union of Public Employees, Tanganyika Railway African Union, Tanga Dockworkers and Stevedore's Union, Transport and General Workers' Union. There was also trade unions not affiliated to the TFL, such as Tanganyika Asian Civil Servants' Association and Tanganyika Civil Servants' Association.

These developments were facilitated by the 1956 Ordinance that enforced compulsory registration of all trade unions in the territory. However, the legislation restricted trade unions from participation in politics. Despite this, trade union leaders clandestinely provided support in the struggle for independence.

The TFL became a staunch supporter of TANU in its struggle for independence from the British. Clearly, trade unions were political breeding grounds in many ways. They, for example, provided financial support, office accommodation and encouraged members to become TANU members. It was a marriage of convenience.[1] As a result, support to and from each other became a norm.

Trade union members (workers) became key torchbearers in the nationalist struggle as they enlightened relatives over support of TANU. Soon after its establishment, TANU joined hands with the ethnic organisation, the Sukuma Union, to protest against some colonial agricultural policies such as livestock destocking in Sukumaland that is Western Cotton Growing Area (Sukumaland). By the end of 1945 Sukumaland was estimated to have 1,728,400 head of cattle.[2]

In 1947, it had 1,747,860 head of cattle, 606,218 sheep and 720,322 goats and by 1950 there were 1,314,491 head of cattle, 725,602 sheep and 679,208 goats.[3] Thus, Sukumaland was declared grossly overstocked and such number of livestock was viewed as the cause of soil erosion. Destocking was therefore considered necessary to avoid further environmental degradation. Compulsory cattle destocking and culling were employed under NA Ordinance Section 72.[4] The Ordinance fixed the number of livestock for a household. The excess had to be sold with prices fixed by the colonial authority which were disappointingly so low that the Sukuma Union among others demanded a better price for livestock, and challenged the unfair destocking procedure.[5]

---

[1] R.S. Mukandala, *Trade Unionism in Tanzania* (November 1999) p. 9
[2] Lake Province Book
[3] TNA/215/36, Culling in Sukumaland
[4] TNA 215/2348/vol. II, Mwanza Veterinary: Cattle Culling
[5] TNA 2397 Lake Province Annual Report; 1954; G. Maguire, *Towards 'Uhuru' in Tanzania: The Politics of Participation* (Cambridge: University Press, 1969) p. 147

The measure was also enforced through livestock taxation. A livestock head tax was viewed not only as an effective instrument of destocking, but also a potential source of government revenue. The Wasukuma, however, did not appreciate it and voluntarily implemented the destocking scheme. Livestock keepers thought destocking was designed to push them into poverty[1] as they would have no cattle, being denied manure generated by their animals.[2] TANU strongly opposed the policy because it was unpopular to growers who were also livestock keepers and viewed it as ruinous because buying cattle was part of the investment farmers made from selling cotton. This suggests that livestock keepers were victimised as they were not a source of the problem. Consequently, the colonial authority called off the policy; and banned TANU from conducting political activities in the WCGA.

Compulsory land terracing on the Uluguru Mountains which was part of the Uluguru Land Usage Scheme[3] and Usambara Mountains as well as in Mbulu[4] was protested against by residents in the respective localities. Some protest leaders objecting to the compulsory land terracing on the Uluguru Mountains were TANU members who actively supported the party's policies.[5] Similarly, TANU exploited Uluguru Mountain range residents' grievances for its political advantage.

TANU's predecessor TAA opposed the land alienation plan popularly referred to as the Meru Land Case at Engare Nanyuki and Leguruki in the Northern Province in 1951.[6] Japhet Kirilo, Secretary of TAA's Arusha Branch stood against eviction of Africans who were rightful occupants of alienated land. The protest was fought on various fronts that in the end generated nationalistic sentiments against colonial rule: in the court of law, petition to the Colonial Office[7] and on 30 June and 21 July 1952 at the UNO's Trusteeship Council. The Meru land case and the inability of African LEGCO members to defend it, resulted in TAA members splitting, with the majority rallying around the radical nationalist struggle.

The Meru land case had support from Lord Fenner Brockway who was the Labour Party's Member of Parliament. Lord Fenner Brockway argued

---

[1] John Iliffe, *A Modern History of Tanganyika*, p. 505
[2] TNA 2397 Lake Pprovince Annual Report; 1954; G. Maguire, p. 147
[3] James L. Brain, The Uluguru Land Usage Scheme: Success and Failure, *The Journal of Developing Areas*, vol. 14, no. 2 (College of Business, Tennessee State University, 1980) pp. 175-90
[4] Lowe Börjeson, A History under Siege: Intensive Agriculture in the Mbulu Highlands, Tanzania, 19th Century to the Present (PhD Thesis, Stockholm University, 2004)
[5] Brain, The Uluguru Land Usage Scheme, pp. 175–90
[6] Iliffe, *A Modern History of Tanganyika*, p. 451; TAA 3rd Conference at Dodoma, 24 March 1945, pp. 1-11
[7] Kirilo Japhet & Earle Seaton, *The Meru Land Case* (Nairobi: East African Publishing House, 1967) p. 46

against land alienation in the House of Commons.[1] Eventually the issue was known not only in Britain but also in the United States of America. It was this case that raised Japhet Kirilo's political profile particularly through political campaigns across the country after his return from Britain in 1953. During his political rallies under the auspices of TAA, Kirilo urged Tanganyikans to press for independence which was viewed as a way to prevent potential further land alienation and other injustices.[2] Similar attempts to alienate land emerged in the Southern Province. The colonial authority in Tanganyika argued that land alienation would provide employment to the rural population. Yet, the colonial authority downplayed the fact that people in earmarked land alienation projects would be rendered landless which became a central point of contention against the move.

TANU participated in the 1957 LEGCO elections in which some individuals, like Paul Bomani from Victoria Federation of Co-operative Unions (VFCUs) and George Kahama from Bukoba Co-operative Union (BCU), were elected TANU's representatives. Bomani and Kahama's candidacy had nothing to do with the co-operative movement which in principle was barred from participation in politics.

Moreover, TANU was formed during the co-operative movement renaissance which was why its popularity within the co-operative movement was never challenged. It intensified its political campaigns with the fight against exploitation being one of its key policy initiatives. This commitment was stipulated in the TANU constitution, Section *(f)* where its principal object *is to see that the government actively assists the formation and maintenance of co-operative organisations.*

In the first democratic election, held in 1960, TANU won 70 out of 71 seats in Parliament. In the election, 10 European and 11 Asian seats were won by TANU candidates and one TANU independent candidate, Hermangild Sarwatt who won the Mbulu consituency. TANU candidates in 58 constituencies did not face opposition. In this election Julius Kambarage won 1,123,553 votes against 21,279 for Mr Zuberi Mtemvu.[3]

This election result concluded British colonial rule and independence of the territory under the the Colonial Office's Marlborough House Constitution granted on 9 December 1961. In Tanzania a one-party system was largely based on the election result in which TANU won the majority votes. This was the case from 1958 with the first LEGCO election held in Tanganyika and it remained the same in all successive elections: 1959, 1960

---

[1] Japhet & Seaton, *Meru Land Case*, p. 46

[2] Lionel R. Cliffle, Nationalism and the Reaction to Enforced Agricultural Change in Tanganyika during the Colonial Period, *Taamuli* 1 (1972): 7

[3] P. W. B. McAuslan, The Republican Constitution of Tanganyika., *The International and Comparative Law Quarterly* 13, no. 2 (1964) pp. 502-73. http://www.jstor.org/stable/756206

and 1962. This justified the Presidential Commission in establishing a one-party state under TANU.[1]

Table 3: Election Results 1960

Party	Votes	Percentage	Seats
TANU	100,581	82.81	70
Independent	20,527	16.90	1
ANC	337	0.28	0
	121,455	99.99	71

Source: Wolfgang Fengler, Kenya, in D. Nohlen, M. Krennerich, & B. Thibaut (eds) *Elections in Africa: A Data Handbook* (Oxford Publishers, 1999) pp. 879, 882

The decision to embrace a one party system was neither driven by intention to stamp out political opposition nor political repression. It was motivated by the popularity that TANU had from all walks of life such as workers, students and farmers as well as the general electorate who voted 58 out of 59 seats to TANU in the 1960 elections. One seat was won by an independent candidate who was also a TANU member. Other political parties such as African National Congress, People's Democratic Party, and the People's Convention Party did not win a seat in the election.

In addition, some political parties like the All-Muslim National Union of Tanganyika (AMNUT) opposed granting independence to Tanganyika. The AMNUT was registered on 8 August 1959. It was led by Arab descendants who contested parliamentary seats, but failed to win. Despite its election loss, the AMNUT believed it was a popular political party that should not be undermined. For example it protested to the Visiting Mission that:

> There are some people, especially, in the Trusteeship of the United Nations who believe that there is only one political society in Tanganyika named TANU, which represents the nine million Muslims and Non-Muslims of Tanganyika, but this is not so, as TANU only represents its people, and not all Africans.[2]

The AMNUT petitioned against granting independence to Tanganyika. The few African Christians with a higher education were overwhelmed by the majority who were African Muslims, and without necessary education, such self-government would result in political chaos and disparity.[3] A party like AMNUT could be regarded as lacking patriotism by preferring continuation of colonial rule. Its argument was 'not to have self-government before a higher education to African Muslims first,' as they were seen to be lacking knowledge, which was an issue especially as they were the majority

---

[1] Report of the Presidential Commission of the Establishment of a Democratic One-Party State, Paragraphs 25-32
[2] AMNUT to The Chairman, Trusteeship, United Nations, Ref. 2965/9/59, 15 January 1960
[3] Ibid.

community.[1] This was followed by various legal mechanisms to eradicate opposition to TANU, and to consolidate its political power.

1.7: Consolidation of TANU political power

In the 1960 Presidential election Julius Kambarage Nyerere defeated Mr C.S.K. Tumbo, the African National Congress (ANC) candidate.[2] Nyerere won 99.2 per cent of the votes cast in the 1962 presidential election, compared to 0.8 per cent cast for the only opponent, Zuberi Mtemvu of the African National Congress.[3] As a result of losing, Mtemvu dissolved the ANC, and rejoined TANU, a move endorsed by its members. Some Asian members who contested for TANU's ticket won. Moreover, Julius Nyerere appointed seven Africans, four Europeans and one Indian, A.H. Jamal, to his cabinet. This prompted nearly half the members of the Asian Association between 1962 and 1964 to join TANU.

During this time, the United Tanganyika Party (UTP), which was oriented to the European population, won only one seat, and the African National Congress, a breakaway party from TANU, won none.[4] From these elections Julius Kambarage Nyerere developed the idea that culminated in the one (single) party state. He argued that the overwhelming electoral support for TANU showed the public did not understand the notion of an opposition party.[5] Further, Nyerere suggested that a multiparty system was more democratic. He pointed out that with multiple parties, parliamentary representatives are under pressure to support their party, and thus do not vote according to their conscience. If there is a single party, and if that party 'is identified with the nation as a whole, the foundations of democracy are firmer than they can ever be where you have two or more parties, each representing only a section of the community.'[6] At this juncture, the political opposition was placed in a difficult position due to repressive legislation, the Preventative Detention Act of 1962. Under this law, it was legal for the government to detain anyone thought to be a 'danger to peace and good order.'

In 1963, TANU's National Executive Council (NEC) decided to make Tanganyika a one party state. In 1965, the recommendations by a presiden-

---

[1] Ibid.

[2] Kibuta Ong'wamuhana, *Party Supremacy and the State Constitution in Africa's One-Party States: The Kenya-Tanzania Experience* (Third World Legal Studies, 1988) pp. 77, 83

[3] International IDEA, *Political Parties in East Africa: Diversity in Political Party Systems* (Stockholm: International IDEA) p. 31

[4] Ong'wamuhana, Party Supremacy pp. 77, 83

[5] Julius K. Nyerere, Democracy and the Party System 1-2 (1962) Substantial excerpts of this pamphlet appear in Julius K. Nyerere, Freedom and Unity: *Uhuru na Umoja*: A Selection from Writings and Speeches 1952-1965, at 195-96 (1967); Julius K. Nyerere, Democracy, supra note 26, at 4

[6] Nyerere, Democracy, supra note 26, at 7

tial commission on constitutional matters were adopted that led to amendment of the constitution. Political activities could only be conducted after a review by TANU.[1] Back in 1964, Nyerere, by then Tanganyika's President in addition to TANU Chair, appointed the Presidential Commission on 28 January 1964 to make recommendations on how one-party rule could be implemented and specifically on how citizen participation could be ensured.[2] The terms of reference for the Commission were:

   a. Tanganyika to remain a Republic with an executive president;
   b. Equality for all citizens;
   c. Maximum political freedom within the context of 'a single national movement';
   d. People's free choice of their representatives in the legislature;
   e. People's participation in the government and their ultimate control over state organs; and
   f. Observance of the Rule of Law and independence of the Judiciary.

Ideally, the terms of reference in this case determined the results and expected recommendation.

The commission could not contravene the terms of reference and when it submitted its report in March 1965 it recommended one-party rule. The Constitution however, was deemed interim. Section 3 of the Interim Constitution which was adopted on 11 July 1965 stated that 'there shall be one political party,' and that 'all political activity in Tanzania, other than that of the organs of State ... shall be conducted by or under the auspices of the Party.'[3] The Constitution was termed Interim because of the unresolved complications associated with the Union between the two recently merged countries: maintaining the ruling parties, that is TANU for Tanganyika and Afro Shirazi Party (ASP) for Zanzibar. The interim constitution paved the way for TANU consolidating power through abolition of opposition parties. In 1964, Tanganyika and Zanzibar (which achieved independence in 1963) united and became the United Republic of Tanzania. Under the Interim Constitution approved in September 1965, the President, assisted by two Vice Presidents, exercised executive power.

Nevertheless, this development was hailed by Julius Kambarage Nyerere, who outlined in his speech to the National Assembly on 8 June 1965, that the structures and institutions provided under the Constitution would

---

[1] A.N. Kweka, One-Party Democracy and the Multi-Party State, Colin Legum & Geoffrey Mmari (eds) *Mwalimu: The Influence of Nyerere* (Trenton, NJ: Africa World Press, 1995) p. 67
[2] Y.P. Ghai & J.P.W.B. McAuslan, Constitutional Proposals for a One-Party State in Tanzania, East Africa Law Journal, vol.1, issue 2 (1965) pp. 124-147
[3] The Interim Constitution of Tanzania, confirmed by An Act to Declare the Interim Constitution of Tanzania, No. 43 of 1965, Tanganyika Revised Laws Cap.596 - Supp. 65, § 3(1), reprinted in 2 Constitutions of African States 1517 (Asian-African Legal Consultative Committee, 1972)

suitably serve Tanzania's circumstances. While the Constitution promoted the ruling party status it reduced the National Assembly to a committee of the National Conference of the ruling party. Against this backdrop, individuals who supported the ruling party had a chance for nomination to Parliamentary seats during elections, unlike critics.

At the time, Zanzibar and Tanganyika each had a dominant political party (the ASP and TANU, respectively), thus the notion of a one-party state faced an obstacle. The Interim Constitution solved this obstacle to an extent in its provision that contemplated an eventual merger between TANU and the Afro Shirazi Party: 'Until the union of the Tanganyika African National Union with the Afro-Shirazi Party (which United Party shall constitute the one political Party), the Party shall, in and for Tanganyika, be the Tanganyika African Nation.'

After independence, trade unions had several demands that pressured the post-colonial government. Some concerned trade union autonomy by providing space for more trade unions, decentralisation of the TFL powers, allowing workers to strike and Africanization of civil service recruitment. The waves of worker strikes gained momentum in the early 1960s demanding better working conditions, higher wages and less oppressive management. Such demands and actions were viewed by the post-colonial authority as provocative and non-patriotic.

Moreover, the trade union movement was a well-organised independent pressure group after independence. At this stage the government had to act against TFL. Thus, post-independence, TFL had to be cut short following a growing rift with the government.[1] The government sought to contain it by appointing some of its leaders. The Secretary of the Tanganyika Railway African Union (TRAU), Mr C.S.K. Tumbo, a critic of government was appointed High Commissioner to London but resigned only to form the opposition political party, the People's Democratic Party (PDP) and Michael Kamaliza, was appointed Minister for Health and Labour. Hence, the Trade Unions (Settlement) Act, 43 of 1962 was promulgated in which strikes technically became illegal and settlement of labour disputes had to go through complex procedures. Moreover, the Trade Union Ordinance (Amendment) Act of 1962 practically made the TFL the only trade union in the country.[2]

The trade union legislation was designed not only to weaken the TFL influence but also to bring the trade union under control of the government, hence the Trade Unions Ordinance (Amendment) Act, 51 of 1962. Under Sections 7, 13 and 14 of this amendment, the Minister for Labour was granted powers to appoint any federation of workers' trade union as a

---

[1] W. Tordoff, *Government and Politics in Tanzania* (Nairobi: East African Publishing House, 1967) pp. 147, 163

[2] Government Notice 351 of 1962

designated federation to which every registered trade union was obliged to affiliate.

In a move to arrest strikes, the Trade Disputes (Settlement) Act, 43 of 1962 was repealed and replaced with the Trade Disputes (Arbitration & Settlement) Ordinance, Cap.296 which made strikes and lockouts an offence. The law made provision for setting up an industrial dispute settlement procedure and machinery which involved negotiation, conciliation and arbitration.

Additionally, in an attempt to further control trade unions, the National Union of Tanganyika Workers (Establishment) Act 18 of 1964 (Cap.555) was introduced by the government. Under this legislation, the TFL was dissolved and lost legitimacy. In its place, the National Union of Tanganyika Workers (NUTA) became the only workers union in the country. The National Union of Tanganyika (Workers Establishment) Act of 1964 brought in some government interference on matters associated with the democratic election of office bearers by trade union members.

In a move to ensure the labour movement was closelely controlled by the government and TANU, the NUTA Secretary-General and his deputy had to be appointed by the President of the country. Hence, Minister for Health and Labour, Michael Kamaliza, was NUTA's first Secretary-General. The creation of NUTA was nothing other than integrating the trade union movement with the political system as the secretary-general became a member of the Executive Committee of the ruling party, TANU. In 1991 the Organisation of Tanzania Trade Unions (OTTU) was established under Section 4 of Tanzania Trade Unions Act, 20 of 1991. As a result, JUWATA was renamed OTTU in 1992 and all members of JUWATA automatically became members of OTTU. This signified a formal split between the trade union, the government and ruling party. At its 1995 Congress OTTU changed its name to the Tanzania Federation of Free Trade Unions (TFTU).

In the early 1960s, more political parties were formed after independence such as the People's Democratic Party (PDP) by Kasanga Tumbo and People's Convention Party (PCP) which opposed TANU's multiracial education policy that was geared towards ending racially separate schools.[1] Others were religious-based such as the All Muslim National Union of Tanganyika (AMNUT) and People's Convention Party led by Christians,[2] and some were confined within ethnic/tribal affiliations such as the Chagga Democratic Party among the WaChagga of Kilimanjaro,[3] the Hehe Democratic Party among the WaHehe of Iringa[6] and Kianja Labour Association which was confined to Kianja in Bukoba

---

[1] Bienien, *Tanzania: Party Transformation* p. 58

[2] Ludwig, *Church and State in Tanzania*, p. 66

[3] Kathleen M. Stahl, The Chagga, in P.H. Gullier (ed) *Tradition and Transition in East Africa: Studies of the Tribal Factor* (London: Routledge, 1969) p. 219

district.[1] For the newly independent country this was viewed as disintegration of the country into religious and ethnic backgrounds.

To achieve national unity, legal steps were taken which had political implications. Such measures involved the African Chief (Repeal) Act 13 of 1963 that brought indirect rule, a chief-based administrative system introduced in 1926, and the Native Authority to an end. The system was replaced by elected district councils. The Chiefs (Abolition of Office: Consequential Provisions) Act, 1963, made it illegal for former chiefs to reclaim or challenge their lost position and a number of them became civil servants. Such reforms were designed to stamp out chiefs who opposed the ruling party TANU before and after independence. In so doing it provided for centralised political power under TANU. This was a significant step in stamping out tribalism which posed a threat to national unity.

2. Promotion of Cash Crop Farming

The British administration was confronted with innumerable difficulties when it took control of Tanganyika. Such challenges included trade and revenue having fallen to less than half of what they were before the war. The Germans had been expelled from the plantations and commercial enterprise as well as from mission stations, these holdings being held together precariously either by the administration in the case of plantations and commercial enterprises or by missionaries from allied countries in the case of the latter. Sir Horace Byatt, the first British governor of the territory, had to rescue Tanganyika from the economic crisis.

Understandably, to prevent extra financial burdens on the British tax payer, all British colonies were to comply with the financial self-sufficiency policy which guided the colonial administrations from the 1920s to the 1940s.[1] The realisation of financial self-sufficiency required the colonial authority to engage every adult in economic activities, either cash production or working in the various economic sectors, and to pay tax (poll, hut, and head taxes) in cash. This enabled the colonial authority to generate revenue for the colonial annual budget.

Since the economic welfare of the natives depended upon agriculture, promoting and engaging Africans to produce crops, mainly for export, was therefore a priority. The Native Authorities and Agricultural Department passed a series of agricultural regulations that provided for compulsion of small-scale growers to produce prescribed crops. The colonial state passed the Native Authority Ordinance of 1926, enabling Native Authorities to force people into cash crop cultivation. Bye-laws obliged African small-scale farmers to cultivate a minimum acreage of export crops. The growers responded to the demand in order to generate money and avoid punishment. In turn, growers managed to pay taxes that were collected by the chiefs and village headmen who were vested with the task.

The most important established revenue source by the Native Authorities was the native hut or poll tax imposed by colonial authorities on Africans. The Native Authorities established in 1925, included overseeing local chiefs who were responsible for collecting taxes on behalf of the government. Taxation of natives was also a means to force them to grow cash crops for foreign markets especially in Britain and European countries.[2]

---

[1] British Aid – 5 Colonial Development: a factual survey of the origins and history of British aid to developing countries (London: The Overseas Development Institute) p. 6
[2] Walter Rodney, *How Europe underdeveloped Africa* (Dar es Salaam: Tanzania Publishing

Table 4: Number of tax payers in all Provinces, 1931

Province	Number of tax Payers	Exempted	Additional taxes (polygamy families)
Central	205,023	2,748	28,660
Eastern	157,628	5,483	20,366
Iringa	115,327	4,610	20,427
Lake	377,118	26,256	49,197
Lindi	146,097	8,569	14,204
Mahenge	59,284	6,781	8,675
Northern	104,222	1,727	15,091
Tanga	132,369	3,908	13,021
Western	291,496	16,834	37,385

Source: Tanganyika Report by His Majesty's Government to the Council of the League of Nations on the Administration of Tanganyika Territory, 1931

The NA treasuries were created which also fell under the chiefs. The treasuries raised revenues from various sources including taxes (poll and hut). Part of the collected revenues were kept and the other disbursed to the central government. Revenue collected by the chiefs was spent on aspects such as salaries, development of infrastructure and provision of social services (health and education).[1]

Tax paid in colonial currency rather than in-kind was essential to produce the desired outcome as well as monetise the African communities.[2] The governor had power to reduce the tax in less developed districts, and there was no reason why the tax had to be uniform throughout any given territory. Taxation facilitated the primitive accumulation of capital and creation of markets among Africans for imported goods to generate further revenue for the colonial administration.[3]

In addition, some locations were specifically set aside for the supply of labourers to other sectors where they were paid salaries, part of which was used to pay taxes. In such places as Kigoma and Songea, people were strongly discouraged from undertaking other cash production activities thereby curtailing access to alternative income sources, except wage labour. This forced them into migrant labour and subsistence production.

The interwar years saw a steady supply of migrant workers in the territory. The 1938 reports show that 10,000 laborers were from Lake Province, 9,000 from Southern Highlands with 6,500 from Central

---

House, 1973)

[1] British Aid – 5 Colonial Development: a factual survey of the origins and history of British aid to developing countries (London: The Overseas Development Institute) p. 6

[2] Walter Rodney, *How Europe underdeveloped Africa* (Dar es Salaam: Tanzania Publishing House, 1972)

[3] Report of East Africa Commission 1925, presented by Secretary of State for Colonies to Parliament by command of His Majesty (London: HMSO, 1925)

Province.[1] Most labourers were deployed to work in sisal plantations. However, following outbreak of the Second World War, sisal plantations in Tanzania faced serious labour shortages. This was prompted by the colonial authority prioritising war efforts. Therefore, the war and sisal industry found themselves in competition for labourers. At the outbreak of World War Two, sisal gained a strategic importance when Indonesia fell to the Japanese[2] that created scarcity and eventually demand increased. This was a time when the British Ministry of Supply had to incorporate sisal into war-time Defence and Emergency Orders.

The colonial authority could not restrict the industry recruiting labourers. As a result, the plantation owners set up the Sisal Labour Bureau (SILABU), in 1944 that had its headquarters in Tanga, to facilitate conscription and regulation of labourers on sisal plantations. As a result, Songea district, Kigoma and Tabora (then in Western Province), and Rukwa and Njombe (then in Southern Highlands Province), were set aside as labour reserves to supply *manamba*, that is migrant labourers, to sisal plantations along the coast[3] where monthly wages were Shs. 20/- plus a Shs. 5/- bonus.[4] Some labourers from WCGA were sent to work on the sisal plantations in Tanga and Arusha Provinces as punishment for neglect of their cotton farms.[5]

The NAs had responsibility for conscription and labour recruitment. This was in response to the demands made upon NAs by the colonial authority for the war effort. The NAs thus played a part in the supply of their people to serve in the KAR and as labourers for the sisal plantations.[6] In 1944 about 30,500 and, the following years to 1946, 26,200 labourers from labour reserve areas were recruited and transported to work on sisal plantations. SILABU recruited most plantation labourers from various parts of the territory and several from neighbouring territories as Rwanda and Burundi, Zambia, Mozambique and Malawi.[7] The labourers from neighboring countries came to Tanganyika, particularly to work for a wage. This recruitment of labour from neighboring countries was however brought to an end in 1950[8] in favour of expanding to cover more districts

---

[1] John A. Noon, *Labour Problems of Africa* (Philadelphia: University of Pennsylvania, 1944) p. 105

[2] Andrew Coulson, *Tanzania: A Political economy* (Oxford: Clarendon Press, 1982) p. 49; I.G. Shivji, *State and the Working Class in Tanzania* (London: James Currey, 1986) p. 49; Isaria N. Kimambo, Gregory H. Maddox & Salvatory Nyato, *A New History of Tanzania* (Dar es Salaam: Mkuki na Nyota, 2017) p. 211

[3] Kimambo, Maddox & Nyato, *A New History of Tanzania*, p. 211; Shivji, *State and the Working Class in Tanzania*, p. 14

[4] TNA 16, 13/25: Annual Labour Report for 1953, p. 270

[5] TNA 215/665, vol. I: Maswa DC to PC, Lake Province, Ref. 402/3676, 16 May 1933; Shinyanga District Book

[6] Coulson, *Tanzania*, p. 49; Shivji, *State and the Working Class in Tanzania*, p. 44

[7] Noon, *Labour Problems of Africa*, p. 105

in the territory in addition to the reserve areas.¹

Apart from paying taxes, workers were lured to plantations by the need to buy imported manufactured goods. This together with other incentives were instrumental for the small-scale crop growers to engage in cash crop farming. This is demonstrated by the argument that 'the backward condition of the people and their preference for agricultural pursuit offer the prospect of continued markets for manufactured goods'.² In this respect, the taxes imposed were obligatory, to be paid even in the face of declining prices. This made a very effective economic policy and laid a concrete foundation for cultivation of 'economic' crops.

From the late 1860s, the politicians and public in Britain were divided over whether the colonies were worth keeping. This was the era when William Ewart Gladstone was British Prime Minister and when pro-colonists had the view that colonies were vital for the British economy, for the supply of foodstuffs and raw materials, industrial employment in the colonialising European metropoles and as markets for manufactured goods.³ Those who opposed having colonies were of the view that colonies were an extra financial burden on British tax payers. The consensus was that for the colonies to be maintained they should be financially self-sufficient (self-supporting).⁴ This was primarily to ensure that, all British colonies covered their administration costs and were not dependant on the United Kingdom Treasury for finance. For the policy to be achieved, political control and restructuring of the African subsistence economy was fundamental for both the production and supply of raw materials, marketing and revenue generation.

However, the advent of the Great Depression heightened the need for the colonial power to assist its colonies. This led to setting up the Colonial Development fund in 1929,⁵ which aimed at aiding colonial economic

---

[8] Francis Wilson & Christpher Clapham, *Labour in South Africa Gold Mines* (Cambridge: University Press, 1972) p. 123

[1] TNA 460, 8/94/Vol I: Labour Commissioner John V. Shaw to TSGA Labour Bureau, 6 January 1951; Walter Rodney, Migrant Labour and the Colonial Economy, W. Rodney, K. Tambila & L. Sago (eds) *Migrant Labour in Tanzania During the Colonial Period: Case Studies of Recruitment and Conditions of Labour in the Sisal Industry* (Hamburg: Institut fur Afrika-Kunde, 1983) pp. 4-28

[2] FJD Lugard, *The Dual Mandate in British Tropical Africa* (London: Frank Cass & Co, 1965) pp. 4, 13, 268, 277

[3] Paul Knaplund, *Gladstone and Britain's Imperial* (New York: MacMillan, 1927)

[4] British Aid – 5 Colonial Development: a factual survey of the origins and history of British aid to developing countries (London: The Overseas Development Institute) p. 6

[5] Frank, The Formation of British Colonial Development Policy in the Trans World Wars Two Period, 1942-1953: With special reference to central and Southern Africa (unpublished PhD thesis, Edge Hill Lancaster University, 2002) pp.17-20; Fabian Colonial Bureau, *A Report from a Special Committee to the Fabian Colonial Bureau on Co-operation in the Colonies* (London: George Allen & Unwin) p. 21

development.[1] It was made by the colonial power basically to increase its foreign trade so as to create employment in Britain which was seriously affected by the economic depression.[2] The British colonial power was compelled to support its colonies financially because the depression caused a substantial fall in government revenue. By and large small-scale cotton production proved flexible and important in stabilising the country's economy through compulsory minimum acreage that led to expansion of production. In response to the economic crash colonial government made efforts to bolster the territory's finances through an 'Increase Production Campaign'. This was an attempt to counterbalance the price decline of exported cotton by increasing output. At the time, coffee production in settlers' estates was also destabilised and declined due to a drastic fall in price and increased production costs. As a result, some settlers abandoned production, but African growers continued with production and their number kept increasing as they increased acreage and output.

2.1: Characteristics of the agricultural sector

During the German colonial era (1885-1919), agricultural production in Tanzania was characterised by having two parallel competing agricultural sectors, split between European planters and settlers and native small-scale growers. The British adopted the system when they took over the German-controlled territories after WWI. The planters focused on sisal farming that was dominant along the coast, whereas the settlers were mainly occupied with coffee farming in Kilimanjaro and Meru districts. In the Southern Highlands, mainly in Rungwe district, settler farming failed to prosper and they abandoned coffee farming, a vacuum that was filled by small-scale growers. However, given the capital demand to develop the sisal industry, natives could not afford to participate in that sector but were exploited as labourers. Coffee farming in Kagera, like cotton farming in both Eastern and Western Cotton Growing Areas, remained native-dominated industries.

Clearly, the colonial agricultural policy in Tanganyika had been a dual agricultural economy whereby the commercial estates sector existed side by side with peasant agriculture. The commercial estates sector under European settlers and planters occupied alienated land for coffee, tea, tobacco and sisal plantations, creating an environment that attracted German and Greek settlers to invest in coffee farming from 1898.[3] The policy considered small-scale crop growers essential for increasing the export of raw crops,

---

[1] Meredith and Havinden, *Colonialism and Development*, pp. 140-206
[2] Frank, Formation of British Colonial Development Policy, p. 17
[3] Tanganyika Territory 1947 Report of Arusha – Moshi Land Commission, p. 16; Helmut Glenk, Horst Blaich, & Peer Gatter, *Shattered Dreams at Kilimanjaro* (Trafford Publishing, 2011) p. 12; R.W. James, *Land Tenure and Policy in Tanzania* (Toronto: University Press, 1971) p. 13

and thus increasing revenue obtained from exported crops.[1] Additionally, maintaining settler and small-scale grower co-existence would ensure that both African agriculture and European plantations would enable effective economic integration beneficial to all parties.

Under the terms of the peace treaty, all Germans, missionaries as well as settlers, were required to leave Tanganyika, surrender their property and vacate their plantations. This action might have been prompted by the terms of the peace treaty itself since it was silent on estates and land formerly alienated by German settlers until the Tanganyika Order in Council that set up the Mandate was published by Governor Sir Horace Byatt. The Order set about framing legislation for land control and distribution that was in favour of natives. For example, in his speech to the London Chamber of Commerce on 22 May 1922, Horace Byatt catagorically argued that the future lay in developing native cultivation.[2]

The earliest British agricultural policy encouraged small-scale growers to utilise their own land for cash crop production by maintaining the landholding system which was based on customary laws. This was provided for in the Mandate Agreement, Article 22. The policy was implemented by the Germans and later by the British which provided small-scale growers access to land for crop cultivation. Encouragement of small-scale growers was supported and reinforced by the policy that provided access to land as provided under the Land Ordinance (Cap.68) of 1923, which was based on the Northern Nigerian ordinance of 1907. More so, the law resolved land disputes and provided for restriction over land alienation for settlers.[3] The British colonial authority supported the policy and made its commitment clear that the future of the territory required prioritisation in developing native agriculture.[4] The legislation provided for safeguarding natives access to land that they had to use for settlement and production of crops both for food and export. The legislation, unlike in some countries where the settler economy was dominant as in Kenya and Zimbabwe, did not racially segregate the natives into reserves. Importantly, under the legislation further land alienation was not precluded by taking into primary consideration the needs of the particular historical period and its future; as a result in the mid-1920s, the settler community in Tanganyika had to lobby, but failed, for transfer of land lying between Meru and Kilimanjaro Mountains to be transferred to Kenya where land alienation policy was applied. It is worthy to note that settlers in Kenya unsuccessfully attempted to have access to

---

[1] Archibald Church, *East Africa a New Dominion: A Crucial Experiment in Tropical Development and its Significance to the British Empire* (London HF & G Witherby, 1927) p. 87
[2] Dar es Salaam *Times*, 3 June 1922
[3] Report on Tanganyika Territory Armistice, 1920 (London: HMSO, 1921)
[4] Byatt, Sir Horace, *Journal of the Royal African Society*, XXIV (1924) pp. 1-5

land in Tanganyika, having lobbied for closer political union of East African countries.[1] The implementation of the policy, therefore, provided for the predominance of small-scale growers in Tanganyika unlike in Kenya and Zimbabwe.

Native Authority Ordinance 8, 1926, Cap.72 authorised power to issue bye-laws regulating land by the Native Authorities.[2] In an attempt to protect native rights, land occupancy was redefined in 1928 to include the title of a native[3] community lawfully using or occupying land in accordance with customary law. This was to accommodate crop cultivation by small-scale growers and recognised land occupation by natives.

The policy was implemented as an important measure to revive the economy, which was brought to a standstill by the war and to raise revenue to cover administrative costs by enabling growers to generate revenue to pay taxes. As a result of implementing both the League of Nation's commitment and the need to generate revenue, there was a predominance of small-scale growers who were preoccupied with the production of food crops for their own consumption as well as cash crops such as coffee, cotton and tobacco, mainly for export. The cultivation of export crops by African small-scale growers represented an important and long established economic activity during the colonial period. The engagement of African small-scale growers in the cash crop export market was principally to benefit the colonial government and later the post-colonial government. Farming of export crops by small-scale growers was by and large a policy that integrated them into the foreign export market to which they had no direct access as access was dominated by marketing boards or merchants who determined the prices for the produce. The policy gained significance during the Great Depression when Britain exploited small-scale growers to solve the economic crisis in the metropole.

Encouragement of cash crop production by small-scale growers was the most effective strategy because it was the cheapest way to obtain raw materials for export. African growers were, unlike settlers, a viable option because they had to utilise their own land for the production of prescribed crops; as a result they became the main cash crop producers. The approach was further maintained through taxation that was paid in cash thereby creating an effective mechanism to stimulate cash crop production among the natives. Thus, land policy and encouragement of natives in producing

---

[1] Ali A. Mazrui & Michael Tidy, *Nationalism and New States in Africa, from about 1935 to present* (Nairobi: Heinemann, 1984) p. 75; E. Huxley, *White Man's Country: Lord Delamere and the Making of Kenya*, vol. 1, 1870-1914; vol. 2, 1914-1931 (New York. Praeger, 1968)

[2] The Native Authorities Ordinance, no.8 of 1926, Cap 72 was revised in 1947 and then replaced in 1953 by the Local Government Ordinance Cap 333 which established local government authorities instead of the native authorities.

[3] Native was defined as Native of Africa not being European, Somali, Asiatic or Arab descendants.

cash crops proved fruitful as in 1925, 51 per cent of total coffee exports and about 75 per cent of cotton was produced by small-scale growers. More so, the law resolved land disputes and provided for restrictions over land alienation by settlers.[1] The British colonial authority supported the policy and made its commitment clear: the future of the territory lay in developing native agriculture,[2] providing an opportunity for Britain to exploit colonial resources for its own economic benefit.[3] Against this backdrop, Britain complied with the obligation of incorporating the colonised into cash crop production.

The policy emanated from the land tenure system under Article I of 1895 through which the Germans issued an Imperial Decree that all land, whether occupied or not, was to be treated as public; ownership was invested in the Empire (crown land). The British put in place the Land Ordinance (1923) in which land rights were vested in the governor who was empowered to lease public land. The land policy, following promulgation of the Land Ordinance which, among many aspects, prohibited further land alienation in the Central, Northern and Tanga Provinces.[4]

Through amendments of the Ordinance made in 1928 it ensured and allowed Africans to utilise *vihamba* (clan land)[5] among the WaChagga of Kilimanjaro and *Nyarubanja*,[6] the quasi-feudal system, among the WaHaya of Bukoba where coffee was grown. Similarly, in cotton growing areas, the Ordinance accommodated land occupation in accordance with customary law but precluded land transfer from Africans to non-Africans. Access to land and its utilisation was enhanced by the administration's compliance with the League of Nations' encouragement of indigenous Tanganyikans to join in efforts in utilising the land for economic purposes, mainly the production of cash crops for export. The encouragement of small-scale growers to produce cash crops was that they were much cheaper in that the government would not be required to invest capital and use its own land for crop production. Additionally, growers were viewed as more reliable in meeting production targets.

The land legislation gave rights to farmers to use land to cultivate crops. Through indirect rule, the British governor encouraged indigenous Tanganyikans to join in efforts to produce cash crops for export, thereby expanding small-scale grower agriculture. Ordinances were the major instruments used to achieve agricultural development under small-scale grower management. The dual agricultural economy was therefore significant in the devel-

---

[1] Report on Tanganyika Territory Armistice, 1920 (London: HMSO, 1921)
[2] Sir Horace Byatt, *Journal of the Royal African Society*, XXIV (1924) pp. 1-5
[3] L. Hadden-Guest, *The Labour Party and the Empire* (London: 1926) pp. 3, 83-90
[4] Dar es Salaam *Times*, 31 December 1921
[5] Moshi District Book
[6] Bukoba District Book

opment of the coffee industry in Tanganyika, particularly for indigenous growers who employed on their own farms the knowledge and experience acquired as labourers on settler and missionary coffee farms in Kilimanjaro.

With the increased tax burden, growers had to borrow money from money lenders to meet the obligation and purchase other necessities. Several defaulted or could not afford to repay because of crop failures which resulted in land confiscation. In response the British colonial authority stepped in by enacting the Native Credit Ordinance which clearly supported small-scale crop growers as it provided protection for their land. Philip E. Mitchell, then a district Commissioner in Tanga, wrote, 'The Credit to Natives Ordinance fills a long felt want and will do more than anything to prevent the African from selling or encumbering his land';[1] hence assurance of the cultivation of both food and cash crops.

The encouragement of small-scale growers by missionaries had support from the colonial government on realising that the small-scale grower could offer a cheaper alternative to produce export crops than the estates. Such support was significant in the expansion of coffee cultivation, not only in Kilimanjaro but also in Bukoba. This was an important policy development that engaged Africans in cash crop production and meant a departure from subsistence economy.

The European coffee planters in Tanganyika lobbied the colonial authority to displace growers in the suitable coffee growing areas on the slopes of Mount Kilimanjaro, Pare Mountains, and the Matengo highlands in Ruvuma, Rungwe and Meru districts.[2] These settlers consistently demanded restrictions be imposed because growers lacked expertise in coffee farming and because their crops allegedly were a source of pests and disease, which could have infected planters' farms, resulting in loss of the invested capital.[3]

Hundreds of farmlands were alienated to make room for settler production of coffee in Rungwe, an area considered by Lord Delamere suitable for white colonisation.[4] Kilimanjaro and Meru districts experienced land alienation for the same reason.[5] In Rungwe, in Meru district, the settlers succeeded in their intent, whereas in Kilimanjaro it was the colonial authority who quashed the idea. The failure in Rungwe was prompted by the huge debts that settlers experienced during the economic depression, while the failure in Meru can be attributed to bankruptcy and drought, which incapac-

---

[1] TNA 1733/23 Tanga district Report, by P.E. Mitchell, 1923, p. 1

[2] Iliffe, *A Modern History of Tanganyika*

[3] A.J. Wakefield, Native Production of Coffee on Kilimanjaro, *The Empire Journal of Experimental Agriculture*, Volume IV (Oxford: Clarendon Press, 1936) pp. 97-109

[4] Church, *East Africa: A New Dominion*, p. 279

[5] T. Spear, *Mountain Farmers* (Dar es Salaam: Mkuki na Nyota, 1997) p. 142; N.N. Luanda, *European Commercial Farming and its Impact on the Meru and Arusha Peoples of Tanzania, 1920-1955* (University of Cambridge, unpublished PhD thesis, 1986)

itated a significant number of settlers from developing the industry further.

All in all, the cultivation of some export crops by native growers represented an important and long-established economic activity during the colonial period that was then the main cash resource. The export crops policy extensively promoted peasant agricultural development . To achieve these initiatives which were implemented initially by missionaries, the Department of Agriculture assumed responsibility for agricultural development and promotion. The integration policy was designed principally to benefit the colonial government, and later the post-colonial government, to meet financial self-sufficiency through the realisation of revenue by encouraging growers to participate in production.

2.2: The Agricultural Department

The Agricultural Department and competent staff were key to the Colonial Office and Corporation to ensure industry success. In this, a number of policy issues, most of which emanated from Major Hastings Horne's report on the cotton industry, were given priority by the Colonial Office and the government.[1] Firstly, setting up the Agricultural Department.

In the early 1920s, Horne recommended the recruitment of European experts to facilitate the formation of a department to co-ordinate not only cotton cultivation but all other crops, such as coffee and tobacco. To accomplish this, the Empire Cotton Growing Corporation (ECGC) was assigned the task given that it had experts at its disposal. The ECGC appointed Cotton Specialist R.C. Wood, who was first stationed at Mpanganya which was potentially to become the department headquarters. However, Wood decided to move the office to Morogoro where he eventually set up the Agricultural Department because of access to transport services.[2] Wood established the department in 1921 with the revival and expansion of the cotton industry as one of its chief objectives.

Horne recommended recruitment of the experienced cotton extension staff to work in the department. To him, they were vital to the success in widening and extending the industry.[3] As a result, the ECGC made available some of its own experienced staff in matters related to cotton to assist the department.[4] One of its experts was appointed Assistant Director of Agriculture who was stationed in Mwanza, charged with responsibility to

---

[1] H. Horne, *The extension of cotton cultivation in Tanganyika Territory: Report to the Committee on tour in Tanganyika territory Nov 1920 – July 1921* (London: The Empire Cotton Growing Corporation, 1922)

[2] The Empire Cotton Growing Review, *Journal of The Empire Cotton Growing Corporation*, vol. XXVIII, no 1, January 1951

[3] Horne, *The extension of cotton cultivation*

[4] Bulletin of the Imperial Institute, *A Quarterly Record of Progress in Tropical Agriculture and Industries and the Commercial Utilisation of the Natural Resources Of the Dominions, Colonies and India*, vol. XX (London: Hasell, Watson & Viney, 1922) p. 176; TNA, 215/665, vol. I

promote and oversee cotton production in the Western Cotton Growing Area (WCGA).[1]

To facilitate production of cotton in the WCGA, the Corporation recruited ten cotton experts who had to strengthen the capacity of the local Department of Agriculture and develop the industry to enhance and stimulate cotton production in the British colonies.[2] A team of three agricultural instructors were recruited on a temporary or part-time basis; all European supervisors specialised in cotton.[3] Obviously, such intervention by the Corporation was significant to reinforce the department given that production of cotton and other crops formed, the mainstay of the economy of the colony. Clearly, this signified a commitment of the Corporation to develop the industry. It also assumed cotton policy dominancy of the department.

The Agricultural Department was of primary importance in agricultural development. For this reason, the number of officers with higher education rose from 127 in 1950 to 232 in 1960. This changed the overall outlook of the Agricultural Department where the work which was carried out by 756 instructors with hardly any training in 1950 was then in 1960 carried out by 815 assistant field officers, who had completed a two-year course at the agricultural school in Tengeru (Northern Region) and Ukiriguru (Lake Region). In addition, 1,210 instructors without formal training were employed in 1960.

Table 5: Staff of the Agricultural Department 1950-1960

Year	Agriculture officers	Specialists officers	Field assistants	Field instructors	Agriculture instructors
1950	39	17	71	-	756
1951	46	21	79	-	-
1952	52	23	91	-	971
1953	48	24	101	-	1512
1954	47	21	91	414	1442
1955	50	20	97	527	1264
1956	49	20	103	322	920
1957	66	25	112	411	872
1958	70	28	114	608	1246
1959	69	30	138	700	1272
1960	74	33	125	815	1210

Source: Report of the World Bank, Table 16, p. 61

---

[1] Bulletin of the Imperial Institute, *A Quarterly Record of Progress*
[2] N.R. Fuggles-Couchman, *Agriculture Change in Tanganyika: 1945-1960* (Stanford: California: Food Research Institute, Stanford University, 1964) p. 17
[3] TNA 26298/8, Lake Province, PC, to CS, Ref. 26298/29, 14 February 1940

2.3: Agricultural Research

Agricultural research, as an organised, state-sponsored activity, began with the development of botanical gardens that were established by the colonial powers to select desirable plant materials that were transferred to the colonies. One such research initiative was Kew Gardens in Britain, where the rubber tree was introduced in southeast Asia, tea was introduced in Ceylon (now Sri Lanka), and Cinchona (quinine) to India. In 1919, the British set up the Colonial Research Committee that facilitated funds to assist crop research in the colony.

The Germans similarly had experimental initiatives that began in the 1850s, and France soon followed. Whereas the stations located in Europe tended to focus on food crops, those in the colonies emphasised export crops that would provide exotic foods (bananas, sugar and coconuts), exotic drinks (coffee, tea) and raw materials (cotton). It was only after the end of World War II, and especially after independence of the former colonies, that research on food crops became a significant part of African research agendas.

The German Colonial Administration established a research station (Biologisch–Landwirtschaftliches Institut) at Amani in 1902 where they conducted basic research on crops such as coffee.[1] When the British took over after World War I, they utilised the station to service the British East African colonies of Kenya, Uganda, and the British Protectorate of Tanganyika. After World War II, the British Colonial Headquarters for Regional Research in East Africa moved from Amani to Muguga outside Nairobi.

The ECGC made grants available to the Agricultural Department for the maintenance of cotton experimental stations at Ilonga and Kingolwira in Morogoro, Ukiriguru in Mwanza, Lubaga in Shinyanga, Uzinza in Geita, and Mpanganya in Lindi. In 1939, a training school was set up at Ukiliguru, mainly to train staff for extension work.

Several other research stations were opened by the British in Tanganyika. Amongst the principal experimental stations in Tanganyika was the Coffee Research and Experiment Station at Lyamungo, near Moshi, established in 1934, which has ever since enjoyed a worldwide reputation. The Coffee Research and Experiment Station at Lyamungu usually had a staff of one scientist and two agricultural officers. The work of the station was principally coffee, but bananas, fodder grasses, and a small dairy herd of native cattle were among its other interests. The objective of coffee experiments was to explore different methods of cultivation, pruning, and soil treatment, the control of pests and diseases and irrigation. Clonal selection with a view to producing hardier and higher yielding varieties was a major part of the

---

[1] H. Brode, *British and German East Africa: Their Economic and Commercial Relations* (London: Edward Arnold, 1911) p. 114

work. The results obtained were most promising and of great value to planters.[1] Maruku station, comprising 869 acres of land, near Bukoba town, was opened in 1951 with a grant of £26,679 from the Development and Welfare Fund. The object of the scheme was to conduct research on Robusta coffee.

In summary, this chapter examined efforts by the British colonial and colonial authority in Tanzania in the promotion of agricultural export crops such as coffee, cotton and tobacco among African small-scale growers. The engagement of the African small-scale growers in the agricultural export crops was facilitated by free availability of approved seeds, and farming and post-harvest guidelines to ensure recommended quality of the produce was attained. The African small-scale growers who were encouraged to grow produce on their farmland were supported by the legislation.

The engagement of the African small-scale growers to produce cash crops went hand in hand with the erection of a concrete foundation that paved the way for the success of the industry. This comprised stakeholders in the textile industry in Britain engaging and deploying experts to determine the potential to develop cotton farming in Tanganyika. Some organizations like the Empire Cotton Growing Corporation (ECGC) made resources available to fund cotton development research and create the Department of Agriculture. The ECGC made available cotton experts to serve the Department, arguably to ensure that textile mills in Britain were successfully served. Similar development was also observed in the improvement of coffee production.

The promotion of agricultural export crops was enforced through compulsory crop farming measures among African small-scale growers by the district officials and local leaders provided by Native Authority legislations. The next chapter examines production of the agricultural export crops such as coffee, cotton and tobacco by African small-scale growers in various districts in the territory.

---

[1] Tanganyika Territory, Department of Agriculture, Annual Report, 1945, and Twelfth Annual Report of the Coffee Experimental Station, Lyamungo (MNCB, 1945).

3 Cash Crop Farming Among Smallholders

3.1: Cotton farming in the Western Cotton Growing Area

During the late 1890s, the farming economy of Tanganyika was basically subsistence, based on shifting cultivation.[1] Although wild cotton was found in the WCGA prior to the colonial period,[2] it was under German colonial rule from 1884 to 1916 that cotton cultivation was introduced as a cash crop to supply cotton to the textile mills in Germany, so as eventually to reduce dependence of supply on the United States of America (USA). The Germans devoted a great deal of attention to the development of the crop,[3] which was introduced to the area in 1904 by German settlers, but the attempt failed. One such attempt was by German settlers in Korogwe.

As a result of failed cases, the Germans had to learn from the success of the British methods in Uganda where cotton was produced by small-scale growers. However, the Germans compelled growers to produce the crop, especially in the Eastern Cotton Growing Area (ECGA) in such districts as Rufiji, Kilwa and Morogoro. Promotion of the crop was characterised by brutality and intimidation of growers. As a result, growers took up arms against the Germans in what was referred to as *Maji-maji* resistance from 1905-1907.

In the WCGA, production of the crop was introduced by White Fathers Missionaries on Ukerewe island. Development of the cotton industry in the country during German rule enjoyed technical expertise from the *Kolonialwirtschaftliches Komitee* (KWK) that earmarked the WCGA and Eastern coastal belt for cotton cultivation due to their suitable climate, soil and the availability of native labourers. In a move to support cotton growing in these locations, the KWK under the German government's auspices set up experimental stations.

During WWI, cotton cultivation in the WCGA and the rest of the country virtually ceased. The two British organisations with an interest in cotton, the ECGC and British Cotton Growing Association (BCGA), were

---

[1] M. Little, Colonial Policy and Subsistence in Tanganyika 1925-1945, *Geographical Review*, vol. 81, no. 4 (Oct., 1991) pp. 375-388; HR Webb, *Cotton in Tanzania* (United States of America: Department of Agriculture, 1970)

[2] C.P.K. Norris, *Cotton British Production in East Africa* (Washington, DC: United States Department of Agriculture, 1937); Annual Report of British Cotton Growing Association, General Items and Reports Manchester Association of Importers and Exporters, *The Journal of the Textile Institute*, vol. XIII, 1922, p. 132

[3] Annual Report of British Cotton Growing Association, General Items and Reports Manchester Association Of Importers And Exporters, p. 132

heavily involved in recovering the cotton industry. When the British took over, cotton production was a priority given the high price of imports from the United States of America that were hurting British textile mills. Production of cotton in a newly acquired colony,[1] it was thought, would contribute to the economy and supply stability. The ECGC was given responsibility by British textile mills and the British government to explore developing the cotton industry in Tanganyika.[2]

The ECGC employed Major H. Hastings Horne who spent from November 1920 to July 1921 in various districts investigating the potential to grow cotton.[3] Hastings' investigation report was published in 1922 which indicated his conviction and recommended that cotton could be established as the lead economic crop of Tanganyika in the coastal belt, Morogoro Region (Eastern Cotton Growing Area – ECGA), and Lake Victoria Basin (Western Cotton Growing Area – WCGA).[4]

His report showed that both areas proved successful during German colonial rule,[5] and it was clear that the WCGA was most preferred for cotton production. The area covering 40,000 square miles and Ukerewe Island[6] with 300 square miles were found suitable for cotton cultivation.[7] Importantly, the entire WCGA had 800,000 people who were potential labourers and sufficient rainfall for cotton cultivation.[8]

By then, the DCs were considered important officials to facilitate introducing the industry.[9] The agriculture instructors' functions were to facilitate distribution of seed, ensure that fields were planted at the proper time, and give instruction as to the methods of sowing and cultivation. The agriculture instructors surveyed and identified suitable soil for cotton cultivation and assisted farmers in cotton production methods.[10] The suggestion was made that bonuses should be given to responsible chiefs and headmen who directly stimulated cotton growing and enforced the policy by providing

---

[1] Speeches at Banquet given to Winston Churchill, 7 June 1921, BCGA no. 74
[2] Bulletin of the Imperial Institute: *A Quarterly Record of Progress in Tropical Agriculture and Industries and the Commercial Utilisation of the Natural Resources of the Dominions, Colonies and India*, vol. XX (London: John Murray, 1922) p. 173
[3] His report was titled 'The Extension of Cotton Cultivation in Tanganyika Territory,' and was issued by the ECGC (London: 1922).
[4] Report to the Board of Trade of the Empire Cotton Growing Committee Presented to Parliament by Command of His Majesty (London: HMSO, 1920) p. 33
[5] Bulletin of the Imperial Institute: A Quarterly Record of Progress in Tropical Agriculture and Industries and the Commercial Utilisation of the Natural Resources of the Dominions, Colonies and India. VOL. XX (London: John Murray, 1922) p. 173
[6] Ukerewe Islands is in Lake Victoria.
[7] Bulletin of the Imperial Institute, 1922, p. 173
[8] Bulletin of the Imperial Institute, 1922, p. 196
[9] Ibid.
[10] TNA 215/665, vol. I: Maswa DC to the Lake Province Provincial Commissioner Agricultural Cotton General, Ref. 301/2, 9 October 1933

close supervision of planting, weeding, harvesting and uprooting plants after crops were harvested.

The colonial power, textile mills, as well as ECGC and BCGA embarked upon implementation of Hastings' recommendations. The ECGC's tasks included formation of the Agricultural Department, training of agriculture extension staff employed by the department, production and breeding cotton seed varieties. Importantly, Agricultural Department staff in the country and local chiefs had various roles to play that included supervisory, advisory, and enforcing functions around cotton farming: thinning, picking, post-harvest marketing and ginning legislation and regulations.

The BCGA's expertise was evident in cotton ginning and marketing and provided advice around quality control.[1] The association deployed its experts to work in Tanganyika for three to five years of whom one was P.W. Briggs who was seconded from Uganda[2] and posted in the WCGA.[3] Inspector and expert salaries along with other incentives (Briggs' salary was dictated by the association to be £560 and not £500 per annum)[4] were paid by the Tanganyika government.[5] Most experts were posted in the WCGA and other cotton producing areas.[6] The ECGC's support was accepted by the colonial administrators in Tanganyika.[7]

With a view to stimulating progress in the WCGA, the BGCA acquired ginneries in Mwanza, Kwimba and Biharamulo districts which formerly belonged to the German firm of Hansing & Company.[8] However, the BCGA ginnery business was a disaster owing to competition for cotton supply from Indian merchants who had similar business interests in the area. By 1932 the BCGA decided to sell its ginneries to the Native Authorities (NAs) but the idea was discouraged by the colonial authority as it could not accommodate the NA being embroiled in commercial ventures.[9] In-

---

[1] TNA 21032, Proposal to Purchase Ginneries of the BCGA in Mwanza, Kwimba and Biharamulo districts from Colonial Office, London, to CS Despatch no. 828, 19 November 1934

[2] TNA 21032, Proposal to Purchase Ginneries of the BCGA

[3] TNA 21032, Proposal to Purchase Ginneries of the BCGA, CS to DA, Secretariat no. 21032, 20 December 1934

[4] TNA 21032, Proposal to Purchase Ginneries of the BCGA, Manchester to Colonial Office, London, to CS 17 December 1934

[5] TNA 21032, Proposal to Purchase Ginneries of the BCGA, CS to Secretary of State for Colonies, Ref. 25020/34, 26 October 1934; from DA to BCGA, Jinja, Uganda, Ref. 281/512, 19 January 1935

[6] TNA 21032, Proposal to Purchase Ginneries of the BCGA, Ref. 25020/34

[7] Ibid.

[8] TNA 21032, Proposal to Purchase Ginneries of the BCGA; W.H. Himbury (General Manager, British Cotton Growing Association), Empire Cotton Supplies, Meeting at Institute, Manchester, 31 October 1922, *The Journal of the Textile Institute*, vol. XIII, 1922. p. 194

[9] TNA 21032, Proposal to Purchase Ginneries of the BCGA in Mwanza, Kwimba and Biharamulo districts from CS to BCGA, Mwanza, 25 July 1932; from Colonial Office,

stead, the BCGA donated its Biharamulo ginnery to the NA in the district[1] and those in Mwanza and Kwimba district were sold for £3,000.[2]

During the 1920s new cotton production efforts focused on smallholder production in both the ECGA and WCGA as well as many other locations. The Agricultural Department was charged with responsibility for the supply of seeds to small-scale farmers. The task was carried out by extension officers who also provided instructions on proper farming practices.[3] In 1922, seed cotton imported from Uganda was distributed by the Agricultural Department to growers, from which 5,000 cotton bales were produced in the 1922/23 season.[4] During the early years of British colonial rule, seed supply to growers was through the local chiefs in Shinyanga district in the WCGA. This was so in other years as shown on the Table 6.

Table 6: Cotton seed distribution to growers in 1922-1927

Years/seasons	Seed distributed (tons)	Yields (tons)
1922	1.5	n/a
1923	10	37.8
1924	55	207.5
1925	180 (only 255 issued & planted)	540.6
1926	160	875.7
1927	113	565.0

Source: Lake Province districts' Report Book I

In 1925, as demand for cotton cultivation in the district grew, the chiefs proposed a seed farm to facilitate the smooth supply of seeds. The authority and Agricultural Department took this up by opening a farm at Ibadakuli in Shinyaga Township. This was an attempt to develop a reliable supply of a cotton seed strain suitable for the district. The supply of cotton seeds to growers was important throughout the colonial period. Seeds were bred in experimental stations and supplied by Agricultural Department staff, local chiefs (*Mtemi*), sub chiefs (*Bambilija* or *Balamji*) and village headmen (*Banangwa*).[5]

London, to CS 26 October 1934 (signed W.C. Bottomley); from PC, Lake Province, Ref. 476/191, 11 November 1934

[1] TNA 21032, Proposal to Purchase Ginneries of the BCGA, Mwanza to CS, 22 November 1934; BCGA, Manchester to Colonial Office, London, to CS 29 October 1934 (signed W.H. Himbury)

[2] TNA 21032, Proposal to Purchase Ginneries of the BCGA, Manchester to Colonial Office, London, to CS 29 October 1934

[3] TNA 215/665, vol. I: Letter from Maswa DC to the Lake Province Provincial Commissioner Agricultural Cotton General with Ref. 402/3676, 16 May 1933

[4] Norris, 1937

[5] H. Horne, *The extension of cotton cultivation in Tanganyika Territory: Report to the Committee on tour in Tanganyika territory Nov 1920 – July 1921* (London: The Empire Cotton Growing Corporation, 1922)

In 1924, the Department of Agriculture distributed 1,000 tons of cotton seed to growers across the country. This was an increase of approximately 100 per cent over the previous year, 1923. The chief cotton producing district where cotton seed was distributed to natives was Mwanza in the WCGA, where growers received 338 tons, whilst the ECGA of Morogoro got 208 tons, Lindi had 160 tons, Rufiji got 120 tons, and Tabora received 68 tons.[1] Cotton lint produced by small-scale growers during the 1923/24 season in the WCGA, particularly in Mwanza, Shinyanga and Nzega districts was 1,750,000 pounds, Morogoro was 448,000 pounds, Lindi was 248,000 pounds and Rufiji was 238,000 pounds.[2]

Legislation, such as Cotton Ordinance, 1920, was passed by the colonial authority geared towards pressing natives to increase cotton farms and modernise farming practices. The legislation proved important during the world economic crash between 1929 and the early 1930s which caused a substantial fall in government revenue.

The economic depression had an impact on growers too, mainly due to violent price fluctuations as they received poor pay for their produce and had to reduce their cultivation acreage. Since the colonial government had a duty and responsibility to bolster the territory's finances, it launched an 'Increase Production Campaign' to offset depression deficits. The campaign prioritised cash crops but also covered food crops. Under the campaign, growers were heavily engaged as it was compulsory to increase farm sizes and hence production of both cotton and food crops for export, as argued by the colonial authority, to facilitate maintaining their income to what it had been in previous years.[3]

To stimulate cotton production among the natives the policy was reinforced through legal measures provided under Circular 36 of 1931. For example, households were compelled to cultivate cotton. Each household was required to utilise one-quarter of their farm for cotton farming in 1931 and in 1933 farms had to dedicate half their land to cotton in Ubinza chiefdoms.[4] The expansion of farms imposed great strain upon land that led to debilitation.[5] Specified acreage was meant to move growers towards commercial production, thereby facilitating an increase of crops. Growers who failed to grow cotton were punished by being sent to work on sisal plantations in Tanga and Arusha provinces.[6] In return, they conformed to

---

[1] Report of the East Africa Commission, The Secretary of State for Colonies to Parliament by Command of His Majesty, April, 1925 (London: HMSO) p. 117

[2] Report of the East Africa Commission (1925) p. 117

[3] TNA 26054, DA to CS, Ref. 35/1237, 15 February 1946

[4] TNA 215/665, vol 1, Maswa DC to PC, Ref. 301/2, 9 October 1933

[5] TNA 26054, Confidential 'Consideration which may led to an Agricultural Policy', Agriculture General Policy

[6] TNA 215/665, vol 1, Maswa DC to PC, Lake Province, Ref. 402/3676, 16 May 1933;

regulations on cotton cultivation.[1] The Increased Production Campaign led to successful cotton production that increased from 20,000 bales in 1930 to 56,000 in 1935 despite low prices, namely three cents per pound and six cents per kilogramme.[2]

The compulsion measures, obviously a violation of the 1930 Geneva Convention on compulsory labour, was ratified by the British government on 3 June 1931. That the British Government ignored the Geneva commitment, is seen in Article 19 which was silent on matters regarding compulsory cultivation provided that it was for educational purposes, and in such instances meant to stimulate native production of marketable crops.[3] The policy was ignored as it facilitated government revenues and commitment to self-finance colonial administration.

Public opinion was that any compulsion was wrong and unethical. Despite this, more measures were brought in during the 1930s by the government whereby the Native Authority (Extension of Powers) Cultivation of Cotton Order, 1935 and Government Notice 75, 1935, targeted lazy or idle growers and also sanctioned those who made no attempt to work their cotton plots. However, to evade criticism the government employed and exercised measures provided under the Emergency Power (Defence) Act, 1939, and Supplies and Services (Transitional) Power Act, 1945, set out in Section 8 of Cap.47 meant for community service. Other measures employed were Government Notice 177, 1942, amended by Government Notice 37, 1946 Section 101. These measures, together with other activities, were designed to improve production, and existed for five years.[4] These Rules were also promulgated to stabilise or increase cotton production. Evidence shows that in 1932 production was 2,065 bales, the following year, 1933 it was 2,615 bales, and in 1934, there was a marked improvement of 7,871 bales bought from across all ginneries.[5]

In addition, the Cotton Rules provided, under Government Notice 84, 1931, a basic guideline on cotton cultivation, seed for distribution, sale and purchase of cotton and ginning licensing.[6] The 1931 Rules were amended in 1933 and in 1934 to ensure growers were seriously committed to cotton

---

Shinyanga District Book
[1] TNA 215/665, vol 1, Maswa DC to PC, Lake Province
[2] TNA 26054, Memorandum on cotton marketing in Tanganyika, Director of Agriculture, 17 January 1936
[3] Lord Hailey, *An African Survey: A study of Problems Arising in Africa South of Sahara* (London: Oxford University Press, 1938), pp. 630-631
[4] TNA 215/1423A, Memorandum on Cotton Marketing in Tanganyika Territory, 17 January 1936
[5] TNA 251/1423A, PC, Lake Province to CSC confidential, Ref. 302/42, 16 December 1935; TNA 215/1423A, Memorandum on Cotton Marketing
[6] TNA 1423C, Government Notice 84, Co-operative Cotton Buying and Ginning in the Lake Province

production.[1] For example, Rule 10a) empowered the Director of Agriculture to issue orders for picking cotton. Such orders targeted native growers who deliberately neglected to pick their produce. Under the Cotton Rules, it was made compulsory for growers to tend their crop from planting to picking. The *Mtemi, Bambilija* and *Banangwa* enforced these Rules. Local leaders were made responsible for enforcing the policy in their administrative localities through closer supervision of growers at all stages, namely planting, weeding, picking, uprooting and burning plants immediately after harvest. In accordance with Horne's suggestion that bonuses be paid to *Mtemi, Bambiliji* and *Banangwa* who were directly involved in stimulating cotton growing in their respective administrative areas,[2] the colonial authority began paying bonuses to *Mtemi, Bambiliji* and *Banangwa* who were exemplary in stimulating cotton growing.[3]

It is worthwhile to mention that unlike coffee, better farming implements were important for cotton cultivation. Usually, growers used rudimentary tools for farming such as a *jembe* (hand hoe).[4] Better farming implements were therefore introduced to ease the burden and importantly to facilitate expansion of cotton farms and increase production. By then, Horne was of the opinion that introducing the good English hoe and plough to replace primitive native implements was vital to improve and ease cultivation. The native *jembe* was light and fragile and could not break up the dry, hard soil to any real depth, which was necessary for commercial production. Axes were also recommended for clearing new farm land.[5]

A hoe and axe obviously would not be useful for commercial production, so in a further development, 'progressive growers' were persuaded to use light ploughs drawn by trained oxen. These were introduced in the district in 1923 by the Director of Game and Preservation, C.F.M. Swynnerton, as part of experiments in connection with tsetse control[6] using funding through the 1929 Colonial Development Act.[7] The use of ploughs was successful as it led to advances in farming and demand increased so that by 1927, there were 130 ploughs under group ownership. However, ploughs were not well looked after, especially when broken as there had been no one responsible to repair them. This suggests that the scheme lacked governance mechanisms such as bye-laws and maintenance rules that would have

---

[1] TNA 215/1423C Government Notice 78, Co-operative Cotton Buying and Ginning in the Lake Province

[2] Horne, *The extension of cotton cultivation in Tanganyika Territory*

[3] TNA 215/665, vol. I, Maswa DC to PC, Ref. 301/2, 9 October 1933

[4] TNA 26054 Agriculture General Policy, confidential 'Consideration which may led to an Agricultural Policy'

[5] Horne, *The extension of cotton cultivation in Tanganyika Territory*

[6] Lake Province Districts' Reports Book I

[7] L.P. Mair, *Welfare in the Colonies* (Bombay: Oxford University Press, 1944) p. 85

facilitated routine upkeep of equipment. Therefore, the department decided the ploughs should be allocated to individuals for private ownership.[1]

3.2: Coffee farming in Kilimanjaro Region

Records show that in the early years small growers in Marangu, Old Moshi and Mamba engaged with the industry seriously. This was partly attributed by the support they had from their chiefs (*Mangi*). The *Mangi* of Old Moshi was one who positively and voluntarily responded, and had cultivated coffee as early as 1902. By 1916, there were 14,000 coffee growers in Kilimanjaro, a number which increased year after year as a result of government encouragement (see Table 7).

Table 7: Coffee growers and farm size from 1928/29 – 1939/40

Season	Number of growers	Acreage
1928/29	9,000	4,000
1929/30	10,000	4,300
1930/31	11,000	4,600
1931/32	11,800	4,900
1932/33	12,530	5,160
1933/34	16,800	6,700
1934/35	18,550	7,560
1935/36	21,740	9,380
1936/37	24,280	12,450
1937/38	25,230	14,790
1938/39	25,730	14,440
1939/40	26,270	15,170

Source: KNCU 1946/47 Annual Report, Moshi KNCU, Appendix B

Some chiefs or *Mangi*, like Marealle of Marangu and his wife, followed suit in 1906. Historical records show that de L. Crore, the Italian settler, who had a coffee plantation in Marangu assisted some individuals like Sawaya Mawala and Chief Marealle of Marangu to plant coffee trees in 1900. In 1930, Sawaya Mawala had 20 acres. Other growers from Marangu, such as Joseph Merinyo, responded in 1908 following persuasion by his employer, Dr Förster, a German settler.[2]

The Germans who first colonised Tanganyika realised that small-scale growers could offer the cheapest alternative to produce export crops than the estates. However, the settlers did not like the co-existence policy that encouraged both European plantation and smallholders. Their criticisms emerged in 1907 when they complained of the danger of disease spreading to their plantations from African-grown coffee. Such complaints were

---
[1] Lake Province Districts' Report Book I
[2] TNA 13060, A.L. Pennington, Report on the Kilimanjaro Planters Association

Table 8: Cotton Bales sold by Ginners 1935-1946 (each bale had 400 lbs.)

Zones	1935	1936	1937	1938	1939	1940	1941	1942	1943	1944	1945	1946
Nassa	5,212	5,755	3,137	1,700	5,717	5,708	4,859	3,253	2,844	2,242	3,814	4,220
Nyambiti	3,078	5,074	2,764	1,429	4,336	4,257	4,235	2,562	2,515	2,121	3,520	3,665
Malampaka	2,507	4,274	3,539	3,905	6,599	6,340	6,969	4,657	1,550	250	3,033	1,067
Ihale	3,870	2,808	1,848	909	2,870	3,349	3,831	2,414	1,751	1,185	1,902	2,830
Bukumbi	2,611	3,836	2,527	2,240	1,924	2,972	2,625	1,560	1,018	405	1,417	1,335
Mwanza	7,373	5,362	4,222	2,073	3,648	4,579	4,139	2,953	2,795	1,404	2,472	2,670
Pambani	4,582	3,743	2,557	2,620	3,448	3,054	3,446	1,441	1,342	410	3,081	3,385
Usogore	4,620	5,137	4,974	2,943	4,407	4,757	9,046	6,705	4,183	863	4,590	1,235
Murutunguru	3,871	3,997	2,968	1,706	5,021	4,708	5,081	2,171	3,151	4,076	4,035	5,900
Mugango	1,501	2,302	1,580	488	1,703	774	2,002	1,102	590	749	2,063	2,900
Buchenzi						775	3,882	1,932	2,303	2,081	2,983	3,510
Luguru								2,971	761	1,385	2,468	1,100
Total	39,226	42,288	30,116	20,103	39,643	40,273	50,115	33,721	24,713	17,171	35,378	33,817

Source: TNA 215/1423/A, Cotton Marketing

rejected by the German governor in Tanganyika and he encouraged the natives to grow coffee for export.[1]

Crucially, the influx of settlers played a part in encouraging small growers to farm crops, especially amongst those employed on settlers' farms. Through such employment, they learnt coffee farming skills that they employed on their own farms. The training covered such aspects as cultivation techniques and processing of the produce for marketing. Local labourers took advantage of the opportunity to plant coffee on their farmland. For example, they collected rejected seedlings and some were given seedlings as presents, while others were given plants by employers such as Mr de Croce and Dr Förster who were based in Marangu.

However, during the First World War, growers could not market their produce. As a result, many abandoned farming as it was no longer profitable. But, the new colonial power saw a need for recovery of the crop and immediately provided support to small-scale coffee growers.[2] Sir Charles

---

[1] J. Iliffe, The German Administration in Tanganyika, 1906-1911: The Governorship of Freiherr von Rechenberg (Ph.D. dissertation, Cambridge University, 1965) p. 297

Cecil Farquharson Dundas,[1] who was first the district Commissioner (DC) of Moshi between 1919 and 1924 spearheaded the support.[2] Dundas did much to encourage coffee growing by the local population in Kilimanjaro. He undertook initiatives in collaboration with local chiefs (*Mangi*) who were charged with responsibility to mobilise and enforce coffee farming practices among subjects.

Given previous economic benefits accrued by coffee growers, the natives quickly responded by cleaning bushes, weeding farms, pruning coffee trees, and spaying fungicides as well as pesticides.[3] This led to the recovery of the industry which was further stimulated when the British colonial authority passed Land Ordinance (1923) to ensure that African land rights were secure and thus growers had access to land for cultivation.

The next step was to make the crop an economically viable proposition by persuading more people to grow it, and expand the industry. The government was prompted to employ agriculture officers from 1922 to provide guidance on coffee farming. This was achieved largely because the growers were highly motivated by the availability of the market locally, selling their produce to settlers, Greek and Indian traders and of course, good prices were obtained. This significantly stimulated more growers to plant coffee, whereby in 1916 there were 16,000 growers, the number was 125,000 in 1922. Records from the Agricultural Department show that in 1922, in all chiefdoms, over 50 per cent of the coffee trees were in Marangu where Mwika chiefdom had 263 trees, Old Moshi had 350 with only 45 trees in Rombo, most of which were at Mashati.[4]

Table 9: Names of outstanding small-scale coffee growers 1920s – 1930s

Name	Location	Number of coffee trees
Shangali Ndeserua	Machame	12,082
Jacob Kihawi	Kibosho	11,892
Lerda Tukia	Uru	10,892
Gideon Masuwa	Machame	7,212
Chief Mashingia	Kirua Vunjo	5,625

Source: Pennington Report on the Kilimanjaro Native Planters Association, TNA 13060

---

[2] TNA 13060, A.L. Pennington, Report on the Kilimanjaro Native Planters Association, p. 4
[1] Charles Dundas was Secretary for Native Affairs from 1925 to 1929. In 1929 he was appointed Governor for the Bahamas.
[2] TNA 13060, Pennington, Report on the Kilimanjaro Native Planters Association, Attitude of the KNPA; R.J.M. Swynnerton, A.L.B. Bennett & H.B. Stent, *All About KNCU Coffee* (Moshi: KNCU, 1948) p. 4; Iliffe, (1979) p. 154
[3] Wakefield, Native Production of Coffee on Kilimanjaro, pp. 97-107
[4] Ibid.

There were also prominent individuals, such as Joseph Merinyo who had been in the industry for a while, who became Dundas' right-hand man. This was pivotal in motivating him and he became a selfless exemplary as he used the opportunity to freely distribute new coffee seedlings to small-scale holders.[1]

In support and recognition of Merinyo's efforts, Dundas created a revolving fund amounting to 25 rupees[2] to establish coffee tree nurseries. Merinyo made available mature seedlings to growers at low prices for those who could afford them. The *Mangi* from other locations in Kilimanjaro who heard of this development made study tours in Old Moshi. During their visits, they met Dundas with whom they discussed tree planting. In appreciation of his effort to promote coffee farming, which the settlers opposed, Dundas was given the title of *Wasahuye-o-WaChagga* (Elder of the Chagga).[3]

3.2.1: Role of the Colonial Authority

Arguably, by having an export crop in place, this fulfilled the government's obligation towards realisation of the self-sufficiency policy. This was also in compliance with the United Nations' recommendation, which stressed that native production should be encouraged, with training and supervision available. Training of native growers improved their coffee farming knowledge and skill, making them better and more progressive agriculturists on their own land.[4] Dundas encouraged coffee farming in Kilimanjaro to enable farmers to have a reliable source of income and money to pay taxes that facilitated administration of the colony.[5] The crop farming revival went hand in hand with access to markets of the produce. The initiative led to the tremendous and rapid growth of acreage in production (see Table 10).[6]

By 1936, the volume of coffee produced by growers surpassed that of the European planters.[7] Increased production, however, did not necessarily imply opening up new farms or additional land because coffee was in home gardens (*vihamba*) where banana trees were grown under the inter-cropping system.

---

[1] TNA 13060, Pennington, Report on the Kilimanjaro Native Planters Association, p. 4

[2] The German and Indian Rupee was a currency in circulation until 1925 when the conversion of circulating rupees was completed and replaced by florins and shillings which was carried out by the British colonial power East Africa Currency Board.

[3] TNA 13060, Pennington, Report on the Kilimanjaro Native Planters, p. 4

[4] Report of the East Africa Commission Presented by The Secretary of State for Colonies to Parliament by Command of His Majesty, April 1925 (London: HMSO) p. 36

[5] TNA 3864/2, Dundas to Chief Secretary June 1024; Dundas to Chief Secretary June 1924; TNA 26207, DC to PC Ref. 23/13, 21 April 1936

[6] TNA 13060, Pennington, Report on the Kilimanjaro Native Planters; TNA 3864/2, Dundas to Chief Secretary June 1924; TNA 26207, DC to PC Ref. 23/13, 21 April 1936

[7] TNA 26207, DC to PC Ref. 23/13, 21 April 1936

Table 10: Coffee producers and acreage

Season	Growers approximate	Average approximate Acreage
1923/33	12,530	5,160
1933/34	16,800	6,700
1934/35	18,550	7,560
1935/36	21,740	9,380
1936/37	24,280	12,450
1937/38	25,230	14,790

Source: Tanganyika Legislative Council: A Report on the KNCU (Dar es Salaam: Tanganyika Government Printer, 1937)

During the 1920s, Merinyo was not only the leading coffee entrepreneur, but also a pioneer in Kilimanjaro. He spent much of his time touring locations and villages around Kilimanjaro Mountain encouraging the Chagga to plant coffee; his campaigns were successful. Some cultivated farms were adjacent to those of settlers, which posed a threat to settler prosperity. Such farms like those owned by Chief Gideon Masuwa of Machame had over 4,000 coffee trees by 1915, and records show an average of about 350 trees for every farmer in 1932. Some of them were most outstanding.[1]

In Kilimanjaro, there was a considerable number of Greek, Dutch, and a few English, coffee planters.[2] Thus, a parallel coffee farming system was in existence: the European planters and settlers, and the natives, WaChagga small-scale growers. This led to tension between the two as the expansion of smallholdings was resented by settlers who responded by exerting pressure on the colonial administration to rescind the policy.

3.2.2: Settler reaction

In 1921, over 12,000 natives owned coffee trees in Kilimanjaro.[3] This led to agitation which was intense between 1922 and 1925. The settlers challenged the colonial authority for allowing WaChagga, the natives of Kilimanjaro, into the industry.[4] They argued that having inexperienced and unknowledgeable natives in the industry posed a risk for the spread of coffee pests and diseases that were likely to infect their trees, menacing their crops, and negatively affecting their investment.[5] They also argued that there was a risk of theft of coffee by Africans.

Understandably, the settlers' concerns were relevant. However, their approach was misguided. One would have expected the settlers to emphasise promotion, to ensure availability of the extension services to small-scale

---

[1] KNPA newspaper *Uremi*, 4 August 1932
[2] Report of the East Africa Commission Presented by The Secretary of State for Colonies to Parliament by Command of His Majesty, April 1925 (London: HMSO) p. 116
[3] J. Huxley, *Africa View* (London: Chatto & Windus, 1932) p. 55
[4] TNA 13060, Pennington, Report on the Kilimanjaro Native Planters Association
[5] Wakefield, Native Production of Coffee on Kilimanjaro, pp. 97-107

growers and extensive application of insecticides and pesticides to eliminate insects that were damaging coffee plants. This would have eliminated the tension.

A negative attitude and policy towards small-scale growers reigned over the settlers' opposition. The settlers resented not only the fact that the African farmers were beginning to out-produce them (largely due to the practice of inter-cropping coffee with bananas, as opposed to the single-crop farming style used by the settlers) but also that their success made them less likely to work as labourers on settler estates.

In reality, the settlers' main concern was not fear of the spread of disease, but the shortage or curtailment of cheap labour for their farms as local Africans were not available to provide labour because they were attending their own crops. It was obvious that the settlers underpaid growers for laborious and long hours at a time when they had to concentrate on their farms from which they were earning a reasonable income. It was essentially important that natives were reduced to labourer status to work on plantations. Forced to labourer status would reduce native growers to the weakest economic autonomy thereby prompting them to accept work for poor payment in order to pay hut and poll tax.

Apart from attempts to force the natives from coffee farming by the settlers, water used for irrigating crops was an issue of dispute too. For decades, much of the native banana and coffee land was irrigated during dry seasons using numerous traditional canal systems that drew water from rivers that orginate in the Mount Kilimanjaro glacier. Distribution of water to the crops was, and still is, regulated by customary law of which each individual cultivator had his share of water with a quantity and time.[1] Thus, the natives were the beneficiaries, unlike the settlers whose farms were located at the bottom of Mount Kilimanjaro. In several instances, the native cunningly diverted water essential for the European planters. Diversion of water often caused tension between settlers and natives, who controlled the system, which had a detrimental effect on European farming.[2] As a result, settlers petitioned the governor to prohibit natives growing coffee.

3.2.3: Grower reaction against settler agitation

Regardless of the opposition from settlers, native coffee planting kept expanding and growers became more determined to engage in the industry, which was economically lucrative. Due to such agitation, natives banded together against a move to restrict them growing coffee.[3] For them, such

---

[1] Huxley, *Africa View*, p. 66; Lord Hailey, *An African Survey*, p. 1044; Mattias Tagseth, The Expansion of Traditional Irrigation in Kilimanjaro, Tanzania, *The International Journal of African Historical Studies*, vol. 41, no. 3, pp. 461-490

[2] J.A. Kieran, The Origins of Commercial Arabica Coffee Production in East Africa, *African Historical Studies*, vol. 2, no. 1 (1969) pp. 51-67

opposition was viewed as nothing other than jealousy. By 1925, there was further increase in the number of coffee farmers despite settler opposition (see Table 10).

Such agitation by settlers posed a threat to the natives' livelihood and left them with unanswered questions about their coffee farms. Joseph Merinyo[1] who worked in the agriculture office came across such complaints which he shared with Dundas. In their discussions, it was agreed Dundas would meet the farmers to find out more. During a meeting between Dundas, Merinyo and growers at Kibosho, it was suggested to form a marketing organisation. The idea was to form the Kilimanjaro Native Planters Association (KNPA), which Dundas approved.[2] The growers proposed a name for the organisation which sounded like the Tanganyika Planters Association (TPA), which was the settlers' organisation. Upon election of its leaders, Joseph Merinyo was its first African President and Stefano Lema was Secretary.[3]

The formation of the KNPA was prompted by two major factors. First, to protect African producers from the settler community who strongly opposed seeing Africans producing coffee. Second, it met the colonial government demand for production of raw materials. The objects of the KNPA were:[4]

a) The marketing of native coffee and other native crops to ensure the best price for native producers;
b) To make provision for sanitation of native coffee crops by supplying lime sulphur to producers;
c) To establish stores in which producers could obtain goods of every kind; and
d) Doing all such things incidental or condusive to the attainment of the above objects.

Moreover, the colonial government position was that KNPA was the appropriate institution to enforce the provisions of the Coffee Industry (Registration and Improvement) Ordinance and Plant Pest and Disease Regulations of 1928. Rules enacted by the Native Authority on the advice of the Agricultural Officer brought native coffee under strict control and adherence to stipulated conditions with planting approved by the NA and Agriculture Officer.[5] The task was performed by KNPA's *wawakilishi* or *wakili* (representatives) elected by producers. The *wawakilishi* were responsible for providing practical educational instruction on coffee cultivation,

---

[3] Wakefield, Native Production of Coffee on Kilimanjaro, pp. 97-107
[1] Merinyo was a civil servant working at the Agriculture Department in Moshi district.
[2] TNA 13060, PC Northern Province to CS, Ref. 80/iii/248, 24 February 1931
[3] TNA 13060, Pennington, Report, p. 5
[4] TNA 13060, Minutes of the Inaugural KNPA's Meeting held on 15 January 1925
[5] Wakefield, Native Production of Coffee on Kilimanjaro

spraying insecticides and pesticides to protect trees from being damaged and infected.[1] In addition, they kept records showing details of each plantation, those inspected, and reported diseased or dirty coffee plantations to the coffee officer.[2]

The KNPA was considered a useful institution to enforce Native Authority passed rules that were approved by the governor. Some rules compelled individual planters be a member and sell his coffee to the association. It can therefore be argued that the force behind the creation of the KNPA was to combat the strong settler opposition to coffee growing by natives.[3]

Furthermore, the government responded in several ways to protect the industry and to ensure the success of native coffee growing in the Kilimanjaro area, while safeguarding both native and European plantations against disease, an experienced European coffee officer was recruited. The officer was deployed in Kilimanjaro to supervise native coffee growing and advise European planters.[4] If that was not enough, government deployed an agricultural entomologist to inspect native coffee farms. According to the entomologist's report it was shown that native farms were better attended than settlers' were. In response, in 1926, the governor made it clear that he had the power to prohibit natives growing any crop if he felt it was right. But he reiterated that it was his duty to encourage the prosperity of the colony by encouraging native production.[5]

Interestingly, in the 1930s, members of KNPA brought to the attention of the Department of Agriculture cases of unattended European coffee plantations for action.[6] During the same year, over 50 native small-holders were prosecuted and several others were fined a maximum of 8/- shillings for failure to properly attend their coffee trees, for example, pruning them as required under the Plant Pest and Disease Control Regulation of 1928. Apart from agricultural extension services, the KNPA managed to influence the government to grant it a monopoly over the market for native produced coffee in the Moshi district.[7]

---

[1] TNA 13060, PC Northern Province to CS, Ref. Confidential/80/iii/258, 12 March 1931
[2] TNA 13060, Minutes of the Inaugural KNPA's Meeting held on 15 January 1925; Report by His Britannic Majesty's Government on the Administration Under Mandate of Tanganyika Territory for the Year 1924 League of Nations Geneva, 1925
[3] Swynnerton, Bennet & Stent, *All About KNCU Coffee*, p. 12-13
[4] Report by His Britannic Majesty's Government 1924
[5] Huxley, *Africa View*, p. 55
[6] TNA 13060, Northern Province Agriculture Department Report on Pest and Disease Control in Moshi district, 1930, p. 3
[7] S.M.L. Seimu, The Growth and Development of Coffee and Cotton Marketing Co-operatives in Tanzania (PhD Thesis, University of Central Lancashire, 2015)

3.2.4: Colonial Authority reaction to settler agitation

Dundas and Sir Horace Byatt, the first British Governor of Tanganyika between 1919 and 1925, opposed the settlers' grievances as baseless.[1] This was at a time when native production surpassed the settlers' combined tonnage, giving Byatt courage and confidence to support the Africans.[2] Moreover, it was a responsibility of the colonial authority to comply with the League of Nations, making it clear that no more land on the mountain could be alienated to non-native enterprise.[3] It was also argued that:

> Suppression of coffee planting was out of the question. The British government could not suppress development initiated by the Germans and no rules for suppression of the Native enterprise would ever have been permitted by the government or countenanced by the League of Nations. Moreover, no government could set out to root up trees, which had stood for 15 years and were bringing in secure and ample income. It is clear therefore that before the British government entered in the administration of Tanganyika certain of the WaChagga had already seen and had experience of benefits to be derived from the cultivation of coffee.[4]

Clearly, the colonial authority had a vested interest in the settlers and in the economy of the colony; and it was unable to prohibit a thriving native coffee industry. Consequently, the government not only preserved WaChagga cultivation privileges, but also expanded its support.

The colonial authority's commitment to encourage the natives to cultivate coffee in Kilimanjaro attracted many more into the industry. For example, by the end of 1929 there were over 12,000[5] and in early 1930, 12,025 small-scale growers in Kilimanjaro who owned 5,949,902 trees on 8,064 acres (see Table 11).[6] Such growth was partly a result of government policy, the leadership of Kilimanjaro Native Association (KNPA), later Kilimanjaro Native Co-operative Union (KNCU), and its affiliated societies' encouragement. By 1936, the volume of coffee produced by growers surpassed that of the European planters.[7]

In 1929, Britain established the Colonial Development Fund which aimed at aiding colonial economic development and was made available by the colonial power to increase its foreign trade to create employment in Britain, which was seriously affected by the economic depression.[8] In

---

[1] Charles Dundas (1955) pp. 123-25
[2] TNA 13060, Pennington, Report in Coffee Ordinance and Regulations
[3] Report of the East Africa Commission, Presented by the Secretary of State for Colonies to Parliament by Command of His Majesty (London: HMSO, April 1925) p. 116
[4] TNA 13060, Pennington, Report on the Kilimanjaro Native Planters Association
[5] Huxley, *Africa View*, p. 55
[6] TNA 19126, President of KNPA to PC North Province, July 11 1930
[7] TNA 26207, DC to PC Ref. 23/13 ,21 April 1936

Tanganyika, the fund was utilised to expand coffee production among small growers and for a coffee research station, mainly the development of facilities at Lyamungo, a few miles from Moshi town. Increasingly, colonial government support led to the expansion of Wa-Chagga coffee cultivation (See Table 11) that contributed to the realisation of financial self-sufficiency.

Table 11: Coffee trees owned by KNPA members, 1930

Location	Growers	Trees	Acres
Kibongoto	198	28,597	27
Masama	1,128	63,2013	587
Machame	1,694	746,402	696
Kindi	111	42,855	39
Kibosho	1,579	2,062,001	1,917
Mbokomu	280	103	21
Kima Vunjo	874	237,610	26
Kilema	1,010	324,745	3,019
Marangu	1,066	900,186	836
Mamba	686	182,710	169
Mwika	57	85,269	81
Mengwe	53	10,413	9
Keni	168	32,300	30
Mkuu	260	39,425	35
Mrao	27	5,402	5
Mashati	31	3,912	3
Olele	57	2,440	2
Useri	85	1,058	0.5
Usangi	255	46,246	42
Ugweno	85	12,840	11
Gonja	125	25,286	23
Kirua Rombo	190	2,308	12
Total	12,025	594,902	8,064

Source: KNPA to PC North Province, 11 July 1930, TNA 19126

3.3: Coffee farming in Kagera Region

The German colonial administration in Tanganyika was short, 1890-1914. During this period, it devoted much money and energy to the development of transport infrastructure and plantation agriculture, including the introduction of Arabica coffee in Bukoba.[1] It encouraged natives to plant coffee for export purposes.[2] The pioneer of these initiatives was the German officer Emin Pasha who established Arabica nurseries from which seedlings

---

[8] Frank, The formation of British Colonial Development Policy, p. 17

[1] T.S. Jervis, Control of the coffee berry borer in Bukoba, *East African Agricultral Journal*, September 1939

[2] A.E. Haarer Modern Coffee Production (London: Leonard Hill, 1923)

were distributed to farmers and *Omukama*.[1]

However, the response of farmers was disappointing as they maintained a belief that the coffee plant belonged to *Omukama* and the royal family. Pasha embarked upon campaigns against such restrictions by convincing the *Omukama* of the importance of coffee farming. The colonial administrators played a significant role in convincing the *Omukama* to relax conditions that restricted their subjects from planting coffee. When the *Omukama* of Kiziba allowed his subjects to cultivate coffee, from 1903, the area under coffee cultivation gradually increased and exports rose from 214 tons in 1906 to 681 in 1913.[2]

3.3.1: Coffee industry under British rule, 1916-1961

Under Article 3 of the Mandate Agreement, Britain was responsible for safeguarding the material well-being, of native interests and social progress of the Tanganyika population.

The immediate responsibility of the new colonial power was reconstruction of the economy and transport infrastructure devastated during the war. It also established the Native Authorities at local level, for example the eight chiefdoms of Karagwe, Ihangiro, Kyamtwara, Kianja, Kiziba, Bugabo, Misenyi and Kinyengereko in Kagera Region who were charged with responsibilities such as carrying out judicial and administrative duties under the supervision of superior European administrative officers.

Given the economic difficulties, the new territory had to comply with financial self-sufficiency to cover its administrative costs to avoid draining an already depleted London Treasury. The self-sufficiency policy had to be achieved through:[3] first, the revival of agriculture, mainly for export crops such as sisal and coffee. Attracting former investors back, and new ones, for plantations and estates formerly owned by Germans. However, attracting new investors was not promising given Mandate policies that sounded unfavourable to long-term investment in agriculture. This necessitated the colonial power to adopt a second initiative, which was to encourage farming among native small-scale holders to produce cash crops such as coffee, cotton and tobacco.

The second policy was realised by ensuring that small-scale holders had access to, and ownership of, land provided under the Mandate Agreement, Article 22. There was a steady increase in revenue from rather more than half a million pounds during 1919-20 to over a million in 1923-24.[4] By 1935

---

[1] Jervis (1939)

[2] Ibid.

[3] Havinden & Meredith (1993); TNA 26054, Extract from minutes of meeting of the Directors of Agriculture for East African countries (Kenya, Tanganyika and Uganda) held in Nairobi on 12 June 1946

[4] Tanganyika Territory Annual Report (1926)

there were 60,000 to 70,000 growers who produced 3,409 tons of Arabica which was also exported, earning £88,956, and 7,473 tons of Robusta that had a value of £160,688.[1]

Table 12: Coffee production and value for 1928–1929

Variety	1928	Value (£)	1929	Value (£)
Robusta	1,019	57,571	1,693	116,405
Arabica	1,767	105,661	1,118	79,486

Source: DAO to DA, Ref. S/26/122, 6 March 1929, TNA 24545

3.3.2: Response from growers and chiefs

Encouragement of coffee cultivation among small-scale growers outside Ngara district in Kagera Region took a different dimension compared to Kilimanjaro. The local population, the WaHaya and WaNyambo ethnic groups, lacked the European example and familiarity with coffee farming like those in Kilimanjaro. They planted coffee haphazardly amongst the bananas that provided them their staple food and beer.[2]

Robusta coffee was more popular amongst the growers owing to its high yield, minimum labour needs and being less suseptible to pests, unlike Arabica. However, the preference of the colonial authority was Arabica of which 100 Arabica coffee seedlings were made available in the 1920s from Kilimanjaro and Uganda for each household required to plant on their farms.[3] The village headmen were charged with supervision, which they failed to do, resulting in poor harvests.[4]

Understandably, chiefs and headmen had no coffee husbandry experience and were untrained. Despite this, the total export in 1923 was 4,047 tons, consisting of 2,562 tons of native-grown Robusta coffee from the Bukoba district, and 177 tons, of which natives produced 20 tons, of Arabica coffee. A colonial official judged this as disastrous given the number of growers.[5] It was disappointing to the colonial authority merely because there was low Arabica production and export volume. The Colonial Office preference was for Arabica due to its better price in the European markets compared to Robusta. Robusta coffee was exported to North African markets and some to Holland and Central European markets.[6]

The colonial authority had to act to realise its projected revenue collec-

---

[1] TNA 24545, Northcote 1936 Inquiry Report on Bukoba Coffee Industry in Report on Bukoba Coffee Marketing
[2] TNA 11969/19, Harvey (undated)
[3] Ibid.
[4] TNA 24545, Harvey (undated); TNA 11969/19, DA to CS (November 1928)
[5] Ibid.
[6] Report of the East Africa Commission, 1925

tion. For example, between 1925 and 1927, the Director of Agriculture (DA) established Arabica nurseries at Nyamihanga village in Karagwe chiefdom or district and provided supervision. In this regard, it was decided that the local chiefs and some exemplary headmen could assist the Agriculture Department to supervise growers. Again, most chiefs lacked relevant knowledge and experience. By the late 1920s, 64,000 acres of Arabica coffee were farmed by smallholders with approximately 25.5 million trees. By then, the region had one agriculture officer and one coffee officer who were able to visit each area only once a year. The expansion was obviously impressive, necessitating the governor to consider the urgency to deploy qualified officers to provide supervision of coffee growing in Bukoba.[1]

For a considerable number of years coffee farming in all districts in Kagera (with the exception of Ngara district, which was then a division in Biharamulo district) was characterised by compulsion measures to increase production, which unfortunately had disastrous results.

The colonial authority introduced more compulsory measures to stimulate further coffee farming among smallholders. These comprised a series of Ordinances, Regulations and Orders in 1927. The Native Authorities, in particular the local chiefs and headmen, were made responsible to enforce the Ordinances, Regulations and Orders to enhance coffee improvement through better husbandry.[2] This was due to the inadequate number of trained agricultural extension officers, regardless of the fact that the local chiefs and headmen were untrained and lacked knowledge of their new duties. For example, evidence shows that two officers of the Agricultural Department were available to attend all growers in the region who in total had 64,000 acres and 25,250,000 coffee trees by 1928.[3] They managed only one visit in over two years, and this for a fortnight.

Regardless of encouragement of smallholders by the colonial authority to cultivate Arabica, understandably, growers were more inclined to Robusta coffee, which they had been growing for decades.[4] Evidence shows that in 1928 the total export volume was of Robusta 1,693 tons, whereas Arabica was 1,019.[5] In 1929, tons of exported Robusta rose to 1,767 and Arabica was better but low, of which 1,118 tons were exported.[6] Robusta accounted for two-thirds of the total coffee exported from Tanganyika which was an indication of its economic potential regardless of disfavour by the colonial authority due to its low price on international markets.[7]

---

[1] TNA 11969, DA to CS (November, 1928)
[2] TNA 24545, Northcote, 1936; TNA 26054 Report on Agriculture Policies, June 1932
[3] TNA 11969/19, Harvey (undated)
[4] Ibid.
[5] TNA 11969, DA to CS (November, 1928)
[6] TNA 11969, DA to CS (March, 1928)
[7] TNA 11969/9, Governor to DA (May 1928)

Table 13: Tons of coffee exports and revenue in GBP (Bukoba & Tanganyika)

Year	Tons Bukoba	Price/ ton	Revenue Bukoba	Territory production	Territorial revenue
1922	2,899	39.1	113,387	4,271	N/A
1923	2,562	45.5	116,678	4,047	204,986
1924	3,608	64.9	234,026	5,261	352,529
1925	4,150	77.3	320,745	6,009	481,055
1926	4,650	69.7	324,094	6,539	495,199
1927	3,943	54.7	215,845	6,595	463,420
1928	7,832	61.1	478,311	10,431	739,657
1929	6,794	58.9	400,011	8,857	588,671
1930	7,369	26.3	194,012	11,547	387,040
1931	6,586	20.2	133,261	9,251	247,037
1932	7,107	37.3	264,785	11,362	463,597
1933	7,922	28.7	227,006	12,718	429,523
1934	10,231	32.2	329,682	14,766	595,237
1935	10,865	22.9	249,645	N/A	N/A
1936	6,504	24.8	161,204	12,320	609,691
1937	9,540	28.4	270,797	N/A	N/A
1938	8,295	20.2	167,890	16,170	742,904
1939	12,028	20.6	247,677	N/A	N/A
1940	7,787	20.5	160,000	17,490	664,975
1941	6,697	26.9	180,000	N/A	N/A
1941	6,697	26.9	180,000	N/A	N/A
1942	8,111	32.5	263,583	16,610	656,695
1943	7,265	44.5	323,583	10,898	553,741
1944	6,095	43.5	265,584	15,561	852,332
1945	8,105	52.4	424,377	14,441	896,301
1946	4,358	54.4	237,175	10,021	675,580
1947	9,533	62.2	592,953	13,858	976,741
1948	5,768	66.1	38,059	11,259	879,068
1949	7,470	89.3	667,017	16,560	1,821,000
1950	11,451	122.6	1,404,135	16,500	4,125,000
1951	11,665	136.2	1,589,000	17,500	4,400,000
1952	9,278	365.0	3,386,000	18,300	4,715,000
1953	11,000	309.0	3,400,000	N/A	N/A
1954	10,187	402.0	4,077,000	N/A	N/A

Sources: R.C. Northcote, Report on Bukoba Coffee Marketing, 1936 (App A), TNA 24545; Tanganyika Territory Annual Reports for 1920-1930; BCNB 1947 & 1954 Annual Reports

Irrespective of the achievements shown in Table 13, the colonial authority was dissatisfied with the development, given the region was endowed with resources such as land, good climate, and labour.[1] The dissatisfaction was grounded in poor cultivation and managing the coffee trees that resulted in low yield. For example, at one point, the Agriculture Officer observed that:

> Coffee grows without proper attention, almost like weed. It was badly planted, much too close to each other, hacked about with axes, and chopping knives/*panga* in lieu of pruning. The womenfolk on the other hand, do all the work and coffee growing has been forced upon them by their menfolk whose one aim has been to harvest the crop and take the profits for themselves. The womenfolk, who were never taught how the coffee should be grown, must look upon their coffee as an extra burden that brings little advantage to them.[2]

Further encouragement was part of government's 1933 Increase Production Campaign. The campaign stressed that every individual planting coffee had to have no less than 250 trees with desired tree spacing. This was enforced through penalties if not adhered to, for example trees were uprooted, and growers evicted from their land.[3] In addition, the *bashuti* performed most of the cultivation, harvesting tasks, and delivering the crop at buying posts. It is alleged that hired labourers under-performed thus threatening coffee production. Coffee plant pruning, reducing the number of banana trees, mulching and weeding helped curb the spread of diseases, along with proper spacing so plants could produce more coffee. However, farmers were reluctant to implement such measures.

The Agriculture Officer was also of the view that Ordinances, Regulations and Orders did not bring immediate and desired changes to improve coffee husbandry. The officer was of the opinion that the Ordinances, Regulations and Orders were relevant but improvement was insignificant. For him, this was attributed by:[4]

a) Reluctance to enforce the regulation;
b) Lack of authority among chiefs and sub-chiefs;
c) The inadequacy of timing as corrective measure;
d) Lack of initiative on the part of the NA.

The disappointing response by the local chiefs and headmen was in the opinion of the District Agriculture Officer due to NA negligence and lack of commitment. Hence, slow progress. The District Agriculture Officer further pointed out that the Native Authority either could not, or would

---
[1] TNA 11969/19, District Agriculture Officer to DA (October 1930)
[2] TNA 11969/19, Haarer to DA (October, 1930)
[3] Seimu, The Growth and Development of Coffee and Cotton Marketing Co-operatives
[4] TNA 11969/19, District Agriculture Officer to DA (October 1930)

not, attempt to shoulder responsibility for the enforcement of their own coffee regulation.[1]

Several other issues disappointed the District Agriculture Officer. For example, in his assessment, he established that 75 per cent of the cases heard in NA courts had been the result of direct activities of officers of the Agricultural Department, often with the assistance of the DO. Chiefs and village headmen had not taken their responsibilities seriously and had excuses. For instance, when asked why, on innumerable occasions, 'I have complained to chiefs and village headmen of their slackness in prosecuting the owners of dirty plantations,' they invariably answered, '*Bwana* (Sir), we no longer have any authority over these people.'[2]

The engagement of the chiefs and headmen by the colonial authority did not take into account that most were illiterate and could not understand the guidelines.[3] Obviously, they were not trained to execute the colonial government's prescribed crop husbandry and management practices. In such a situation, it was evident that growers lacked proper guidance on prescribed crop husbandry and management practices for which the colonial government was responsible, but it failed to deliver its responsibility.

The complaints raised by the Agriculture Officer demonstrated that chiefs and village headmen were not effectively enforcing Regulations and Orders such as fines in their *Gombolola* (chief's administrative area). According to the Agriculture Officer, the imposition of fines as a form of punishment was an absolute failure. Most of them regarded payment of a fine as a guarantee of a certain period of immunity from the unwelcome attention of the village headman.[4] This was in addition to the NA making a genuine attempt to administer Regulations which were forced upon them by the Department of Agriculture.[5]

On the other hand, payment of fines mostly among 'rich' growers did not lead to improvement of their farms as they could afford the fine, and there was no pressure to hire labourers for the task. The Agriculture Officer was of the opinion that this was because natives saw money as insignificant.[6] He further argued, based on experience, that when a native had money he paid fines cheerfully.[7] For them, fines led to further neglect of coffee farming and attending trees, for example, banana trees that were co-planted with coffee were not pruned.

---

[1] TNA 11969/19, District Agriculture Officer to DA (October 1930)
[2] TNA 11969/19, District Agriculture Officer to DA (4 October 1930)
[3] Seimu, The Growth and Development of Coffee and Cotton Marketing Co-operatives
[4] TNA 26054, Report on Agriculture Policies, June 1932; TNA 11969/19, District Agriculture Officer to DA (4 October 1930)
[5] TNA 26054, District Agriculture Officer to DA, 4 October 1930
[6] TNA 26054, Report on Agriculture Policies, June 1932
[7] TNA 11969/19, District Agriculture Officer to DA (4 October 1930)

Markedly, chiefs and village headmen were coffee growers too. Some chiefs' farms were dirty and they were also, on occasion, fined for an offence. Such fines drained their income. Having plots poorly managed was yet another bad example to their subjects.[1] This obviously annoyed chiefs and village headmen who probably felt embarrassed by the colonial authority officials' bully behaviour and disrespect of their position.

Consequently, coffee trees were exposed to disease and pest risks. This threatened the realisation of self-sufficiency targets. Hence, the colonial authority had to intervene under the leadership of the DA to improve the situation. For example, in 1933, an Assistant District Officer was deployed in Kagera to assist the Agricultural Officer to deal with coffee problems in the region, however, limited progress was achieved.[2] The mentioned production was from small-scale growers who were in the majority, and who produced five to eight Frasilas (equivalent to 36 pounds) of coffee annually. At the same time there were some individuals who produced three tons.[3] All in all, Robusta coffee export was the highest.

In 1937, the DA introduced comprehensive extension services such as guided methods of sowing, planting, cultivation and thinning overcrowded banana trees and pruning leaves. The objectives of the colonial agriculture extension services were designed to make sure that cash crops production met a certain level of productivity and quality influenced by the importing market consumers. New seedlings were distributed across all chiefdoms in the region (Table 14).

Table 14: Number of coffee trees in Kagera Region by 1937

Chiefdom	Robusta	Arabica	Total
Kianja	620,271	2,381,818	5,002,089
Ihangiro	2,012,763	1,271,337	3,284,100
Kiziba	1,462,927	262,176	1,725,103
Karagwe	195,203	121,1670	1,406,873
Kiamtwara	28,7051	143,316	430,367
Buyobo	499,539	25,681	525,220
Kanyangereko	167,695	92,327	260,022
Misenyi	11,071	66,794	176,865

Source: Coffee Cultivation in Bukoba, TNA 1196/19

The distribution of seedlings to growers aimed to improve future productivity. This went hand in hand with extension services introduced by the DA under strict measures supervised by the Agriculture Officers and police officers.[4] Such measures included spacing, by uprooting banana plants, and

---
[1] TNA 24545, Northcote, 1936
[2] TNA 24545, DA to CS (April 1937)
[3] TNA 24545, Northcote, 1936

pruning of banana leaves to enable more light to reach the coffee trees.¹

These measures were not friendly to growers and created widespread fear of an outbreak of famine, as banana was the staple food for the WaHaya and WaNyambo, and an ingredient for making beer, *rubisi*.² It was the natives' fear of implementing coffee improvement measures that culminated in resistance by growers in the form of riots in 1937.³ The colonial authority fiercely quelled the riots using deployed police officers from across the border, Uganda.⁴ Nevertheless, no matter how successful the colonial authority was in arresting riots there was an oversight of the need and necessity to have experts assist growers to improve cultivation methods. None of the existing literature mentions colonial authority reaction towards the riots in Bukoba.

The riots prompted more stern measures. However, these measures were implemented by the District Office. As previously mentioned, the Agriculture Office failed owing to its reliance on the chiefs and headmen who failed to deliver. Evidence shows that the District Officer (DO), Major O.A. Flynn, had to resort to political measures by removing disobedient chiefs from office. It was argued that the removal of chiefs from office was to ensure the maintenance of law and order and sent a message to chiefs who were in power that their disobedience would not be tolerated.⁵

In effecting disciplinary measures, Flynn boasted that, 'I ably handled by removing two chiefs who supported the rioters from their position and ring leaders were punished to restore order.' This measure proved successful as Flynn pointed out that 'it has led to the adoption of coffee improvement measures and expansion of the crop in the region'.⁶

While there was an appreciable improvement in coffee farming practices among small-scale growers, some challenges remained. One was how the coffee bean was processed. Such coffee bean processing methods had been practised for decades.⁷ This was a traditional and rudimentary method at a low technological level referred to as *olwazi ne ibalelyokusa* in Kihaya.

In the process, coffee beans are spread on the outcrops of flat rock and a boulder attached to rope is pulled round and round to crush the coffee.⁸ The method was used because it could easily hull a huge volume of coffee

---

⁴ TNA 24545, DA to CS (April 1937)

¹ Ibid.

² R.A Austen, *Northern Tanzania under German and British rule* (New Haven: Yale University Press, 1979); Iliffe *A Modern History of Tanganyika*; Haarer, *Modern Coffee Production*

³ TNA 26298/8, PC, Lake Province to CS (December 1939)

⁴ Ibid.

⁵ Ibid.

⁶ Ibid.

⁷ Ibid.

⁸ TNA 11969/19, vol. II, C. Harvey (undated)

in a short time unlike a wooden mortar/huller (*kinu*).¹ However, this process resulted in damaging or breaking coffee beans, into small pieces, thereby creatng marketing impediments.²

Evidence shows that broken coffee beans received little interest from foreign buyers but those willing to purchase them, paid poor prices.³ In both instances, broken beans posed a foreign revenue loss or poor return. The colonial authority was not happy with this loss of coffee market, thus it had to intervene, for example in 1929 when the Agriculture Department involved itself mainly in a supervisory capacity.⁴ In the same year, legislation and regulations were put in place. These were the Bukoba Produce Export (Coffee) Rules and the Export Inspection. In addition, the Coffee Industry (Registration and Improvement) Ordinance, coupled with the Grading and Inspection Regulations provided under Ordinance 7 of 1929 and the 1929 Coffee Export Rules, set out by the DA were added to the coffee improvement list. The legalisation, rules and regulations were drafted and passed by the Legislative Council.⁵

However, the colonial authority did not consult key stakeholders such as coffee merchants, Chamber of Commerce and colonial officials in the region in enacting the laws and regulations. Consequently, they were all opposed by the Indian business community in the region,⁶ as well as the provincial colonial authority.⁷ Ultimately, the governor advised the CO to intervene,⁸ prompting withdrawal of the policy by the CO.⁹

3.4. Coffee production in the Southern Highlands

According to Rungwe district records, the missionaries introduced Arabica planting among native growers in several villages such as Kyimbila, Rutenganio, Isoko and Itete, Manow, Mwakaleli, Mbozi and Rungwe in 1900. In 1924 or thereabouts, British and German planters commenced coffee planting on a commercial scale. These planters obtained seedlings from missionaries who had coffee estates in Mbeya and elsewhere. In 1929, drought affected their farms so much that all, but seven, planters decided to abandon farming. Some abandoned plantations were taken over by planters who decided to continue farming, so that the seven planters owned 551 acres of which 504 had coffee bearing trees and 47 non-bearing trees.

---

[1] TNA 24545, Northcote, 1936
[2] TNA 11969/19, vol. II, C. Harvey (undated)
[3] Ibid.
[4] TNA 11969/9, DA to CS (November 1930)
[5] Seimu, The Growth and Development of Coffee and Cotton Marketing Co-operatives
[6] TNA 41011, Indian Association Memorandum to CS (May 1929) & Indian Association Memorandum to Governor (June 1929)
[7] TNA 41011, PC to CS (April 1929)
[8] TNA 41011, Governor to CO, Dispatch no. 424 (April 1929)
[9] Seimu, The Growth and Development of Coffee and Cotton Marketing Co-operatives

The local small coffee growers in Rungwe district were also encouraged by colonial officials to plant coffee on the land they used to cultivate food crops, especially within banana plots, most of which were around 1.3 acres. Given that coffee was a new crop among local growers, the colonial officials took responsibility to train them at demonstration farms which were established in most villages in the district.

The Rungwe Native Authority established its demonstration model plot at a school in Mpuguso village, and employed coffee instructors who provided guidance to growers. Also, the Native Authority encouraged growers to keep some cattle through which they could obtain manure to apply to their coffee trees. In a move to expand the industry, the Rungwe Native Authority established hundreds of coffee tree nurseries from which they obtained seedlings that were distributed to growers.

During 1927 and 1928, the European planters in Rungwe started campaigning against Arabica growing by natives. They pressurised the colonial authority to bar natives from growing the crop. In response, the colonial authority restricted missionaries from supplying seedlings to growers. However, in 1927, the colonial authority made a u-turn as it allowed natives to keep growing coffee, but it was the Robusta variety which settlers regarded as inferior and suitable for natives.

As a show of commitment to small growers the colonial authority supplied seedlings to growers. This was supported by legal mechanisms. In 1929, the Registration of Plantation Act was passed and a year later, that is 1930, it deployed an agricultural officer in Tukuyu chiefly to organise and control the native coffee industry. However, Robusta failed to thrive as climatic conditions and the soil were not suitable for the variety. Native growers were so disappointed that many abandoned the industry. At the same time, settlers failed to develop the industry owing to debts generated out of the economic depression.

The abandonment by native growers and collapse of settlers' farms drew colonial authority attention that led to intervention and a review of the restriction of natives growing Arabica that became a priority from 1934. As a result, communal Arabica coffee plantations and extensive coffee planting was evident between 1936 and 1938 when the Rungwe Native Authority established nurseries from which seedlings were distributed to growers.

Table 15: Coffee seedlings distributed to growers

Year	Seedlings distributed	Source of Seedlings
1933	35,000	Mbeya farms
1934	200,000	Moshi, Blue Mountain (Arusha)
1935	550,000	Blue Mountain (Arusha)
1936	600,000	Blue Mountain (Arusha)
1937	500,000	Blue Mountain (Arusha)

Source: Rungwe District Book

As coffee farming among small-scale growers was gaining pace, marketing of the crop was considered. This was achieved through establishing and organising coffee crop markets. The success of the campaign was due to the creation of administrative units to facilitate monitoring. The NA across Rungwe district grouped growers into nine production zones, and drafted local chiefs and headmen as supervisers (Table 16).

Table 16: Coffee production zones in Rungwe and Mbozi

Group 1	Undali area
Group 2	Kiwira area
Group 3	Masebe area
Group 4	Masoko area
Group 5	Manow area
Group 6	Selya area
Group 7	Mwakaleli West area
Group 8	Mwakaleli East area
Group 9	Mbozi area

Source: Rungwe District Book

Table 17: Coffee production in tons

Production in tons	1932	1933	1934	1935	1936	1937
	24	31	54	65	58	72

Source: Rungwe District Book

3.4.1. Coffee producing areas Rungwe and Mbozi districts

At one time, it was considered that cultivation of coffee by natives in the Rungwe district would lead to the introduction of disease into European owned plantations and the native industry was therefore discouraged. However, the non-native industry turned out a complete failure, thus leaving the road free from obstruction for native coffee growers, so that by the end of 1933 there were 1,380 native coffee planters owning 272,457 trees, while 1934 saw an increase to 2,888 growers with 356,554 trees with an output of 25 tons of clean coffee, which realised Shs. 12,549/80 in total.[1]

Table 18: Coffee production in Mbeya and Rungwe districts

Coffee production in Mbeya district

Years	1932	1933	1934	1935	1936
Number of growers	-	1,000	1,020	1,203	1,286
Number of coffee trees	-	64,000	73,900	121209	2,100,762

Coffee production in Rungwe district

Years	1932	1933	1934	1935	1936
Number of growers	1,349	1,663	2,688	3,801	5,777
Number of coffee trees	238,500	242,457	356,654	465,473	830,678

Source: TNA 22983, PC Southern Highland Province to Chief Secretary, 2/44/66, 20 March 1936

---

[1] Provincial Commissioner, Southern Province to CS, Ref. 2/10A/226

Table 19: Coffee production groups in Rungwe Clusters

Group	Number of growers	Production in kilogrammes
Undali	1067	11,300
Kiwira	1148	14,021
Masebe	694	9,362
Masoko	493	902
Manow	425	4,587
Selya	735	3,206
Mwakaleli East	783	5,696
Mwakaleli West	432	2,833
Mbozi	286	10,300

Source: TNA 22983, Director of Agriculture to Chief Secretary, Ref. 482/233, 13 January 1937

3.5. Rice production in Mbeya and Songwe Regions

Rice was first introduced to the lakeshore (Kyela) of Rungwe district in 1896. Arabs from Malawi (then Nyasaland) supplied seeds to Sultan Koroso and a headman named Mwakilima. In 1898, the Moravian Missionaries and Swahili traders introduced more rice varieties in Kyela. Having observed success amongst traders who farmed rice, the locals followed suit. This marked the beginning of the industry in Kyela. By 1932, several rice varieties were being cultivated in Kyela.

Table 20: Rice varieties

Rice Varieties	Year introduced	Development
Mwakilima	1896	Very poor quality, very little grow
Bungara	1899	Good quality, extensively grown
Marura	1907/8	Fair quality, extensively
Hujeni	1907/8	Poor quality, small area grown
Msafiri	1907/8	Good quality, extensively grown
Marija	1917	Good quality, extensively grown
Mbonera	1918	Fair quality, small area grown
Faya	1929	Excellent quality, very extensively grown
Kingoma	1929	Poor quality, very little grown
Korosso	1929	Good quality, small area grown
Mwanguru	1926	Good quality, extensively grown
Lady Wright	1932	Excellent quality
Calorina Storm Proof	1932	Good quality
Carolina Edith	1932	Good quality
Mexican Edith	1932	Good quality
Rufiji	1932	Fair quality

Source: Rungwe District Book

By 1930 the rice harvest was 250 tons and in 1934 it was 800 tons, which was consumed locally with some exported. Before the outbreak of World War II, production amounted to 400 tons. However, a proper rice marketing system was absent, preventing the generation of clear figures of rice sales. The Indian traders were the main buyers, especially in Kyela and Mwaya (in Mbeya Region) where they paid 12–18 cents per kilogramme. In many instances barter trade dominated, for example, growers were given a piece of cloth per 100 kilogramme-bag of rice. This practice changed from 1939 when the government intervened through bye-laws that provided for the setting up of a marketing system and opened buying posts in various locations. Kyela and Mwaya were the biggest rice markets in which the Native Authority and merchants were key buyers.

In 1943 and 1944, the colonial government intervened by encouraging growers to expand rice farming. In so doing, it appointed E.L. Shipman to guide growers in modern rice farming and in the pricing of rice, as well as facilitating marketing of the crop to South Africa, Malawi, Zanzibar and other towns in Tanzania. Such efforts led to increased production.

4. Post-WW2 Agricultural Colonial Policy

At the end of World War II, the British encouraged immigration and settlers to invest in the Tanganyikan agricultural sector with attention being given to reviving plantations abandoned as a result of the war. Plans were put in place to alienate more land for the settlers. However, the Labour Party won the election in 1945 and under its socialist policy considered it appropriate, and necessary, to address the exploitation of the working class by the private sector, and to address poverty and colonial development through 'development and social welfare'. With this view, policy changes were made that impacted on economic development in the colonies. Such changes were in response to the aftermath of the Second World War when Britain experienced shortages of food and raw materials and had a balance of payment problem, mainly being short of USA dollars to meet importation costs. The colonies were of priority to help reduce the large deficits Britain was facing. Also, it was believed that economic development required investment in infrastructure to increase and improve production which caused the government to become directly involved.

The overall effect of these altered economic conditions prompted a new 'development policy' towards the colonial territories. However, there was uncertainty in the Colonial Office over how to achieve increased production of raw materials and foodstuffs in the sterling currency zone. This was due to the slow pace of economic development in the colonies since the CO lacked expertise and could not operate in every colony. To accelerate economic development a central body that could carry out major projects independently of existing colonial authorities was required.

To meet this commitment, the Overseas Resource Development Bill was introduced in the House of Commons in 1947 by the Minister of Food, John Strachey, who argued that the Bill was intended to initiate productive activities in hitherto undeveloped areas. Sir Stafford Cripps, Minister for Economic Affairs, addressing a conference of sceptical colonial governors in 1947, stressed the urgency of the situation and the central importance of Africa:

> it is essential that we should increase out of all recognition the tempo of African economic development. We must be prepared to change our outlook and our habits of colonial development and force the

pace. An occasional failure is the necessary price of adventurous development and we must not allow safety first to be the key note of our work ... the whole future of the Sterling Group and its ability to survive depends in my view on a quick and extensive development of our African resources.

Two statutory bodies were formed: the Overseas Food Corporation that came under the Ministry of Food, and the Colonial Development Corporation (CDC)[1] under the Colonial Office. The latter was charged with facilitating international finance capital, backed by the state, to encourage the private capital moving into important areas of colonial economies. The Overseas Food Corporation (OFC) encouraged private capital investment in food crop production projects in colonial territories. An example was the groundnut scheme in Tanganyika which was quashed in 1956 for failure to meets its objective.[2] The Colonial Development Corporation was also charged with improving the standard of living of the colonised people by increasing their productivity and wealth.

To enhance agricultural productivity, the British government had the political will and commitment to modernise subsistence agricultural production. In 1955, it commissioned a study by the East Africa Royal Commission, whose report, published the same year, established the challenges: mainly poor farming practices, such as cut and burn, that were uneconomical and posed a threat to soil fertility; this according to the commission was due to the land tenure system. Thus, the colonial authority blamed small-scale farmers for the ecological crisis; this was, according to the colonialists, caused by either overpopulation or primitive and careless farming practices. In implementing the commission's recommendations, the government had to compel small-scale farmers to adopt modern methods of agriculture embodied in the Land Development and Soil Conservation Schemes. Compulsion was enforced through either threats of fine or imprisonment; they were further enforced through bye-laws laid down under the 1927 Native Authority Ordinance by the chief and native courts, on their failure to undertake agricultural practices which were deemed correct by the government.

There was a period after the Second World War when six major schemes were undertaken in Tanganyika. The largest of these Development Schemes were the Sukuma, Mbulu, Usambara, Upare, and Iringa Cattle Dipping Scheme. These schemes were of doubtful value and their manner of

---

[1] The ORD established under the Overseas Resources Development Act was amended in 1951 and 1954. In 1951 ministerial responsibility for the Overseas Food Corporation was transferred to the Secretary of State for Colonies.

[2] Stefan Esselborn, Environment, Memory, and the Groundnut Scheme: Britain's Largest Colonial Agricultural Development Project and Its Global Legacy, *Global Environment* 11 (2013) 58-93

imposition upon the people caused considerable resistance and, in some instances, violent clashes.

Colonial government policy shifted in 1955 from preserving small-scale crop farming as recommended by the Royal Commission of Land and Population in East Africa, to one where the communal land tenure system was replaced with individual ownership. A number of arguments were presented: first, it was thought to create a wealthy class of farmers (*kulaks/ yeomen*) who would check political instability that the subsistence growers could not, as experienced in Kenya under the Mau Mau.

Second, support for progressive farmers was unveiled. Conducive conditions were created for progressive farmers by providing incentives for investment and land improvement. The policy was geared towards fostering a yeoman class of capitalist farmers. In 1958, the colonial government embarked on changes to the land policy and law that transformed traditional customary property rights, which guaranteed *kulaks* or yeomen access, to freehold land ownership to enhance agricultural productivity and develop a rural capitalist class. Under this approach growers or tenant farmers were resettled in disastrous groundnut schemes set up between 1947-51 such as Urambo who were encouraged to grow tobacco.[1] During the same period, the British American Tobacco (BAT) had tobacco plantations in Urambo. Nevertheless the interest was small-scale growers. The preference over small-scale growers was envisioned to stimulate mechanisation and the economies of scale in agriculture.[2] Under settlement schemes the tenant farmers were allocated plots of land for farming, on condition that they complied with rules and regulations that defined 'modern' agricultural techniques.[3]

Progressive farmers comprised a handful of growers selected from tens in a village, basically to hasten agricultural development on realisation that perpetuation of subsistence farming was not sustainable. It was envisaged that such farmers would cause a multiplier effect in increasing crop production, not only to themselves but to the entire crop producing community in a given area. The progressive farmers were given technical advice so as to diffuse modern farming techniques and support, and could access credit and use their land as security, which would ultimately instil a sense of commercial farming.

However, the selection of farmers produced mixed results; for example,

---

[1] M. Agarwal & D. Linsenhmeyer, *Smallholder Tobacco Development in Tanzania: A Review of Urambo and Tumbi Schemes* (Washington, D.C.: World Bank, September, 1974)

[2] Göran Hydén, *Beyond Ujamaa in Tanzania. Underdevelopment and an Uncaptured Peasantry* (London: Heinemann, 1980) p. 71; Coulson, *A polotical economy*, p. 145

[3] Walter Scheffler, Tobacco Schemes in the Central Region, in H. Ruthenberg (ed), *Smallholder Farming and Smallholder Developmet in Tanzania* (Munich: Weltforum Verlag, African Studies #24, 1968)

some misused their credit by diverting funds to social functions. Others were reluctant to provide support to unselected farmers who, as a result, were then viewed as arrogant which disqualified them as an example to emulate. The impact of the policy was that inequality began to emerge in rural areas:

> a class of African rich peasants was emerging which ... had already achieved a substantial degree of economic and political control at the local level, through improved access to resources related to its domination of the co-operatives and most other local administrative and decision-making bodies.[1]

In 1954 the OFC projects were transferred to the Tanganyika Agricultural Corporation (TAC) to perform dual functions: (a) to bring to a feasible conclusion the investigative work in establishing permanent systems of self-supporting agricultural production in three former groundnut areas at Kongwa, Urambo, and Nachingwea; and (b) to promote, develop, and manage planned settlement schemes and such other agricultural projects as might be considered by the government to be in the best interests of the economic development of the country. Some of the TAC's economic activities were:

a. production of variety of crops
b. operation of a livestock ranch at Kongwa
c. establishment of tenant farmers in Urambo (tobacco), Nachingwea and
d. the Ruvu ranching project.

---

[1] P. Raikes, The state and the peasantry in Tanzania, in: J. Harriss (ed), *Rural Development: Theories of Peasant Economy and Agrarian Change* (London: Routledge, 1982) pp. 350-380, 359

5. Post-Independence Agriculture Policy

After independence in 1961, rural development was given priority with emphasis on increasing the production and living standards of the rural population which was by then 95 per cent of the total Tanganyikan population. The World Bank recommended two approaches to achieve rural development, particularly improvement in agricultural production among the peasants, and transformation approaches.[1] The improvement approach was designed to gradually increase household agricultural output, mainly in coffee and cotton through the provision of extension services and agricultural inputs; whereas transformation was meant to bring about radical change in agriculture with attention and focus being the demise of settler colonial agricultural capital development schemes. These were incorporated into the Five Year Social and Economic Development Plan of 1 July 1964 to 30 June 1969.

5.1: Agricultural development schemes

The policy envisaged the introduction of technical and legal systems which allowed the exercise of modern agricultural techniques to enhance productivity. It involved regrouping and resettling farmers in identified schemes or settlements[2] such as Kerege in Bagamoyo district, Kabuku in Handeni district, Upper Kitete[3] in Karatu district and Mlale in Songea district, which were established specifically for the purpose. In both schemes the settlers or villagers were required to engage in modern farming under supervision of government officials or experts. Until 1965 there were 23 such schemes across the country, farming over 15,000 acres, most of which were cash crops like tobacco.

The critical challenge faced by this approach was reluctance of farmers to engage with selected schemes. Those who were willing lacked skills for mechanised farming and funding, as such schemes depended on financing from donors. The *kulak* class of farmers and income disparities emerged in rural areas as a result of implementation of the approaches and land individualism led to rural inequality in the WCGA where there were half a million cheap labourers being hired. For example it was estimated that 77 per cent of the hired rural labourers were in Usmao, 34 per cent in Luguru, and 34 per cent in Maswa district.[4]

---

[1] URT, *National Human Settlement Development Policy* (Dar es Salaam: Government Printer, 2000) p. 11

[2] Ibid., pp. 10-11

[3] For wheat production

5.2: Socialism and self-reliance

The lessons learnt by the government of Tanzania from these approaches played an important role in the revision of its economic and rural development policies that led to official withdrawal of the early 1960's rural development policies in 1966. An alternative approach was considered: Vice-President Rashid Kawawa pushed for expansion of the co-operative movement, whilst Julius Nyerere developed *Ujamaa*, and embraced the Arusha Declaration in February 1967 that revolved around Socialism and Self-reliance. Implementation of the *Ujamaa* policy in rural areas was guided by the Socialism and Rural Development document published in September 1967. The document and further elaborations by Julius Nyerere, President of Tanzania, envisaged the organisation and mobilisation of rural communities based on socialist principles whereby small-scale agricultural crop-growers would not only live together as a village but also work together in groups conducting agricultural practices. This would lead to a realisation that co-operative production and marketing could foster socialist principles and rural transformation.

The post-independent government viewed the early 1960s more capitalist approaches as unsuitable and inherently linked to colonialism which rested on the exploitation of man by man. It was held that Tanzania was fertile ground for the germination of Socialism which was by and large in harmony with African communal society (egalitarianism), whereby kinship ties were strong and maintained communally owned land. In this respect, development of agriculture placed the politicians in a dilemma. It is believed that the improvement approach led to the emergence of private agricultural production resulting in the growth of *kulaks*, viewed by politicians as a rural exploitative class. It was also conceived that small-scale growers were not potentially economically viable, thus state farms were considered a suitable option in which the government itself engaged in agricultural production. Under this policy it offered feasible ways for direct state control of production and marketing, thereby bringing the entire economy automatically under the control of the state.

The post-colonial government viewed co-operatives as the vehicle to achieve the government's rural development and also to facilitate unity among growers. At independence the NAs were abolished in favour of Village Development Committees. They were found in every village where a ten-cell leadership position was created to replace the village headmen position. The vacuum created by abolished NAs and district councils necessitated the promotion of co-operatives to take over development

---

[4] H.V.É. Thoden van Velzen, *Staff, Kulaks and Peasants: A Study of A Political Field, Rural Development* Paper 8, Rural Development Research Committee (Dar-es-Salaam: University of Dar-es-Salaam, 1971)

function at grassroots level to administer projects by targeting individuals who were not organised in groups; also to facilitate increased production and productivity in agriculture. This represented continuity of colonial agricultural policies. The co-operative movement would play a part in the modernisation of agriculture as a medium for providing knowledge and skills to enable growers to improve and learn modern farming practices.

The First Five Year Plan[1] marked the beginning of a political shift away from capitalism towards socialism unveiled in the Arusha Declaration (ArD) of 5 February 1967.[2] Under the ArD the major means of production and exchange were extensively nationalised and placed under the control of the workers and small-scale growers through the government and co-operatives. With the nationalisation of estates and plantations the government could not cope with managing nationalised farms due to lack of staff and funding. Therefore it had to rely on the co-operatives, so, for example, the KNCU was given nationalised coffee plantations. Thus the movement became an integral part in the control of all the major means of production and exchange. It was argued that:

> To build and maintain socialism, it was essential that all the major means of production and exchange in the nation were controlled and owned by peasants through the machinery of their government and their co-operatives.[3]

To this effect, the government strengthened the administrative apparatus responsible for co-operation, adjusted co-operative legislation to fit the new strategy, and became subject to strictly political and ideological imperatives. It was also envisaged that under the policy the co-operative movement would engage Tanzanians in achieving economic independence and self-reliance.

As part of the First Five-Year Development Plan, the Presidential Special Committee of Enquiry into the Co-operatives Movement and Marketing Boards was appointed in 1966 amid complaints from growers and co-operative members about the terms of payment on their produce. The Committee was given terms of reference that was entailed:

> To review the staffing and, where necessary, the organisational structure of the co-operative movement and Marketing Boards in order to recommend what steps should be taken to strengthen them for the maximum benefit of producers and consumers alike.[4]

---

[1] URT, *First Five-Year Plan for Economic and Social Development* (1964-1969), vol. I (Dar es Salaam: Government Printer, 1964) p. 43

[2] J.K. Nyerere, *Ujamaa: Essays on Socialism* (Dar es Salaam: Oxford University Press, 1968) pp. 13-37

[3] J.K. Nyerere, *Freedom and Socialism.* (Dar es Salaam: DUP, 1968) pp. 233-234

[4] URT, *The Presidential Special Committee of Enquiry into Co-operatives Movement and Marketing Boards* (Dar es Salaam: Government Printer, 1966) p.1

The 1966 Commission of Enquiry recommended strengthening of the Co-operative Unions. Consequently, a number of developments took place. First, Paper 4 of 1967 was published that provided a new policy direction that the movement should embark upon. Second, the policy recommended the creation of multi-purpose co-operative societies intended to replace 14,000 Asians who majority-controlled retail and 4,000 in wholesale businesses where the number of Africans was negligible.[1] It was envisaged that for effective utilisation and profit realization the co-operative movement had to diversify to include marketing food crops, processing plants and agriculture production so that they become multi-purpose.[2] This signified a shift of emphasis by having co-operatives undertake new businesses. However, this was in addition to serving affiliated primary societies resulting in over-burdened plans, performance and progress. This overwhelmed their managerial and financial capacity and exposed a lack of knowledge in executing some of the new business.

---

[1] Gerald Albaum and Gilbert L. Rutman, 'The Co-operative-Based Marketing System in Tanganyika', In *Journal of Marketing*, vol.31, No 4, Part 1 (October 1967) pp.54-58
[2] URT, *The Second Five-Year Plan for Economic and Social Development*,(1964-1969) (Dar es Salaam: Government Printer, 1969) pp. 31-32

6. Cash Crop Marketing

Incorporation of small-scale native growers in cash crop production was fundamental to the growth and development of the embryonic agricultural marketing co-operative societies during the inter-war and post-war years. This was the same in Uganda because they had no co-operative law, until one was promulgated after World War II. In Kenya small-scale growers' marketing associations were restricted as the colonial authority considered the co-operative law passed in 1931 unsuitable for promoting co-operatives among natives. The policy remained so until after World War II. Native growers in Kenya had sold their produce to settlers who sold it through their associations and from 1932 via co-operatives.[1] The marketing of crops produced by settlers was in the hands of the producers themselves with some statutory regulation, whereas African-produced crops were actively controlled by government.

6.1: Coffee marketing by the KNPA

Until the mid-1920s, coffee marketing in Kilimanjaro was under the control of Indians, Greeks, missionaries and some civil servants. The direct involvement of growers began in 1925 when KNPA was formed with approval by Charles Dundas. Basically, the association was formed to protect the growers from settler agitation against a policy that accommodated small-scale growers in coffee cultivation. The involvement of KNPA in crop purchase was emulated from the settlers' coffee bulk marketing scheme. Essentially, the association was not legally allowed to conduct coffee marketing but the colonial authority accommodated it because the produce was sold in British markets. The association charged commission and some fees were used to develop the industry, for example the purchase of seedlings. The colonial authority viewed the association as an institution which enabled tax collection.

To facilitate the KNPA, it was given a mandate and monopoly over coffee marketing under Section 15 of Native Authority Ordinance 18, 1926, which compelled native coffee growers in Moshi district to sell their coffee produce through the association from 1 April 1929. Consequently, this policy brought coffee marketing under the association culminating in a takeover of coffee marketing from Indian control. Under such policy direction, coffee quality was emphasised to encourage demand for Kilimanjaro-grown coffee on the world market. Various stakeholders were involved

---

[1] Kenya Colony & Protectorate, *Colonial Annual Report on the Social and Economic Progress of the People, No. 1659* (London: HMSO, 1932)

in facilitating the attainment of coffee quality such as government agriculture officers and the NA's agricultural extension officers and coffee instructor. Similarly, the growers had an advantage, learning from the settlers the best coffee processing practices that together enabled them to be successful.

6.2: Coffee marketing in Bukoba

In Bukoba, coffee marketing was under the control of middlemen and merchants, the same as Uganda. This was accidentally influenced by two factors. Following the defeat of the Germans in World War 1, the Belgians occupied Bukoba until when they evacuated, the British took over. It thus became necessary to engage Ugandan marketing policies, largely because Bukoba was considered to be technically part of Uganda since it utilised its rail outlets to Mombasa. At the time, there were poor roads and no railway transport to Dar es Salaam. It was therefore essential to maintain a parallel coffee marketing scheme with Uganda. However, the Ugandan influence was not meant to dominate permanently.

In 1929, there were 6,000 coffee dealers (Indians, Arabs and Africans) who purchased 8,000 tons, mostly from unregistered buying posts, mainly *shambas* or illegally at night in *dukas*; buyers convinced growers to mortgage unharvested coffee, a system referred to as *okulangula emwani* in Kihaya. Such practices intensified competition for the community but quality was compromised. These dealers and practices were gradually eliminated by the government so that by 1939 there were only 1,500 and the number was further reduced to between 750 and 900 in 1947. Among the traders were Africans which suggests they were not excluded from participating in coffee marketing. These dealers were either agents of traders based in Bukoba or were self-employed.

Table 21: Licensed and *abalanguzi* traders, 1930–1936

Year	Non Natives	Natives	Itinerants (*abalanguzi be emwani*)
1930	325	497	2440
1931	307	360	850
1932	340	490	1785
1933	352	498	1640
1934	365	515	1510
1935	335	475	915
1936	278	310	98

Source: R.C. Northcote Report on Bukoba coffee marketing (Appendix E)

Under such trading practices, cheating was widespread as both category of traders operated in Bukoba town. This was also happening in other trading centres where traders paid prices fixed by their financiers who in turn paid the growers a much lower rate. They also cheated on weight, taking advantage of growers' illiteracy. Generally, barter trade was widespread and alarming; for instance, coffee was exchanged for meat, fish, cigarettes, and salt, in which exchanged volumes of the crop were determined by a buyer using, in most instances, inaccurate scales.[1]

In view of the escalating problem, R.C. Northcote, the Registrar of Co-operative Societies, was invited in 1936 to investigate and advise on the marketing undertaken in Bukoba, which was described as 'in far worse state than the produce market in Sukumaland prior to the establishment of Native Authority markets.'[2] Northcote established that native producers were receiving unfair prices for their coffee and were cheated by both natives and non-natives, since they were ignorant.

The Northcote findings coincided with a colonial economic development circular issued by the Secretary of State for Colonies, Sir W. Ormsby-Gore, on 22 June 1937. It stressed that colonial authorities had a responsibility to promote colonial economies. This was based on the view that prior to the First World War, crop marketing efforts were not only sporadic but also uncoordinated. The establishment of the boards was strongly emphasised in the circular, in which their functions were to encompass promotion of production, and to enhance crop marketing efficiency and crop research. The circular was so comprehensive that it emphasised building and maintaining links with local trade associations and agencies that were already in place in East Africa, Sri Lanka (Ceylon), the West Indies, and Malaysia (Malaya).

6.3: Statutory Marketing Boards

The Ormsby-Gore memorandum had in some ways provided a solution to the problem that gripped coffee marketing in Moshi district where throughout 1936 there was growing discontent among the natives, which culminated in rioting in the area in 1937. The rioters complained that owing to heavy overhead expenses the Union paid lower prices than they could obtain outside. This was a result of the Chagga Rule, of 1934, ordering all natives in Moshi district to market their coffee produce through KNCU.

However, the Chagga Rule was considered a temporary measure pending amendment of Section 36(1) of the Co-operative Ordinance. Some growers, not satisfied, instituted a law suit to challenge the compulsion measure on grounds that it was repugnant to the general laws of the territory and was unreasonable to the welfare of growers. Again, it was viewed by the colonial authority that the legislation had drawn the NA into coffee industry economics.

---

[1] TNA 24545, Northcote 1936 Inquiry Report on Bukoba Coffee Industry in Report on Bukoba Coffee Marketing, p. 12
[2] Ibid.

As a result of the riots and legal challenge, it was decided that new legislation should be passed specifically for the control of African-grown coffee, and enforcement of the legislation had to be the government's business. In drafting new legislation it was carefully considered to exclude European planters but it had to be so to African growers who, it was thought, could not manage the industry on their own. Consequently, the native coffee industry was brought under more direct government control using the Coffee (Control & Marketing) Ordinance 26 of 1937.

In practice, the Ordinance empowered the governor to set up the MNCB which was charged to give direction on the method of sowing, planting, cultivation, harvesting or preparation and marketing of native coffee by appointing native agents to facilitate purchasing from growers. The establishment of the MNCB, and Cocoa Boards in West Africa, revolved around addressing growers concerns with regard to poor prices paid for their produce. This ordinance was envisaged to apply first, only, in Kilimanjaro so as to gain experience on how effective the MNCB was before being replicated in other parts of the country. The plan was unveiled when the Lake PC showed interest in setting up a similar board in Bukoba,[1] and he was informed that:

> it is not desired to appoint Coffee Boards at that particular time any place except the Kilimanjaro area, (…) firstly, the members of the LEGCO (Legislative Council)[2] were informed that the Government principal objective in passing the Native Coffee Ordinance was to control the cultivation and marketing of coffee in that area alone, and secondly, because it desired to gain experience of the working of the Moshi Native Coffee Board.[3]

The Indian traders were displeased with the Ordinance which perpetuated a coffee marketing monopoly, but in any case the compulsory element was in place. The Fabian Colonial Bureau was also critical of this crop marketing arrangement, arguing that the appointment of KNCU to act as the agent for the board was somewhat chequered.[4] The publication of the bill and the Ordinance's promulgation was strongly opposed by the Indian community, particularly traders across the territory. They viewed it as prejudicial to them given their status as major buyers of crops produced by Africans.[5] In this respect they demanded it be abandoned largely because it was designed to

---

[1] TNA 25442, Native Coffee Board Moshi District: Establishment and Membership, from PC Lake Province to CS, telegram 390, 23 December 1937
[2] LEGCO was set up in 1926.
[3] TNA 25442, CS to PC Lake Province, Ref. 25442/39, 4 January 1938
[4] Fabian Colonial Bureau, *Co-operation in the Colonies: A Report from a Special Committee to the Fabian Colonial Bureau* (London: George Allen & Unwin, 1945) p. 38
[5] TNA 25038, India Association, Bukoba to CS 30 September 1937; Secretary of State for Colonies Ref 25 141/1938 7/2/1938

introduce principles of monopoly which proved repugnant to the interest of growers and free trade, and against the spirit of the mandate. Despite criticism and opposition, the monopoly was upheld by having the Ordinance stipulate that those who did not comply, would have penalties imposed, such as a fine or imprisonment.

On 12 February 1938, the legislation was approved and applauded by Ormsby-Gore,[1] when he was informed by the CS of the governor's approval on 20 November 1937. The legislation came into effect on 9 December 1937.[2] Under Section 6 of the Ordinance, coffee produced by natives in Moshi district had to be sold through such agencies as the MNCB directed. In this regard, the Ordinance provided an assurance that all produce exports be diverted from Germany and Japan to Britain.[3] However, the appointment of KNCU as the MNCB agent was viewed as somewhat chequered[4] and controversial. It was seen as an attempt by the government to exert control of over production on racial lines as depicted in Section 36 of the Co-operative Societies Ordinance. It became clear that government practically limited discrimination bias on racial lines.

The experience gained with the MNCB led to the establishment of a similar localised board, the Bukoba District Coffee Board, to serve the same but limited functions in 1942. The BDCB was not granted a marketing mandate and monopoly which suggests that *laisser-faire* prevailed. It was also decided that the legislation could be applicable in other coffee producing areas, such as Bugufi, Tukuyu and Songea, when the need arose. Again, this suggests that a focus was Moshi district and Bukoba where the board employed coffee instructors, inspectors and extension officers to help farmers to improve and modernise coffee production. The board staff were assigned to enforce regulations and were charged with engaging growers in mulching. This clearly, suggests that the government took responsibility to intervene in both production and marketing.

Within two years of implementating the Ormsby-Gore policies, the Defence Acts were put in place which directed that food and raw materials produced in the colonies be marketed through recommended outlets. This was a result of the outbreak of World War II in 1939 under which the colonial governors issued orders regulating crop cultivation and exports. This included the Defence Coffee Control Board regulations issued in 1940 to direct coffee produced by both natives and non-natives to be sold to the British Ministry of Food through the KNCU.[5] In 1942 the government set

---

[1] TNA 25038, Secretary of State for Colonies to CS Dispatch 25, 4 January 1938; TNA 25147, Marketing of Colonial Produce in the UK and Overseas

[2] TNA 25038, CS to Secretary for Colonies, 7 February 1938

[3] *The Tanganyika Standard*, 22 September 1937

[4] Fabian Colonial Bureau, *Co-operation in the Colonies: A Report from a Special Committee to the Fabian Colonial Bureau* (London: George Allen & Unwin, 1945) p. 38

up the Bukoba Coffee Control Board (BCCB) under General Notice 329 of 8 April 1941 to replace the BDCB. The new board took over the BDCB functions which were extended to include marketing and it entered a long-term contract with the Ministry of Food to ensure coffee was supplied to Britain during the war. When the war ended in 1945, colonial government intervention took a new turn as far as coffee marketing was concerned, by replacing the BCCB with the Bukoba Native Coffee Board (BNCB) in 1947 under Government Notice 169, 1946, formally ending BCCB operations on 31 October 1947. The BNCB undertook the responsibility of delivery to the Ministry of Food under a five-year agreement. Bukoba thus experienced and witnessed three board changes substantially geared towards creating one that would target and service coffee produced by African growers.

Setting up a new board in Bukoba was necessary for quality control of coffee produced by Africans. The new board was charged with marketing, unlike the previous one whose function was limited to supervision of coffee farming. Unlike before, the colonial government was brought into direct intervention in coffee marketing. When the new board took over, it established the zonal scheme and erected hulleries in each zone to ensure quality was maintained. It also began to fix prices for coffee, delivered by top growers at buying posts, based on grades or quality of coffee. This was implemented in accordance with the powers conferred upon the BNCB by Native Coffee (Compulsory Marketing) Order, 1947.

BNCB was appointed the sole purchaser of all native coffee in Bukoba as per Ordinance 26 of 1937 Section 6.[1] The buyers or agents were appointed to buy coffee in the zones on behalf of the board under a contract that lasted seven years from October 1947 to 31 October 1954. The Order made clear that all coffee produced by Africans in Bukoba district should be sold to the board through the zonal agents. The agents were required to buy coffee from producers at a fixed price. The agents then sold both Arabica and Robusta to the board at a fixed price.

However, the contract with the Ministry of Food was received with mixed feelings. Traders protested largely because the contract was unfair and frustrated free trade competition. Indian merchants were unhappy with the contract, and judged 'it is undesirable to introduce monopolistic ignorant and not capable of looking after their own interest.'[2] They felt that their interests were in jeopardy as the monopoly was designed for African

---

[5] M. Yoshida, *Agricultural Marketing Intervention in East Africa* (Tokyo: Institute of Developing Economics, 1984) p. 77

[1] TNA 11969, extract from minute of meeting of the standing committee held in April 1947

[2] *The Tanganyika Herald*, 3 September 1947

interests over other nationals.¹ They thus urged the government to postpone the scheme until an investigation was conducted by the Chamber of Commerce with agreement on the best modalities to implement.² Furthermore, they expressed their grievances and opinions to the Chief Secretary, which in their opinion was a threat to the livelihoods of hundreds of Indians. Apart from that, involvement of Africans in the industry did not offer a solution to improving the quality of the produce.³ Finally, Indians strongly protested against government interference in coffee marketing which they viewed as unfair.⁴ The print media was also critical of the scheme, referring to it as the 'monopoly evil'.⁵

However, the protest did not deter the colonial authority from implementing the order which saw the reorganisation and streamlining of the whole marketing structure by setting up 12 zones which were allocated to traders who were considered financially sound to facilitate the excise. It was envisaged that the establishment of the zonal coffee buying arrangements was to ensure that coffee growers were brought into closer contact with the board. Contact with the farmers was made through committees in each zone which had one representative elected by growers from each *Gombolola*.⁶

The creation of zones had some impact such as the elimination of itinerants and middlemen but generated new challenges: smuggling, involving traders who were not part of the contract; and cheating with scales by Asian traders.⁷ Coffee smuggling in Bukoba was a critical challenge that threatened the financial survival of the BNCB. Smuggling was disruptive and rendered the BNCB, the co-operatives and Native Authority powerless before the growers as well as traders.⁸

Several meetings were held to discuss mechanisms to curb coffee smuggling from the area. At one BNCB meeting held on 26 July 1951, a number of smuggling factors were shared. One was the low price paid to growers by the BNCB through the zonal agents and the co-operatives, unlike the payment received from traders. Another was lack of control of coffee

---

[1] *The Tanganyika Herald*, 6 July 1947

[2] TNA 29585, BNCB Bukoba District from Tanganyika India Chamber of Commerce and Agriculture to CS on 21/8/1947

[3] TNA 11969, Tanganyika Indian Chamber of Commerce and Agriculture to Chief Secretary, 21 August 1947

[4] TNA 11969, Indian Chamber of Commerce to CS, telegram, 10 May 1947

[5] *The Tanganyika Herald*, 3 September 1947

[6] According to Gabriel Kagaruki – Gombolola administrative area in the chiefdom that was under the sub-Chief; BNCB Annual Report November 1947-1948, pp. 14-16

[7] BNCB Annual Report, November 1947-1948, pp. 14-16

[8] TNA 41011, Organisation of Bukoba Coffee Marketing: From BNCB to Members of Agricultural and Natural Resources, Ref. C.1/92, 26 November 1951

produced by non-natives and the existence of a huge number of licensed traders, 200 non-natives and 400 Africans, who were operating in the zones.[1] They called for a reduction of the number of traders,[2] as well as restrictions on issuing licenses; an increase in coffee prices; co-operatives to be promoted and a monopoly to be granted in coffee marketing.[3] Another measure considered vital was to end all shipments through Bukoba port.[4] Implementation of these measures was felt necessary, not only to rescue revenue sources for the BNCB but also for the co-operatives and Native Authority.

These measures were submitted to various authorities for implementation and to consider legislation that would provide the BNCB and co-operatives with a monopoly in coffee marketing. The Commissioner for Co-operative Development declined the proposals on grounds they were impractical;[5] a long term contract with zonal agents was expected to expire in October 1954.

Table 22: Zones and appointed agents

S/N	Zone	Sub-chiefdoms	Appointed Agents
1	Muleba	Kahengere, Bukoba, Ilamera, Mubunda, Karambo	Sharrif Jiwa & Co Ltd
2	Nshamba	Kashasha, Mbatama, Kishanda, Nshamba, Birabo	Messers MN Patel & Co Ltd
3	Kamachumu	Ibuga and Kamachumu	Messrs Rashid Maledina & Ltd
4	Muhutwe	Izigo, Muhutwe, Rwagati, and Minazi	JS Patel & Co
5	Ikimba	Kabirizi, Mikoni, Ibweru, Kishogo, and Kaibanja	Messers Rashid maledina & co
6	Maruku	Kanyangereko chiefdom	JS Patel & Co
7	Kiziba	Kiziba chief	Messrs JS Patel & Co
8	Bugabo	Bugabo chiefdom	Sheriff Jiwa & Co Ltd
9	Kyaka	Misenyi chiefdom	Messers Shah & Co
10	Karagwe	Karagwe chiefdom	Messers Shah & Co
11	Bukoba	Kyantwara chiefdom	Mr Kassamali Allarakhusa
12	Bumbire	Ihangiro	The BCU (11 affiliated co-ops)

Source: Compiled from the BCNB 1948 to 1953 Annual Reports

---

[1] TNA 41011, Extracts from BNCB Minutes no. 394, for a meeting held on 26 July 1951
[2] TNA 41011, BNCB to Chairman of Licensing Board, Confidential C.1/64 2 August 1951
[3] TNA 41011, Extracts from BNCB Minutes no. 394, for a meeting held on 26 July 1951; TNA 41011, BNCB to Chairman of Licensing Board, Confidential C.1/64 2 August 1951
[4] TNA 41011, BNCB to Members of Agricultural and Natural Resources, Ref. no. C.1/92, 26 November 1951
[5] TNA 41011, Commissioner for Co-operative Development to PC, Lake Province, 2 September 1953

On 17 September 1948 it was outlined in the British Parliament by the Chancellor of Exchequer that Britain would enter into a long term contract of ten years for many colonial products to encourage the economic and political advancement of the colonies. A long term contract to continue purchasing Bukoba coffee was viable given that coffee takes over three years from planting to bearing age. It was envisaged that such contracts would be negotiated between the producers and purchasing department of the United Kingdom government.[1]

The direct negotiations were meant to be encouraged and statutory marketing negotiations were expected to be given priority based on British requirements. However, the British government dominated and controlled the terms of the agreements. This reflected in quantities or volumes that were ordered. In many instances, production surpassed the order, thus what was produced remained unsold. The British government fixed prices for commodities; the statutory marketing boards did the same when purchasing in local markets. Despite control and domination of terms for coffee trade, the agreements had some positive aspects as they encouraged production to meet the targeted volume.

During implementation of the contract with the Ministry of Food, new legislation, The African Agriculture Products (Control & Marketing) Ordinance, 1949 (57) was passed, followed by the Order passed by the governor under Sections 3 and 17 of the African Agricultural Products (Control And Marketing) Ordinance, 1947 for coffee produced in Bukoba district. The Order established that the Bukoba District Native Coffee Board be given powers to control and regulate the production, cultivation and marketing of coffee grown and produced by Africans. The Ordinance clearly recognised and emphasised the existence of the co-operatives which had to be accommodated in crop marketing.

In Kilimanjaro, the Ordinance reinforced and justified the existence of the KNCU. It was envisaged that the co-operatives would take over as the board's sole agent,[2] that it paved the way for the formation and setting up of the co-operatives as from 1950 in Bukoba. Unlike in Kilimanjaro, private traders were accommodated in Bukoba to operate in specified zones alongside the co-operative which was given one zone. This is evidence that it was not necessary to provide the co-operatives with a monopoly in coffee marketing.

The establishment of a co-operative in Bukoba was facilitated by the 1949 African Agricultural Products (Control & Marketing) Ordinance which the Registrar of Co-operative Societies drafted[3] and which was

---

[1] TNA 25147, Marketing of Colonial Produce in the UK and Overseas,

[2] BNCB Annual Report 1953, p. 13

[3] Tanganyika Government, Annual Report on Co-operative Development (Dar es Salaam: Government Printer, 1947) p. 6

passed into law by the LEGCO in 1949. The legislation was designed to foster and promote co-operatives with assistance from the boards. It was stressed that existing agricultural marketing societies should be the agents of the boards. This legislation took into consideration that co-operatives were unable to raise funds for the purchase of crops and erection of storage facilities, thus it made clear that short- and long-term loans would be available to societies with approval from co-operative officers.

Additionally, the impact of this Ordinance was proved by the formation of the co-operatives in Bukoba. This was to a limited degree in the WCGA, given that the Lint and Seed Marketing Board (LSMB) was not in existence but cotton produced in this area was handled by the Uganda LSMB which complicated the matter even further. However, the 1949 African Agricultural Products (Control & Marketing) Ordinance did not only control the industry, but also the surplus generated was transferred to collective co-operative funds and union reserves for further promotion and development of co-operatives under Section 46 of the Ordinance Cap.211.

Price control was relaxed under a 1951 Order so that by 1952 coffee trade was less controlled. Thus there was no longer any reason for the control of Tanganyika coffee under long term contracts. However, the Bukoba coffee purchase contract was extended in which 2,000 tons had to be supplied in 1952/53 and the same in 1953/54.[1] However, such negotiation was declined by the KNCU[2] which was approached by the Ministry of Food to supply coffee at reasonable prices to enable it to be available to customers in England. The request was declined given that:

> our growers have made a considerable contribution to alleviate the difficulties but time has arrived when we must concentrate on their (growers) needs. A reasonable price inflicted a loss to growers who were paid 80% of the f.o.b. value of their coffee after deduction expenses, taxes, levies under which they ended up earning only £30 annually.[3]

It was pointed out that for five seasons KNCU coffee had been sold to the Ministry of Food, and that the coffee growers in Kilimanjaro intended to gain some profits from the crop. They were well aware that the depreciation of the Pound sterling meant the determined price was only two-thirds of the free market price during 1951/52, which was too low to be paid to growers. Some growers also complained, one being Charles Ndetanyo, then a member of Kirua Vunjo Co-operative Society, that for 20 years the Chagga growers had been paid below costs they incurred in production.[4]

---

[1] TNA 37200, Ministry of Food to DA, Ref. CS/CP 30G, 23 April 1952

[2] TNA 37200, KNCU to Ministry of Food

[3] Ibid.

[4] TNA 37200, Purchase of Coffee Crop by Ministry of Food, Charles Ndetanyo, 15 May 1950

The contract according to him was unfair and inconsiderate of growers' fate; consequently, their livelihoods had been affected. Thus, he recommended the board consider a more profitable market such as auction, which was adopted by the KNCU with effect from 1952 in its own building in Moshi town.

6.4: Cotton marketing in the WCGA

The marketing of cotton can be traced from when the ECGC began its cotton promotion in the WCGA. The colonial authority in Uganda and Tanzania as well as the ECGC encouraged cotton buyers in the WCGA not only to purchase cotton but also undertake ginning. The policy issued by the Empire Cotton Board in 1920 stressed that 'it is necessary that there should be available an agency independent of government, whether local or imperial to conduct business and able to do so efficiently', and a fixed or minimum price.[1] From the 1920s, Indian cotton merchants flocked to the WCGA where some erected ginneries and engaged in buying cotton following an invitation from the Tanganyika colonial government.[2] Those allowed to erect a ginnery were required to have capital of about £10,000 to £20,000.[3]

In an attempt to improve the quality and price of native cotton, the department, in 1922, established an auction system in WCGA districts where cotton production had just started.[4] The growers had their cotton produce sorted into three different grades categorised by quality then delivered to markets where it was sold under auction. On certain days, cotton buyers would bid for the right to purchase the whole crop of the district. By this means, it was believed that growers secured protection against unfair weighing, and that they could ensure being paid in cash. In some cases, because of competition among bidders, growers also received higher prices than in districts where the open market prevailed. On one hand, some growers believed that the winner of the bid profited at the expense of the producer when market prices increased. On the other hand, traders opposed the auction scheme because it limited competition. With the growth of cotton cultivation, it became impossible for agricultural officers adequately to supervise the auction system. Thus, it was abandoned.

During the second half of the 1920s, NAs were given responsibility for overseeing cotton marketing. The NAs were responsible for the quality of the cotton delivered by growers for marketing. The NAs were brought in

---

[1] TNA 23218, *Report to the Board of Trade, the Empire Cotton Growing Committee, CMD 523* (London: HMSO, 1920) p. 9; Charlotte Leubuscher, *Tanganyika Territory: A Study of Economic Policy under Mandate* (Oxford: University Press, 1944) pp. 51-52

[2] TNA 21238, DA to CS, Ref. 6/5389, 24 July 1935

[3] TNA 22813, Extracts from Tanganyika Memorandum on Cotton Marketing presented by Chief Secretary to the Legislative Council, 1934

[4] Raymond Leslie Buell, *The Native Problem in Africa* (New York: Macmillan, 1928) p. 475

because the BCGA struggled and proved a failure as it could not provide supervision across the WCGA owing to staff shortages, and instead had to rely upon local leaders who lacked experience and knowledge of quality control.[1]

In this regard, there were widespread incidences whereby cotton growers compromised cotton quality. In several instances, traders pushed prices down and cheating of growers was widespread. Cotton buyers were also competing against each other for bigger volumes. The situation prompted intervention by the colonial government which conducted an investigation in 1923.[2] This investigation established widespread cheating of growers that partly demoralised their participation in cotton production. Cotton merchants were also dishonest and unscrupulous. They cheated growers by under weighing, under grading and under paying their delivery.[3] Consequently, the government was prompted to form the Cotton Advisory Board in 1927 charged with responsibility to curb cheating, approving and issuing cotton marketing licenses.[4]

As far as cotton ginning was concerned, throughout the 1920s there was only one ginnery in the entire WCGA, located in Ukerewe.[5] More ginneries were erected in the 1930s, each separated by a radius of 10 miles to reduce competition, by having each supplied with sufficient cotton. The promulgation of the Cotton Ordinance was followed by a number of applications presented by ginners to the government which granted permission for erecting ginneries. For example, Ladha Meghji erected ginneries in Luguru;[6] also in Uzinza and Mugango.[7] The Mugango ginnery was meant to serve cotton produced in Busegwe, Ikizu, Ushahi and Bukwaya. The British East Africa Corporation erected a ginnery at Usogore in Shinyanga district but in 1933, it transferred ownership to Ladha Meghji.[8] Baghwaji Sundweji & Company, the biggest ginner in the WCGA with five ginneries, also erected a ginnery in Uzinza.[9]

A controlled marketing system was not in place and competition between cotton traders as well as ginners resulted in increased speculation.[10]

---

[1] TNA 23218, DA to CS, Ref. 6/5389, 24 July 1935; TNA 23218, DC Shinyanga to PC Lake Province, Ref. 62/38, February 1936
[2] TNA 23218, PC Lake Province to DA (copy to CS), Ref. 1302/150, 24 August 1935
[3] TNA 215/1423/A, Popat Ranji to Lake Province PC 20 June 1947 & 19 August 1947, 22 December 1947 to Bishop of Mwanza; TNA 215/1423/A, Uzinza Farmers Association to Ibanza (Council of Chiefs), 2 October 1950
[4] TNA 34953, DA to CS, Ref. no. 473/3878, 23 July 1927
[5] The Empire Cotton Growing Review, *Journal of The Empire Cotton Growing Corporation*, vol. XVI, 1939; Horne, *The Extension of Cotton Cultivation in Tanganyika Territory*
[6] TNA 215/772, Ladha Meghji to DA, 15 March 1935, Cotton Ginneries
[7] TNA 215/772 A, Willis on behalf of Ladha Meghji to DA, 9 January 1935
[8] Chairman (E.H.M. Leggett) British East Africa Corporation to DA, 14 November 1933
[9] TNA 215/772, Baghwaji Sundweji & Company to DO Mwanza district, 13 March 1935

The critical problem was that the ginning of cotton was marred by defects that led to deterioration of its quality. The concern was also the spread of diseases and pests that could curtail production. Under these circumstances, the colonial authortiy intervened as it was increasingly evident that the producer could no longer be left to sow, cultivate and harvest his crop without government playing a bigger role, while the control of marketing would be the business of ginners.[1]

Furthermore, the legislation and regulations were put in place in an attempt to curb indiscriminate buying and to control uneconomic competition that attracted investors who applied for a license. Cotton marketing and ginneries/ginning were confined to a single buyer, licenced to operate in a specific production zone.[2] It was therefore recommended that a centralised marketing system be established to control both the cotton producers and buyers. Subsequently, in 1926, a Cotton Ordinance was passed and in 1931 cotton rules were in operation designed to control the industry. Amendments made in 1933 and 1934 were meant to increase production and provided for the control of cultivation, marketing, and ginning. The rules required a ginner to develop the area where it operated, and deliver cotton seed to natives for planting.

Legislation and regulations were followed by the creation of cotton buying posts in the early 1930s.[3] The Ordinance reorganised cotton growing areas into zones to curb the spread of diseases, and licensing purchase was introduced that confined buyers to operate in a specific zone. The cotton rules aimed to curb indiscriminate buying and to control uneconomic competition which could adversely affect cotton quality.

Cotton production and harvesting was meaningless without access to markets. The cotton rules of 1931 stipulated a system for cotton purchase from farmers. It categorised purchase as follows:

a. ginneries under Rule 15;
b. ginnery buying posts; here cotton was exclusively bought by a specific ginnery as per Rule 2 of the cotton rules.
c. cotton markets with special arrangements provided under Rule 15.

The cotton buying centres were further categorised under Cotton Ordinance 12 of 1937. The centres were in four categories. The first three were allocated to specific buyers: the pioneer buying posts allocated to the nearest ginnery; second, ginnery buying posts where a storage facility was obligatory and comprised all centres within proximity to the ginnery; third, ginner cotton markets where production volumes ranged from 100–400

---

[10] TNA 23218, PC Lake Province to DA (copy to CS), Ref. 1302/150, 24 August 1935
[1] TNA 23218, DA to CS, Ref. 6/5389, 24 July 1935 in response to CS to DA, Ref. 10844/533
[2] Government Notice 84 of 1931 amended in 1933 under Government Notice 78
[3] TNA 23218, PC Lake Province to DA (copy to CS), Ref. 1302/150, 24 August 1935

tons; and fourth, the public ginnery or free zone centres which were not allocated to a specific buyer but where only one buying centre was allocated to whoever was interested.

The creation of cotton buying zones and ginning within the allocated zone was meant to avoid mixing varieties, maintain quality and control the spread of diseases in compliance with Cotton Rule 12 that forbade the removal of seed cotton from one district to another unless authorised by the Director of Agriculture. Importantly, the Cotton Rule was to encourage ginners, middlemen and merchants to take an active interest in marketing and processing cotton in the allocated zone; also it led to monopolisation of marketing and ginning by a few Asian traders.

Despite a series of measures, irregularities remained common in cotton marketing, for example itinerant or unlicensed traders operated cotton purchase in various locations in the WCGA.[1] As a result, further improvements of marketing systems were made under Cotton Ordinance 12 of 1937 which was passed alongside the native coffee control and marketing legislation. The Ordinance marked a shift from depending on, and employing, local chiefs and Native Authorities in encouraging and enforcing cash crop production and supervision to direct colonial authority intervention.

6.4.1: Cotton transportation in the WCGA

Transport was a serious challenge in the WCGA when the British took over Tanganyika. During Hasting Horne's visit in the early 1920s to investigate the potential to develop the crop, the WCGA lacked reliable transport connectivity within and outside the region.[2] This jeopardised cotton industry development as it was difficult to transport bulk products over its vast area.[3] Yet, shipment could be across Lake Victoria then by railway from Kisumu to Mombasa. This was the most serious obstacle for Tanganyika not having direct transportation to Dar es Salaam harbour. It was considered important by Horne to extend the central railway line from Tabora to Mwanza that would directly link the region with Dar es Salaam. The corporation lobbied for the line's construction to Mwanza and finance was sanctioned in 1924 by the British government.[4]

Nevertheless, links within the WCGA, allowing growers to transport their produce to marketing centres as well as to ginneries then to a ship, mainly from Mwanza town remained a critical challenge. Improvement of roads was carried out by the Native Authorities; and in many instances ginners funded roads to their ginneries and shipment points. Generally,

---

[1] TNA 22813, DA to CS, Ref. 58/1310, 22 February 1935, Tanganyika Police, Lake Province to DA, 30 January 1935
[2] Horne, *The Extension of Cotton Cultivation in Tanganyika Territory*
[3] Iliffe, *A Modern History of Tanganyika*
[4] The Empire Cotton Growing Review

throughout the 1920s to 1940s, road improvement lacked a coordinating institution and reliable funding. The challenge took a new direction in the 1950s. At the time, these networks were named cotton roads. The LSMB funded a road survey, improvement, and construction not only of roads, but also of bridges across the WCGA.

These developments had an economic impact in facilitating cotton output and the supply of seeds. A significant amount was allocated by LSMB for road works. For example, Geita district received £45,000.00 in 1955 and a lorry was procured to facilitate the ferrying of road construction materials.[1] Kwimba received £175 for construction of twenty bridges.[2] Other districts had funds allocated to them too for the purpose as shown in Table 23.

Table 23: Road funding in some Districts in the WCGA

District	Amount in £
Ukerewe	150.00
Kwimba	1,200.00
Mwanza	700.00
Musoma	600.00

Source: TNA 2283/Volume II, Provincial Commissioner of Members of Communication Committee, 28 December 1955

In the 1950s, the LSMB embarked upon the construction of cotton storage facilities for bales awaiting transportation. Such facilities were erected at various railway stations such as Fela Malampaka and Shinyanga, and locations further away from rail lines such as Buchosa and Nansio.[3]

6.5: Tobacco marketing in Western Province

Formation of co-operatives during the post-war era was not successful everywhere. The evidence shows that in 1947 native tobacco growers in Biharamulo, in the Lake Province and Kibondo Division in Western Province (today Kigoma Region), had shown a desire to form a co-operative society. But while the wish was present, the capacity to operate a society was lacking because the standard of literacy was so low that clerical staff could not be recruited from within the district.[4] Therefore, the option available was to have the board undertake the marketing functions. Such functions were provided under Section 6 of the Native Tobacco (Control & Marketing) Ordinance.[5] However, this was translated by the Commis-

---

[1] TNA 2283/Volume II, Geita to Provincial Commissioner, Lake Province, Ref. R/4/1/120, in Improvement of Cotton Roads

[2] TNA 2283/Volume II, Kwimba district Commissioner to Provincial Commissioner, Lake Province, Ref. R.4/1/131 in Improvement of cotton roads

[3] Lint and Seed Marketing Board, 1953 Report by the Executive Committee

[4] TNA 36883, PC, Lake Province to CS, Ref. 1154/1265, 20 November 1947

sioner of Co-operative Development, Robin Sydney Wyld Malcolm, as an obstacle towards promoting co-operative societies.[1] Understandably, such a view was reflected on the role of Registrar of Co-operative Societies which included not only registering but also establishing, promoting and strengthening co-operative societies.

In a move envisaged to facilitate tobacco marketing in Biharamulo the Native Tobacco Board was formed. This was provided under Subsection 1 of Section 6 which led to the Native Tobacco Board of Biharamulo and Ngara districts in Lake Province and Kibondo Division in Western Province being formed in 1948. On 2 March 1948, the board was reconstituted under Government Notice 44, only to be renamed the Nyamirembe Native Tobacco Board. The board was charged with control, preparation, and marketing, of native produced tobacco and MacGregor[2] was appointed its first manager.[3] Under the legislation all native tobacco growers were compelled to sell their produce to the board which had a monopoly over handling the produce.

---

[5] TNA 36883, DA to PC, Lake Province, Ref. 804/9484, 16 October 1947
[1] TNA 36883, Commissioner of Co-operative Development to Members of Agricultural and Natural Resources, Ref. Co-op. 1183/30, 11 April 1950
[2] TNA 26563, C.J. MacGregor was Senior Agricultural Officer in the South West Circle throughout 1940s, before this, the Songea district Native Tobacco Board
[3] Extracts from His Excellency's Visit to Biharamulo district, 15-7 February 1950

7. Emergence of Co-operatives

The epicentre for the co-operative movement in Tanzania is Kilimanjaro which dates from 1925 when the WaChagga coffee growers formed KNPA which was registered under the Indian Act, 1913 Section 26, because there was no legislation on co-operatives. The Association was formed in response to the need to combat the strong settler opposition to coffee growing by natives.[1] By the end of the 1920s and early 1930s much of the settler opposition to natives growing coffee by settlers had died down but had been replaced by the allegation that the association was a political menace and as such should be supressed. This view was widespread among colonial officials at district and provincial levels.[2]

The KNPA was distrusted by the colonial authority due to its involvement in politics, contrary to its vested objectives. This prompted the colonial government to consider restructuring it into a co-operative society and to set up a new co-operative system. The idea was given impetus by a number of related developments within the country and in Britain. First, the idea was affirmed by the Permanent Mandate Commission in July 1929.[3]

Second, the earliest official development emerged in October 1929 when the governor called a conference in Dar es Salaam on agricultural co-operatives to be attended by Senior Administration Officers. In his presentation the Secretary for Native Affairs (SNA) stressed a need for promoting co-operatives in the territory by citing cases of the KNPA and similar arrangements as for the rice crop in Mahenge district.[4] He pointed out that such organisations could only be successful by prioritising training of civil servants in Sri Lanka, particularly District Officers (DOs), on co-operative methods and management to provide proper guidance to members in managing their societies. The SNA reiterated that trained officers should work with little interference or restriction.

The conference unanimously affirmed a resolution that 'in any district or Province where interest to form co-operatives has been shown should be encouraged and officers be assigned to facilitate formation of societies to facilitate agriculture development'.[5] Consequently, considerable co-ordinat-

---
[1] Swynnerton, Bennett & Stent, *All About KNCU Coffee*, pp. 12-13; P.W. Westergaard, Co-operatives in Tanzania as Economic and Democratic Institutions, in Widstrand (ed), *Co-operatives and Rural Development in East Africa* p. 124

[2] TNA 13060, PC North Province to CS, Confidential, Ref. 80/iii/248, 24 February 1931

[3] TNA 13698, Extracts from Minutes of Permanent Mandate Commission 15th Session on 1 July 1929

[4] TNA 13698, Memorandum of SNA on the Agricultural and Credit Co-operative Societies

ed initiatives were launched. Thus the colonial government had to seek assistance from the CO and direct communication with various countries for assistance to develop the co-operative movement in the country.

After the conference, the government dispatched a memorandum to PCs in the territory regarding promotion of co-operatives, either agricultural or credit, or both, in their respective administrative areas. The decision taken in Tanganyika at the October 1929 conference was backed by the Colonial Office in its memorandum to all British colonies in which it was pointed out that the 'time was thought to be ripe for development of co-operative methods for agriculture'. It emphasised that it was important for each colony to consider providing staff qualified for the purpose: 'staff should be of first class to provide supervisory function and must have specialised training in co-operation and inspection as has been the case in Ceylon (Sri Lanka), Malaya (Malaysia), and Gold Coast (Ghana)'.[1]

The CO's memorandum challenged the colonies that lacked sufficient provision for adequately trained staff and placed emphasis on the education of co-operators in their responsibilities and duties towards their societies. It was further stressed that the Horace Plunkett Foundation should open its doors to train colonial staff on co-operation as well as to research in the field.

All mentioned developments took place between 1929 and 1930 at a time when the Labour Party was in power in Britain. This had an impact on the emergence, growth and development of co-operatives in Tanganyika, demonstrated by the personal commitment of encouraging the movement by Colonial Secretary Sidney Webb (Lord Passfield). For example, Webb chaired the 1930 Governors' Conference where he emphasied the importance of having co-operatives, affirming that 'development of co-operation within the colonial empire is a subject to which the Secretary of State wishes to direct the special attention of colonial government.' It was emphasised that 'co-operation relieves [the] indebtedness burden on small producers and provides for training on the responsibilities of a simple form of self-government'.[2] It was also argued that since small producers could not compete against large units, co-operatives would have to facilitate such capabilities. In order to develop co-operation in the colonies it was urged that local customs and conditions be taken on board, to assign duties and responsibility and that staff be trained for proper execution of their functions.[3]

[5] TNA 13698, Extracts from Minutes of Conference of Senior Administration Officers, 21–24 October 1929
[1] TNA 13698, Colonial Office Memorandum: Co-operation in the Colonies, Protectorates and Mandated Territories (HMSO, 21 May 1930)
[2] Ibid.
[3] Ibid.

The 1930 Governors' Conference had provided an important impetus for policy implementation in regard to co-operative development in Tanzania.[1] The colonial authority acted in accordance with the conference resolution on two major aspects.[2] First, it appointed a committee charged to consider the marketing organisation of native and non-native produce.

Significantly, a focus of the committee[3] was on Africans. This is evident in its report which indicated: 'we consider that the actual line of advance for Africans is through the channel of co-operative societies but they will need the continual guidance and supervision of a trained officer'. It also recommended that a Registrar or Director of Co-operative Societies be appointed to organise and control such societies wherever he found groups of Africans capable of understanding the simple principles of such bodies. It further recommended that the co-operative ordinance should confer the same powers to the Registrar as those granted in various European and Asiatic countries, and emphasised that, 'the Ordinance will no doubt make these powers applicable to European as well as African societies'. Finally, the committee recommended that an experienced man would know how to 'adjust the use of his powers to the capacity and understanding of groups with which he is dealing'.[4]

The implementation of the resolution in Tanganyika began in August 1930, partly in response to the Governors' Conference and a dispatch memorandum from the Colonial Office (CO) regarding co-operation in the colonies, protectorates, and mandated territories. In order for co-operative societies to be introduced in the country a decision was made to send an officer to study the working of co-operative societies.[5] Sri Lanka and the Federated Malay States (Malaysia) were considered by the CO as suitable for training because they had many years of experience of co-operative movement practices.

The CS expressed an intention to establish co-operatives in primitive and ignorant societies.[6] This indicated that the colonial authority was committed to address backwardness and ignorance among the colonised of which the co-operative movement was considered a suitable solution. The aim of

---

[1] TNA 13698, Conversation between Secretary for Native Affairs with C.F. Strickland on the organisation of co-operative societies in Tanganyika between 21 & 23 March 1931
[2] TNA 19595, CS to PCs of Tanga, Northern and Lake Provinces, Ref. 13698/97, 10 December 1930, Co-operative Societies Ordinance
[3] TNA 19595, CS to PCs of Tanga, Northern and Lake Provinces informing them on appointed committee members who were P. Wyndham, A.J. Wakefield, F.J. Anderson, RR. Staples (Secretary) and A.B. Dumas
[4] TNA 19005, Extract from a report of a committee appointed to consider the marketing organisation of native and non-native produce
[5] TNA 13698, CS to Director of Agriculture, Ref. 19005/15, 8 May 1930; CO Memorandum
[6] TNA 13698 CS to Plunket Foundation, 21 November 1930

intervention suggests an intention to promote the movement through a top-down approach by borrowing ideas from other countries and experienced individuals. In a letter to Sri Lanka, the CS pointed out that 'our problem is rather to harness co-operation as to influence an experience that proved successful in South America among the Negro'.[1]

In further developments the governor asked the Secretary of State for Colonies for C.F. Strickland to advise on reconstruction of the KNPA and overhaul coffee marketing in Kilimanjaro.[2] In response, the Colonial Office facilitated the availability of Strickland who was commissioned on a similar task in Zanzibar to provide advice on the formation of co-operatives.[3] When Strickland met the CS they discussed several issues and policy aspects such as types of co-operatives, appointment and training of the Registrar, the Co-operative Ordinance and Rules, formation of a co-operative department and location of the Registrar's office.[4]

The meeting to discuss the Co-operative Societies Ordinance in Dar es Salaam, attended by Strickland, colonial officials, Phillip E. Mitchell the CS and Secretary of Native Affairs Charles Dundas. The Attorney General, Joseph Alfred Sheridan was also consulted on the matter.[5] Owing to the vast experience and success of Asian countries, the Co-operative Societies Ordinance borrowed heavily from Indian Co-operative Act 2 of 1912 and the 1927 Act of Myanmar (Burma).[6] Some clauses with modifications were borrowed from British Columbia, Malaysia (Malaya's 1922 Co-operative Societies Ordinance), Sri Lanka's Co-operative Societies Ordinance 34 of 1921 while other elements were drawn from Jamaica, and Queensland Australia;[7] as well as South Africa's 1922 co-operative legislation.

From this meeting it was agreed that Strickland would prepare a draft co-operative legislation. The matter was presented to the Chief Secretary and the Council who approved funds for the 1932/33 financial year. The matter was also presented to the Attorney General who approved Strickland's drafting of the Co-operative Societies Ordinance.

In the discussion it was emphasised that the legislation should bring the KNPA onto a legal footing. When the Bill was presented to LEGCO it was made clear by colonial officials that 'the immediate necessity is to save the KNPA (so as) to organise itself in a manner known to the law and under certain amount of control'.[8]

---

[1] TNA 13698, SNA to Sir Charles Campbell Woolley (Sri Lanka), 6 December 1929
[2] TNA 13698, Telegram 252 Governor to Secretary of State for Colonies, December 1930
[3] TNA 19595, Secretary of State (Passfield) for Colonies to Governor, Dispatch 867 (Confidential), 8 November 1930 & further confirmation provided on 29 January 1931
[4] TNA 19005, Extract from Conversation between the SNA and C.F. Strickland
[5] Ibid.
[6] TNA 19595, vol I Co-operative Societies Ordinance, Note on the Draft Ordinance
[7] TNA 19005, Extract from Conversation between the SNA and C.F. Strickland

Unlike credit societies in India and Burma, the agriculture marketing co-operative appeared most relevant in a Tanganyikan context. It was agreed that the legislation had to be comprehensive with emphasis on agricultural marketing co-operatives. The colonial authority had two major reasons: to provide for the restructuring of the KNPA which was then becoming subversive; and to compel growers to sell their produce through co-operatives.

A completed draft Co-operative Societies Ordinance was made available to the Colonial Office for approval. In his dispatches G. Stewart Symes, the governor, appealed to the CO to support the Tanganyika colonial authority to accomplish the mentioned objectives. The governor further proposed that the Ordinance be enacted in the January 1932 LEGCO session with a determination to restructure the KNPA.[1] The same message was conveyed in Chief Secretary Douglas James Jardine's dispatch arguing that 'to enable this to be done I seek your approval to the early enactment of a Co-operative Ordinance on the lines of the draft Ordinance'.[2]

Sidney Webb was impressed with the draft Ordinance, but proposed postponement suggesting 'it is desirable and commended for a fully informed Registrar to be available to guide the progress of the movement in its early stages'.[3] The correspondence shows the extent of consultations with the CO by the Tanganyika colonial authority. This was not the case with India, indicating that Tanganyika did not have the same autonomy. It could also be viewed as a cautionary measure given that Tanganyika was under Mandatory agreement, where restructuring of the KNPA was done with great care to avoid breaching British commitments in administering the country.

A dramatic development took place just after the departure of Webb from the Colonial Office in August 1931 following the Labour Party defeat in the general election. This coincided with a change of governorship in Tanganyika where George Stewart Symes took over from Donald Cameron, and Sir Douglas James Jardine became CS. In the first place, the governor pressed ahead with the appointment of A.B. Bennett as Association Manager. Second, he advised the Colonial Office to discontinue incorporation of the KNPA as a company in accordance with the amended provisions of the Companies Ordinance (46 of 1931) because it did not appear to be practical, and it was quite clear to him that the correct course

---

[8] TNA 13060, LEGCO Proceedings February 1932

[1] TNA 13060, Governor to Secretary of State for Colonies (confidential) 23 April 1931 & 20 November 1931

[2] TNA 13060, Governor to Secretary of State for Colonies (confidential) 20 November 1931; Douglas James Jardine was Deputy Chief Secretary 1927-29, CS from 1928-1934 & acting governor in 1929, 1931, 1933, 1934

[3] TNA 13060, Passfield to Governor Dispatch 507, 22 July 1931

was formally to constitute the enterprise as a co-operative society.[1]

The departure of Webb created an opportunity for the colonial authority in Tanganyika to pursue and implement what they viewed as proper for developing the co-operative movement. Although the governor in his dispatch to the Secretary of State for Colonies[2] seemed to concur with Webb's recommendation, maintaining that any attempt to develop the co-operative elsewhere in the territory must wait until it became possible to provide a fully informed Registrar. The governor pursued the matter with the Secretary of State, Sir Phillip Cunliffe-Lister (later Lord Swinton), who approved the application of the Ordinance with effect from 23 May 1932.[3]

Approval of the Ordinance by Cunliffe-Lister demonstrated policy inconsistency on the part of the CO which ignored Webb's view that better preparation and planning was required before embarking upon developing co-operatives. There were two main requirements: staff to deal with co-operative society matters and members' education, and a co-operative department to administer co-operatives. It also illustrated approval was a matter of urgency for both the CO and the colonial authority with no regard to availability of qualified staff. In an attempt to fill the gap, on 4 March 1932, CS Jardine on behalf of the governor appointed Acting Registrars of Co-operative Societies and then Acting Land Officers.

The urgency was also evident in Moshi district where registration of societies was about to start which led to the appointment of A.O. Flynn as provided for under Government Notice 61 of 1932 issued on 4 March under Section 3 of the Co-operative Societies Ordinance, 7 of 1932. Flynn was appointed the Assistant Registrar of Co-operative Societies, based in Moshi, to provide services to facilitate the formation and registration of the KNCU affiliated primary co-operative societies in Kilimanjaro.[4] The appointment of Flynn was recognition of his role to counteract the KNPA which the colonial authority labelled as subversive. A similar approach was adopted in other districts when there were no trained officials.

By then, lack of trained staff in other parts of the country was no longer an excuse for failure to promote co-operative societies among some colonial staff at provincial and district level. Colonial officials were enthusiastic when the governor visited Lake Province in October 1933.[5] However, the governor insisted that promoting co-operatives should be considered when staff were available for the purpose and showed no interest in either

---

[1] TNA 13060, Governor to Secretary of State for Colonies (confidential) 20 November 1931

[2] Ibid.

[3] TNA 19595, Approval of the Co-operative Societies Ordinance 7, 1932

[4] TNA 19005, Memorandum on the Working of the Co-operative Societies Ordinance, November 1934

[5] TNA 19005, Extracts of notes taken on HE's safari in October 1933 in Lake Province

appointing or assigning civil servants on a short-term basis at district level, as happened in Kilimanjaro. Some district officers had their own plans to promote co-operative societies in their respective district, for example in Biharamulo district where initiatives were in place by the end of December 1933.[1] Overall, the governor maintained a biased position in his presentation at the East Africa Governors' conference. For him, promotion was to be restricted and confined within Kilimanjaro. He further insisted that where necessary it had to wait until a trained registrar was available for the purpose.[2]

Given that the position of Registrar of Co-operative Societies was managed by an Acting Officer, the colonial authority was tirelessly occupied with a vetting exercise to have an official appointed on a permanent basis. The attributes that were strongly recommended by the CS in his letter to Central,[3] Lake[4] and Tabora[5] Province PCs included eight years of service in the country with good knowledge of the territory. In addition, the candidate needed to have an appreciation of the natives particularly, their modes of life, prejudices, agriculture, etc. Academically, it was considered desirable that he should have political science and economics in his university studies.[6]

Both the Central[7] and Lake PCs[8] replied with regret that they had no suitable candidate available in their respective provinces. The Western (Tabora) PC proposed R.C. Northcote as suitable for the post;[9] a proposal that was accepted by P.E. Mitchell, then the CS,[10] who subsequently appointed him, while Governor Symes, informed the Colonial Office of the appointment.[11]

Since Northcote had no background of co-operatives for executing his duties, the colonial government considered his training a priority. It was decided that the United Kingdom, Sri Lanka, and Malaysia were the most suitable countries for him to study due to their experiences in promoting co-operative societies.[12] Northcote accepted the offer and confirmed his

---

[1] TNA 19005 DO, Biharamulo district to CS and SNA, 22 December 1933
[2] Extracts from a paper by the Governor of Tanganyika presented at the East Africa Territories Governors' conference, April 1932
[3] TNA 19005, CS to Central, PC Ref. 19005/20, 9 September 1930
[4] TNA 19005, CS to Lake PC, Ref. 19005/18, 9 September 1930
[5] TNA 19005, CS to Tabora (West Province) PC, Ref 19005/22
[6] TNA 19005, CS to Tabora, Central & Lake Province PCs, Ref. 190005/33, 30 September 1930
[7] TNA 19005, Central PC to CS, Ref. 1/1/26, 6 October 1930
[8] TNA 19005, PC, Lake Province to CS, Ref. P./18/37/4, 9 October 1930
[9] TNA 19005, Tabora PC to CS, Ref. P./18/37/2, 9 October 1930
[10] TNA 19005, CS (P.E. Mitchell) to R.C. Northcote, Ref 19005/27, 18 November 1930
[11] TNA 19005, Governor to Secretary of State for Colonies, Ref. 372, 23 April 1931, telegram 205, 3 July 1931
[12] Ibid.; Governor to Secretary of State for Colonies, telegram 205, 3 July 1931

availability to visit.[1]

By then Tanganyika had no funds to send Northcote on the study tour. The funds were supposed to be made available by the CO but none were available, due to the economic depression.[2] It is obvious that under such circumstances funding for training was not a priority. The governor was advised by the CO to postpone the activity whilst efforts to establish funding were underway.[3] Further soliciting for funds was made by the colonial authority, for example the CS contacted Dr J.H. Oldham, Director of the International Institute of African Languages and Culture, who was asked to forward the Tanganyika colonial interest to the Carnegie Foundation for its consideration to fund training of the designate Registrar of Co-operative Societies.[4] Oldham convinced Carnegie to consider both West and East African countries, with Tanganyika given special treatment,[5] hence the Carnegie Corporation Scheme released funds.[6] The fund was sufficient to cover a six-month study tour to several countries from August 1934 to April 1935.[7] Countries visited included India, Burma, Zanzibar and Sri Lanka.[8]

On his return in May 1935, the Registrar designate published a report[9] that recommended a road map for co-operative development in which he proposed types of co-operatives covering credit, dairy and livestock in the colony. He also emphasised co-operative education. Importantly, setting up the Co-operative Department and tertiary (apex body) society were recommended.

In his report,[10] Northcote criticised Sub-Section 36 of the co-operative legislation that provided for the compulsion of membership of a co-operative society. This was because the compulsion provision was contrary to the co-operative principle of voluntary association. Similarly, the sub-section provided for compulsory marketing of the produce by growers to a co-operative society. This provision, criticised by Northcote, was taken from

---

[1] TNA 19005, Northcote to CS, Ref. 22/28, 6 December 1930
[2] TNA 19005, CS to PCs & copy to Northcote with Ref 19005/27, 18 November 1930
[3] TNA 19005, Colonial Office (signed by Passfield) to CS Dispatch 507, 22 July 1931
[4] TNA 21103, CS to Dr Oldham, 12 September 1932
[5] TNA 21103, Dr Oldham to CS, 20 October 1932
[6] TNA 19005, Governor of Tanganyika to Secretary of State for Colonies, Dispatch 1235, & 23 December 1932, Extract from Secretary of State for Colonies to Governor of Tanganyika, Confidential, 23 January 1933, Mitchell, CS & SNA to F.A. Stockdale of Trinidad, 30 November 1933
[7] TNA 22929, Phillip Cunliffe-Lister, Secretary of State for Colonies to CS Dispatch 695, 29 September 1934
[8] TNA 22919, Report on Co-operation by Northcote, letter from CS to all Provincial Commissioners, Ref. 22919, 28 October 1936, p. 19
[9] Ibid.
[10] TNA 22919, Report on Co-operation by Northcote, 21 May 1935

the South Africa 1925 compulsory principle, mainly for co-operative marketing.[1] However, its application in South Africa was to control adulteration by a minority of growers who ruined sale schemes. Additionally, under the South African legislation the Minister of Agriculture was empowered to compel products to be sold through co-operatives.[2]

Clearly, the timing of Northcote's submission of the report was wrong. It was at a time when government officials' mind and policy were not the same as the senior colonial officials. For example, P.E. Mitchell, who was Secretary for Native Affairs and CS, was appointed Governor of Uganda in 1935 and later to Kenya. New officers were Sir Harold MacMichael, the Governor, while acting CS was W.E. Scupham until Henry Charles Donald Cleveland Mackenzie-Kennedy[3] took office in 1935.

The new colonial authority officials were much irritated by such criticism that for example, in his comments on Northcote's report[4] the acting CS, Gerald Fleming Sayers, expressed scepticism about co-operative policy: 'it must be understood that the government has no doctrinaire (or other) predilection for co-operation and has no wish to urge it on anyone, nor on any group, European, Asiatic or African. And no Co-operative Department be set up, nothing of that kind (whatsoever) is needed, at any rate but, if there is a genuine local desire on the part of anybody'.[5]

A refusal to support development of co-operatives by senior colonial officials was a significant policy shift. The colonial authority had no interest in promoting co-operatives regardless of interest shown, and the provision of education to instil an understanding was ruled out. This decision ended the enthusiasm shown in the late 1920s and early 1930s. Furthermore, the CS opposed Northcote's recommendation to set up the Co-operative Department noting that 'to establish such a Department will only result in drowning a possibly useful development in ink'.[6] Clearly, the CS incarcerated the Registrar's ideas. Thus, the CS stalled the growth of co-operatives in Tanganyika throughout Northcote's tenure in office. He used his powerful political position to undermine the Registrar's responsibilities and abused his power to undermine Northcote's expertise and eventually suffocated

---

[1] TNA 24870, ILO, Union of South Africa: A Review of the Co-operative Movement, *Co-operative Information*, 1:12, 1936, p. 73, C.F. Strickland, *The co-operative movement in South Africa* (undated) http://afraf.oxfordjournals.org/content/XXXVI/CXLV/461.full.pdf, pp. 461-468, accessed 19 July 2013; R. Rhodes, *Empire and Co-operation: How the British Empire used Co-operatives in its Development Strategies 1900–1990* (Edinburgh: John Donald, 2012) p. 142; Hailey, *An African Survey*, p. 1471

[2] Ibid.

[3] Mackenzie-Kennedy was CS in Tanzania from 1935 to 1939

[4] TNA 25147, Extract from Minute C8, 23 May 1935, Marketing of Colonial Produce in the United Kingdom and Overseas

[5] TNA 22919, CS (C.F. Sayers) to all Provincial Commissioners, Ref. 22919, 28 October 1936; Extract Minute from CS to the Governor, 23 May 1935

[6] TNA 22919, Extract Minute from CS to the Governor, 23 May 1935

the Registrar's vision in promoting co-operatives in the country.

Against this backdrop, Northcote's proposals were rendered inoperative and it became difficult for the co-operative movement to be promoted. This ended Northcote's ambition to be a game changer as far as the development of the co-operative movement in Tanganyika was concerned. As a result, a lack of policy or policy consistency and non-existence of planning strategies had played their part.

The policy direction of Tanganyika's new officials, especially the CS, was significantly different from its predecessors. In the first place, the colonial authority and officials, particularly the CS, disassociated themselves from the Northcote report. Specifically, it was argued that 'the government would like to make (it) clear that the opinions formed and views expressed by the author (Northcote) do not necessarily indicate the policy which the government consider should be followed and sending him for study does not imply a desire on the part of government to impose co-operatives on anyone'.[1] It was also made clear by the CS that neither staff nor funds would be made available for the purpose.[2]

In one instance, Northcote was invited by the Central Provincial Commissioner to his province to initiate creamery co-operatives.[3] The CS authoritatively disclaimed any attempt for co-operation or any official wish to urge it on anyone and put Northcote's invitation on hold. It was alleged by the CS that this would remain the position pending approval from the Secretary of State. The alleged need for approval was just an excuse to stamp out any emerging interest from the provincial and district officials; it had to emerge spontaneously from the growers.[4] Ideally, a co-operative society should be a spontaneous growth, springing from the needs of the people/members with a determination to improve their economic conditions through the principle of mutuality. This demonstrated the single-minded character of the CS who put forward an excuse that had an unequivocal detrimental effect not only on the envisioned creamery co-operatives, but for the development of an entire movement in the country. The CS was determined to suppress any initiatives from the Provincial Commissioners, the latter being informed that 'Northcote was assigned other duties (not co-operation) to which more of his time has to be devoted'.[5] It was emphasised by the CS that Northcote would be available to help with advice and organisation, but that he was employed merely in a

---

[1] TNA 22919, Report on Co-operation by RC Northcote: Minute by the CS, folio 83
[2] TNA 33017, W.K.H. Campbell, Report on Development and Reconstruction Establishment of co-operative societies visit by 29 July 1944
[3] TNA 22919, Central Province, PC to CS, Ref. 20/32/4, 14 June 1935
[4] TNA 22919, CS to all Provincial Commissioners, Ref. 22919, 28 October 1936
[5] TNA 22919, CS to PCs, Ref. 22919/84, 29 June 1935

consultative capacity.¹ With such a limited role assigned to the Registrar, the movement could hardly take off.

The CS's letter to the Secretary of State for Colonies further demonstrated his averseness in promoting co-operatives. He pointed an accusing finger at Northcote's report, which was contentious. The CS argued that 'to be frank, his report is disappointing and contains some extraordinary opinions to which this government could not subscribe and paid no attention to non-natives mainly, Europeans and Indians and too much on natives that would raise all sorts of misunderstandings'.²

In bolstering the decision, the CS sent the same content in a letter to the Carnegie Foundation in which he made clear that 'Mr Northcote's report contained a good deal of matter of theoretical and contentious nature that the government cannot subscribe to'.³ Additionally, it was maintained by the CS that 'there was no question to set up a Department or Organisation to deal with co-operation'.⁴ It was also strongly emphasised that 'Northcote would only be able to act in a consultative capacity, mainly to advise when a genuine local desire for co-operation emerged'.⁵ He ordered that such matters be referred to him regardless of Northcote's appointment.⁶ Clearly, this indicated that support from the colonial authority for Northcote's co-operative development was ended, as the CS stressed that there would be no suggestions that any special department be set up and no financial help or subsidy, direct or indirect, would be given.⁷ Northcote's recommendation was rendered useless and an attempt to reform the way co-operative movements were being developed was crippled. This is a clear indication that there was a lack of commitment in promoting co-operatives within the colonial administration and the CO, as no action was taken by the latter against the Tanganyikan colonial authority.

The CS emphasised that 'co-operatives should emerge spontaneously'.⁸ Again, this was a failure to acknowledge the low knowledge level of growers to co-operatives in Tanganyika's rural areas. The spontaneous growth of the co-operative movement was desirable, but the colonial authority had to address the difficulties facing the growers. Having the CS maintain a spontaneous growth policy illustrates an attempt by the colonial authority to distance itself from providing the growers with a chance by creating the

---

1 TNA 22919, CS (acting) to all PCS, Ref. 22919/79, June 1935
2 TNA 22919, Minute by CS
3 TNA 22919, CS to Carnegie, Ref. 22919/423, 12 September 1935
4 TNA 22919, Clerk of Executive Council minute, August 1935 in Report on Co-operation by Northcote, District Officer, 1935
5 TNA 22919, Clerk of Executive Council minute, August 1935
6 TNA 22919, CS (Scupham) to all Provincial Commissioners, Ref. 22919, 28 October 1936
7 TNA 22919, CS (acting) to all PCs, Ref. 22919/79, June 1935
8 TNA 22919, CS to Carnegie, Ref. 22919/423, 12 September 1935

necessary conditions under which co-operation could be propagated, thrive and develop. Therefore, by limiting the Registrar's role to a consultative capacity, the CS hindered the growth of co-operatives. Historically, the spontaneous growth principle belonged to the nineteenth century during the *laissez faire* epoch in Europe, where the Rochdale and Raiffesein pioneers commandeered high levels of exposure. For example, Strickland pointed out in 1933 that 'it appears that Co-operation is almost unknown in tropical Africa',[1] suggesting that the conditions which led to the emergence of co-operatives in Europe did not exist in colonies like Tanganyika where most societies commanded subsistence economy (*ujima*), and the Rochdale, Raiffesein co-operative principles were unheard of among the illiterate rural growers.

Despite obstruction by the CS, various types of co-operatives were formed. The development was, however, slow and disappointing due to the colonial authority's position. For example, five credit co-operative societies were formed and registered. These societies would probably not have emerged without the promotional effort by the Aga Khan Foundation. Apart from promoting these societies, the Aga Khan Foundation provided capital. These were the Tanganyika Ismailia Credit Co-operative Society Ltd (registration number 3938, which had 1,559 members in 1947) based in Dar es Salaam; Moshi Ismailia Credit Co-operative Society Ltd (registration number 39, with 476 members in 1947), Mwanza Credit Co-operative Society Ltd (registration number 41, and 212 members in 1947), all of which were registered in 1938. The Dodoma Ismailia Credit Co-operative Society Ltd was registered in 1946 (268 members in 1947) and the Tanga Ismailia Credit Co-operative Society Ltd was registered in 1947.

Noticeably, the credit societies comprised the Indian community, mainly Ismailia sect.[2] The Aga Khan Foundation's provision of a loan at six per cent interest was for both members and non-members of these societies.[3] All societies had 2,677 members and in 1951 had 2,889 members,[4] they accessed funds from the Diamond Jubilee Trusts, and by 1949 had borrowed £3,250. Such financial loans had an obvious far-reaching effect on the availability of capital for small-scale traders to both start and expand their businesses.

In the late 1920s an attempt to promote credit societies among Africans failed. The initiative was made by the Post Office officials among African cotton growers.[5] This was a time when the money economy among the

---

[1] TNA 24870, C.F. Strickland, Co-operation for Africa, *Journal of the International Africa Institute*, vol. 6, no. 1 (January 1933) pp. 15-26
[2] TNA 37192, Tanganyika Government, *Report on Co-operative Development* (Dar es Salaam: Government Printer, 1947) p. 8, Appendix 4
[3] Ibid.
[4] Ibid.

small-scale African growers was at infant stage. Second, the scheme failed because there was no interest from among Africans in the district. Third, these were years when the country was recovering from the First World War and was characterised by wide-spread mistrust among the Africans to the credit societies that the Post Office was trying to promote. Mistrust was generated from experience owing to a loss of their savings accumulated in credit societies by the Post Office following the ejection of Germany as a colonial power. As a result of this loss, the Africans buried their money (cash) or placed it under their beds, believing it was more secure. Additionally, Africans were not confident they would be able to withdraw their money if they moved away from Bukwimba chieftaincy.[1]

Promotion and registration of co-operative societies were nevertheless taking place in some places, but, disappointingly, progress was slow. For example, in Kilimanjaro which was the colonial authority's main interest, the Acting Registrar pointed out that 'for two years since the Co-operative Societies Ordinance was passed [1932] only 21 societies have so far been registered and in the last 12 months only one application was submitted from the European society which was also based in Moshi'.[2] By 1944 the number of societies in Moshi district was 27.[3]

The slow progress in Kilimanjaro affected other types of co-operatives, as the colonial authority's attention and preference was primarily AMCOs. Where in 1941 the Chagga Transporters Co-operative Society was registered with registration number 52, by 1947, the society had 72 members.[4] The transport society's principal task was to ship coffee from various KNCU affiliated primary societies to the union warehouse in Moshi town. Individual members owned the vehicles transporting passengers, coffee and other commodities. The society function was largely to receive and arrange orders, and the bulk purchase of fuel and spare parts on behalf of members; a position made difficult during World War II. The transport society also had a license to operate in the Central Province particularly in Kongwa and Mpwapwa where the Overseas Food Corporation (OFC) had a groundnut project.[5]

Coffee transportation was crucial given that the KNCU had an obligation to ensure coffee was collected in Moshi town. At the outbreak of

---

[5] TNA 20999, Extracts from a report published by Post Master General in *Mambo Leo Newspaper*, 27 July 27 1927

[1] Ibid.

[2] TNA 19005, Minute from Ag Registrar to the CS, 5 November 1934

[3] TNA 37192, Northcote to J.D. Rheinallt Jones, Director of South African Institute of Race Relations, Ref. Co-op/1058/17, 11 December 1944, Co-operative Development, 1946-1950

[4] TNA 37192, Tanganyika Government, *Report on Co-operative Development* (Dar es Salaam: Government Printer, 1949)

[5] Horrace Plunket Foundation, *Year Book of Agricultural Co-operative* (London: Basil Blackwell, 1958) p. 307

World War II, the native coffee industry in Tanganyika fell under the bulk purchases' long-term contracts from 1940 to 1952 to ensure supplies to the United Kingdom. As a result, procuring and directing supplies and controlling prices has been imposed under war conditions. Thus, coffee produced by natives in Kilimanjaro had to be sold to the Ministry of Food and Supply of which the KNCU was appointed the Ministry of Food's agent. Under such conditions, African transporters had been encouraged by the colonial authority to form a co-operative society committed to the transportation of coffee in Kilimanjaro.

Despite hesitation and obstruction to promote co-operatives, the co-operative legislation for the territory, drafted by Strickland, made an impact in Africa, Europe and China. This came at a time when co-operation was embodied as a means of rural development in developing countries. Having legislation in place paved the way to technical collaboration between the League of Nations and China and W.K.H. Campbell, formerly Registrar of Co-operative Societies in Ceylon, was entrusted by the League of Nations with assisting the Chinese government in this respect. The League of Nations pointed out that 'it would be of great assistance in advising the national government of the republic of China on co-operative assistance'.[1]

Other countries requested copies of the Ordinance. The Nyasaland (Malawi) colonial government requested its officials have a study tour on modalities to establish societies.[2] The governments of Kenya,[3] Uganda, Cyprus[4] and Southern Rhodesia (Zimbabwe)[5] were all interested to learn and replicate Tanganyika's Ordinance and made inquiries. In Kenya, the legislation provided for compulsory marketing for producers of wheat and pyrethrum to the government appointed agency, the Kenya Farmers Association.[6]

7.1. The Co-operative Societies' Ordinance

The colonial authority in Tanganyika was preoccupied with supporting the KNPA, fought against it and eventually strangled it through the legal mechanism, the 1932 Co-operative Ordinance. The Ordinance was clearly controversial. The Ordinance did not imply that co-operatives could be promoted in the country during the inter-war years. Some co-operatives

---

[1] TNA 19005, League of Nations, China to CS Tanganyika territory, 22 October 1935
[2] TNA 19005, CS Malawi to CS Tanganyika, 23 March 1936
[3] TNA 19005, Secretariat (Acting Colonial Secretary), Kenya, Ref. C/Agr.1/15/76, 16 March 1934 to CS Tanganyika
[4] TNA 19005, CS Cyprus to CS Tanganyika Ref. 1240/20, 2 November 1934
[5] TNA 19595, Department of Native Development, South Rhodesia (Zimbabwe) to CS Tanganyika Ref. 193/1671, 17 July 1932
[6] TNA 24870, A Report by the International Committee for Inter-Co-operative Relations, 1937 on Cameroon, Ghana and Kenya

were, however, established but the initiative lacked a road map due to absence of central co-ordination. In districts where co-operatives were successfully promoted, the initiatives were accidental and not guided by a common political stance and policy from the colonial authority.

Clearly, a commitment to promote AMCOs in the territory was a scapegoat as the whole scenario was driven by political decisions such as the strangulation of the KNPA which was the main focus of the colonial authority in the territory.

It was obvious that all aimed to undermine the KNPA. To achieve this intention, C.F. Strickland who was assigned to draft the law was given terms of reference to use as guidance. The terms highlighted overhauling coffee marketing in Kilimanjaro,[1] and revolved around replacing the association and the need to put native coffee growers under obligation to market their produce through co-operative societies.[2] Strickland advised against the compulsion measure[3] but was convinced when he was informed of its necessity, which was to protect native coffee growers from unscrupulous Indian traders:

> no satisfactory marketing arrangements can be made until every native grower is compelled to sell his coffee through the Association as this would eliminate the local buyers from competing with the Association. It also ensures that the association remains in existence.[4]

Thus, Section 36 of the Ordinance provided that growers (who made up 75 per cent of all producers in the territory) were required to sell their produce through co-operative societies. In 1933, KNCU applied to the colonial authority to enforce Section 36 (i and ii) of the co-operative legislation.[5] This was when the colonial officials noticed the 'discrepancy'. Several consultations were made to resolve the 'controversy'. The Section implied that European coffee planters were also answerable to the law. When the discrepancy was noted, the colonial officials sought advice from Strickland, the colonial co-operative expert, who argued that 'it was unreasonable to expect these different types of coffee to be bulked and marketed through the same agency'.[6]

In a speech to the East African governors, Strickland affirmed that the Ordinance for Europeans should exclusively be for them as one for the natives did not suit them and if it was necessary to have the same there should be clauses separating the two.[7] This would imply the natural end of

---

[1] TNA 13698, Telegram 252 Governor to Secretary of State for Colonies, December 1930
[2] Ibid.
[3] TNA 13060/261, 15 April 1930
[4] TNA 13060, Terms of Reference for Reorganisation of the KNPA
[5] TNA 20378, KNCS to Chief Secretary on 22 April 1932 signed by Joseph Maliti (President), Stepano Lema (Secretary) and A.B. Bennett (Manager)
[6] Strickland, *Co-operation in the colonies* p. 78

their organisation, the TPA in the same manner as the KNPA. When criticism raged on, Strickland defended this in his publications, claiming that the section establishing obligatory membership could not be described along racial lines. More so, he admitted that the practice provided under the law was wrong.[1]

The idea of separate legislation for the settlers was however null and void as it would be a violation of the Order of Mandate that prohibited racial segregation. All in all, separate legislation was the only option to keep European planters safe and immune from the provision. The colonial authority therefore had to mastermind a way forward against a defective and unfriendly legal position.

In an attempt to overcome this defect in the co-operative ordinance the government had to bring forward a specific section for WaChagga growers. It was decided that the ordinance, the Coffee (Moshi district) Rules popularly referred to as the Chagga Rule or *Masharti* in Kiswahili, should be included under Section 15 of the NA Ordinance.[2] The colonial officials prepared the *Masharti* draft, which was ready by August 1934 and passed by the Chagga Council without any consultation: it compelled native growers to sell coffee exclusively through the KNCU.

The passage of *Masharti* demonstrated success on the part of the colonial government in delegating powers to the NA to pass the law as provided for under the Indirect Rule policy. The policy was made acceptable on the premise that it reinforced the protection of the native coffee industry. However, it primarily envisaged protection of the settler coffee grower industry. The *Masharti* stipulated that:

> In exercise of the powers conferred upon Native Authorities by Section 15 of the Native Authority Ordinance, the following rules are hereby made:
> a. These rules may be cited as the Coffee (Moshi district) Rules, 1934 and shall apply to Moshi district. They shall come into force on the first day of ... 193...
> b. Every native planter of coffee shall market his crop through the Kilimanjaro Co-operative Union and for this purpose deliver his crop at such place as the Union require
> c. Any person who contravenes any of the provisions of the rules, shall be liable to a fine not exceeding one hundred shillings. Default of payment to imprisonment either description for a

---

[7] TNA 19005, Extract of Strickland's Speech to the conference of the Governors of the British East Africa Territories, 17 January 1932
[1] TNA 19005, Strickland, Co-operation for Africa, pp. 15-26
[2] TNA 25038, Legislation on Control Native Agriculture and Industry, History of the Chagga Rule

period not exceeding one month for a first offence, and for subsequent offences to fine not exceeding shs 200/- or to imprisonment of either description for a period not exceeding two months, or both fine and imprisonment.

In ensuring that European coffee planters were not affected, two aspects were raised: first, it was justified by application of Section 36 of the co-operative legislation that they had to sell their produce only to the European planters' co-operative society. This provision laid the foundation for the formation and registration of all types of societies on the basis of racial lines (African, European and Asian). In a move to keep the settlers away from natives, a safety valve was implemented, namely the Tanganyika Coffee Growers Association (TCGA) which was the European-only co-operative society created in 1935 so that their coffee produce could be sold through a non-native society. The TCGA had several branches in coffee producing locations across the country as shown in Table 24.

Table 24: Societies affiliated to the TCGA

Name of the Association	Location
Kilimanjaro Coffee Growers Association	Kilimanjaro
Mbeya Mountain Coffee Planters Association	Mbeya
Mbozi Planters Association	Mbeya
Oldean Planters Association	Arusha
Meru Coffee Growers Association	Arusha
Usa River Planters Association	Arusha
Ufiome Planters Association	Mbeya
Usambara Planters Association	Lushoto

Source: TNA 19595, Secretary Kilimanjaro Planters Association to DA, 18 July 1932

7.2: Merchant opposition to the Co-operative Ordinance

Despite widespread interest in the Co-operative Ordinance, it was not popular among Indian traders in Tanganyika. The traders opposed it on the grounds that the policy represented nothing other than involvement of the government in commerce. The traders passed a resolution during the merchant chambers' conference in Dar es Salaam on 31 December 1933. The resolution stated: 'the co-operative ordinance is repugnant to the interests of the Indian community for it has an element of monopoly'.[1] The Chamber argued that the natives are not in a position to understand co-operative principles prevalent in civilised countries and urged the government to repeal the ordinance quickly.

In the Chamber of Commerce Conference held in Tabora, criticism over the co-operatives emerged. They argued that the co-operative ordinance was repugnant to free trade and would create artificial barriers against the

---
[1] TNA 13698, Telegram 252 Governor to Secretary of State for Colonies, December 1930

movement and investment of private capital and that the existing stage of economic development of the territory did not warrant restriction of free trade. Further protests were echoed in the Indian Federal Chamber of Commerce meeting held in 1935 in Dodoma which argued that government was moving too rapidly in promoting co-operatives in an immature economic system. In their resolution it was stated that:

> This Federation is further of the confirmed opinion that the government is moving too rapidly towards the augmentation of co-operative systems which has already resulted in the displacement of the trading population concerned which remains unabsorbed in suitable manner. It also reiterates that its strong belief that the system of co-operation is quite primitive in the infant economic circumstances of the territory. Therefore, it urgently requests the government to stop the advancement of the co-operative system until the Territory is placed on a basis of intensive and extensive production and industrial development so that the trading population which might be displaced by co-operative institutions might be suitably absorbed in other spheres of economic fabric of the Territory.[1]

The merchants' concern was not ignored by the colonial administration. It was taken by the government that encouragement of the co-operative policy was a response to the demands for co-operative societies in various parts of the country.[2] The Indian trading community, for its part, resented the growth of co-operatives because they posed a threat to their position as middlemen. So, they vigorously fought and obstructed its development in every possible way. The arguments and proposals presented by Indian traders reveal their anxiety and the threat posed to them by co-operatives. It demonstrated their perpetual desire to monopolise crop marketing at the expense of the producers. It also illustrates their desire to exploit producers. They wanted producers kept at a lower level in the social stratification.

However, the Indian business community did not undermine government's commitment. The government's *laissez faire* economic policy was not accommodated but involvement of the government in regulation of the economy was important by the control of growers through their own organisation; a commitment embedded in its duty to protect the interests of the growers and support producers to market their produce through co-operatives.

---

[1] TNA 19005, Extracts from Resolutions the Chamber of Commerce Conference held in Tabora during 1935 Easter

[2] TNA 19005, CS to Honorary Secretary Federated Chambers of Commerce Section, the Indian Association, Ref. 21884, 24 June 1935

8. Strangulation of the KNPA &

Emergence of the KNCU

Promotion of the co-operative movement by the British colonial authority in Tanganyika took centre stage in October 1929 at the District Officers (DOS) and district Administrators (DAS) conference.

In principle, the colonial authority was committed to weaken the KNPA. The association was formed in 1922 following a threat from the settler community on the slopes of Mount Kilimanjaro who strongly opposed Africans producing coffee. The KNPA was one of the first ever indigenous associations for small-scale African coffee farmers in Tanzania.[1] It was registered in January 1925 under provisions of the Indian Companies Act 1913 Section 26. The association's objectives were coffee marketing and defending members' interests. The settlers objected to the colonial government policy that encouraged natives to grow coffee, believing they were inexperienced, which would lead to the spread of pests and diseases that could infect the white plantations.[2] The industry would be harmed as the export of ill-prepared native coffee would damage the reputation of white coffee in the London market which fetched high prices, as well as in other European markets.[3] They were of the view that coffee was a European crop and that natives should grow food crops to feed their family members and not be allowed to grow cash crops such as coffee.

The attempt by settlers primarily aimed at displacing growers to compel them to become labourers on settler coffee plantations, where they would be paid low wages. Labour shortages were prevalent as most labourers committed their time to their own farms.[4] Thus, the KNPA primarily aimed to counterattack pressure from settlers and defend the interests of native coffee growers.

Historically the Chagga, the natives of Kilimanjaro, had for years engaged in coffee production and marketing. Such agitation by settlers obviously posed a threat to their livelihood and their coffee farms. In a move towards protecting themselves, the native growers in Kibosho with guidance from Joseph Merinyo, who worked in the district colonial agriculture office, presented their request to the DC of Moshi, Major Charles Dundas,

---

[1] Westergaard, Co-operatives in Tanzania as Economic and Democratic Institutions, p. 124

[2] TNA 13060, Pennington Report, p. 4

[3] Ibid., p.203-234

[4] Hyden, *Beyond Ujamaa in Tanzania. Underdevelopment and an Uncaptured Peasantry* p. 53

to form an association with similar objectives as the Kilimanjaro Planters Association, which had members drawn from the settler (European) coffee growers' community. Dundas approved the formation of the association in 1922 and named it the Kilimanjaro Native Planters Association (KNPA).[1]

The association elected Theodore Mchau and Stanlaus Ndaskoi as the first representatives (*wawakilishi/wakili*) of the organisation. They were from Kibosho, a few kilometres from Moshi town. More *wawakilishi* were nominated by producers in other areas where Merinyo met them, for example, Lyimo Shaushi from Kilema and Bernard Mallya from Uru. It was 15 January 1925 when the *wawakilishi/wakili* from all over Kilimanjaro held a general meeting. The meeting selected Lt. Commander A.M. Clark who succeeded Major Charles Dundas (following his appointment as Secretary for Native Affairs[2] in June 1924 as Moshi DC) to act as its first President and Secretary until G.D. Patterson was appointed honorary secretary.[3] At the end of 1925, the colonial officials resigned their positions and were replaced by Joseph Merinyo who became the President and Stefano Lema the Secretary.

The association received government technical support that included developing a co-operative marketing scheme to help members sell their produce. Apart from protecting the interests of native growers as its primary goal, the association had a monopoly over coffee marketing in the Moshi district granted by the colonial authority. The association was also appointed by the government to implement and supervise, throughout the district, the Coffee Industry (Registration and Improvement) Ordinance and Plant Pest and Disease Regulations of 1928. The legislation was significant as pointed out by the DA that 'my definite policy is to make the KNPA an efficient instrument for looking after coffee cultivation'.[4]

This was evident, as the association was required by law to enforce the aforementioned coffee industry improvement Ordinance under which chiefs had to submit to supervision of the KNPA in implementing the policies and legislation. This meant that the KNPA was administering and controlling the chiefs in the same manner as growers. Chiefs viewed this as an infringement upon their political authority.

The colonial authority was equally concerned as it viewed the association as the leading organisation that opposed colonial policies. For example, the KNPA opposed attempts by the colonial authority to transfer land to

[1] TNA 13060, Pennington Report, p. 4
[2] In 1934 this office merged with that of Deputy Chief Secretary, the reason given being that supervision of native affairs should be the concern of the whole administration rather than of a specialist officer.
[3] Swynnerton & Bennett, *All About KNCU Coffee*, p. 4; TNA 13060, Minutes of the KNPA Inaugural Meeting held on 15 January 1925
[4] TNA 11908, DA to Governor, 16 April 1929, Ref. 50/11908

Kenya so settlers could alienate it. Such an attempt was viewed by the KNPA leadership as necessary to protect its members and the native coffee industry. However, land alienation policy was not applicable in Tanganyika as it was a Mandated territory where most policies had to have the League of Nations' approval. At the same time, the KNPA opposed census and land registration exercises that had been carried out by provincial and district officials which aimed to establish acreage and coffee trees owned by growers. The exercise was meant to determine how much tax growers would have to pay as reflected by his/her land and farm size. The KNPA opposed the coffee tree census and land registration because it suspected the government was preparing a list of plots for confiscation. The KPNA opposition infuriated the provincial and district colonial officials who concluded that the association no longer stood for the interests of the country and posed a threat to colonial commitments.

Effectively, the association lost the trust in their chiefs as well as colonial officials at provincial and district level. For example, the DO of Moshi pointed out that 'the KNPA has outgrown its usefulness and is inefficient, unable to deal with cultivation and care of coffee plantations'.[1] The Northern Province Commissioner, Hallier, alleged that the KNPA had a bad relationship with Native Authorities. Such opposition against government policies resulted in the KNPA being labelled as subversive and that it should be brought to an end. The colonial officials in the province viewed the KNPA as shifting away from its core business into politics. This heightened tension amongst the Provincial Authority, which failed to convince the CS to abolitish the association. Instead, Governor Sir Donald Cameron defended the association. He stressed the need for the association to continue if coffee cultivation was to do so and if the 1928 Coffee Ordinance and regulations were to be carried out.[2] The governor stressed the significance of the association. He reminded the Provincial Commissioner that KNPA duties could not be handled by the NAs. He also reminded the DC that the association was formed to protect native coffee growers from unscrupulous Indian traders. This again, intensified hostility because the governor's decision was interpreted as a triumph for the KNPA against its enemies (district and provincial authorities).

Furthermore, in March 1931 the KNPA indicated its desire to recruit a manager with responsibility to facilitate coffee marketing and export. This was viewed by the colonial authority as an attempt to divert coffee exports to destinations other than Britain. Thus, the colonial authority intervened by taking over the organisation. While doing so, the colonial authority replaced the management, suspecting it of embezzling association funds.

---

[1] TNA 11908, DO Moshi to Commissioner North Province, 7 October 1929, 88-8
[2] TNA 12809, Minute to Commissioner North Province, 12 November 1928

However, this did not lead to the takeover of the association by the colonial authority. The financial crisis that the association was facing was taken as management failure. Difficulties to sell produce during the 1929 great depression was an excuse for the colonial authority to judge it as a failure following its inability to provide and deliver services and its lack of commitment to coffee growers who were its members. Thus, the colonial officials in the province embarked upon placing the KNPA under its management. This began with a takeover of KNPA's functions facilitated by the governor appointing a caretaker manager to run the association.[1] A.L. Pennington, Assistant District Officer, was seconded for special duty[2] which was primarily to prepare a road-map for the restructuring and takeover of the KNPA.

In executing its duties, the colonial authority gave Pennington terms of reference. The official was to investigate association affairs and produce a recommendation for restructuring. In his report, Pennington pointed out that 'the KNPA was deeply in debt'.[3] Therefore, technical support was necessary to rescue it from the financial crisis, which ironically occurred during the economic depression of the 1930s, when the KNPA failed to pay coffee growers on delivery of coffee due to lack of a market.

The financial crisis identified by Pennington presented an opportunity for the colonial authority to provide free services to the association. Obviously, this was a move meant to infiltrate it and establish an influence within. The influence began by having Joseph Maliti as the new association President. Maliti was appointed at a meeting chaired by A.O. Flynn, the DO of Moshi.[4] Maliti's appointment was crucial in asserting government control over the KNPA. Pennington's position was to facilitate a rescue mission by providing commercial management support, which was crucial to strangle Merinyo's influences. New KNPA committee members were appointed to replace Merinyo's[5] die-hard supporters. The new committee members were carefully brought on board by selecting suitable candidates, especially those who would collaborate with the colonial authority.

The recruitment of the managerial team was considered necessary by the colonial authority because the financial crisis was not the only challenge that faced the association. Other challenges were ignorance of business, lack of

---

[1] TNA 13698, Extract from Minutes of Conference of Senior Administration Officers held in Dar es Salaam, 21-24 October 1929 at which the governor mentioned the idea to appoint a European manager for the KNPA; TNA 19126, Minutes of Pennington meeting with KNPA committee, 4 November 1930

[2] TNA 25777, Governor to Secretary of State for Colonies, 16 May 1931

[3] TNA 13060, Pennington to PC, Northern Province, Ref. B/2, 23 September 1930; TNA 19126, Minutes of Pennington meeting with KNPA committee,4 November 1930

[4] TNA 13060, Governor (Symes) to Secretary of State for Colonies (confidential, 20 November 1931

[5] TNA 13060, CS to Secretary of State for Colonies (cConfidential), 20 November 1931

organisational experience and misfortune in the choice of collaborators.[1] A vacancy was advertised within Tanganyika, in provincial and district offices, as well as in some newspapers. Several applicants applied for the position. These applicants were Molloy, Major Perkins, Arthur Leslie Brice Bennett and H.P. Smith. Bennett, the ex-colonial labour officer in the Northern Province, was the colonial authority's favoured candidate. However, some government reports show that Bennett was appointed following consultation of the association with the colonial authority.[2]

The governor saw Bennett's appointment as a significant achievement. He sounded optimistic in writing to the Secretary of State for Colonies, in which he explained that 'it is anticipated that he will be a thoroughly satisfactory Manager and a great assistance and future progress of the Association is assured'.[3] He was also described by the Northern Province Commissioner as 'whole-heartedly and able to co-operate with the government and thus, he has confidence that the Association was in good hands which is an essential factor for a successful society'.[4] The Moshi DC described him as 'being a man of absolute integrity, with long business training and experience, equitable temperament, knowledge of Kiswahili. In addition he's known and liked by a large number of WaChagga. It was also argued that the KNPA was fortunate to obtain his service'.[5] The WaChagga honoured him as *Mbuya-o-WaChagga* (the intimate friend of the WaChagga).[6]

In a further development, a new organisation was established to take over KNPA functions. This was the Kilimanjaro Native Co-operative Society (KNCS) on 30 May 1937.[7] This was the landmark in replacing the KNPA orchestrated by colonial officials Pennington and A.O. Flynn. Thus, the KNCS became not only a new co-operative society but also the first organisation named 'co-operative' in the country. It is also important to note that the KNCS was formed without the CO's consent. Apparently, if it was so, the CO was ill-advised. This advice was also communicated to the LEGCO over the intention to have the co-operative ordinance to basically allow the 'restructure' of the KNPA, which was not the case.[8]

Upon creation of the KNCS, the KNPA's members and membership were automatically transferred to the new organisation.[9] The transfer of

---

[1] TNA 37192, Tanganyika Territory, *Report of the Co-operative Development* (Dar es Salaam: Government Printer, 1948) p. 1
[2] TNA 37192, Tanganyika Territory Annual Reports on Co-operative Development (1948); TNA 13060, Governor (Symes) to Secretary of State for Colonies (Conf.) 20 November 1931
[3] TNA 13060, Governor to Secretary of State for Colonies (Conf. 20 November 1931
[4] TNA 20378, Northern Province, PC to CS (conf.), Ref. P. 377/416, 18 September 1931
[5] TNA 20378, Extracts from reports on the reorganisation of the KNPA, Confidential 14 September 1931
[6] Dundas (1955) p. 125
[7] *Uremi*, 2, June 1932
[8] TNA 13060, Governor to Secretary of State for Colonies (conf.), 20 November 1931

members to KNCS signified a step toward weakening KNPA. Making KPNA a useless organisation and technically null and void forced it to cease trading and dispose of its assets and liabilities to the KNCS. Furthermore, A.L.B. Bennett was hand-picked by the colonial authority to manage the KNCS with effect from 30 May 1932.[1] Maliti, the KNPA committee members as well as Bennett comprised a team that was charged with managing the KNCS. Immediately, campaigns were placed in motion under which chiefs, the KNCS committee, Bennett and, of course, the colonial officials in the district participated. Thus, some primary societies were established in various villages on the slopes of Mount Kilimanjaro.

During the campaigns, Bennett assured growers that the society would address all problems that the KNPA failed to resolve. It was made clear that the society would help coffee producers within a short walking distance and facilitate coffee marketing by setting up marketing posts at village level. The colonial authority portrayed the passage of the Co-operative Societies Ordinance as a measure intended to restructure the KNPA. The colonial officials maintained that the legislation was to provide legal backing for having co-operative societies, as the Ordinance under which the association was registered proved unsuitable; thus, it had to be disregarded. Under the Industrial Society Ordinance, it proved difficult to subdue as the ordinance provided for registration of a company in which the Registrar could not directly intervene.

The legal difficulties provided by the Industrial legislation made it difficult for the colonial authority to replace or conspire in getting the KNPA replaced. Nevertheless, the stated association's problems were excuses that colonial officials exploited as reasons to replace it. By the early 1930s, the co-operative legislation to provide a legal ground for sidelining the association was presented and approved by the LEGCO. While presenting the Bill to the LEGCO, the colonial authority argued that the objective 'was to save the KNPA (so as) to organise itself in a manner known to the law and under a certain amount of control'.[2]

Soon after approval of the Bill at the LEGCO, the governor presented the legislation to the CO. The governor appealed to the CO that primary objectives were to weaken the powers of the KNPA and to give the colonial authority control over native produced coffee in Kilimanjaro. He further insisted that new legislation was important because the 1913 Indian Industrial Act which provided for registration of the association proved unsuitable and would not place it under government control.[3] However, the CO

---

9 *Uremi*, 2, June 1932
1 TNA 13060, Governor (Symes) to CO (conf.), 20 November 1931
2 TNA 13060, LEGCO Proceedings February 1932
3 TNA 13060, Governor to Secretary of State for Colonies (conf.), 20 November 1931

which was under the Labour Party declined to approve the legislation because by then Tanganyika had to 'appoint the Registrar of Co-operative Societies to facilitate guidance to the co-operatives'.[1]

The colonial authority considered the appointment and training of the Registrar to meet a long-term measure. This came as early as 1931 when it was made clear that the Registrar should be recruited from among the local colonial civil servants and Ronald Cecil Northcote was appointed. In addition, the colonial senior officials discussed where to locate the co-operative department in Moshi, which was established as the right place given the experience, gained from the KNPA in crop marketing; whereas Mpwapwa, Tabora and Morogoro were rejected because they lacked experience.[2] None of the decisions, training the Registrar nor establishment of the Co-operative Department was immediately implemented due to financial constraints.

Although the administrators were occupied with setting up co-operative models, technicalities, vetting of the Registrar of Co-operative Societies, they also had in mind to have a Kiswahili term for co-operative. Research to establish a term was assigned by the authority of the Inter-Territorial Language Committee, which originally identified two terms, *Ushirika* and *Ujima*. It was finally concluded that *Ushirika* was appropriate which by then translated as 'work of the activities of the society', also 'participation in the results of the activities'. Literally, *Ushirika* is a Kiswahili term that implies co-operation. Whereas *Ujima* was viewed as unsuitable as it translated to 'work done with assistance', e.g. crop cultivation, house building.[3] The official incorporation of the term, *Ushirika* by the government provided co-operation a unique stature and status that was not only accepted in Tanganyika but across Kiswahili speaking countries.

8.1: Imposition of the KNCU on coffee growers

The promotion and registration of co-operative societies in Kilimanjaro was triggered by political developments in Britain when the Conservative Party defeated the Labour Party in the general election of October 1931. The defeat of the Labour Party meant its political influence in the colonies was lost and with the assumption of power by the Conservative Party, new colonial policies were unveiled. The co-operative legislation was approved, prompting appointment of the Registrar of Co-operative Societies.

The political development in Britain coincided with a change of governorship in Tanganyika that created an opportunity for the colonial authority

---

[1] TNA 13060, Passfield to Governor Dispatch 507, 22 July 1931

[2] TNA 19005, Mitchell report on discussion with Strickland on organisation of co-operative societies in Tanzania, 23 March 1931

[3] TNA 19005, Secretary Inter Territorial Language Committee to CS, Dar es Salaam, Ref. 139/119, 14 January 1933; Memo 19005/125, 23 January 1933

to influence the CO to approve the application of the Co-operative Ordinance with effect from 23 May 1932. This was a time when the colonial government was whole-heartedly prepared to spare an officer for the purpose as it was viewed as a proper way for the prosperity and development of the co-operative movement. It should be noted that the co-operative legislation however, provided a politically expedient solution to sideline the KNPA with the formation of the Kilimanjaro Native Co-operative Society (KNCS), which took over the association's functions.

The 1932 co-operative legislation culminated in not only sidelining the KNPA but also punishing it. This treatment was provided for and implemented under Section 36 of the legislation in which all growers in the district were compelled to be members of a co-operative society, most of which were in the villages. Implementation primarily deprived the KNPA of membership and eventually it lost its base in the villages. Additionally, all coffee growers had to sell their produce to the co-operative societies, making the KNPA redundant and dysfunctional as far as the coffee business was concerned. This was not an outcome of a popular demand, but was essentially the act of a government anxious to set up co-operatives for growers. The strategy was nothing other than an imposition of KNCU and affiliated societies and members. Moreover, the KNCU emerged as the dominant and unchallenged organization with excessive government intervention through market monopoly legislations.

Sub-section 36 of the co-operative legislation was not only designed to suffocate the KNPA by denying it access to coffee produced by Africans. The very sub-section was the colonial authority drive and mechanism towards controlling the native growers and coffee through co-operatives. The KNPA protested Section 36. The essence of its objections was a distrust of measures designed to stabilise native enterprise. Moreover, having Section 36 in place was not economically motivated but rather a political manoeuvre through which the co-operatives were granted a monopoly over coffee; whereas the local chiefs were granted the political authority to control people who were, of course, coffee producers. Thus, enforcement of coffee production and tax collection mechanisms were put in place.

The KNCS with support and guidance by the colonial authority in Tanganyika utilised the political development in Britain to its advantage. In this, several societies with affiliation to the KNCS were formed, basically to ensure the KNPA lost its support at grassroots level by having co-operative societies with a deep-rooted base within each village. To ensure the KNPA lost its following among coffee farmers, the DO of Moshi, Flynn, created a new structure for the KNCS. The structure was embedded under KNCS bye-laws to operate at division level.[1] The CS strongly indicated approval to

---

[1] Land Department to CS, Ref. E.852/1250, 27 May 1932

the Land Department, which was in charge of co-operative development in the country, of a structure for the KNCS proposed by Flynn. In his approval the CS pointed out that:

> it strikes me, however in a discussion with DO, O.A. Flynn on the structure of co-operative movement in Kilimanjaro whether to have a number of separate societies for each division in the district namely Kibosho, Usa, Moshi, Kilema, Marangu, and Machame; and that this society should be members of central society or a union.[1]

The CS stressed that the KNCS manager, Bennett, and acting co-operative Registrar in Moshi district, Flynn were to acquaint themselves with co-operative principles and practices as well as ways in which societies could be controlled, and about the county's co-operative legislation and bye-laws.[2]

Noticeably, an affiliation of co-operatives with the KNCS was meant to ensure that coffee marketing was administered at division level in order to place delivery stations closer to growers. It was also partly to curtail the KNPA by having all growers in each village became members and to deliver their commodity to a nearby primary society. The members were required under the law to sell their produce to a co-operative society. Consequently, the KNPA lost members at grassroots level and was deprived of business as it became illegal for growers to sell coffee to the association.

In October 1932, the KNCS and its affiliated societies submitted registration applications,[3] which were duly accepted. Registration started in January 1933 in which the KNCU was given registration number 12. Another 11 affiliated co-operative societies were registered on 1 January 1933 out of which Kibong'oto Co-operative Society Limited was the first. These were the first 12 registered societies not only in Kilimanjaro but also in Tanzania.

According to the bye-laws, native coffee growers were to be members of the KNCU affiliated co-operative societies,[4] and all registered societies in Moshi had to be affiliated to the KNCU. By 1934, 27 societies were registered with 12,000 individual growers as members.[5] The creation of the union at the top and primary societies, as in the case of KNCU and for all other AMCOs, in Tanzania was a replication of the unified co-operative, which is vertical in structure. This model was common in all British colonies and characterised by a disintegrated and disjointed relationship as the co-operatives were distinguished by type. As far as crop marketing is

---

[1] TNA 19595, Director of Land Department to CS, Ref E.852/1251/850, 27 May 1932
[2] TNA 19595, CS to Land Department February 1932
[3] TNA 25777, KNCU to CS, 8 May 1933
[4] TNA 25828, Bye-laws of the KNCU and affiliated societies, p. 10
[5] TNA 19005, Memorandum on the working of the Co-operative Societies Ordinance, November 1934

concerned, the vertical integration had its origin under Section 36 of the 1932 co-operative legislation. Under this Section AMCOs were geographically confined. There was no horizontal connectivity or integration as provided under the ICA's sixth co-operative principle. The principle emphasis is on co-operation among co-operatives geared to strengthen the movement by having them collaborate with each other.[1]

Under Section 36, growers were compelled to sell their produce through co-operatives, and compelled to be members of a society which was primarily meant to deprive the KNPA not only membership but also to handle coffee produced by native growers. However, the Section had further implications whereby the settlers were trapped. Under such circumstance the settlers had to sell their produce to the KNCU and its affiliated societies, hence the colonial authority was hesitant to apply the Section. Several consultations were made to resolve the 'controversy'. For example, Strickland, considered the colonial co-operative expert, argued that 'it was unreasonable to expect these different types of coffee to be bulked and marketed through the same agency', and that as 'the ordinance for Europeans should exclusively be for them as one for the natives does not suit them [and if] it is necessary to have the same there should be clauses that separates the two'.[2]

8.2.1 Section 36 of the co-operative legislation

Under Section 36 (Sub-Section i and ii) of the 1932 Co-operative Societies Ordinance 7, all growers in the region were compelled to sell their produce through KNCU and its affiliated co-operative societies. The section was used by the colonial authority to control coffee marketing in Kilimanjaro and primarily to suffocate the KNPA. Section 36 (Sub-Section ii) laid down that 75 per cent of the producers in an area had to sell through one agent.

In principle the sections formed the bedrock to the cash crop marketing policy in Tanganyika but its significance has been seriously neglected in existing literature, and where attention is paid it is treated in isolation with native-produced crop marketing policies. Strickland, who drafted the legislation, pointed out that this section provided for obligatory membership that cannot be described as a native co-operative.[3] The section also provided that non-members of the organisation were automatically members of the society and could sell to the organisation or its affiliated societies.

---

[1] Suleman Adam Chambo, *Agricultural Co-operatives: Role in Food Security and Rural Development*, Paper Presented to the United Nations Organisation Expert Group Meeting on Co-operatives held 28-30 April 2009, New York, www.un.org/esa/socdev/egms/docs/2009/co-operatives/Chambo.pdf, accessed 12 May 2014

[2] TNA 19005, Extract of Strickland's Speech to the conference of the Governors of the British East Africa Territories, 17 January 1932

[3] TNA 19005, Strickland, Co-operation for Africa

In 1933, KNCU applied to the colonial authority to employ Section 36 (i and ii) of the co-operative legislation.[1] However, the colonial authority was hesitant to approve its implementation in Kilimanjaro due to the existence of both settlers, mostly European, and small-scale Chagga or native growers. The hesitation was obviously due to its impact on European coffee planters who had to sell their produce through the KNCU and its affiliated societies. However, having separate legislation was a violation of the Order of Mandate that prohibited racial segregation;[2] Strickland interestingly admits it is wrong.[3] Basically, it was viewed an impractical proposition by the colonial authority to have members comprising both natives and non-natives.

Several attempts by the colonial authority to separate African and European settlers were made. The natives, especially those in Kilimanjaro were guided by the Chagga Rule policy that excluded the settlers. This rule came into effect on 1 October 1934 and applied to all Chagga coffee producers in Moshi district. It recognised and empowered the KNCU as the only legal institution to purchase and sell native grown coffee and compelled producers to sell their coffee to co-operatives.

8.2.2: The Chagga Rule

The idea of Chagga Rule originated from the colonial government, who persuaded the Chagga Council to pass it. This was an attempt by the colonial government to delegate powers for promulgating native legislation in accordance with the Indirect Rule policy, primarily as a cover to protect native coffee growers, but intended to protect European coffee growers from being compelled to market their produce to co-operative societies of which the majority of members were natives. The policy was justified by the colonial authority:

> No satisfactory marketing arrangements can be made until every native grower is compelled to sell his coffee through the Association as this would eliminate the local buyers from competing with the Association. It also ensures that the Association remains in existence.[4]

It is obvious that engagement of the NA was to keep the colonial authority from being implicated with racial policies which were against the Mandate policy. Understandably, the Chagga Rule was rooted in racial segregation that compelled native growers only to market coffee to the co-operatives.

---

[1] TNA 20378, KNCS to Chief Secretary, 22 April 1932 signed by Joseph Maliti (President), Stepano Lema (Secretary) and A.B. Bennett (Manager)
[2] TNA 357883, Extract from Lord Winster speech 1-3 March to House of Lords; Strickland, *Co-operation in the Colonies* (London: George Allen & Unwin, 1945) p. 78
[3] Strickland, *Co-operation in the Colonies*, p. 78
[4] TNA 13060, Report on the Reorganisation of the KNPA

All in all, the colonial authority was responsible for creating racial barriers by providing guidance and pressuring the NA to promulgate the legislation. As a result, the NA and chiefs found themselves embroiled in the affairs of growers and societies without their participation. Compulsion or automatic membership never existed in ICA's co-operative principles or that of Rochdale's. This clearly suggested a violation of the co-operative principles, regardless of the pretext that they were designed to protect growers from unscrupulous traders and to develop the native coffee industry.

The employment of the Chagga Rule coincided with the collapse of the coffee price in the world market from which Kilimanjaro, especially Wa-Chagga, coffee was not spared. The 1934/35 coffee season saw a drastic drop in coffee price triggered by the flooding of the market with produce from Brazil.[1]

Table 25: Coffee Production (in tons) and payment, 1932–1946

Season	Coffee crop parchment (in tons)	Amount paid in £ to growers	Price per lb. paid to growers
1932/33	1,072	35,426	29.55
1933/34	1,167	35,384	27.03
1934/35	1,587	35,456	19.85
1935/36	1,684	33,995	16.94
1936/37	882	18,707	18.95
1937/38	1,472	33,336	20.16
1938/39	1,959	58,747	26.78
1939/40	2,680	72,275	24.17
1940/41	4,063	84,798	18.53
1941/42	1,948	52,184	23.97
1942/43	3,103	145,399	41.96
1943/44	2,114	131,012	57.49
1944/45	3,974	276,380	62.96
1945/46	3.102	173,032	49.81
Total	30,807	1,186,131	

Source: Moshi District Book I 1939/40 to 1943/44 seasons & KNCU 1946/47 Annual Report. Appendix B

Table 25 shows payment trends in which advances paid for the 1934/35 season were only -/16 cents per pound of parchment coffee delivered. It shows a sharp fall in 1935. The crisis was so serious that the KNCU could not pay growers a second instalment (*mabaki* in Kiswahili). The KNCU issued a communiqué through its monthly bulletin, *Uremi*, on 22 August 1935, informing members of the impending problem of not being able to

---

[1] T.S. Jervis, Marketing of Coffee, *East Africa Agricultural Journal*, May 1957, pp. 459-464, in Bukoba District Book

sell much of the coffee to the London market.¹ However, the message did not explain why coffee could not fetch a buyer, nor gave a reason for the fall in prices. Despite this, the growers showed trust in the KNCU and there was no reaction from them. At the same time, the KNCU had to embark upon measures to resolve financial problems to meet its commitments to pay growers in the 1934/35 season.

In contrast, the settlers, especially of German origin, were not affected by the crisis since they exported their coffee direct to Germany and fetched a higher price that was fully paid in cash. Simultaneously, there were several traders, mostly Asian, German and British settlers, missionaries and traders who paid better prices than the union. For example, the KNCU paid 15 cents per pound, while companies such as Sheriff Jiwa paid 20 cents and H. Bueb paid 21 to 25 cents, depending on the quality of the delivered coffee.² The German settlers offered between 10 and 15 per cent above the market price on condition that part of the payment be spent on purchasing agricultural implements that they were selling. To this effect, growers demanded to sell coffee wherever and to anyone provided they were able to pay well and promptly.³

8.2.3: Riots against poor coffee price

For two seasons, 1934/5 and 1935/6, the growers received poor prices for coffee sold to co-operative societies compared with what settlers were paid,⁴ and in 1937, the growers rioted, in what is popularly referred to as 'Coffee Riots'.

There was widespread feeling among native growers that they were underpaid and could not see the KNCU justification for paying them low prices. They felt cheated. This generated criticism and by November 1936 growers/members could no longer hold their patience. The growers pressed for implementation of various alternatives to resolve the problem. First, they withdrew from the KNCU in preference of an open market where they could fetch better prices; and second, removed society leaders from office for failing to defend their interests and welfare in union forums. Such societies were Machame Central and East, Marangu Central and East; however, their decisions were revoked by the KNCU because they were contrary to the Chagga Rule.⁵

In 1935 the colonial authority relaxed restrictions over growers selling their coffee to any buyer who offered better rates but cancelled the decision

---

¹ *Uremi*, 22 August 1935

² TNA 13060, Coffee Ordinance & Regulations Attitude of the KNPA: History of the KNPA

³ Hailey, *An African Survey*, pp. 1472-1473

⁴ TNA 26207, Moshi DC to PC, Northern Province, Confidential 23/13, 21 April 1936

⁵ TNA 5/243, Bennett to Chief Shangali of Machame & Marrealle of Marangu, Folio

in 1937. This cancellation fuelled further discontent and dissatisfaction amongst WaChagga coffee growers. The discontent was widespread over the whole mountainside, engineered by some individuals; but more so in Machame Central and East and Marangu East societies that comprised about 3,784 members who owned 24 per cent of the total crop produced in Kilimanjaro. On 15 September 1937, riots broke out in these societies and for two days, 16 and 17 September 1937, there were riots in Marangu East, where members replaced existing leaders with men who 'refused to recognise the existing bye-laws'.[1]

The riots spread to 27 primary societies including Lyamungo, Masama, and Machame North, in which the primary society's stores were ransacked.[2] The rioters complained that owing to heavy overhead expenses the union paid lower prices than they could obtain outside.[3] Campbell analysed the riots.[4] However, his analysis has not shown how the issue was resolved and its impact on the crop marketing policy in Kilimanjaro and the country in general.

To arrest the riots the government drafted in the police and air force. Around 70 rioters were apprehended and sentenced to jail while others were deported.[5] This indicated to growers that they were meant to take any price given to them by a buyer regardless of how low it was. The ring leaders were imprisoned and about 14 others deported to Singida, Iringa and Sumbawanga in the Southern Highlands of Tanzania.[6] Deportations, imprisonment and other threats, in addition to measures set out in Section 36 of the 1932 co-operative legislation, compelled growers to become members of the co-operative movement.

Apart from riots, other societies which were affiliated to the KNCU decided to split from the union for failure to meet its obligations.[7] In response, the KNCU suspended sending money to all societies where riots had taken place. This created an impasse that forced the PC and Moshi DC to intervene. The PC had meetings in Marangu and Machame which successfully ended with restoring the societies' committees.[8] In 1939, the

---

[1] TNA 19005, Tanganyika Territory LEGCO, *A report on the Kilimanjaro Native Co-operative Union* (Dar es Salaam: Government Printer, 1937) p. 9 & a speech to the Registrar of Co-operative Societies from the President of the KNCU, Appendix J, p. 59

[2] Tanganyika Territory LEGCO, *A report on the KNCU*, p. 9

[3] Hailey, *An African Survey*, p. 1472

[4] W.K.H. Campbell, *Practical Co-operation in Asia and Africa* (Cambridge: W. Heffer & Sons, 1951) pp. 196-197

[5] TNA 255442. PC, Northern Province to CS, Ref. 377/7/180, 10 November 1941; TNA 25400, Disturbances at Moshi in Connection to KNCU

[6] TNA 5/24, Report to the League of Nations on Tanganyika Territory, 1937, pp. 206-13; TNA 25442, PC, Northern Province to CS, Ref. 25442/30, 22 December 1937

[7] Government of Tanganyika, Annual Report, Northern Province (Dar es Salaam: Government Printer, 1937) p. 40

Moshi District Officer, Bruce Hunt, set out to reorganise such societies to get them back within the KNCU framework. In one instance, the DO wrote to *Mangi* Addiel Solomon of Mwika asking him to facilitate the exercise for West Mwika Primary Co-operative Society in his chiefdom.[1]

It was viewed by the colonial administrators that the riots were politically motivated because a number of the German settlers, about 882 in total for the whole district, Asian traders, Greeks, teachers and missionaries in the area, were reported by the Registrar of Co-operative Societies, Northcote, to have instigated the agitators[2] by exploiting the poor price paid by the KNCU as a means to accumulate coffee. Northcote's allegations were adopted by Leubuscher in her argument.[3]

The accusation of the traders illustrates the prevalent understanding that the growers were too ignorant to protest and, under the same premise, were expected to be obedient to the Chagga Rule. The chiefs were also accused by growers to have conspired in the passage of the Chagga Rule. Therefore, chiefs were seen to be against the economic interests and welfare of the growers. Additionally, Northcote's accusations might have been based on a coincidence of riots with German campaigns for the return of colonies mentioned by Hitler in conversation with Sir John Simon on 25 March 1935. At the time, Germany was lobbying for membership of the League of Nations so that the country could qualify to administer colonies. However, Britain not only had no mandate for a German proposal, but was not supportive of the idea as reflected in parliamentary statements for three years from 1936 to 1939. Rejecting the German idea was obvious to prevent losing sources of raw materials and food supplies to the enemy.

According to Lord Winster in his speech to the House of Lords, one reason for the riots was the lack of effort to educate the members of the union in co-operative principles. This was depicted by members' refusal to adhere to the society bye-laws.[4] The KNCU reacted by suspending such societies and withheld coffee payments and advances, even though the Chagga Rule was applicable.[5]

In a communiqué, the DC ordered members to re-join the society which

---

[8] TNA 19005, Tanganyika Territory LEGCO, *A Report on the KNCU*, p. 9

[1] TNA 25777, DO to Mangi of Mwika Abdiel Solomon, Ref. no. 237/7, 29 June 1939

[2] Session Paper no. 4, 1937, p. 9; TNA 5/375C 24/13, KNCU School Lyamungo; TNA 25400, Memorandum of Disturbances in the Moshi district, pp. 208-209; Government of Tanganyika, Annual Report, Northern Province (Dar es Salaam: Government Printer, 1937) pp. 9-10; Interview with Emanuel Kitely Mbowe, Joseph Mchomba, John Joseph Munishi (24 October 2012)

[3] Charlotte Leubuscher, Marketing Scheme for Native-Grown Produce in African Territories, *Journal of the International Institute of African Languages and Cultures*, vol. XII, no. 2 (April, 1939) pp. 163-188

[4] TNA 357883, Extract from Lord Winster speech 1-3 March to the House of Lords

[5] TNA 19005, Tanganyika Territory, LEGCO, *A report on the KNCU*, pp. 9-10

was the only option open to them to sell their 1939 produce.[1] This was government interference and an obvious compulsion that became a dominant factor; the legislation was criticised by Strickland as deviating from co-operative practice.[2] It was stressed that only if society affiliates returned to the union could they sell their produce. In accordance with the law of the land they were obliged to comply by selling through a society and the KNCU, which in Kiswahili was '*ni lazima wafahamu ya kwamba ni lazima wote wawe chini ya masharti ya KNCU na basi hawataweza kukifungua chama chao na Union*'. This memo was communicated to growers by the *Mangi* at a meeting held on 1 July 1939.

At the meeting the *Mangi* managed to convince his subjects and it was decided to elect new leadership 'dedicated' and committed to comply with KNCU bye-laws. The new leaders were Marua bin Kishimbo elected as Chairperson, Abel bin Maktano, vice-Chairperson and Yohanne bin Manaseh as Secretary. In light of this, *Mangi* asked the DO to restore West Mwika Primary Co-operative Society onto the list of KNCU affiliated societies; and asked for permission to have the society's office opened for business to serve his subjects. This was interpreted by *Mangi* Abdiel Solomon as a significant step towards restoring confidence in the union[3] at a time when growers had lost trust in it. However, the political leadership and government authority had demonstrated an upper hand on issues affecting the movement.

All in all, the riots generated nervousness amongst the authority concerning the co-operative movement. There was also a fear of repetition and spread of such troubles where societies existed. This was seen as a political risk, particularly if promoted throughout the country. The authority would have difficulty controlling societies if the growers rose against them. This study is of the opinion that this was a contributing factor that led to delays and uneven promotion or accommodation of co-operatives in other parts of the country. The lesson learnt was sufficient to warrant the colonial authority to introduce appropriate legislation that provided for the formation of the Moshi Native Coffee Board (MNCB) in 1937.[4]

As a result of the riots, the government decided that the native coffee industry was one that should be brought under more direct control with effect from October 1937 when Native Coffee (Control & Marketing) Ordinance 26 was passed replacing the Chagga Rule. The Ordinance provided for control of the native coffee industry and compulsory market-

---

[1] TNA 25777, DO to Mangi of Mwika Abdiel Solomon, Ref. 237/7, 29 June 1939
[2] Strickland, Co-operation in the Colonies
[3] TNA 25777, Mangi of Mwika, Abdiel Solomon to DO, Ref. L. 9/6/39, 14 July 1939
[4] Francis Lyimo, Peasants Production and Co-operative Experiences in Tanzania: Case Studies of Villages in Moshi Rural and Urambo districts (PhD Thesis, University of Wisconsin-Madison, 1984) pp. 57-58

ing of the produce. Promulgation of the new policy can be viewed as a victory for the growers. But it was embarrassing for chiefs and central government because the Chagga Rule had to be revoked by the governor on 21 December 1937.[1] This was in response to the recommendation made by a committee formed to investigate the crisis/riots that faced the KNCU.[2]

Having the Chagga Rule replaced with legislation to control coffee indicated that the colonial government was not prepared to lose control of the native coffee growers. In reality, the legislation was not a significant departure from the Chagga Rule. The important contrast with the Chagga Rule was that the Native Coffee Ordinance did not specify to which organisation growers were compelled to sell their produce, but only mentioned an agency that the board could suggest. Given that in Moshi the KNCU and its affiliated societies were already in place, they were granted a monopoly to purchase native-produced coffee. No other organisation had been allowed as per the Chagga Rule. This provided an indirect integration of the co-operatives into marketing policy. Under the legislation all growers were restricted from selling coffee in an open market. Similarly, no organisation, apart from the KNCU and affiliated societies, was allowed to operate coffee marketing in the district.

The legislation targeted native coffee growers and ensured that European growers were not compelled to sell their produce through the KNCU and its affiliated societies. Thus, the native coffee industry was brought under more direct control than that attainable through the Co-operative Societies Ordinance Section 36 (Part 1). The Ordinance led to the formation of the Moshi Native Coffee Board (MNCB), which under Section 6 compelled all producers of native coffee in Moshi district to sell coffee produce to the agency chosen by the board.

The MNCB was empowered to control and market native-produced coffee. This further reinforced Section 36 of the 1932 Co-operative Societies Ordinance that provided for the compulsory sale of the produce through a registered society, clearly demonstrating that the co-operative legislation provided for a violation of the co-operative principles. However, the measure was justified as necessary by the colonial authority so that 'no satisfactory marketing arrangements can be made until every native grower is compelled to sell his coffee through the Association'.[3] A compulsion measure was pursued by the government in the expectation that members would remain loyal as they were during the KNPA and later KNCU periods, which protected them from attempts by the settlers to supress

---

[1] TNA 25442, CS to PC, Northern Province, 21 December 1937

[2] TNA 19005, Tanganyika Territory, LEGCO, *A report on the KNCU*, p. 41

[3] TNA 13060, Coffee Ordinance and Regulations: Attitude of the KNPA in Report on the Reorganisation of the KNPA

them, but the timing of the policy proved problematic as its implementation took place when the coffee price plummeted.

By having the MNCB and KNCU with affiliated societies below the marketing ladder, a three-tier marketing system was established whereby primary societies were at the bottom, the union in the middle and the board at the top of the structure. Under the system, primary societies collected the produce from growers and sold it to the KNCU which forwarded it to the board. This was applauded by the Agriculture Secretariat, who pointed out that 'the MNCB now has a weapon to use'.[1] This illustrates that the colonial authority had meant for the economic subjugation of the growers. It was also pointed out that the Chagga Rule was an embarrassment that placed the NAs on the same footing as a Department of State.[2] The establishment of the MNCB rendered the Chagga Rule inoperative.

In addition, the Coffee Industry Ordinance marked the official end of the application of Chagga Rule on 21 December 1937. The replacement of the Chagga Rule was a decisive step in restoring the confidence of chiefs and the NA amongst growers, especially when no challenge against them cropped up. The calm acceptance could also be due to the threat growers experienced when the government intervened to quell the riots. The replacement of Chief Abdiel Shangali as paramount chief of the WaChagga, for his support of the growers' demand for a better coffee price and the 'riots', was a strong message to chiefs who failed to collaborate with the colonial authority and support its policies.[3] Of course, the legislation strengthened government's grip over the KNCU, and ultimately the affiliated societies and growers through the MNCB. The control of marketing by the boards implied that co-operatives were curtailed from fully applying their roles which crippled their capability as independent organisations.

To avoid future embarrassment as experienced under the Chagga Rule, growers were kept well informed by provincial officials, especially C.F. Hallier, of this new development and the appointment of the KNCU as MNCB's agent. Such awareness and updated development were communicated to growers in public meetings and articles in *Uremi*. The PC made tours in Kilimanjaro where he informed chiefs and growers of the government decision to abolish the Chagga Rule. He also informed them of the setting up of the MNCB whereby KNCU would be appointed as its agent. This announcement was met with great satisfaction by growers because it meant the government was ready to listen and address their concerns. This was so for chiefs who had long been conscious of the anomaly of their positions as sponsor of the Rule which brought them into conflict with

---

[1] TNA 25442, Secretariat to PC, Northern Province, Ref. 25442/30, 22 December 1937
[2] Ibid.
[3] K.M. Stahl, *History of the Chagga People of Kilimanjaro* (London: Mouton & Co, 1964) p. 37

their subjects. From meetings and *Uremi* articles it was concluded that 'the withdrawal of the Chagga Rule and its replacement by the MNCB are fully and widely understood in Kilimanjaro'.[1]

Coincidentally, the setting up of the statutory board came at a time when the coffee price was improving which generated and restored grower confidence in both co-operatives and the board. It was the view of government officials that such development was met with great satisfaction since it was seen to protect growers' interests as well as their organisation. Importantly, unlike the Chagga Rule, MNCB members were drawn from government and growers as well as co-operative societies, so growers felt represented.[2] It also appointed one of the deportees as a board member. All in all, the use of force to quell the riots, imprisonment and deportation tactics employed by the colonial authority contributed to a 'forced' confidence.

Additionally, forcing growers to sell coffee through the agency (societies) appointed by the board was a feature that dominated for decades. The pre-riot era and legislation saw the colonial authority directly involved through the MNCB in which those who did not adhere were liable to penalty or imprisonment or both under Section 14 of the Native Coffee Ordinance 26 of 1937. In this regard, the KNCU became part of the government machinery for organizing the compulsory marketing of native produce that was utilised by the colonial power and colonial authority during WWII and for almost a decade after the outbreak of the war to handle coffee from growers. Control of coffee by the post-colonial government through the co-operatives was envisaged to facilitate development of the industry.

8.2.4: The Native Agriculture Control Bill

The colonial government was not prepared to lose control over native produced crops and therefore prepared a new Bill that was circulated by the Provincial Commissioners throughout the country.

The Bill borrowed some provisions from the Kenyan Coffee Industry Ordinance of 1934[3] and the 1934 Zanzibar Clove legislation, where it was decreed that only the Clove Growers' Association was allowed to buy cloves. The colonial government gave reasons for introducing the Bill:[4] to enable the Kilimanjaro Native Co-operative Union (KNCU) to market coffee and deal with crop plant diseases without the aid of the Native

---

[1] TNA 25442, F.C. Hallier, Northern Province, PC to CS, Conf., Ref. 377/7/96, 28 December 1937

[2] TNA 25442, PC, Northern Province to CS, Conf., Ref. 77/7/96, 28 December 1937

[3] J.H. Vaughan, Acting Attorney General, the Native Coffee Industry (Marketing and Control) Ordinance, 1936: TNA Legal Report, 26 October 1937

[4] TNA 25038, CS to Provincial Commissioners, Ref. 377/7/35, 8 September 1937

Authority Ordinance. Second, the law was to empower the governor to establish agricultural marketing boards for the purpose of advancing and improving the cultivation of native grown crops and to promote the organised marketing of the selected crop. The board established under the ordinance could pass compulsory marketing orders but only with the consent of the Legislative Council (LEGCO). Third, the legislation served to advance and improve the cultivation of coffee.

The government circulated copies of the Bill to all Indian business associations and chambers across the country for comment.[1] A stream of protest telegrams from Indian merchant associations reached the Chief Secretary in Dar es Salaam as the Indians thought they would be driven out of the coffee business, and considered the Bill unfair, discriminatory, iniquitous and against free trade principles. Thus, many demanded its withdrawal; some asked the government to postpone it by submitting it first to LEGCO for debate and only after that passing it into law. In response to merchants' reactions, the government clarified that it was unable to postpone the Bill until the next session of LEGCO.[2]

The editorial comments in *Tanganyika Opinion* were among the most critical of the Bill. It was argued that those suffering most under the Bill were natives who unfortunately were not organised enough to voice their protest in an effective manner.[3] Thus, they would be compelled to sell to the board regardless of the availability of sources that could pay them better prices. The newspaper also pointed out that there was no justification for the law because natives were making more money than they needed by selling some of their produce in open and competitive markets. For all these reasons, the Bill was undesirable as it deprived Indian merchants of all sources of livelihood so that many would be repatriated to India.[4] The President of the Tanganyika Indian Association requested the Indian National Congress to table a demand to India's colonial authority and the League of Nations to intervene and pressure the Tanganyika colonial authority to withdraw or at least postpone the scheme.[5]

The native business community jumped on the bandwagon as the government did not inform them of the Bill, and they only heard of it from Indian merchants. They asked for a copy of the Bill in Kiswahili, demanding

---

[1] TNA 25038, CS to Indian Business Associations in Mpwapwa, Morogoro, Seke, Ngerengere, Mwanza, Bukene, Kintinku, Singida, Bahi, Iringa, Kilosa, Tanga) also the Mwanza Chamber of Commerce and Lake Province Ginners Association, 30 September 1937, Ref. T. 25038/29

[2] TNA 25038, CS to Indian merchants, 29 September 1937

[3] TNA 25038, *Tanganyika Opinion*, 22 September 1937

[4] Ibid.

[5] TNA 25038, Resolutions of Tanganyika Indian Association meeting held in Dar es Salaam, 25 September 1937

details of the plan to end the free market for coffee and the possibility that the same law would be applied to other crops. Despite not having a proper knowledge of the content of the Bill, they too demanded its cancellation because it was damaging native interests.[1]

In response, the government pointed out that it had no intention of being stampeded or perturbed by uninformed criticism.[2] In late September 1937, it stressed that it had informed the merchants and LEGCO members of its intention to bring the native coffee industry, especially in Kilimanjaro, under control, for which special legislation was necessary.

8.2.5: Statutory marketing boards

The merchants' outcry did not deter the colonial authority. The Native Produce Board could, with approval of the director of agriculture, give direction and make orders with regard to the cultivation, preparation, grading and packing of regulated products; with the approval of the governor in council, it could even order that all producers sell such products to the board or agency. Under Clause 3 of the Ordinance, LEGCO was empowered to declare native coffee in Kilimanjaro a regulated product and thus, despite criticism by the Moshi district, to be sold through the agency appointed by the board under Section 4 of the Ordinance. Section 4 prescribed that the MNCB was the sole buyer of native-produced coffee in the Moshi district, thus granting the MNCB the monopoly over native-produced coffee.[3] On the same premise, it was empowered to appoint agents who were compelled to sell the coffee produce to the agency chosen by the board.

Until the outbreak of the Second World War in 1939, the MNCB was the only statutory organisation in the country. The need for similar organisations became evident after the end of the war. At this juncture boards were in fact necessary to facilitate procurement of strategic agricultural produce like tobacco and sisal.

The Lake Provincial Commissioner showed an interest in setting up similar boards in Bukoba.[4] But, the Provincial Commissioner was informed of the intention to have legislation providing for the formation of the Moshi Native Coffee Board to control the cultivation and marketing of coffee in Kilimanjaro from where the government would gain experience of how effectively it worked.[5] However, in the early 1940s the board formed in Kagera Region was necessitated by three main factors. First, to invigorate

---

[1] TNA 25038, The Tanganyika African Welfare and Commercial Association, Ref. C/S/117, 27 September 1937
[2] TNA 25038, The Secretariat to Indian Association, Ref. 25038, 25 September 1937
[3] TNA 27317, Agricultural Policies in the Colonial Empire
[4] TNA 25442, Telegram PC Lake Province to CS, telegram No 390, 23 December 1937
[5] TNA 25442, CS to PC, Lake Province, Ref. 25442/39, 4 January 1938

the growers' interests in the industry and bring further development of the crop by supplying seedlings to growers for planting. Second, to provide supervision of native coffee extension services, particularly guidelines on pruning, fumigation and weeding. Finally, improving quality of processed coffee beans and streamlining coffee marketing that for decades had been miserable.

Hence, extensive state control was reinforced following the outbreak of the Second World War that culminated in the formation of the Bukoba Coffee Control Board (BCCB) in 1941 (General Notice 329 of 8 April 1941). The BCCB was set up under War Emergency Orders Ordinance of 1939 and 1940 that also enabled the governor to appoint it to supply coffee to the British Ministry of Food under a five year contract that was further extended in later years. The BCCB's functions were to supervise cultivation of native produced coffee and market the crop.

In 1942, the BCCB was renamed the Bukoba District Coffee Board (BDCB) under General Notice 503 to control native-produced coffee provided under Native Coffee (Control & Marketing) Ordinance, 1937. The BDCB and BCCB indiscriminately controlled both African and non-African produced coffee. However, the BDCB failed to improve coffee quality. This prompted the Director of Agriculture to re-organise it in April 1946, granting it more responsibilities. The new entity known as the Bukoba Native Coffee Board (BNCB) started operating when the BDCB formally ceased operating on 31 October 1947. Reconstruction of the board was necessary to provide legal grounds for supervising the implementation of a long-term contract meant to supply 4,000 tons of coffee annually to the Ministry of Food and to undertake the responsibility of delivery to the same under the five-year agreement.[1] The BNCB only controlled and handled coffee produced by Africans in accordance with the powers conferred upon the BNCB by the Native Coffee (Compulsory Marketing) Order, 1937, Section 6.[2] Although non-natives had coffee plantations in Bukoba, they were not subject to the Native Authority and were not required to sell coffee through co-operatives nor to the BNCB.[3]

The Director of Agriculture outlined the following: the BNCB to be appointed as sole purchaser of all native coffee in Bukoba district; that the exporting companies operating in Bukoba were offered zones to purchase coffee on behalf of the board under two year contracts with an option of renewal; that zonal agents were required to buy coffee at a fixed price from producers, and had to export it to various markets abroad or to an auction in Mombasa.

---
[1] TNA 37200, Note on Coffee Licensing, June 1950; TNA 37200, Foreign Agriculture, September, vol. XII, no. 9, 1948, p. 102
[2] TNA 11969, Extract from the Standing Committee meeting April 1947
[3] TNA 41011, Bukoba Coffee: Marketing Organisation

During World War II, the British Ministry of Supply imported agricultural products from colonies that were sold in the United Kingdom with others re-exported to other countries. The board proved useful for facilitating coffee exports following appointment by the British Ministry of Supply under a long-term contract. The supply remained valid throughout the 1940s into the early 1960s.

When the board took over, it established the zonal scheme hulleries erected in each zone and furial processing was carried out in one plant in Bukoba town to ensure quality. A fixed price was set that growers were paid based on grades or quality of coffee delivered at buying posts. This was implemented in accordance with the powers conferred upon the BNCB by the Native Coffee (Compulsory Marketing) Order, 1947.

However, the Indian community was against the introduction of the long term agreement and zonal coffee marketing scheme. They argued against the monopoly favouring those 'not capable of looking after their own interest,'[1] and began to feel their interests were in jeopardy as the monopoly was designed to put African interests over Indian nationals.[2] They urged government to postpone the scheme until the Chamber of Commerce had conducted an investigation and agreed on the best modalities to implement.[3] In spite of protests, a zoning scheme including exclusive buying rights for select merchants was effected from 1 October 1947.

In an attempt to restore the previous marketing system, the Indians formed the Joint Action Committee to protest against the scheme and approved a lawyer to challenge in court. The African growers and Bukoba Chamber of Commerce formed their memoranda protesting against the Bukoba Coffee control scheme. The scheme was implemented when the Bukoba Coffee (Compulsory Marketing) Order was passed in the LEGCO.

Consequently, native coffee cultivation and marketing in Kilimanjaro and Kagera Regions were placed under the control of the colonial authority. These boards were responsible for the management of coffee nurseries; providing instructions to growers on methods of planting, cultivation, harvesting or preparation and marketing of native coffee.[4] Production of crops remained in the hand of growers, but under control of the colonial authority.

During the war, direct government intervention in coffee marketing was placed under Emergency Order. The matter was further aggravated by adoption of Native Coffee (Control & Marketing) Ordinance 26 of 1937

---

[1] *The Tanganyika Herald*, 3 September 1947

[2] *The Tanganyika Herald*, 6 July 1947

[3] TNA 29585, Tanganyika India Chamber of Commerce & Agriculture to CS, 21 August 1947

[4] TNA 24/13, KNCU School (Lyamungo) from MNCB to the Secretariat Members of Agricultural and Natural Resource, Ref. 75/273, 20 February 1954

that led to setting up the Bukoba Coffee Control Board in 1941. Implementation of this policy came at an important time when the emphasis was primarily geared towards rationalisation and synchronisation of crop purchase in favour of a single government appointed buyer. With this effect, the BNCB was from 1942 charged with supplying coffee to the Ministry of Food under a long-term contract under Defence Ordinance and Orders of 1939 and 1940. In an attempt to ensure that supply of coffee was maintained, marketing zones were set up and agents appointed to handle coffee from growers.[1] This development complicated the promotion of the cooperatives idea in the region.

The evidence shows that in 1947, native tobacco growers in Biharamulo and Ngara districts in the Lake Province and Kibondo Division in the Western Province had shown a desire for the creation a co-operative society or organisation. The Department of Co-operative Development doubted their abilities, mainly due to consideration of the low literacy standard.[2] Therefore, the board would undertake the functions as ruled under Section 6 of the Native Tobacco (Control & Marketing) Ordinance 1948.[3] However, this was translated by the Commissioner of Co-operative Development, R.S.W. Malcolm, as an obstacle to promoting co-operative societies.[4]

In a move envisaged to facilitate tobacco marketing in Biharamulo, the Native Tobacco Board was formed under the Native Tobacco (Control & Marketing), Ordinance of 1948. On 2 March 1948, the board was reconstituted under Government Notice 290, only to be renamed the Nyamirembe Native Tobacco Board, charged with controlling, preparation, and marketing of native-produced tobacco. C.J. MacGregor[5] was appointed its first manager.[6] Under the legislation, all native tobacco growers were compelled to sell their produce to the board.

---

[1] SML Seimu, The Growth and Development of the Coffee and Cotton Marketing Co-operatives in Tanzania, 1932-1982 (Unpublished PhD Thesis, University of Central Lancashire, 2015)
[2] TNA 36883, PC, Lake Province to CS, Ref. 1154/1265, 20 November 1947
[3] TNA 36883, DA to PC, Lake Province, Ref. 804/9484, 16 October 1947
[4] TNA 36883, Commissioner of Co-operative Development to members of Agricultural and Natural Resources, Ref. Co-op. 1183/30, 11 April 1950
[5] TNA 26563, MacGregor was Senior Agricultural Officer in the South West Circle throughout 1940s before being appointed to the Songea district Native Tobacco Board
[6] TNA 36883, Extracts from His Excellency's visit, Biharamulo district 15-17 February 1950

9. Bugufi and NGOMAT

9.1: Bugufi

Throughout British colonial rule it was stressed that production of cash crops was one of the colonial authority's self-sufficiency policies in Tanganyika. The self-sufficiency policy was emphasised to ensure that each colony covered administration costs with limited dependence on the United Kingdom Treasury.[1] In this regard, self-sufficiency was achieved through two important interrelated policies.[2] First, the development and increase in agricultural production for export. Second, encouragement of small-scale growers in cash crop cultivation to provide growers with opportunities for income.

Implementation of the self-sufficiency policy was evident in Bugufi where coffee farming among small-scale native growers, just as in many other parts of the country, was widely encouraged. Coffee farming in Bugufi, in the north-west of the territory then part of Biharamulo district, but now in Ngara district, was also geared towards utilisation of labour, and use of coffee farming and management expertise within the district. This was meant to curb labour migration to Bukoba or even Uganda where people worked on coffee farms to generate money to pay hut tax.[3]

The promotion of the coffee industry in Bugufi came after preliminary research conducted in 1925 by A.H. Savile, Biharamulo District Agricultural Officer. The research established the suitability of land and climate for coffee, and recommended establishing coffee nurseries, mainly for Robusta but including Arabica, in Bugufi, following which the Department of Agriculture established coffee nurseries in villages such as Nyamihanga, Mukiboye, Mwivuza and Mukigoye in 1925. As a result, 2,000 Arabica coffee seedlings were, from 1926, distributed to small-scale native growers by A. Young who was the agricultural extension officer. When he was transferred in 1934, F.H. Brett took over in 1935. Later, training for coffee management was provided; with those trained becoming local instructors.[4] This increased the availability of extension services in the district.

---

[1] TNA 26054, Extract from minutes of meeting of the Directors of Agriculture for East African countries (Kenya, Tanganyika and Uganda, held in Nairobi on 12 June 1946; Frank, The formation of British Colonial Development Policy, p. 16

[2] Melville J. Herskovits, *The Human Factor in Changing Africa* (New York: Alfred A. Knopf, 1952) p. 219; Michael Havinden & David Meredith, *Colonialsm & development: Britain and its tropical colonies* (London: Routledge, 1996) pp. 299-301

[3] A.H. Savile, District Agricultural Officer, 6 September 1929, Biharamulo District Book

[4] Extract from A Report By District Agricultural Officer (Savile), 6 September 1929, Biharamulo District Book

A census of coffee farmers conducted in March 1929 showed that coffee in Bugufi was being cultivated in fourteen out of fifteen villages where there was a total of 1,000 and 2,000 Arabica and Robusta[1] trees respectively. During the 1930s, more seedlings were distributed to growers. For example, 6,000 were made available to 400 growers. This went hand in hand with the deployment of an Agricultural Assistant in 1930 who introduced coffee seedling nurseries that had 270,000 seedlings which when matured were transplanted by growers in 47 villages. By 1931, 50 per cent of all adults who were eligible to pay taxes in Bugufi were producing coffee. Such success was followed by recruitment of agriculture instructors who were pivotal in providing guidance to coffee growers.[2] This was a success of the colonial policy and commitment in promoting the industry throughout the 1930s and early 1950s as shown in Table 26 below.

Table 26: Coffee production (tons) in Ngara, 1936/37 to 1950/51 seasons

1936/7	1937/38	1938/39	1939/40	1940/41	1942/43	1943/44
34	66	36	51	86	222	55

1944/45	1945/46	1946/47	1947/48	1948/49	1949/50	1950/51
201	142	132	59	59	78	228

Source: Registrar of Co-operative Societies, Ngara; TNA, 23752, The Bugufi Coffee Co-operative Society Inspection Notes, Co-op.28/B/BM 17 August 1951

In 1935, the Bugufi Coffee Co-operative Society was established. The society was registered in 1936[3] with registration number 28, with five coffee handling posts established in a number of villages.[4] Coffee marketing in Bugufi was guided under Section 36 of the 1932 Co-operative Legislation and Section 15 of the Native Authority Ordinance to ensure that all coffee produced in Bugufi was marketed through a society. Such coffee marketing compulsion was to ensure that the produce was not smuggled to the neighbouring Belgian colonies of Burundi and Rwanda.[5] In 1959, the Coffee Society was transformed into a co-operative union.[6] The Colonial Development Fund made available £3,000 at 3.5 per cent interest per annum to facilitate the formation of Bugufi.[7] This loan was used as capital

---

[1] Arabica coffee was introduced by Bugufi natives who brought seeds/seedlings from Uganda and Bukoba where they served as coffee farm migrant labourers (*bashuti*).

[2] TNA 23556, Memorandum by Agricultural Assistant on Native Coffee Development in Bugufi, Biharamulo, Bugufi Coffee Society: Question Connected with

[3] TNA 37192, Tanganyika Government, *Report on Co-operative Development* (Dar es Salaam: Government Printer, 1947) Appendix 1-6

[4] TNA 23556, Government General Notice, 19 October 1936

[5] TNA 23556, PC Lake Province to CS, Ref. 1257/326, 29 July 1936

[6] Seimu, The Growth and Development of the Coffee and Cotton Marketing Co-operatives in Tanzania; Somo ML Seimu, Politics and Politicisation of the Tanzania's Agricultural Marketing Co-operatives, *European Journal of Business and Management*, www.iiste.org vol. 7, no. 25 (2015)

for purchase of coffee, storage facilities and housing for managers.

Under the coffee marketing compulsion, growers were compelled to join the Bugufi Coffee Co-operative Society through coffee handling posts that were set up in five locations of which their number and respective villages are shown in Table 27. By 1944 it had 6,000 members.[1]

Table 27: Coffee Buying Posts and Production (tons) in Bugufi

Buying posts	Villages	Number of Members	Production (tons)
Mukarahe	Mukubogoye	667	80
	Mukarahe		
	Kamasi		
	Murugurama	54	
Mususenga	Mubuhororo	222	63
	Kabalenzi	346	
	Muheza	294	
	Kibubwe	53	
	Murugurana	151	
	Mukasenyi	143	
	Muruvigira	79	
	Narukinginye	78	
	Ntarentare	41	
	Kanazi	44	
Ngudusi	Mabare	230	90
	Ngudusi	233	
	Mukufigiri	167	
	Mabawe	160	
	Kabanga	85	
	Mukitamu	81	
	Murukukumbo	71	
	Kichacha	65	
	Ibuga	55	
	Mzaza	53	
	Mwivusa	1,013	6

Source: TNA 23556, Secretary (KD Semugaruka) Bugufi, Biharamulo, Bugufi Coffee Society to PC Lake Province, 19 October 1936, Appendix D and F

9.2: NGOMAT

Growers in many parts of the country produced tobacco. Production of the crop was partly for domestic use and was processed in the form of a roll for sale and barter in parts of the country where tobacco could not grow and for export to Somaliland amongst other places.[2] The industry in Songea district in then Southern Province, located in the south-west of the

---

[7] TNA 22919, Minute from Northcote to CS, 6 May 1935

[1] TNA 37192, Northcote to Rheinallt Jones, Director of South African Institute of Race Relations, Ref. Co-op/1058/17, 11 December 1944

[2] TNA 28978, PC Southern Province (Lindi) to CS, Ref. 15/28/109, 3 November 1947

territory started in 1928. The tobacco crop was first experimented with by A.S. Stenhouse, then District Agricultural Officer in Songea. The officer produced and made tobacco seed available to village headmen[1] who prepared seedbeds in which they planted seeds and seedlings for distribution to growers. This was part of Britain's efforts to ensure tobacco was produced within its colonies to replace at least a portion of the large quantities of leaf imported annually from the United States of America and elsewhere.

The industry reached commercial/economic scale and kept expanding year after year owing to intervention by the Agricultural Department as shown in Table 28. However, there was a decrease in production in some years. This was attributed to two factors: lack of guidance and supervision through frequent changes of staff responsible for providing extension services to growers; as well as falls in commodity prices that demoralised growers from expanding tobacco farming. However, Songea district was a leading tobacco producer, which for example in 1939 had 7,000 growers farming the crop who produced 400 pounds per acre.[2]

Table 28: Tobacco production in Songea district

Year	lbs
1930	1,660
1936	265,678
1937	393,063
1938	848,819
1939	1,121,087
1943	1,260,000
1944	428,000
1945	398,000
1946	716,000
1947	480,000
1948 (estimated)	800,000

Source: TNA 118, Director of Agriculture, Tanganyika Territory, 1947

In 1930, growers produced 830 kilogrammes of tobacco, which were bought from growers. In 1936, they produced 5,009,585 kilogrammes that fetched £14,500.[3] At an early stage, the Department of Agriculture took responsibility in helping with marketing. Regardless of the CS's reluctance, some agricultural marketing co-operative societies were promoted and registered in some pockets outside Moshi district. The role of the Department of Agriculture was taken over by co-operatives with effect from 1936 when the Ngoni Matengo Co-operative Union (NGOMAT)[4] and its three

---

[1] TNA 11828, DA to CS, Ref. no. 635/4600, 20 May 1929 – Tobacco Industry
[2] TNA 28978, Ref. 15/28/109, 3 November 1947
[3] TNA 28978, Extract from Memorandum of Songea the Executive Council
[4] TNA 37192, Northcote to Rheinallt Jones, Director of South African Institute of Race Relations, Ref. Co-op/1058/17, 11 December 1944

societies were registered in 1936. Its affiliated societies increased to thirteen registered by 1936, which had 6,640 members,[1] and by November 1939 NGOMAT had 6,721 members.[2]

Table 29: Co-operatives, members, Tobacco produce and payments

Primary Co-operative Society	Members	Production (in tons)	Payment
Liula	438	36270	2,540.60
Litola	377	28432.5	2,052.10
Msindo	354	32461	2164.00
Matogoro	263	10414	675.35
Mbinga	170	5200	5,147.35
Lumecha	163	12241.5	531.00
Gumbiro	122	8178	531.40
Lipumba	116	4347	218.90
Ndirima	92	2974	185.95
Likuyu	81	2633	168.85
Namtumbo	65	5671	441.80
Mlali	44	851	55.30

Source: TNA 155, Co-op/27/1, NGOMAT, Report on Tobacco Industry & Ngoni-Matengo Co-operative Union

The formation and registration of the NGOMAT and its affiliated societies was not a defiance against the CS position. The promotion of co-operative societies was partly implementation of the colonial self-sufficiency policy through which colonial officials met their obligation in encouraging cash crop production and ensuring supply of agricultural raw materials. These initiatives enjoyed support from Britain, both political and financial. In this regard, Britain financed £2,000 for promoting societies. However, funding obtained was a loan from the Colonial Development Fund which carrried a 3.5 per cent interest rate per annum, which was calculated to be paid by 1940.[3]

The Colonial Development Fund committed to a loan as motivation for small-scale growers to produce tobacco and provide them with a marketing facility for their produce. The loan was important to facilitate growers to contribute to the colony in realising financial self-sufficiency; importantly, through the supply of cheap native-produced tobacco to Britain.

The colonial authority's role through the Department of Agriculture was further reinforced following the outbreak of the Second World War. The colonial authority's intervention in handling tobacco in Songea was provided for under the war's Defence Ordinance and Orders of 1939 and 1940.

---

[1] TNA 37192, Tanganyika Government, *Report on Co-operative Development*, Appendix 1-6
[2] TNA 5/243, Report to the League of Nations on Tanganyika Territory, 1939
[3] Ibid.

As a result, in 1940 in Songea district, the Native Tobacco Board was set up under Tobacco (Control & Marketing) Ordinance 39 of 1940. R.C. Northcote, Registrar of Co-operative Societies, was appointed as the Board chairperson.[1] Under Defence Ordinance and Orders as well as Tobacco (Control & Marketing) Ordinance legislation, the government's control over the tobacco industry in the district was reinforced.

Similarly, the co-operatives and producers were placed under direct government control. The Songea Native Tobacco Control Board appointed NGOMAT and its affiliated co-operative societies as its handling agents. Consequently, the co-operative societies were granted a monopoly over the handling of small-scale produced tobacco. However, the Order created a vertical crop marketing relationship structure over which the marketing boards, statutory bodies, had exclusive control. The board had the upper hand in deciding and controlling the tobacco price, and control over the export coffee trade. It was granted exclusive power of the industry where co-operative societies were ranked at the bottom only to handle the crop from members/growers on behalf of the board.

This seemingly was a significant step in blending and possibly camouflaging the co-operatives' interest in the board and, surely, demonstrates commitment of the government in exploiting co-operatives for its own interests. Having the Registrar of Co-operative Societies, Northcote, as the board chairperson was an attempt to inculcate a sense of trust among the members or growers towards co-operatives as well as to the board. Such a step was also evidence of the colonial authority attempting to evade a similar crisis to that experienced in Kilimanjaro in 1937, when coffee growers revolted against the Chagga Rule, imposed on native growers in a move to control the industry. Yet, the Tobacco (Control & Marketing) Ordinance provided the colonial authority with entrenched influence and stripped away members' control over a crop they sweated to produce.

Another significant impact was the introduction of the first dark fire-cured tobacco processing factory in Tanzania, in 1936. The factory was established by NGOMAT as a response to the growing demands of the tobacco industry in Ruvuma Region. The need for processing the crop emerged from the broader strategy of improving the value of raw tobacco grown by African farmers. At first the union installed a manual processing plant in Mahenge area in Songea town, which processed all tobacco grown in the Ruvuma Region. However, increased production by African growers resulted in the need to build a modern, technologically superior and larger plant. Consequently, the factory was relocated from Mahenge to its present position, the Songea industrial area. This was due to the need for a new and larger plant house. The task was started in 1948 and completed in 1952.

---

[1] TNA 28978, Extract from Memorandum of Songea Executive Council

10. Failed Attempts

10.1: Western Cotton Growing Area (WCGA)

Attempts to form cotton marketing co-operatives in the Western Cotton Growing Area (WCGA) began in May 1932 with Chief Mgemela of Bakwimba in Kwimba district.[1] His request came at a time of economic recession, when growers' income was seriously affected by the falling price of cotton. For him, co-operatives offered a solution to the problem. Chief Mgemela envisaged that co-operatives would improve their income;[2] and to facilitate building a hospital in his chiefdom because the government was unable to raise £2,000 for its construction.[3] This was a critical period for most sectors in Tanganyika. For example, during the period, particularly, from 1930 to 1934 the colonial authority reduced financial assistance by 45 per cent and the government reduced assistance to mission schools, a very important part of the colonial system, which cut its own education staff by 40 per cent.

However, the attempt to promote co-operatives in Kwimba was unsuccessful, mainly because the co-operative legislation was yet to be approved. Further, the DC of Kwimba informed his chief that it was not necessary to have a co-operative society, as the Native Treasury No. 2 Accounts had effectively been playing the same role.[4] This suggests that by having both in operation was duplication of resources. The matter was forwarded to the senior colonial officials, mainly the CS who also rejected it on grounds that:

> as you are aware, owing to absence of trained staff, this government is at present not in a position to give assistance or encouragement to the development of co-operative societies. However, there are some natives who are capable of managing societies, but it is not possible to contemplate the immediate registration of co-operative societies in either Kwimba or anywhere else with the exception of the KNPA owing to peculiar circumstances.[5]

Apart from Chief Mgemela's failed attempt, the British Cotton Growing

---

[1] TNA 20999, Economic Development: Agriculture Production in the Colonies Extracts from meeting between P.M. Huggis, DO of Kwimba & Chief Mgemela, 20 May 1932; Iliffe, *A modern history of Tanganyika* (1979) p. 295

[2] TNA 20999, Extracts from meeting between P.M. Huggis, DO of Kwimba & Chief Mgemela held on 20 May 1932

[3] TNA 20999, DC, Kwimba to PC Lake Province, Ref. 2/15/16/2, 30 May 1932, DC to PC, Ref. 2/15/16/6, 12 August 1932

[4] TNA 20999, Extracts from meeting between Huggis, DO of Kwimba & Chief Mgemela

[5] TNA 20999, CS to PC, Lake Province, Ref. 2099/15, 19 July 1932

Association (BCGA) in the Western Cotton Growing Area (WCGA) attempted in the early 1930s to convince the colonial authority of increasing interest among natives in cotton marketing co-operatives and entry into cotton ginning.[1] The idea was however, rejected by the colonial authority because the 'time to accommodate them (co-operatives) was not ripe'.[2] Overall, the government was reluctant too. For example, the CS stated that 'as you are aware, owing to the absence of staff', he regrettably indicated, 'this government is at present not in a position to give assistance or encourage co-operative societies'. He justified the decision by arguing that 'in any case there is no sufficient number of natives capable of managing such societies and complying with the requirements of the law'.[3]

He declined the proposal stressing that 'it is not therefore, possible to contemplate the immediate registration of co-operative societies in Kwimba or anywhere else with exception of the KNPA due to peculiar circumstances'.[4] The rejection of both Chief Mgemela and the BCGA attempts by the colonial authority is clear evidence that there was an unsupportive environment for the growth and development of co-operatives in the WCGA.

Failure to promote cotton-marketing co-operatives in the WCGA in the early 1930s was further frustrated by the Indian merchants in Tanganyika and Uganda who had an upper hand in marketing cotton. This was prompted by the existing policies and memorandum of understanding between the Tanganyika and Uganda colonial authorities to overcome the transport challenges: shipping commodities from WCGA to Tanganyika's harbours. Because goods went through Uganda, the Uganda colonial government was dictating the cotton marketing policy mandate in the WCGA.

Against this backdrop, Indian merchants in Uganda opposed a co-operative societies' bill, which was presented to the LEGCO by the Ugandan colonial government in 1935. By then Uganda's Asians, who dominated agricultural commodities, were reputedly in control of 90 per cent of the country's trade.[5] In this regard, opposition to the co-operative bill was essentially to protect their interests. However, the colonial government in Uganda worked tirelessly to have the bill presented to the LEGCO. In 1938 when the bill was presented for the second time, it was emphasised that promotion of co-operatives was integral for development of a cash crop industry among small-scale growers. As in 1935, the bill was rejected.[6]

---

[1] TNA 21032, A.A. Wills to Secretary for Native Affairs, 12 July 1932
[2] TNA 21032, Secretary for Native Affairs to Wills, Ref. 21032/3, 24 July 1932
[3] TNA 20999, CS to PC, Ref. 20999/15, 19 July 1932
[4] Ibid.
[5] Hailey, *An Africa Survey*, p. 402
[6] Horrace Plunkent Foundation, *Year Book of Agricultural Co-operative* (London: Basil Blackwell, 1949) p. 315

Rejection of the co-operative Ordinance in Uganda had direct negative implications for the growth of co-operatives in the WCGA. Additionally, the merchants from Uganda had a strong influence and dictated marketing policies in the WCGA. Against this backdrop, the cotton merchants from Uganda exerted pressure on the colonial authority in Tanganyika where the merchants opposed development of the co-operative movement through their forums, mainly annual general meetings.

The merchants in Tanganyika called upon the government to abandon its commitments to promote agricultural marketing co-operatives because it was too early to promote them; promoting them implied participation of the colonial authority in commerce and the natives were not capable of handling cotton marketing.[1] It must be noted that the question was not about the inability of natives or experiences that the Indian traders had. Promotion of co-operatives was a suicidal threat to their businesses and livelihoods, which is why they strongly discouraged them.

The merchants' power, influence and monopoly over cotton marketing was further entrenched following the outbreak of the Second World War which created more difficulties around promoting co-operatives in the WCGA. Cotton marketing during the war was handled by the East African Exporters Group under bulk purchase contracts in which merchants from Uganda were assigned a role provided for under the Defence (Control of Cotton) Regulation of 1939,[2] 1942 and 1943.[3] This was legislation and policy regarding marketing that was primarily geared to suit colonial power interventions and control over all cotton produced in East Africa. Also, the policy was meant to ensure that all cotton produced in the WCGA was bought from the growers.[4] These developments demonstrate that growers had no stake in the marketing of their produce and any attempt to promote the co-operatives was rendered impossible.

10.2: Southern Highlands

Coffee farming expansion among small-scale growers in the Southern Highlands was so impressive that it drew the attention of the provincial administration to promote coffee marketing co-operatives. In a move to convince the CS, the Provincial Commissioner for the South West Highlands Province (PCSH) argued that a local organisation of the natives of

---

[1] TNA 35783, W.H. Campbell, Report on a visit to East Africa, Kenya, Tanganyika and Uganda (July 1944); Okoro Okereke, *The Economic Impact of Uganda Co-operatives* (East Africa Literature Bureau, 1974) p. 20

[2] TNA 34953, Government Notice 325

[3] TNA 34953, DA to CS, Ref. 100/43, 25 March 1943, Cotton Control and Marketing during Wartime

[4] TNA 34953, Defence Regulation (Control of Cotton) Order, 1943; TNA 34953, vol. II Extracts from meeting of the Cotton Board, held in Dar es Salaam, 4 May 1944

Rungwe and Mbozi for the handling and disposal of their coffee crop was essential, and 'I consider that such an organisation should be constituted into groups of Rungwe and Mbozi natives capable of being affiliated to the co-operative union'.[1]

To facilitate coffee marketing, growers were clustered in nine groups in Rungwe and Mbozi: Undali, Kiwira, Masebe, Masoko, Manow,[2] along with rice-marketing groups in Selya, Mbozi, Mwakaleli East and Mwakaleli West.

To further facilitate coffee marketing, the South West Highlands PC applied to the Colonial Development Fund for a grant amounting to £5,660. The grant was to be spent promoting co-operative coffee marketing societies in his province, particularly in Mbozi and Rungwe.[3] The PC argued that there seemed to be no other method of acquiring the necessary capital other than by a grant or loan from the Colonial Development Fund.[4] 'There can be little doubt that such a grant would confer a great benefit to the co-operatives since it would ensure the future economic prosperity of the natives and would stimulate trade in general by increasing their spending power'. Moreover, if funds were granted for the formation of co-operative societies, 'eventually it might be found advantageous to handle and market such other crops as maize, rice and beans for which at the moment there is so great a local demand'.[5]

The provincial and district officials as well as the NA were highly motivated and well prepared to ensure co-operatives were a success. The commitment to achieve this was not only moral but also financial, whereby the NA made available £2,600 for Mbozi and £3,377 for Rungwe to provide storage facilities and equipment for planned co-operative societies. Despite unveiled financial commitment by the provincial, district officials and NA, the CO was not prepared to provide the grant requested, and stated categorically that it had no money to provide as a grant; but it had some that could be provided as a loan.[6]

Meanwhile, the DA stressed that the KNCU did not receive any financial assistance. Obviously, the DA was committed to ensure that the province managed to implement its activities without external financial support. In this, the provincial and district officials had to ensure they generated funds locally that would facilitate promotion of co-operatives for Rungwe and Mbozi. By then marketing groups in the province earmarked nine natives for transformation. Against this backdrop, it was viewed by the DA, in

---

[1] TNA 22983, PC, Southern Province to CS, Ref. 2/10A/226
[2] Rungwe District Book, 1935
[3] TNA 22983, PC, South West Highlands to CS, Ref. 2/44/66, 20 March 1936
[4] TNA 22983, PC, Southern Province to CS, Ref. 47/17/69, 18 February 1946
[5] TNA 22983 , PC, Southern Province to CS, Ref. 2/10A/226
[6] TNA, 22983 CS to PC, South West Highlands, Ref. 22983, 31 August 1937

principle, a significant step in inculcating self-help initiatives, that demonstrated direction towards building a true principle for co-operative societies. Also, rejection of the loan application by the British colonial power in London was part of its economic and financial self-sufficiency policy that emphasised each colony cover its own administration costs to avoid draining the United Kingdom Treasury.[1]

At the same time, an attempt was made by colonial officials in the province interested in promoting marketing co-operatives for rice produced by natives in Kyela.[2] The rejection of a loan from the Colonial Development Fund for this purpose did not discourage the colonial officials who decided to create a Suspense Account provided for under the Native Authority to facilitate rice handling.

10.3: Kagera Region

The British colonial authority promoted coffee cultivation among small-scale native growers through Denis Lynch Baines[3] who was the first British Administrator when the area came under British rule in 1916 following the defeat of the Germans during World War I.[4] Motivation for encouraging small-scale growers remained the same as in other cash crop producing areas in Tanganyika, such as coffee farming in Kilimanjaro, which was to attain territorial financial self-sufficiency.

Immediately when the British took over the colonial authority in Tanganyika, it invited merchants to the region to buy coffee grown by natives. The policy attracted coffee merchants mostly from Mombasa in Kenya and Uganda. This was prompted by existing policies and a memorandum of understanding between Tanganyikan and Ugandan colonial authorities on handling the crop. The involvement of Uganda was geographic, to ease transport challenges from the region to Tanganyika's Tanga and Dar es Salaam harbours for export. Uganda provided reliable water transport for export of coffee from the region through Lake Victoria to either Kampala or Kisumu in Kenya then by rail to Mombasa.

Thus, the Tanganyikan colonial government had to adopt mechanisms and policies to handle crop marketing in remote locations. To address such challenges the Tanganyikan colonial government was forced to accept the Ugandan colonial government dictating marketing policy for coffee produced in the region. Therefore, Ugandan colonial government involvement had an effect on the growth and development of co-operative movements in the region. In addition, protests by Indian traders against promoting

---

[1] TNA 26054, Extract from minutes of meeting of the Directors of Agriculture for East African countries (Kenya, Tanganyika and Uganda, held in Nairobi on 12 June 1946
[2] TNA 22983, PC, Southern Province to CS, Ref. 2/10A/226
[3] Baines was Bukoba DC from 1916 to 1919 and October 1920 to February 1923.
[4] Bukoba District Book

coffee co-operative societies in Tanzania in the 1930s and rejection of the co-operative bill in the Ugandan LEGCO in 1935 and 1938 had far-reaching effects in the region.

By the mid-1930s, the only coffee marketing co-operative society registered in the region was Bugufi. However, Bugufi was by then in Biharamulo district that was in the Lake Province. In this respect, most of Kagera Region had no registered co-operative society. This was unlike in Kilimanjaro with coffee marketing, and tobacco marketing in Ruvuma, where promotion of cash crops began at the same time with self-sufficiency one of the motivations behind encouraging co-operative societies.

Encouraging traders to purchase coffee from growers in Kagera Region met several challenges. For example, there was laxity in control as there was no legal institution empowered for quality assurance. Neither Tanganyika nor Uganda deployed staff charged with such responsibility. As a result, coffee marketing was marred by an intense struggle among traders, which compromised coffee quality. Moreover, the growers were marketing low-quality coffee beans which buyers did not reject. Growers were processing coffee beans using wooden mortar or huller (*kinu*) and rock outcrop which resulted in 50 per cent of the entire crop being damaged.[1] In addition, growers were convinced by traders to mortgage their produce before harvesting. Under such circumstance, growers or traders were determining prices by assessment of what was on the farm. In most instances it was undervalued, hence payment was low. As a result, cheating was widespread and sporadic marketing was common.

The colonial authority at district and provincial levels were concerned over the difficulties and challenges. In response, Northcote was invited to investigate and recommend appropriate measures. In his report, Northcote pointed out that 'it is evident that the marketing of coffee in Bukoba is not in accordance with modern standards' and it was in far worse condition where barter trade was dominant.[2] Moreover, Indian traders illegally bought coffee in Kagera at night. Most traders were operating *dukas* (retail shops) that led to competition so that crop quality was compromised.[3] He also established that coffee marketing was under the control of big coffee exporters based in Bukoba town, either as principal buyers, as major exporters or acting as company branch managers or agents of big merchants and companies based in Mombasa where coffee was auctioned.[4]

Northcote recommended the establishment of central marketing and

[1] TNA 24545, Northcote Report on Bukoba Coffee Marketing, p. 18
[2] Tanganyika Territory, *Annual Reports on Co-operative Development* (1948)
[3] TNA 24545, Northcote 1936 Inquiry Report on Bukoba Coffee Industry, *Report on Bukoba Coffee Marketing*
[4] TNA 23752, Report on Reorganisation of the Bukoba Native Coffee Industry, 31 March 1949

buying posts, pointing out that for 'any improved marketing, it seems fundamentally necessary for the grower to sell coffee to a central depot or collecting station'.[1] This was meant to change the prevailing market system whereby traders collected coffee directly from growers. Second, it was stressed that licences for coffee buying be introduced which would eliminate and control itinerant traders.[2]

Northcote took the view that co-operatives undoubtedly would be the easiest form for Africans to understand and were more adapted to his financing and organisation capabilities. He argued that 'the first step towards improvement in marketing should be by small co-operative power hulieries in order to improve coffee quality which would secure a better price'. These co-operatives were, according to Northcote to serve growers at family or household level. This suggests that co-operatives were mainly envisaged as family enterprises, focusing specifically on hulling to improve the quality of coffee. For him, hulling co-operatives were envisaged not only to process coffee, but also to facilitate collection of the produce for marketing which they could then develop into a district co-operative union for bulk coffee handling.[3] This approach was likely to reinforce the existing division of activities between coffee traders and merchants who concentrated on marketing and natives who focused on cultivation and processing.

In the region, there was one, unregistered, native owned organisation, the Native Growers Association (NGA) at Kamachumu, which was engaged in handling, bulking, grading and pooling coffee crop from a limited number of growers in a similar way to the KNPA in Kilimanjaro. The NGA was under the leadership of Herbert Rugazibwa, President, and Clemens Kiiza as Secretary.

During his investigation, Northcote had discussions with the NGA leaders. It was established that the NGA had 970 members who produced and marketed an average of 360 pounds or 156 tons of coffee per annum.[4] Such records indicate that the members were coffee producers who were interested in selling their produce in bulk. These members were from all eight chiefdoms.[5] In Kianja there were 186 members, Ihangiro had 111, and Kiziba had 524, while in Kiamtwara, 93 in Kinyangereko, 29 in Bugabo and 27 members were from two other chiefdoms. Having members from all chiefdoms in Kagera region demonstrates that the association had affiliations, regardless of how small, across the regions.

---

[1] TNA 24545, Northcote 1936 Inquiry Report on Bukoba Coffee Industry
[2] Ibid.
[3] Ibid.
[4] TNA 23752, PC Lake Province to CS, Ref. 976/233 6 July 1936; TNA 41011, PC Lake Province to CS, Ref. 9756/233, 6 July 1936
[5] TNA 24545, Northcote 1936 Inquiry Report on Bukoba Coffee Industry

The NGA through members' contributions imported a hulling plant for coffee processing, which was installed in Mbatama village[1] in Ihangiro chiefdom on invitation of Chief Ruhinda. However, its license was withdrawn by the government in 1939 due to its involvement in protesting against coffee rules passed by the colonial authority in 1937.[2] The NGA's Mbatama curing factory license was transferred to Habibu Rajan on 19 December 1945. The transfer included machinery and the land or plot where the factory was located.[3] However, Habibu Rajan was not appointed a zonal agent to handle coffee in Bukoba.[4] This demonstrates that the colonial officials and administrators were solely concerned with maintaining peace and the status quo.

In his report, Northcote appeared to be impressed with the NGA's business potentials. In this regard, he recommended reorganisation of the NGA. He envisaged that the NGA could provide a solution to some challenges facing the coffee industry in the region. For example, the NGA could check unscrupulous buyers by having it operate as a co-operative society. Northcote was aware of other difficulties such as limited membership and prospects of having more growers joining the NGA. For him, growers could be encouraged through propaganda, but this would not happen overnight. He estimated that two years or more was essential to stimulate interest among potential members.[5]

While Northcote viewed the NGA as a prospective organisation there were a few obstacles against his idea or proposal. First, at the time, there was no department, funds or staff in the country to facilitate the propaganda. Second, the proposal was vehemently opposed by various government officials at provincial and territorial levels. They were of the view that the livelihoods of numerous stakeholders, such as Arab and Indian traders, would be threatened thus leading to the eruption of riots.[6] Pressure from Asian coffee traders forced the PC to become more sceptical about promoting the NGA as it feared Asian traders would resist, eventually creating political and racial tension in Kagera that would threaten the stability of the colonial authority.[7] Therefore, promoting or registering spontaneous grower organisations like the NGA was ruled out.[8]

The Northcote report attracted attention from various government

---

[1] TNA 38526, Acting DA (Wakefield) to PC, 10 June 1936; TNA 24545, Report on Bukoba Coffee Marketing, p. 9
[2] TNA 24545, PC Lake Province to CS. Ref. 14/0/80, 22 December 1937
[3] TNA 38526, DA to E.C. Phillips of British American Tobacco, Ref. 676/9318
[4] TNA 38526, DA to members of agricultural & natural resources, Conf., March 1951
[5] TNA 25777/1, Minute to the Lake Province PC by Northcote, 18 May 1936
[6] TNA 24545, DA to CS Ref no. Confidential 1/29/36, 28 November 1936
[7] Ibid.
[8] TNA 24545, PC Lake Province to CS, Ref. 14/0/80, 22 December 1937

officials at territorial levels who also vehemently opposed it. For example, the Director of Agriculture (DA) commented that 'I cannot recommend a drastic change in dealing with Bukoba coffee, the co-operative scheme is not important but where necessary has to be implemented slowly and grow as a result of its value on the industry'. It was his opinion that 'co-operative societies are not desirable'; and envisaged that out of such existing groups a co-operative spirit and attitude would develop and spread.

The DA further ruled out encouraging co-operatives by pointing out that 'a family can own a huller and sell their processed coffee to buyers'.[1] He maintained that efforts should entirely be focused on such groups. Also cultivation improvement to raise the quality of output was where native growers could benefit most, and therefore, the necessity for co-operative societies and organised marketing was not of primary importance. The DA's view clearly demonstrated that the colonial authority opposed any attempt for developing the co-operative movement. Their preference was maintaining the status quo regardless of the prevailing chaotic marketing system. Coffee quality was their priority by encouraging family hulling. This illustrates that the desire was to ensure that growers were not organised outside of the family unit. This again, was evidence that Northcote's recommendation was virtually sent to the litterbin.

The NGA leaders, President Herbert Rugazibwa and Secretary Clemens Kiiza, were the local Tanganyika African Association's (TAA) committee members. Despite its affiliation to TAA, there was separation of function, for example the NGA was predominantly engaged in coffee marketing whereas TAA was occupied with the welfare of civil servants and those employed in private sectors.

The colonial authority took the NGA membership as grounds to reject it, as 'it would be a fallacy to regard it as marketing organisation. It has done little and had no substantial experience in marketing'.[2] They emphasised further that the NGA had no business potential or credibility. This conclusion was based on evidence that it marketed only 11 tons in 1934, six tons in 1935 and none in 1936. Thus, it was concluded that it had no prospect for becoming a successful marketing organisation.[3]

The provincial officials did not see the co-operative scheme as important. This was partly due to pressure from coffee merchants in the country, mainly members of the Chamber of Commerce who were on a number of occasions invited by the colonial authority to discuss issues related to crop marketing in various places around the country.[4] They successfully utilised

---

[1] TNA 24545, DA to CS, Ref Confidential 1/29/36, 28 November 1936
[2] TNA 25777/1, Confidential Report on Bukoba Coffee Marketing
[3] Ibid.
[4] TNA 25777, DA to CS, Ref 25777/6, 14 May 1938

such fora and many others to influence the colonial authority to disregard promotion of co-operative marketing societies in the region.[1] For example, opposition was aired during their conferences held in Tabora and Dodoma in 1935. Here they stressed that 'encouragement of co-operatives will create artificial barriers against free trade'. This was the case in Kilimanjaro when having registered the KNPA and later KNCU, the WaChagga were granted a coffee marketing monopoly provided for under the 1934 Chagga Rule and 1937 native coffee control and marketing legislation.

By 1938, the Lake Province PC, C. MacMahon, remained unmoved regarding promotion of marketing co-operatives. He argued against establishing marketing co-operatives 'even if [they] were shown to be desirable on economic grounds'. To him, so long as there were traders buying coffee from growers, marketing co-operatives were irrelevant. He insisted that it was not necessary and considered 'it would be politically unwise to eliminate the present licensed buyers who are too ready to provide the service'.[2]

MacMahon, was suspicious of the NGA's involvement in politics, but was optimistic that if subjected to supervision the NGA would be more effective at marketing than traders.[3] He, therefore, urged support for the NGA for economic and political reasons, as 'any efforts to guide the Association at infancy stage will be of great assistance not only to the coffee industry, but will also enable us (colonial authority) to restore confidence between the chiefs (NA) and many other educated WaHaya who have lost confidence in their NAs'.[4] This suggests that the colonial authority was anxious to learn from its experiences in Kilimanjaro, where the KNPA had challenged the chiefs and the colonial authority.

The PC for Lake Province warned that the chiefs and NA would regard the NGA as a new centre of political power if it was registered for coffee marketing. He reassured the CS that the NGA would automatically vanish when its members joined newly formed co-operatives.[5] The PC argued that the co-operatives should be formed as hulling groups that would gradually grow into larger societies, but he emphasised that private buyers should remain the only outlet for coffee marketing.[6]

---

[1] TNA 19005, Extracts from Resolutions the Chamber of Commerce Conference held in Tabora during 1935 Easter
[2] TNA 25777, PC, Lake Province to CS, Ref. 24545/95, 18 May 1938
[3] TNA 41011, PC, Lake Province to CS, Ref. 9756/233, 6 July 1936, Organisation of Bukoba Coffee Marketing
[4] TNA 23752, PC Lake Province to CS, Ref. 976/233, 6 July 1936, Native Association Bukoba
[5] TNA 24545, PC, Lake Province to CS, Ref. 1110/80, 23 April 1937; TNA 24545 , PC Lake Province to CS, Ref. 14/0/80, 22 December 1937, Northcote 1936 Inquiry Report on Bukoba Coffee Industry
[6] TNA 24545, PC, Lake Province to CS, Ref. 110/80, 23 April 1937

The Lake Province PC argued further that 'promotion of co-operatives is nothing other than brewing unrest as has been the case with coffee riots in Kilimanjaro', by stressing that 'this would add to unrest in case growers are paid low prices for their produce'.[1] The policy was not only maintained at provincial level but also by senior colonial officials in a move to create business security in Kagera. One such official was the DA who, throughout the interwar period, maintained his position against promoting coffee marketing co-operatives. In so doing he kept on reassuring coffee traders in Kagera and those in Mombasa by stressing that 'they should remove any fear or misapprehension that their interests were endangered in the same way as in Kilimanjaro'.[2]

This chapter has examined policies and political decisions that provided impetus to the development of the co-operative movement in Tanzania. Some political decisions taken by colonial officials undermined the growth of the co-operatives resulting in their uneven distribution in the country. The post-war years saw an intensified policy and political manoeuvre that led to the expansion of the co-operative movement footprint in Tanzania as discussed in the following chapter.

---

[1] TNA 25777, PC, Lake Province to CS, Ref. 24545/95, 18 May 1938
[2] TNA 25777, DA to CS Ref 416/5921, 22 August 1938

11. Post-World War Two Crop Marketing

Immediately after the outbreak of the Second World War, the British government embarked upon measures to keep the supply of food and raw materials stable. In Britain, farmers were encouraged to produce more food, rationing was introduced to help maintain stocks, and price control was put in place to protect consumers from being exposed to profiteering.[1] The British economy became critical in 1942-3, when it began losing its Asian colonies to Japanese expansionism and occupation; the Suez Canal was almost captured by the enemy, jeopardising its trade route to India and its economic strategies were also under threat.

All these developments posed a critical threat through the loss of important sources of raw materials. Hence, government control and supervision of the economy increased to better organise production for sustaining war efforts. Tanganyika and the East African colonies of Kenya and Uganda were expected to contribute to the war effort by supplying food and raw materials. The Ministries of Food and Supply collaborated with the CO and colonial authorities on behalf of the colonial power.

Following the outbreak of World War II the colonial authority brought agricultural produce marketing in Tanganyika under its direct control.[2] The Ministry of Food declared coffee, produced in the British colonies, which accounted for fifty per cent of the entire supply to Britain, as essential commodity, and all colonies were required to ensure a steady supply of coffee to Britain.[3] The colonial authorities appointed agents to handle food and raw materials supply in the colonies.[4]

The colonial authority in Tanganyika had to adjust its marketing policies and so established the administrative machinery to provide for the supply of commodities under bulk purchase agreement. The success of these agreements in procuring and directing supplies, and in controlling prices were demonstrated under war conditions and the Minister of Food showed a commitment to continue importing commodities from Britain's colonies.

---

[1] United States Department of Agriculture (USDA), *United Kingdom Market for United States Agricultural Products Agriculture Information Bulletin no. 104* (Washington DC, USA Government Printing Office, 1953) p. 2

[2] TNA 2514 7, The Long Term Contracts Policy on the United Kingdom Departments and Colonial Agriculture Producer, *Standard Newspaper*, 28 September 1948

[3] TNA 28359/3, Ministry of Food to the British Empire Producer Organisation, Ref. CF/5, 26 September and 2 October 1939

[4] TNA 23218, Lord Listowel, *Commonwealth Future,* Fabian Tract 308 (London: Fabian Society, July 1957) p. 24

The native coffee industry in Tanganyika was included in the bulk-purchase scheme during the war. The bulk-purchase was characterised by short, medium or long-term contracts with marketing boards or co-operative societies required to supply the produce purchased for fixed quantities and prices. The produce was sold to the Ministry of Food, which had exclusive control over food and raw material imports in Britain. Under the legislation food and raw materials produced by Africans had to be compulsorily sold to the British Ministry of Food and Supplies through the recommended outlets, mainly marketing boards. Against this background, the food crop and raw material supplies were secured from the level of growers in the colonies to consumers in Britain.

Under Defence Ordinance and Orders of 1939 and 1940, the colonial authority had powers to appoint an agency to handle agricultural produce from growers in which co-operatives were a priority because, unlike private enterprises, they did not offer conflicting interests with those of the marketing board. The functions of the boards were therefore complementary to the work of agriculture marketing co-operatives. This resulted in intensified control of cash crop marketing by the marketing boards. Under this relationship, the colonial authority employed co-operatives as the principle tool for crop collection.

The colonial authority's role through the marketing board was further reinforced following the outbreak of the Second World War. In 1940 the Native Tobacco Board was set up in Songea district and Northcote, Registrar of Co-operative Societies, was appointed the board's chairperson.[1] Similarly, the co-operatives and producers were placed under direct government control. Ndomba suggests that the Songea Native Tobacco Board (SDNTB) was established in 1940 to take control of the tobacco industry in the Southern Province.[2] Ndomba posits further that since SDNTB was vested with legal power over the tobacco industry, the board restricted the growing influence of NGOMAT in the supervision and marketing of the tobacco industry in the region. This paper concurs with Ndomba in some aspects such as the dates that Songea Native Coffee Board was formed, but not over the circumstances that provided for the board formation. In this, the evidence shows that boards formed during and after World War II were created under the Emergency Order.

Boards like BNCB, Nyamirembe Native Tobacco Board and Songea Native Tobacco Board were formed under Emergency Orders provided for under Defence Ordinance and Orders of 1939 and 1940.[3] The latter

---

[1] TNA 28978, Extract from Memorandum of Songea the Executive Council

[2] Herbert Harald Ndomba, A History of Peasant Tobacco Production in Ruvuma Region, Southern Tanzania, c.1930-2016 (Unpublished PhD thesis, Stellenbosch University, 2018)

[3] TNA 25147, The Long-Term Contracts Policy on the United Kingdom Departments and

empowered the governor to set up boards primarily to facilitate supply of coffee and tobacco to the British Ministry of Supply. Under Section 6 of the Native Tobacco (Control & Marketing) Ordinance the Songea Native Tobacco Board was empowered to appoint NGOMAT as agent in handling the crop from its members, and all native growers in the region as provided for under Section 7 of the contract.[1] Consequently, the co-operative societies were granted a monopoly over the handling of small-scale produced tobacco.

11.1: Repeal of the Agricultural Control & Marketing Ordinance, 1937

The Agricultural Products (Control & Marketing) Ordinance of 1937 was repealed in 1949. The Ordinance was replaced by African Agricultural Products (Control & Marketing) Ordinance 1949 which had been drafted by the Registrar of Co-operative Societies[2] and passed into law by the LEGCO in 1949. Under Section 26 (1) and 28 the board members comprised representatives from producers' associations, the co-operative society, representatives from statutory boards, government nominees and the chairperson who was a government nominee.

The legislation was designed to foster and promote the co-operatives with assistance of the boards. The marketing boards were instituted largely as an interim measure pending the formation of producers' co-operatives, and definite steps were to be taken by boards to promote such societies starting at primary level.[3] It was stressed that existing societies should be the agents of the boards. This legislation took into consideration that co-operatives were unable to raise funds for the purchase of crops and erection of storage facilities thus, it made clear that short and long-term loans would be made available to societies with approval from co-operative officers.

The Ordinance clearly recognised and emphasised the existence of the co-operatives, which had to be accommodated in crop marketing. In Kilimanjaro, the Ordinance reinforced and justified the existence of the KNCU. It was envisaged that the co-operatives would take over as the board's sole agent.[4] This paved the way for the formation and setting up of co-operatives from 1950 in Kagera Region.

Colonial Agriculture Producer, *Standard Newspaper*, 28 September 1948

[1] TNA 37200, Contract on Local Arrangement for Handling of Ministry of Food Coffee, Director of East Africa Produce Disposal and Supply Council (Nairobi), 13 March 1947
[2] Tanganyika Government: *Annual Report on Co-operative Development* (Dar es Salaam: Government Printer, 1947) p. 6
[3] TNA 29585, Secretariat, Agriculture and National Resources, to Songea District Native Tobacco Board, MNCB and BNCB, Ref. 39121/37, December 1949
[4] TNA 41011, BNCB Annual Report 1953, p. 13

11.2: Relaxation of Agricultural Marketing Emergency Orders

Soon after World War II, there were demands for relaxation of the Emergency Order impacting trade controls. Most contracts with the Ministry of Food expired between 1950 and 1955. However, some countries dropped their formal arrangements to supply certain products, often because the United Kingdom could obtain supplies elsewhere at lower prices. Pressure from dominions and East African countries coincided with the newly elected Conservative government's decision to revoke the policy in 1951.

In general, the Conservative government aimed at expanding world trade, multilateralism, and adherence to the General Agreement on Trade and Tariffs (GATT), with no restrictions or discrimination in trade. Thus, bulk-purchase arrangements were brought to an end. Essentially, the Conservative Party had to comply with the GATT to dismantle the bulk purchase arrangements with the colonies which opened a door for private traders with no government interference. The effect was that colonial economies were exposed to the full blast of world price fluctuations. The decision by government in Britain appeared in a joint notice by East African countries (Kenya, Uganda and Tanganyika) on the removal of coffee from export control which stated that:

> The export control of coffee being considered necessary, but has to be removed from the schedule of the export control under Declaration of Export Controlled Goods 1951 Order made under the Government Notice no. 542/51.[1]

In Tanganyika, the members of Finance and Economics Committee exerted pressure on the colonial authority to dismantle marketing control policy in 1950. The members argued the invalidity of the policy which was no longer necessary during peace time,[2] and justified by the fact that most contracts were scheduled to expire in December 1951. The basis for dismantling the policy was in line with other countries such as Australia, and Canada, which demanded the policy be abandoned. This was important for the Tanganyika colonial authority to exploit and to boost its dollar reserve as the high prices of agricultural commodities following the outbreak of the Korean war significantly interrupted the flow and shipment of goods from Asian sources. There was therefore demand for raw materials from Tanganyika to markets worldwide.

Revoking the policy did not halt the supply of coffee to Britain from East African countries. However, under new agreements the East African countries supplied about half of British home needs until 1954.[3] The BNCB for example, was persuaded to sell 2,000 tons of Robusta coffee to the Ministry

---

[1] TNA 37200, Decontrol of Coffee, Press Notice by Ministry of Food, 20 August 1952
[2] TNA 37200, Tanganyika Legislative Council Debates, Hansard, 1950, Session 29, para. 241
[3] TNA 37200, Decontrol of Coffee, Press Notice by Ministry of Food, 20 August 1952

of Food for 1952/53 and the same tonnage for 1953/54[1] for the same price terms as previous contracts. The remaining stock from Bukoba and KNCU coffee, as well as from other East African countries, was sold at auction in their respective countries. Coffee auctions were opened in Nairobi, Mombasa, Moshi and Kampala in 1947 and in the early 1950s attracted buyers from various countries who formerly were buying from the London auction market which was closed soon after the outbreak of the war. The attraction of buyers in the East Africa auctions was a success as the price for Robusta coffee from Uganda was £100 per ton compared with £65 for the same weight paid by the Minister of Food.[2] The coffee traders' attraction to the East Africa auctions was prompted by their desire for the resumption of coffee trading which to some degree was interrupted not only by the closure of London auction but also by bulk purchase of coffee by the Ministry of Food. As a result Tanganyika coffee was exported to various countries, except North Korea for political reasons.[3]

---

[1] TNA 37200, Ministry of Food to DA, Ref. CS/CP 30G, 23 April 1952, DA to CS, Ref. C/135/836, 17 December 1946

[2] Charlotte Leubuscher, *Bulk Buying from the Colonies: A study of the Bulk Purchase of Colonial Commodities by the United Kingdom Government* (London: Oxford University, 1956) pp. 53-66

[3] TNA 37200, Office of High Commission (Nairobi) to Controller of Supplies, Ref. 4148/227, 9 October 1952

12. Agricultural Marketing Co-operatives (AMCOs)

This chapter examines interventions and pressures after World War II that forced the British colonial power to promote co-operatives in some regions in Tanganyika. The attempt is made to link global development with co-operative initiatives in Tanganyika. Interest in co-operative development was discussed at the UN Conference held at Hot Springs in 1943, at a time when the co-operative movement was internationally accepted as an instrument for invigoration of development in poor countries.

The promotion of co-operative movement policy was embedded in the Colonial Office post-war Marketing Policy for Colonial Primary Products which was circulated to the colonies.[1] The policy stresed that producers be organised either in producers' associations or under some form of government statutory marketing organisation so they could market their produce in an orderly manner and obtain the best possible price. However, the use of co-operative societies was the only viable way to exploit colonial resources. By pooling them with an excuse to promote and encourage co-operatives controlled by the government through the marketing boards, societies had no power to bargain prices for commodities.

The post-war days witnessed a new chapter regarding promotion of co-operatives by colonial officials across the country. This was a significant policy shift inflicted by the CO on Tanganyika's colonial officials. At this juncture, the officials evidently were pressured to accept the colonial power's new policy as they argued that the co-operative movement was of the greatest value in constructing a prosperous African community.[2]

In general terms, regardless of internal colonial authority opposition to directly engage and intervene in promotion of co-operatives, progress in Tanganyika was impressive compared to other East African countries where co-operatives faced opposition in the 1930s. However, no matter how impressive the progress was in Tanganyika, it was a matter of concern in the Colonial Office which in 1944 appointed W.K. Campbell to conduct an investigation into opportunities for co-operative development in East African countries. His report made it clear that the time was ripe to embark in promoting co-operatives owing to the prevalence of embryonic associations that suggested some degree of spontaneous growth. This would require legislation and guidance to promote, form and register societies.[3]

---

[1] TNA 37192, Colonial Office, Confidential memorandum on General Price and Marketing Policy for Colonial Primary Products (London: The Colonial Office, February 1947)
[2] TNA 33017, The Co-operative Movement and Post-War Planning, 29 July 1944

The colonial authority in Tanganyika accepted Campbell's recommendations to further efforts to promote co-operatives. For example, between 1945 and 1948 the co-operative and African-produced marketing policy was reviewed, leading to the adoption of Northcote's previously rejected proposals, except setting up of the co-operative apex body due to a shortage of staff. The co-operative legislation was amended in 1945 to provide for setting up the Department under a Registrar of Co-operative Societies, who was charged with giving advice and promoting producers' societies,[1] unlike during the Northcote era.

This new policy development approach saw a positive attitude towards co-operative development as stipulated in the 20 March and 23 April 1946 dispatches from G.H. Hall, Secretary of State for Colonies. In his dispatch a clear positive attitude towards co-operative development was stipulated in paragraph 3, that '... the value of co-operative societies is no longer a matter of any dispute ...' He emphasised that a co-operative '... can provide its members with services which they would be unable to provide themselves individually also the co-operative society has a most important educative value'.[2] Furthermore, he stressed that there should be an officer appointed by the colonial government, namely 'the Registrar of the co-operative societies assisted by staff of the necessary quality and strengths assigned to provide guidance and assist the development of the co-operative movement and there must be a proper legal framework in the form of Co-operative Societies Ordinance and the necessary rules thereunder'.[3]

The Co-operative Societies Ordinance and Rules model was based on the classic pattern of British-Indian co-operation and prepared for state-controlled co-operative development mainly in the Anglophone African countries. The recommendations laid a concrete foundation which became the basis for changes that took place between 1940 and 1955 in almost all colonies. This coincided with the major change in policy in 1940s when it was decided that colonies could provide services which it could afford to maintain from locally, or other, available financial resources. Funds for implementation of these activities were made available under the Colonial Welfare and Development Scheme provided under the Colonial Development and Welfare Act of 1945. Later, after the Second World War, separate Co-operative Departments were established and charged with promoting,

---

[3] TNA 35783, Marketing of Primary Products and Price Stabilisation, Report on a visit to Tanganyika (16-24 July 1944), 29 July 1944; SK Kobia (2011) p. 31

[1] TNA 37192, Tanganyika Territory, Report on Co-operative Development (Dar es Salaam: Government Printer, 1948)

[2] Governments that were published as the co-operative movement in the colonies by HMSO (Col. 199 – Co-operative Movement in the Colonies)

[3] TNA 33017, Colonial Office to Colonial Administrations, Circular Dispatch 199, 20 March 1946

registering and supervising the co-operatives.

Such interventions were closely linked to the extension work of both the Agricultural and Welfare Departments set up in 1939 prompted by publication of the League of Nations' report and Lord Hailey's *African Survey* on the social needs in the colonies. Unlike the pre-1940 years, the post of Registrar of Co-operative Societies was no longer combined with other duties as it separated in 1945, when the staff were recruited and trained. The Co-operative Department was set up to: 1) educate people about co-operatives; 2) carry out economic surveys of proposed business propositions; and 3) 'to inspect' and guide member societies.

The CO's dispatches helped to facilitate the prerequisites for colonial co-operative development, making legal frameworks, dissemination and provision of advisory services available to co-operative movements. With the formation of the Co-operative Department personnel were deployed after training. For example, in Tanganyika, by 1946 provision was made to engage two co-operative experts to train African personnel. Also from 1948, education for co-operative societies became the responsibility of the colonial government so that between 1946 and 1957, 27 officers from the Co-operative Department and employees of co-operative unions in Tanganyika attended the annual overseas course at the Co-operative College, Loughborough. Also, in 1956, 26 departmental officers and employees attended the two five-month courses at the East African School of Co-operation at Kabete, near Nairobi. Others had attended in previous years. Furthermore, a co-operative school for training secretaries and members of committees was started near Morogoro, in Eastern Province.

Late 1940 and early 1950 witnessed an intensification of co-operative activity. In 1945, the office of the Registrar for Co-operative Societies was moved from the Directorate of Lands and Mines to the Provincial Administration, and for the first time given control over its budget. Due to concentration of co-operation activities in Kilimanjaro area in those days, the Registrar moved his headquarters to Moshi in 1947.[1] On 1 January 1950 the Department of Co-operatives ceased to be part of the Provincial Administration and became a separate department. A year later Malcolm was appointed its first commissioner.[2] Due to the rapid expansion of co-operative activities all over the country, the office of the Registrar had to expand accordingly. It became not only responsible for the registration and inspection of co-operative societies but also the promoter of co-operatives through advice and education. As a result of the increased roles given to this department, its headquarters had to be moved from Moshi to Dar es Salaam in 1953.

---

[1] TNA 37192, Tanganyika Territory, Report of Co-operative Development (1948)

[2] W.K. Campbell, *Practical Co-operation in Asia and Africa* (Cambridge: W. Heffer & Sons, 1951) p. 194

12.1: The UNO

The UNO was a key stakeholder in promoting co-operatives among the colonies, most of the latter being under the administration of UNO members. The policy was hotly discussed at UNO's Conference held at Hot Springs, in the United States of America in 1943, where the issue of post-war reconstruction was examined and social and economic adjustments in the colonies called for. Co-operatives were one option to address post-war socio-economic challenges. This was due to the role played by some European co-operatives assisting UNO agencies in providing relief services, rehabilitation and reconstruction programmes during and post-World War II.[1] The conference examined how co-operatives could be employed in post-war reconstruction efforts. It was during this period when co-operative movements were internationally accepted and considered a key instrument for invigorating development in poor countries. UNO agencies such as the ILO, at its 26th Session conference, recommended and stressed the need for colonial authorities to play an integral part in promoting the co-operative movement in the post-war years.[2]

In general, colonial authority intervention in promoting co-operatives in Tanganyika, regardless of slow and stunted development, was impressive compared to other East African countries. However, no matter how impressive the progress in Tanganyika, it was a matter of concern in the Colonial Office, which in 1944 appointed W.K.H. Campbell to investigate opportunities for co-operative development in East African countries.

In his report on Tanganyika, Campbell identified five key factors that contributed to the slow progress: shortage of staff, the KNPA experience as well as nervousness created by the 1937 coffee riots in Kilimanjaro, the inability of growers to manage societies, and fears that the movement would interfere with affairs of the NA. In his report it was made clear that the 'time is ripe to embark in promotion of co-operatives owing to prevalence of embryonic associations that suggest some degree of spontaneous growth that requires legislation and government guidance for their promotion, formation and registration'.[3] He also emphasised that co-operatives should be formed to accommodate soldiers returning from World War II battlefields in Ethiopia and Asia. This was widely viewed as an important policy to defuse or divert their interest from engaging in the struggle against colonial rule.[4]

---

[1] ILO, The co-operative movememtns and present day problems with special reference to rehabilitation and reconstruction (Geneva: ILO, 1953) pp. 149, 173-176

[2] TNA 24870, ILO, *Problems Relating to establishment of Co-operative Movements in Non-Self Governing Territories and Government Solution for their Solution* (Geneva: ILO, 1950)

[3] TNA 35783, Campbell Report of Visit to Tanganyika (16-24 July 1944), 29 July 1944

[4] TNA 35783, Campbell Report of Visit to Tanganyika (16-24 July 1944), 29 July 1944

Campbell[1] revealed further that there was no register of members, no meetings were held, the committee of producers did not manage, and no responsibility rested on producers who had no stake in the venture. In additon, there was no publication or explanation of accounts to the members and no audit by an outside agency. He explained that there was a tendency in some quarters in Tanzania to ascribe complacency to certain marketing operations by the Native Administration as passable institutions of co-operation. Again, as a short view they were performing a useful specific function, but as instruments for helping Africans to do things for themselves and to achieve capacity and self-reliance they could hardly be accepted as a substitute for co-operative societies. Apart from desirability of any development of government, native or otherwise engaging directly in trade, they did nothing to educate the producers in practical economics.[2]

Campbell therefore recommended encouraging growers to form co-operative societies. In the case of Uganda, Campbell stressed that immediate action should be in place to enact the co-operative legislation and importantly to appoint the Registrar charged with responsibility to assist quasi-co-operatives. As a result, legislation was enacted and passed in 1946, and registration of societies begun in September the same year. Ideally, he argued that 'the co-operation ought to spring spontaneously from the people themselves and the government should have no need to help in its propagation'.[3] However, he indicated the inability of growers to form co-operatives without government's encouragement and support. In this case, he believed that 'government intervention is justified' but cautioned the greatest care be taken not to devitalise the co-operative movement that lacked the lifeblood of belief by their members.[4]

The colonial officials in Tanganyika had a contrary view or standpoint. For example, in response to Campbell's recommendation on spontaneous growth of co-operatives, the Tanganyika colonial authority challenged the policy on the view that it would not succeed owing to lack of knowledge about co-operation;[5] also, the experience that Tanganyika had during the years between the two wars when the spontaneous policy failed to bring about changes. In this case, it was strongly held by the colonial authority that the government should intervene in the formation of co-operatives.[6] This confirms the commitment of the Tanganyika colonial authority's training policy towards promotion and performance of the co-operative

---

[1] Campbell, *Practical Co-operation in Asia and Africa*, p. 198
[2] Campbell, *Practical Co-operation in Asia and Africa*, p. 197
[3] TNA 33017, Report of the Central Development Committee, 29 April 1944
[4] Ibid.
[5] TNA 33017, The Co-operative Movement and Post-War Planning, 29 July 1944
[6] TNA 37192, Tanganyika Territory Report on Co-operative Development for 1948

movement. It was part of the colonial authority's post war approach that justified attempts in which a top-down approach was employed in the promotion and formation of co-operative societies. Nevertheless, uncertainties as to how co-operatives could be established remained a critical challenge for the colonial authority. This was reflected in their perception that they had to be formed at every centre of native authority in the country.

12.2: The 1945 Fabian Colonial Bureau Report

The British Fabian Colonial Bureau was in the 1940s an instrumental organisation that successfully pressured the CO to adopt co-operatives as argued by the UNO and ILO. As far as Britain is concerned, the Campbell report coincided with one from the Fabian Colonial Bureau to the Colonial Office. The Fabian report helped influence British colonial policy in relation to co-operatives by outlining the advantages of co-operatives as:[1]

a) Lowering costs of production;
b) Distribution and marketing;
c) Obtaining credit on reasonable terms;
d) Ending the monopolisation of trading by big European firms; and
e) Improving agriculture using better stock and seeds, and by the use of fertilisers, machinery.

The advantages outlined clearly attempt to address the disadvantaged position of many small-scale growers, not only in Tanganyika but also in many other developing countries where they remained side-lined. In general terms, the advantages attempted to end the confinement of growers to agricultural production and to broaden their participation in other economic areas by having growers participate in marketing. However, emphasis remained on promoting agriculture co-operatives. Further impetus for promoting agriculture co-operatives was given by the post-World War II planning committee with emphasis on autonomous status. The committee recommended that:

> on desire being expressed for assistance towards greater co-operative effort at instance of the persons concerned the government should view the matter with sympathy and should do what is possible to assist the movement; but we point out that co-operative societies cannot be made by government they must be stated by the co-operatives themselves.[2]

Although Tanganyika had the highest number of registered co-operatives, their footprint was limited to a few areas. The Fabian Colonial Bureau was

---

[1] Fabian Colonial Bureau, *A Report from a Special Committee to the Fabian Colonial Bureau: Co-operation in the Colonies* (London: George Allen & Unwin, 1945) pp. 14, 193

[2] TNA 33017, Report of the Central Development Committee on Co-operatives, para 303

probably satisfied with development in Tanganyika. However, the limited footprint had ramifications in achieving agricultural development among small-scale growers in the country, which generated disparities. The most important policy recommendation envisaged by the bureau was the role of co-operatives in facilitating modernisation of African societies e.g. in crop production and in achieving the switch-over from a subsistence to cash crop economy.[1] This was in line with the Labour Colonial Development policy on improving the welfare of the people in the colonies.

At this juncture, the Colonial Office policy towards co-operatives was that 'the value of co-operative societies is no longer a matter of any dispute',[2] and it should be used as an instrument for the construction of a prosperous African community.[3] It was assumed by then that encouragement of co-operatives and trade unions for example, would create a wealthy rural and middle class that would facilitate political stability in the colonies. The Colonial Office envisaged that the co-operatives in British colonies would collect and market the raw material and foodstuffs and create markets for manufactured goods. Therefore, a combination of both supportive policies and availability of individuals who were committed to execute the policies was not only an impetus but also unveiled an era of co-operative renaissance in Tanganyika that provided for expansion of the movement to cover areas that were starved or viewed as deserts due to a lack or limited number of societies. But again, the purpose was to facilitate marketing of agricultural produce, most of which was exported to Britain.

12.3: Colonial Office intervention

As World War II neared its end, the Colonial Office appointed a Special Committee to investigate post-war co-operative development in the colonies. The committee published the report in 1945, in which it described co-operative movements as 'all but non-existent in most British colonies' and recommended the setting up of a co-operative department with a central department in the Colonial Office.[4]

In early 1946 George Hall, Under-Secretary of State for Colonies dispatched a circular to the colonies detailing a roadmap for co-operative promotion.[5] The circular provided impetus and confidence to the course taken by the colonial authority in Tanganyika in amending co-operative legislation and adoption of the Northcote proposals. This came at an important time when post-war policy on agricultural produce marketing

---

[1] Fabian Colonial Bureau, *A Report from a Special Committee*
[2] TNA 19005, Co-operative Movement in the Colonies (London: HMSO, 1946) Col. 199
[3] TNA 33017, Extract of Lord Winster's speech in House of Lords, 1-3 March 1944
[4] Fabian Colonial Bureau, *A Report from a Special Committee*, pp. 14, 193
[5] TNA 33017, Colonial Office to Colonial Administrations, Circular Dispatch 199, 20 March 1946, pp. 4-5

was primarily geared towards rationalisation and synchronisation of crop purchase in favour of a single government-appointed buyer which was in line with bulk purchase. The policy was embedded in the Colonial Office post-war Marketing Policy for Colonial Primary Products[1] which stressed that producers be organised either in producers' association or under some form of government statutory marketing organisation so they could market their produce in an orderly manner.[2]

However, the circular did not prescribe approaches under which co-operatives could be promoted; but the ILO's 1944 recommendation on government intervention[3] was seemingly in mind among colonial officials. This suggests that individual territories had a mandate to assess the best way to promote co-operatives, suggesting that growers could dictate colonial authority policy strategy, as seen in Kagera where the top-down approach was employed because of a lack of enthusiasm and obstruction from the BNCB which had legal control of coffee marketing under Native Coffee (Control & Marketing) Ordinance, 1937. It was on this legal basis that the BNCB delayed for over two years in accepting co-operatives into the coffee marketing system and it remained reluctant to foster co-operatives.[4] As pointed out earlier provincial administration had also been reluctant to promote co-operatives.

In the wake of George Hall's report, greater emphasis was placed on co-operatives. For example, in 1947 the Colonial Office appointed an advisor on co-operative movements. B.J. Surridge had served as Registrar of Co-operatives in Cyprus between 1934 and 1943 and later became Vice Chair and Trustee of the Plunkett Foundation. All this provided impetus for promoting co-operatives in British African colonies, accelerated by the Labour Party's victory in the 1945 General Election.[5] From the beginning, the Labour government was overburdened with unprecedented difficulties regarding colonial questions, economic and political. India was on its way to independence, with other Asian colonies following. There was another so-called dollar crisis,[6] which caused problems as Britain had to repay its war debts in dollars, while the export capacity of the damaged economy was still limited.[7]

---

[1] TNA 37192, Colonial Office, Confidential memorandum on General Price and Marketing Policy for Colonial Primary Products (London: Colonial Office, February 1947)
[2] TNA 33017, Colonial Office to Colonial Administrations, Circular Dispatch 199, 20 March 1946 p. 4-5
[3] TNA 24870, ILO, *Problems Relating to Establishment of Co-operative Movements*
[4] TNA 29585, Registrar/Commissioner of Co-operative Development to Chairman, BNCB, Ref. Co-op.29585/IL/485a, 22 September 1949, BNCB, Bukoba District
[5] Frank, Formation of British Colonial Policy, p. 1
[6] Havinden & Meredith, *Colonialism and development*, pp. 266-269
[7] Frank, Formation of British Colonial Policy, p. 75

To lessen the burden of external debts and to finance its domestic move to a welfare state, the Labour government opted for a policy of massive 'export drive' from the colonies. Africa and the Caribbean suddenly became valuable assets for the ailing British economy[1] and this perception led to hasty, reckless agricultural projects such as the highly-mechanised groundnut production scheme in Tanganyika, which was a disastrous failure.

Against this backdrop, colonial authorities in British colonies were called upon to realise a planned development of co-operative associations and enterprises by employing them as instruments in introducing an appropriate and modern agricultural policy. The colonial authority in Tanganyika took Campbell's recommendations seriously to further promote co-operatives in which, among its recommendations was to employ the co-operatives to absorb returning soldiers who had served Britain in the Second World War.

This was further accelerated when Arthur Creech Jones from the Fabian Colonial Bureau was appointed Secretary of State for Colonies. Creech Jones reorganised the Colonial Office to reflect the demand for changes in the colonies and to respond to both international and local pressure for the encouragement of co-operatives.[2] By pressuring colonies to pass or amend co-operative legislation to enable the establishment of Co-operative Departments, was pivotal in fostering co-operation.

12.4: Amendments to the Co-operative Ordinance

The post-war era coupled with pressure for agricultural policy reforms to align with colonial powers' demand for raw materials. Given this was an era when agricultural marketing co-operatives were encouraged, amendments of Ordinances were also part of policy reforms. In practice, co-operative society rules and regulations were put in place under co-operative legislation Amendment 26, 1944. Again, the legislation was amended in 1945 under Government Notice 73, 1945, all in accordance with the guidance provided by George Hall and Northcote in the mid-1930s. This was meant to provide for setting up a fully-fledged department separate from the Departments of Lands and Mines, and placed under the Registrar of Co-operative Societies.[3] The Registrar was charged with giving advice and promoting producers' societies. The department employed two European staff in 1945, also three African clerks and two co-operative inspectors.[4] Moshi became the department headquarters. Training and education for the department as well as of

---

[1] Frank, Formation of British Colonial Policy, pp. 26, 75
[2] TNA 24870, *The Bombay Co-operative Quarterly*, October 1950, p. 90
[3] TNA 37192, Tanganyika Territory, *Report on Co-operative Development* (Dar es Salaam: Government Printer, 1947) paragraph 6; T.R. Sadleir, The co-operative moement in Tanganyika (Dar es Salaam: Tanganuyika Standard Printing, 1963) p.7
[4] TNA 37192, Tanganyika Territory, *Report on Co-operative Development* (Dar es Salaam: Government Printer, 1948)

co-operative movement staff was unveiled.[1]

Creation of the department was important to the Labour government, which, as mentioned earlier, had a strong attachment to the co-operative movement and was committed to facilitate reform and develop agricultural production in the colonies. This signified a major post-war policy shift in favour of co-operatives, unlike during Northcote's era when such policies were primarily rejected by the colonial authority. Therefore, a combination of both supportive policies and the availability of individuals committed to execute the policy led to a new era of co-operatives in Tanganyika.

The CO made available a model co-operative ordinance, which was based on the India Co-operative Societies Act of 1912 and the Sri Lanka (Ceylon) Ordinance of 1936 which were circulated to all British colonies including Tanganyika.[2] The model Co-operative Ordinance, Regulations and Rules was prompted by a desire to have a uniform approach throughout British African colonies. For example, the Co-operative Ordinance sets out several provisions governing the organisation of co-operative societies in which native members must be at least sixteen years of age, or of taxable age.

The policy came at a time when Britain and the colonial authority in Tanganyika were encouraging production of cash crops. Funds were made available under the 1945 Colonial Development and Welfare legislation, intended to invigorate economic development of the country based on modernisation. Encouraging agriculture marketing co-operatives and intervention by the CO clearly illustrates that the intention was mainly to salvage Britain from economic ruin caused by the war. To ensure the policy was enforced, a co-operative adviser and advisory committee was appointed in 1947. The adviser operated from the CO charged with responsibility to monitor progress in the colonies. Similarly, Co-operative Departments were established.

The post-World War II colonial strategy of co-operative development was designed around modernisation. This assumption was strongly underscored by the colonial authority: that it would be beneficial to the overall development process in transforming the rural population;[3] it planned to provide a forum for increasing agricultural productivity and to preserve the communitarian basis of traditional Africa.[4] This was however, a significant departure from the position held by Labour in the 1930s, when the co-operatives envisaged preserving traditional Africa.[5]

---

[1] Ibid.

[2] Campbell, *Practical Co-operation in Asia and Africa*, Appendix 1

[3] Develtere, Co-operatives and Development Towards a Social Movement Perspective, *Occasional Paper Series, #92-03* (Centre for the Study of Co-operatives, University of Saskatchewan) pp. 41-42

[4] Fabian Colonial Bureau, *A Report from a Special Committee*

Promotion of the co-operative movement policy was embedded in the Colonial Office Post-war Marketing Policy provided under the Colonial Primary Products directive, circulated to all British colonies.¹ There is no doubt that the policy took into consideration the success and weakness of the bulk purchase system with its emphasis on marketing while production was neglected. The marketing boards played a part in the supervision of production but were limited as they were not directly in contact with growers. It was envisaged that co-operatives would facilitate improvements in cultivation methods as outlined by the Fabian Colonial Bureau.²

Achieving the improvement policies had one critical challenge: lack of a co-operative movement promotion policy. This is evidenced by the inconsistent approach in promoting co-operatives. The 1937 Native Coffee Control legislation did not facilitate the improvement of crops other than coffee. Thus, a comprehensive agriculture and marketing policy was vital, a point realised when the Colonial Office unveiled its post-war policy on agriculture development.³ The CO policy on agricultural crop marketing prompted amendment of the marketing legislation by the colonial authority that provided for integration of the co-operatives in marketing.

In developing the policy, the Registrar of Co-operative Societies was accorded powers to draft legislation, the African Agricultural Products (Control & Marketing) Ordinance 57, 1949. The Registrar had to ensure that it produced comprehensive legislation that covered all native or African-produced cash crops, and in which co-operative societies played a key role in handling and marketing, just as in Kilimanjaro and other areas in the country.

Unlike the previous 1937 native coffee control and marketing legislation, the 1949 Ordinance recognised the existence of co-operatives and compelled marketing boards to promote co-operatives. In this regard, the department exerted its dominance over policy decisions and direction, ultimately implementing them in favour of promoting co-operative societies. This was a significant step that weakened the powers of the colonial provincial administration and BNCB in preventing the promotion of co-operative societies. As a result, the provincial administration and BNCB were both obliged to engage in promoting co-operatives. Under the Ordinance, the board's functions were further extended to include promotion and development of the co-operative movement.⁴

---

⁵ Paul Kelemen, Modernising Colonialism: The British Labour movement and Africa, *The Journal of Imperial and Commonwealth History*, October 2011

¹ TNA 37192, CO, Confidential memorandum on General Price and Marketing Policy for Colonial Primary Products (London: February 1947)

² Fabian Colonial Bureau, *A Report from a Special Committee* pp. 14, 193

³ TNA 27317, CO, Colonial Agricultural Policy (London: 1945) p. 3, DA Circular despatch to Directors (Veterinary, Tsetse Research), Ref. 27317/33, 15 August 1946

The legislation provided for a forum for exerting pressure on existing marketing boards, mainly the BNCB, to promote co-operatives.[1] The object of the legislation was to foster promotion of co-operatives;[2] the marketing boards were instituted largely as an interim measure pending the formation of producers' co-operatives. Marketing boards, which were instruments of government to promote such societies starting at the primary level for crop marketing, had taken definite steps. Consequently, the legislation weakened the provincial administration and BNCB powers to impede the Co-operative Department's attempts to promote co-operatives by compelling boards to appoint co-operative societies as their crop handling agencies.

Additionally, the legislation went hand in hand with ensuring that surpluses accrued by the boards be returned to growers through the co-operatives, in line with the ICA and Rochdale principles.[3] Thus, the boards no longer retained control of the surpluses. The marketing boards were also required to disburse part of the profits accrued from sales of coffee in accordance with Section 10 of the Ordinance as an incentive to encourage production among the growers with effect from January 1950.[4]

Clearly, the policy was a step to crippling the boards financially and this was significant in compelling the BNCB to provide support to co-operative societies. In a further development, all Provincial Commissioners were informed that the Secretary of State for Colonies had instructed that with effect from 1951 the Commissioner of Co-operative Development became the liaison officer between his department and the boards in all matters regarding co-operatives, marketing and commercial accounting.[5] The CO's intervention further reinforced control over marketing of native produce by the Co-operative Department and weakened the status of the boards. The African Agricultural Products (Control & Marketing) Ordinance, 1949 was not only a key prime lever but also wider in terms of crops involved, unlike the 1937 legislation that provided only for the coffee industry. Thus, it was a facilitating policy for the growth of co-operative movements as it compelled marketing boards to promote the co-operatives, which under previous legislation had immersed power in control of crop marketing. Its application proved effective and successful as far as promotion of coffee marketing co-operatives was concerned.

[4] TNA 11969/9, DA to Secretariat Members of Agriculture and Natural Resources, Ref. 1369/7561, May 1952

[1] TNA 37192, Tanganyika Territory Report on Co-operative Development for 1947

[2] TNA 24545, Registrar of Co-operative Societies to BNCB, 22 September 1949; TNA 28585, DA to Members of Agriculture & Natural Resources, Ref. 1368/7561, 19 May 1952

[3] TNA 11969/9, DA to Secretariat Members of Agriculture & Natural Resources, Ref. 1369/7561, May 1952

[4] TNA 24545, Registrar of Co-operative Societies to BNCB, 22 September 1949

[5] TNA 40657, Member of Agriculture & Natural Resources (C.E.J. Biggs) to All Provincial Commissioners, Ref. 40657, 12 May 1951

In the early 1950s, the CO recommended amendments of several co-operative legislation sections that would enhance control of the co-operative movement. One of these was Section 36 of Co-operative Ordinance 7, 1932 which was contradictory to co-operative principles as it emphasised compulsion measures such as membership and that growers sell their produce through co-operative societies. Understandably, such functions were handed to the marketing boards. During the post-war years, the CO challenged and recommended for either amendment or repeal of Section 36.[1] It was reiterated by the CO that the Ugandan government had decided to amend its co-operative ordinance along the lines of Section 39 of the Cyprus Ordinance.[2] The CO instructed the Tanganyika colonial authority to copy Uganda.[3]

> My attention is on Section 36 of the Co-operative ordinance, which has not been included in the model ordinance. It is appreciated that in certain circumstances the increase of the powers of the registration necessary in the interests of the members whose affairs were being mishandled which proved to be effective in Cyprus.[4]

In response, the Tanganyika colonial authority presented the amendment bill for the Section to the LEGCO in October 1951.[5] Co-operative Societies Ordinance (Cap.211) 55 of 3 December 1952 provided for repeal and replacement of Section 36 of Co-operative Ordinance 7, 1932. The amended legislation was sent to the CO for approval, which was granted. Of course, in support of the amendments, the CO reinforced that 'it is appreciated that in certain circumstances the increase of the powers created by the Section might well be necessary in the interest of the members' of a society whose affairs were being mishandled.[6] This Section was replaced by a new sweeping power granted to the Registrar of Co-operative Societies. This placed the co-operative institutions under control of the government through the Registrar of Co-operative Societies who was given overriding powers to direct and regulate co-operatives. The CO further stressed that 'the power would be exercised in exceptional and appropriate circumstances and that a clear explanation of the reasons for such action would be given to committee and members of the society'.[7]

Repeal and replacement of some Sections of the Co-operative Ordinance was viewed during post-war years as significant. It was argued that repeal of

---

[1] TNA 40657, Telegram CO to Governor Tanzania, 683, 25 July 1951, Nos 423 & 432
[2] TNA 40657, Telegram 432, 9 May 1951
[3] TNA 40657, CO Governor CO to CS, Telegram 426, 8 May 1951
[4] TNA 40657, CO's Circular Dispatch, 20 March 1946
[5] TNA 40657, Commissioner to Governor, Ref. 19595/51, October 1951
[6] TNA 19595, CO to CS Tanganyika, Telegram 426, 8 May 1951
[7] Ibid.

Section 36 and replacement of the Registrar's powers over co-operative societies was intended to prevent abuse and misuse of office.[1] In this regard, Section 36 comprised the following subsections: a) Dissolution of the committee; b) direction that affairs of the society should be managed and administered by a suitable person or persons appointed and that they would serve for a period not exceeding two years. Moreover, Section 19 of the ordinance charged the Registrar with responsibility to audit and inspect a co-operative society. In conducting audits and supervision co-operative societies were required to access services of professional accounting and audit firms. The Registrar was therefore responsible for registration, auditing, and supervision of co-operative societies.

Under the Amendment, whenever the government deemed it necessary for example, the Registrar could dissolve co-operative society committees. Under the same section, the Registrar was granted powers, subject to the governor's approval, to appoint a supervising manager to oversee the management and affairs of any society.[2] The powers to appoint co-operative society managers was effected previously by appointing the KNCU and NGOMAT managers as well as for BCU and Rungwe African Co-operative Union and VFCUs.

Further, each society was empowered to draft its own bye-laws as provided for under Section 68 Cap.211 subject to approval by the Registrar. However, Section 59(1)(2) Cap.211 under which the governor could prescribe the matter in respect of procedure involved referring members to the Commissioner of Co-operative Societies. Largely, this shows that co-operative societies lacked autonomy and were controlled and possibly influenced by the Registrar. Thus, such legislation Sections highlight how societies were deprived of their autonomous status that obviously contradicted co-operative principles.

While the pre World War II years were characterised by uneven development of co-operative movements, legislation led to expansion of the co-operative footprint as seen by several societies in new locations such as Rungwe district in the Southern Highlands of Tanzania and Kagera Regions (then Bukoba district) as shown in Table 30.

Under the marketing legislation, boards retained some powers regarding crop marketing. They had power to appoint an agency in which co-operatives were a priority because unlike private enterprises, they did not offer conflicting interests with those of the board, and by and large were complementary to the work of agricultural marketing co-operatives. Under this relationship the legislation set the co-operative as the principal tool for crop

---

[1] TNA 19595, Registrar of Co-operative Societies to the Member of Agriculture and Natural Resources, 4 January 1952

[2] A.J. Grattan-Bellew, Attorney General

collection. This resulted in expansion in cash crop producing areas which marketing boards intensely supported. It also had an effect in the growth of co-operatives in Kilimanjaro, Bukoba, the WCGA and Southern Province (Mbeya, and Iringa) and Southern (Ruvuma region) but also led to regional inequality as shown in Table 31.

Table 30: Co-operative Unions during the Colonial Era

Name	Date of Registration	Region	Reg. Number	Crop
Kilimanjaro Native	29/12/1933	Kilimanjaro	12	Coffee
Ngoni-Matego	7/ 5/1936	Ruvuma	27	Tobacco
Rungwe African	11/ 5/1949	Mbeya	89	Coffee
Bukoba	1/12/1950	Kagera	144	Coffee
Mbinga	10/ 9/1954	Ruvuma	265	Coffee
Victoria Federation	4/ 7/1955	Mwanza, Shinyanga & Mara	330	Cotton
Bugufi Coffee	17/ 6/1957	Kagera	459	Coffee
Unyakyusa	5/ 4/1958	Mbeya	541	Coffee
Meru/Arusha	23/ 9/1958	Arusha	579	Coffee
Mbeya	10/ 6/1960	Mbeya	707	Coffee
Tambarare	9/ 5/1961	Kilimanjaro	784	Cotton
VUASU	1/ 7/1961	Kilimanjaro	812	Coffee
Usambara	29/ 8/1961	Tanga	830	Coffee

Source: Annual Report on Co-operative Development, Dar es Salaam, 1961

Table 31: Number of Co-operative Societies in 1959 and 1960

S/No	Provinces	Total
1	Northern	61
2	Southern	33
3	Southern Highlands	59
4	West Lake	79
5	Lake	341
6	Tanga	8
7	Eastern	34
8	Western	1
9	Central	1
	Total	617

Source: Tanganyika Territory Annual Report on Co-operative Development 1959, Dar es Salaam

12.4: Reaction to the Recommendations

In Tanzania, the key policy emphasis and recommendations were by the UNO and Fabian Colonial Bureau. The agencies and Campbell envisioned the formation of various types of co-operatives such as agricultural and animal products as well as consumer societies in developing countries. It was established that the policy implementation would be impractical without local initiatives. At the time, external impetus was vital to stimulate a change of attitude and interest among colonial officials in the colonies as local initiatives remained pivotal. This brought successes soon after the end of the war when some co-operative societies were registered in the country.[1] The first society to be registered after the war in Tanganyika was the Mwanza African Traders Consumer Co-operative Society (MATCS) in 1946, which became a driving force giving significant impetus to the growth of cotton marketing co-operatives in the WCGA.

Several other consumer co-operative societies were registered in 1946. These were the Chagga Traders' Consumer Co-operative Society with registration number 57, Tanganyika Co-operative Trading with registration number 58, and Tanga Co-operative Trading with registration number 63. The East African Co-operative Trading Society with its headquarters in Nairobi, Kenya, had branches in Arusha and Moshi, Tanganyika. The Arusha Co-operative Stores Limited with exclusive membership was confined to members of the Ithna-Ashri sect.[2] The formation, and registration, of consumer co-operative societies among Africans was prompted by circumstances around World War II.

During the war, several restrictions and emergency measures were imposed, not only for exported agricultural commodities such as coffee and cotton, but also for individuals to purchase consumer goods in the country. The restrictions imposed upon consumer goods included allocation of quotas on wholesale items. Under such conditions, African traders experienced some difficulties to access or buy goods in bulk from Indian merchants who dominated wholesale businesses. One of the difficulties concerned the quota allocation of goods, most of which were below the requirements and demands from their customers in villages where they were managing *dukas* (retail family shops) or shops. Inadequate supply of goods generated discontent among the African as well as Indian traders. The African traders, however, translated this scenario as discrimination and an attempt to undermine their livelihoods. For them, consumer co-operatives offered a sustainable solution.

---

[1] TNA 33017, The Co-operative Movement and Post-War Planning, 29 July 1944
[2] TNA 37192, Tanganyika Government Report on Co-operative Development (Dar es Salaam: Government Printer, 1949) p. 8

13. Post World War II Co-operative Development

13.1: Southern Highlands Province

It was shown earlier that attempts to form co-operatives proved futile in the second half of the 1930s, which was a disappointment to both growers and colonial officials, who played a key role in stimulating the idea. The formation of co-operatives in Southern Highlands Province (SHP) particularly in the then Rungwe district, rekindled after World War II partly to comply with Colonial Office recommendations on promoting co-operatives in the colonies.

In a move that indicated commitment to promoting co-operatives in the province, on 14 December 1945, the Provincial Commissioner presented a proposal to the CS to register co-operative societies. The Provincial Commissioner detailed financial implications and showed that the senior agricultural officer, assigned to pursue a task throughout the province, and the Native Authority in the province were responsible for facilitating and implementating the policy. Assigning a task to the senior agricultural officer was obviously to address a shortage of staff for such responsibility. Moreover, the proposal indicated types of co-operatives that were to be registered, such as the rice marketing co-operative in Kyela and coffee marketing co-operative societies in Mbozi and Rungwe.[1]

The PC indicated that the province had funds allocated for the purpose to counteract possible rejection by the CS as in the mid-1930s. It was shown that funds were internally generated, mainly from the Native Authorities in the province. A source of funding that was earmarked by the PC was the savings in the Native Authority Treasury, particularly No. 2 Account that had accumulated from marketing crops primarily to promote native co-operative societies. The Native Authority Treasury No. 2 Account was mostly a temporary measure pending transformation of groups into fully-fledged co-operative societies.[2]

Such major crops as coffee and rice, produced by natives in the province, raised revenue through pre-co-operative organisations, which had been organised under crop marketing group membership, following the failure to register co-operative societies in the 1930s. This had been the result of crop marketing restrictions imposed by the colonial authority during and after World War II. These groups were formed as there was no formal organisation to serve as co-operatives.

---

[1] TNA 322997, PC SHP to CS, Ref. 47/17/57, 14 December 1945
[2] TNA 322997, Extract from Proceedings of all PCs

In principle, the CS accepted the proposal from the province. For example, creation and utilisation of funds from the NA Treasury No. 2 Account, which by then had accumulated £4,424 in the 1945/46 season,[1] was commended by the CS as a reliable funding source to all PCs in the country, urging them to utilise it in their endeavour to promote co-operatives in their provinces.[2] The CS gave approval for the process and urged the provincial authority to immediately exploit the opportunity.[3] At this point, the CS gave approval of the intervention and utilisation of funds, mainly NA Treasury No. 2 Accounts.[4]

Apart from a written proposal, the CS had a meeting with the Southern Highland Province PC to discuss promoting crop marketing co-operatives. This provided an impetus and strengthened the Southern Highland Province Provincial Commissioner's commitment to promoting co-operative societies. During the meeting, the PC announced the appointment of E.L. Shipman as a co-operative organiser in the province. It was explained that Shipman would be responsible for promoting rice marketing co-operative societies in Kyela and also coffee marketing co-operative societies in Mbozi and Rungwe districts.[5]

The responsibilities assigned to Shipman were further outlined in the communiqué in which he was tasked by the PC to undertake a feasibility study on the formation of creamery co-operative organisations in the province.[6] The Registrar of Co-operative Societies was also involved in considering the provincial proposal. In his letter to the PC, the CS stressed that the PC should carry out an activity in consultation with the Registrar. The CS insisted that 'approval conveyed therein in respect of rice co-operative societies in Rungwe district; and should also market coffee produced by growers in Mbozi division in Mbeya district'.[7] As far as the CS was concerned, such opportunities warranted registering co-operative societies. In response, the Registrar approved, insisting it was the right time to have the growers engaged in handling their produce. Moreover, the Registrar insisted that the provincial authority consider agricultural marketing legislation by pointing out that whoever and wherever attempts were made to promote co-operative societies, setting up native control and marketing boards was a priority that was not to be ignored.[8]

All these developments indicated support from key government officials

---

[1] TNA 322997, CS to PC SHP, Ref. 32997/45, 3 June 1947
[2] TNA 322997, Extract from Proceedings of all PCs
[3] Ibid.
[4] TNA 322997, CS to PC SHP, Ref. 32997/45, 3 June 1947
[5] TNA 322997, PC SHP to CS, Ref. 47/17/05, 13 February 1947
[6] Ibid.
[7] TNA 322997, CS to PC SHP, Telegram 32997, 10 July 1947
[8] TNA 322997, Registrar to CS, Co-op. 10059/97, 24 March 1947

and departments such as the CS, Co-operative Department, and particularly from the Registrar of Co-operative Societies himself who indicated how important it was. The Registrar revealed the involvement of government and the Native Authority in buying rice produced by small-scale growers for the last five years in Kyela.[1] The DA also provided strong support for promoting rice marketing co-operative societies in Kyela and coffee marketing co-operative societies in Mbozi and Rungwe.[2] The DA not only provided moral support but also pointed to sources of funding from the Economic Control Board's profits which accrued from control of both rice and coffee marketing during and after the Second World War. In a further development, several other co-operative promotion funding sources were identified such as the Agricultural Development Fund.[3]

Approval by the CS and the Registrar, as well as the appointment of the co-operative organiser led to successful promotion of societies. For example, in 1947 ten primary co-operative societies, of which four were rice marketing co-operatives societies registered in Kyela and six coffee marketing co-operatives societies in Rungwe and Mbozi were registered for undertaking bulk sales formerly conducted by local administration through the special Account of the Native Authority.[4]

Table 32: Co-operative societies in Kyela, Rungwe and Mbozi

Rice Marketing Co-operative Societies in Kyela

S/N	Reg. no.	Name
1	73	Itete Rice Growers Co-operative Society Limited
2	74	Kilwa Rice Growers Co-operative Society Limited
3	75	Mwaya Rice Growers Co-operative Society Limited
4	76	Ndamba Rice Growers Co-operative Society Limited

Coffee Marketing Co-operative Societies in Rungwe and Mbozi

1	67	Unyiha Coffee Growers Co-operative Society Limited
2	68	Mwakaleli Coffee Growers Co-operative Society Limited
3	69	Suma Coffee Growers Co-operative Society Limited
4	70	Masebe Coffee Growers Co-operative Society Limited
5	71	Katumba Coffee Growers Co-operative Society Limited
6	72	Kiwira Coffee Growers Co-operative Society Limited

Source: Tanganyika Territory Government, Annual Report on Co-operative Development, 1947

More primary co-operative societies were registered between 1950 and 1957. Some of them are Lwanga which was registered to market rice and Lukata, Mpombo, Kagwina, Kinyala, Katumba, Kandete, Katengele, Mbig-

---

[1] TNA 322997, Registrar to CS, Co-op. 10059/97, 24 March 1947

[2] TNA 322997, DA to CS, Ref. 1174/2817, 25 March 1947

[3] TNA 322997, Memorandum no. 9 for Development Commission

[4] Tanganyika Government, Annual Report on Co-operative Development (Dar es Salaam: Government Printer, 1947)

ili and Iponjola were registered to handle coffee. Clearly, the CS appeared supportive of initiatives and progress that was taking place in the province. For example, he instructed the PC that rice handling by co-operative societies should be in place during the 1948/49 season.[1] CS support was further justified in a feasibility study conducted by Shipman that showed there were sufficient funds available in NA Treasury No. 2 Account, and profit generated by the government through marketing of rice that could serve the purpose.[2] Shipman argued that rice was profitable. He showed that between 1942 and 1946 the profit accrued from marketing rice was only 66,708 shillings and proposed the amount be spent on promoting co-operative societies. The Registrar recommended approval for formation of both rice and coffee marketing co-operative societies in the province, immediately makimg this evidence available to the CS. In giving his approval, the CS insisted that 'approval conveyed therein in respect of rice co-operative societies in Rungwe district should also be taken to the Mbozi coffee growers in Mbeya district'.[3]

However, soon afterwards, the CS's approval was rendered useless; and the excitement of the provincial leadership on kick-starting co-operatives in their province was short-lived. The excitement was seriously frustrated as Shipman had miscalculated available funds. When a request was made to the DA to release funds mentioned by Shipman, it was realised that the amount available was only £832 for promotion of co-operative societies in the province.[4] The fund available was not sufficient. The CS reporting that 'it has been realised that the sum available for payment to the co-operative societies was very much less than originally anticipated'.[5]

Disappointingly, the PC informed the CS that coffee and rice handling by co-operative societies could not start in 1948.[6] The Registrar pointed out that failure to begin intervention was due to discrepancies in the Agricultural Development Fund and inadequate funds; he then concluded and recommended postponing the engagement of co-operative societies in crop handling until the following year when funds would be available. In a move to ensure co-operative societies were fully engaged in marketing rice and coffee produced by native growers, the colonial authority released funds amounting to £2,265 in December 1948.[7] Release of the funds provided a guarantee for co-operative societies to be able to handle crops with effect

---

[1] TNA 322997, CS to PC SHP, Ref. 32997/66, 31 December 1947
[2] TNA 322997, EL Shipman (Co-operative Organiser) to PC, Ref. 9, 23 January 1948
[3] TNA 322997, CS to PC SHP, Telegram 32997, 10 July 1947
[4] TNA 322997, CS to PC SHP, Ref. 47/17/159, February 1948
[5] TNA 322997, CS to Registrar of Co-operative Societies, (Undated)
[6] TNA 32299,7 PC SHP to CS, Ref. 47/17/159
[7] TNA 322997, CS to Registrar of Co-operative Societies, Ref. 322997/127, 20 December 1948

from 1949. Further effort and commitment was evident as the CS stated that 'the government will make its effort available to support the co-operative societies to be able to purchase rice in Rungwe; and this has to be effected by guaranteeing a bank overdraft or by other means'. One of the means was an overdraft of £30,000 obtained from the Colonial Standing Finance Committee. Release of funds was justified by the Finance Committee on the pretext that employing co-operative societies in Rungwe was advantageous for economic control.[1]

Understandably, funding commitment by the Colonial Standing Finance Committee was not a grant, but it was a loan to co-operative societies, which had five per cent annual interest.[2] Accordingly, the colonial authority's release of funds to the Department of Co-operative Societies began to register rice marketing co-operative societies in which nine primary societies were registered in Kyela, which had 4,500 members. The £30,000 approved by the colonial government, and transferred into the DC, was all for registered rice marketing primary co-operative societies in Kyela.[3] The evidence shows that development was taking place in other areas, where in early May 1949 the necessary details for registration of the Rungwe Co-operative Union as well as primary societies meant to market coffee were finalised.[4] It has to be noted that primary societies affiliated to the Rungwe Co-operative Union were those registered in 1947. Registration of the Rungwe Co-operative Union was followed by further promotion and registration of other primary societies whereby in 1958 it had 18 affiliated organisations of which 11 were coffee marketing and six were handling rice.[5] In 1958, the amicable intention for breakup of the Rungwe African Co-operative Union into two was reached and the breakup was finalised in 1960 when a new union, the Unyakyusa Co-operative Union was formed and registered. This new union had nine affiliated primary societies that handled rice produced in Kyela.[6]

13.2: The Bukoba Co-operative Union

The Bukoba Co-operative Union (BCU) in Kagera Region (then Bukoba district and West Lake Region) is a peculiar co-operative movement case in terms of how it evolved, and the only co-operative society that handled Arabica and Robusta coffee varieties.

Coffee marketing in Kagera region began at the same time as in Kilimanjaro in the 1920s following maturity of coffee trees which were planted four

---

[1] TNA 322997, Memorandum no. 48 of Standing Finance Committee, 5 April 1949
[2] TNA 322997, CS to Registrar of Co-operative Societies, Telegram 322997, 4 May 1949
[3] TNA 322997, ibid., CS to Registrar of Co-operative Societies, Ref. 322997/167, 27 May 1949, CS to Registrar of Co-operative Societies, Ref. 322997/167, 3 June 1949
[4] TNA 322997, Registrar of Co-operative Societies to CS (undated)
[5] Horace Plunkett Foundation, *A Year Book of Agricultural Co-operation*
[6] Ibid.

years earlier. From the onset, coffee produced in Kagera was bought by merchants from outside the region. Most traders were from Uganda and as far as Mombasa, Kenya. Attraction of the coffee buyers (merchants) was a key factor in encouraging coffee cultivation, and owing to geographical proximity with Uganda special arrangements were put in place in which the Ugandan colonial authority could dictate, and had the mandate for, the policies that governed coffee marketing in the region.[1]

Importantly, a racially free coffee marketing policy was a dominant feature in the regions where traders, mainly Indians, Arabs and Africans, were encouraged into coffee marketing.[2] Such integration persisted largely because they had well established trade relations and ability locally to collect coffee; a task that was easily done owing to acquaintances and trust by growers.

Table 33: Licensed Coffee Dealers in Bukoba District Chiefdoms

	European	Indian	Arab	African	Total
Kianja	2	50	34	11	97
Ihangiro	-	8	23	45	76
Kiziba	-	13	7	36	56
Kinyengereko	-	2	23	25	50
Kiamtwara	-	24	14	36	74
Karagwe	-	1	7	4	12
Bugaboo	-	1	-	14	15
Misenyi	-	2	-	4	6

Source: Northcote 1936 Report (Appendix H)

One effect of the participation of natives in commerce in Kagera resulted in harmonious relations that minimised conflicts, hence, a drawback in demand for the formation of co-operatives as in Kilimanjaro. Nevertheless, this illustrates that the natives operated in the villages. This was as per licences granted to them; but they were not issued a licence for exporting coffee to the world markets as they had no chance to learn and practise international business. Such licences were reserved for Asians who kept a watchful eye on whether or not they were granted to Africans.[3] In this regard, division of function and role was clear – local traders were accommodated when they could be useful in the use of local languages, Kihaya or Kinyambo, for business transactions. The mentioned traders were operating in all eight chiefdoms.

Coffee traders of Indian and Arab background from Uganda and as far

---
[1] The Defence (Control of Cotton) Order of 1944, Section 4
[2] Kenneth R. Curtis, Cooperation and Cooptation: The Struggle for Market Control in the Bukoba district of Colonial Tanganyika, *The International Journal of African Historical Studies*, vol. 25, no. 3 (1992) pp. 506, 508, 509
[3] John Iliffe, *A Modern History of Tanganyika*, pp. 374- 375

as Mombasa could easily be attracted to the regions by the colonial authority which kept opportunities open for them. It is argued that Africans were introduced to coffee marketing by Asians as agents as well as porters because transport within the region was difficult and it remained so even when the transport infrastructure improved.[1] Indian coffee dealers were either agents of traders based in Kagera or were self-employed, some of whom like Sheriff Jiwa transferred businesses from Moshi after being granted a coffee marketing monopoly by the KNPA and later KNCU. There were also big coffee exporters based in Bukoba town, either as principal buyers and major exporters, or acting as company branch managers or agents of big merchants and companies based in Mombasa where coffee was auctioned.[2]

Coffee marketing in Kagera experienced a number of challenges. For example, there was laxity in control as there was no legal institution empowered for quality assurance. Coffee marketing was marred by an intensive struggle among the traders which compromised coffee quality. For example, growers were marketing poor and broken processed coffee beans where 50 per cent of the entire crop was hulled by growers on wooden huller (*kinu*),[3] and rock outcrop. In addition growers were mortgaging their produce before harvest which led to unfair prices, cheating was wide spread and sporadic marketing was common. All these were of concern to the colonial authority in the district and province. In an attempt to address them they invited Northcote to investigate the problems and recommend measures to improve coffee marketing. Northcote pointed out that marketing 'was in far worse state than the produce market in the Sukumaland (WCGA) prior to the establishment of Native Authority markets' (see cotton marketing in the WCGA for details).[4]

In an attempt to improve coffee marketing Northcote recommended the establishment of central marketing and buying posts. He defended them by arguing that for 'any improved marketing; it seems fundamentally necessary for the grower to sell coffee to a central depot or collecting station'.[5] This was meant to change the prevailing marketing system whereby traders collected coffee directly from growers. Secondly, it was stressed that licences for coffee buying be introduced which would eliminate and control the itinerant traders.[6]

[1] Kenneth R. Curtis, Cooperation and Cooptation, pp. 506, 508, 509

[2] TNA 23752, Report on Reorganisation of the Bukoba Native Coffee Industry, 31 March 1949

[3] TNA 24545, Report on Bukoba Coffee Marketing, p. 18, Bukoba Chamber of Commerce to CS

[4] TNA 24545, Northcote 1936 Inquiry Report on Bukoba Coffee Industry in Report on Bukoba Coffee Marketing

[5] TNA 24545, Report on Bukoba Coffee Marketing, p. 19

One of the measures recommended by Northcote included promotion of co-operatives designed to ensure improved coffee hulling and thus coffee quality in order to fetch a reasonable and better price. These were to serve growers at family or household level. Hulling co-operatives were envisaged not only to process coffee but also to facilitate collection of the produce for marketing that could then develop into a district co-operative union for bulk coffee handling.[1]

However, Northcote was cautious in his recommendation as he argued that 'any attempt to effect many changes all at once might be fraught with disaster and cause serious disorganisation in the disposal of the crop during the transition period'. To avoid a disaster, he maintained that societies offer guidance. He was optimistic that under guidance 'undoubtedly the co-operatives would be the easiest form that Africans […] understand and more adapted to his financing and organisation capabilities.'[2] Although he was optimistic, the expectation was failure as he pointed out that, 'but there is little prospect of success since there is no widespread desire for any co-operative selling agency; nor is there yet any external pressure so strong towards the direction to stimulate interest. This could be achieved through propaganda and explanation over a period of two years or more to encourage interest. Through propaganda growers need to be convinced of the resulting financial advantages so that they can willingly form societies to handle the crop and later stage to form a co-operative union; however, I do not visualise this to happen in a considerable period'.[3]

The recommendation was generally appropriate, but its implementation was unlikely given that his superiors were against such an approach. It will be recalled that Northcote was restricted from stimulating interest in co-operatives to growers, but they could be given guidance only when they spontaneously emerged. It was further argued that given the level of exposure among growers of modern co-operatives it was unlikely that societies would emerge spontaneously. Northcote provided a road map that emphasised sensitisation of growers, which illustrates a desire to instil an understanding that was presumably expected to generate a spontaneous need for the formation of co-operatives. Moreover, Northcote's proposal was fundamentally that success was unlikely because there was no department, funds or staff to facilitate the propaganda.

Northcote reiterated further that promotion of co-operatives was important; the chiefs could be informed, but they should not be actively engaged in the promotion process.[4] Active engagement of the chiefs in promoting

---

[6] Ibid.
[1] Ibid., p. 13
[2] Ibid., p. 21
[3] Ibid.

co-operatives would lead to development, top-down, that the imposed societies would be attached to the establishment and detached from forming voluntary organisations which were insulated from politics. However, his recommendations were seriously affected by decisions taken by senior colonial officials.

13.2.1: Political Decisions

Despite dislike of the DA to see growers organised into co-operatives, by 1936 some Africans in Kamachumu were organised under the unregistered Native Growers Association (NGA) which was under the leadership of Herbert Rugazibwa, President, and Clemens Kiiza, Secretary. Both were TAA committee members. In spite of NGA's affiliation to TAA, it was predominantly engaged in coffee marketing unlike the KNPA whose initial objects revolved around coffee production.

It is obvious that the association was being commercially challenged by coffee merchants. This was reflected in their request during a discussion with Northcote that the colonial authority 'prohibit the middlemen from buying coffee'.[1] They wanted a monopoly, the same as the KNPA and KNCU, and assured Northcote that they were capable of performing a useful role in the marketing of coffee in anticipation of a monopoly being granted at village level.[2] This illustrates that the association envisaged their business to focus on coffee collection from growers which was covered in Section 36 of the 1932 Co-operative legislation. It seems it was planned to operate as the KNPA with no affiliated societies at grassroots level. It also illustrates that the idea was to be appointed as marketing agent; a tactical step in displacing middlemen and iterant traders. In discussion with NGA leaders, it was made clear that NGA would not be allowed to purchase coffee from non-members.[3] Again, this demonstrated a double standard in providing the necessary support to growers who had shown an interest and desire in marketing their produce thereby undermining Section 36 (1) of the Co-operative Ordinance.

The NGA's vision did not portray any intention to be transformed into a co-operative society. They tended instead to operate as a company. But the idea fell short of Northcote's expectation on the premise that Northcote contemplated that 'it is insignificant given that there is no widespread desire for any co-operative selling agency, nor there yet any interest for growers to take joint action to save their own interests'.[4] However, Northcote's arguments might be baseless given that the NGA, regardless of its size, managed

---

[4] TNA 24545, Northcote 1936 Inquiry Report on Bukoba Coffee Industry, p. 2
[1] TNA 23752, PC Lake Province to CS, Ref. 976/233 of 6 July 1936
[2] Ibid.
[3] TNA 25777/1, Appendix M, Summary of conversation with the President of the NGA
[4] TNA 24545, Northcote 1936 Inquiry Report on Bukoba Coffee Industry, p. 21

to establish itself in some chiefdoms where it had members and support from the NA.

Northcote also established that the NGA was financially weak; and none had knowledge of both accountancy or bookkeeping, and business in general was poor.[1] However, Northcote did not consider or suggest an improvement. This was an obvious neglect by Northcote himself, as Registrar of Co-operative Societies, in taking the initiative to guide the association to improve its business knowledge.

That the association had no plans to transform itself into a co-operative society was likely due to lack of knowledge on co-operative organisation, unlike growers in Kilimanjaro who suggested forming the KNPA from experience with the settler organisation, KPA. It seems however, that the discussion was useful to help Northcote draw a roadmap for co-operative development in Kagera.

In June 1936, the Northcote view prompted NGA leaders to consult the PC to whom they presented a request for a loan amounting to £500, equivalent to 10,000/ shillings, so that it could engage in coffee trading.[2] When the PC received the NGA loan application letter he indicated that he could provide funding, but on condition that it should disassociate from politics; which they did and informed him.[3] The PC then asked the police to investigate the activities of NGA officials. The police report confirmed that Rugazibwa and Kiiza had resigned all positions in the TAA.[4] Despite the police report, the colonial authority declined to register the NGA. They were still realing from the KNPA incident. It also demonstrated that government was not willing to support growers' initiatives to engage in crop marketing.

The colonial authority totally undermined any development achieved by the NGA, arguing that 'it would be a fallacy to regard it as a marketing organisation[,] it has done little and not had substantial experience in marketing that was a basis to suggest that the NGA had no business potential or credibility'.[5] The conclusion was based on evidence that it marketed only 11 tons in 1934, six tons in 1935 and none in 1936, thus it was clear that it had no prospect for becoming a successful marketing organisation.[6] The basis for disapproval was the Credit to Natives Ordinance of 1931.[7] This Ordinance restricted Africans from access to credit

---

[1] TNA 24545, Northcote 1936 Inquiry Report on Bukoba Coffee Industry, p. 29
[2] TNA 24545, Report on Bukoba Coffee Marketing 'Confidential'
[3] TNA 41011, PC, Lake Province to CS, Ref. 9756/233, 6 July 1936
[4] TNA 41011, Commissioner of Police to PC, Lake Province, 17 September 1936
[5] TNA 25777/1, Confidential Report on Bukoba Coffee Marketing
[6] Ibid.
[7] Coulson, *Tanzania: A political economy*, pp. 60-61

unless specific permission had been granted by the government, as had been the case with KNCU when it had financial problems in 1934/35.

Both the DA and PC were sceptical about promotion of the NGA, largely because it would pose a threat to peace and order. Under this premise, it was strongly held that if co-operatives were to be allowed into coffee marketing, the Asian traders would resist eventually creating political and racial tension in Kagera. For them, co-operatives were inherently a threat to the establishment and posed a risk for fermenting political awareness and eventually a challenge to both the Native Authority and central government. They, too, indicated that unorganised growers were far better than organised, because unorganised growers could not have a voice and were more easily exploited than the organised who had bargaining power in the marketing of their produce.

The PC Lake Province sounded more anxious that the chiefs and NA would regard the co-operatives as new centres of political unrest, and emphasised that the NGA should be ignored as it would automatically vanish when co-operatives were formed through losing potential members. On the other hand, the PC felt that the focus had to be on hulling groups that, in his view, would grow into large societies and by then private buyers would remain the only outlet for coffee marketing.[1]

The PC Lake Province opposed promoting co-operative societies; they 'would create opposition from groups comprised of Arabs and Asians as well as those who had vested interest in the industry and they would be a threat to the chiefs as they would be a centre for fermenting political unrest'.[2] This suggested that the idea to promote or to register spontaneous co-operatives like the NGA was ruled out in favour of established stakeholders in coffee marketing, and declined for fear that they could pose a threat to the establishment and probably disrupt the whole industry.

Ultimately, Northcote's recommendations for promoting co-operatives were undesirable in some government quarters while others seem to have supported his idea. Generally, the government officials who commented on Northcote's report failed to come up with a time frame and strategy for encouraging co-operatives among growers. Comments and decisions were made by officials without involving or consulting growers on the matter. Thus, the official decisions remained inadequate and biased in addressing the whole question regarding the modality for encouraging co-operatives and a strategy to develop and guide the NGA on co-operative principles.

By 1938, the Lake Province PC decision remained unchanged regarding promotion of co-operatives in Kagera. The PC was not supportive of promoting co-operatives in his own area of jurisdiction. He argued that

---

[1] TNA 24545, PC Lake province to CS, Ref. 1110/80 23 April 1937 & 22 December 1937

[2] TNA 24545, PC Lake province to CS, Ref. 14/0/80, 22 December 1937

'even if it were shown to be desirable on economic grounds,' so long as there were traders buying coffee from growers, the co-operatives were irrelevant. He insisted that 'it is not necessary and consider that would be politically unwise to eliminate the present licensed buyers who are too ready to provide the service'. He further argued that 'promotion of co-operatives are nothing other than brewing unrest as it has been the case with coffee riots in Kilimanjaro' by stressing that 'this would add to unrest in case growers are paid low prices for their produce'.[1]

Consequently, the prospect for the rise and development of the movement in Kagera was placed in limbo and was further delayed due to the outbreak of the Second World War. The matter was aggravated further by adoption of Native Coffee (Control & Marketing) Ordinance 26, 1937 that led to setting up the Bukoba Coffee Control Board in 1941. Implementation of this policy came at an important time when the emphasis was primarily geared towards rationalisation and synchronisation of crop purchase in favour of a single government-appointed buyer. At this juncture opportunities began to appear for promotion of co-operatives.

13.2.2: Development in Bukoba after WWII

Commitment and development in Uganda were very important in providing a kick start to foster and guide co-operatives in the 1940s and early 1950s in Tanganyika. Pressure from UNO and Colonial Office following a report by the Fabian Colonial Bureau and Campbell were also important as they provided encouragement of grower co-operatives in Uganda from 1945. Such pressure had an impact in Tanganyika. Importantly, this was a period when the colonial policies on the co-operative and African produced marketing were under review.

After the war, creation of marketing boards was strongly emphasised by the Colonial Office. This was due to the success of the Cocoa Boards in West Africa in generating revenue for the colonial authority. Emphasis for co-operatives was by and large viewed more complementary to the work of the marketing boards than private traders. Such emphasis was basically designed to align the functions of the board and those of co-operatives. It was during this time that the British government intervened in crop marketing under bulk purchase in which co-operatives, the KNCU for example proved to be more suitable as they did not challenge the policy unlike private traders in the Kagera. Additionally, both co-operatives and government were united in not involving middlemen in crop marketing.

As a result, the DA drew up a Memorandum in 1946 earmarking the following preliminary issues:[2]

---

[1] TNA 25777, PC Lake Province to CS, Ref. 24545/95, 18 May 1938
[2] TNA 25777/1, Extract of Minutes of the 14th meeting of BNCB held on 4 May 1949

a) Bukoba is ready for a co-operative effort which should be actively fostered before the coffee agreement with the Ministry of Food expires on 30 November 1954;
b) To rationalise the industry, coffee crop must be purchased by a single buyer i.e. the government/agent appointed by the government or co-operative society; and
c) The government should provide assistance in teaching co-operative society staff in Bukoba accountancy and bookkeeping.

This commitment signified a new chapter for the promotion of co-operatives in the region, which was a significant step in replacing private firms. Nevertheless, none of the identified priorities earmarked or envisioned the movement in facilitating development. Emphasis revolved around the extraction of coffee and provision of knowledge on how best to manage co-operative accounting. The issue was lack of strategy as the DA's memorandum was more lip-service than a road map for implementation. Similarly, there were difficulties that arose, whereby BNCB, which had legal control of coffee marketing under the Native Coffee (Control & Marketing) Ordinance, 1937, itself did not recognise co-operatives. So it was the board which did not consider co-operatives necessary as private traders and agents were in place handling marketing on its behalf. It was over such legal issues that the BNCB delayed for more than two years in accepting co-operatives in the coffee marketing system.[1]

The Co-operative Department was in favour of co-operatives and viewed them as a suitable single buyer to be accommodated under the new policy. The interest was not just a single buyer, which in this case was the co-operative movement; but was viewed as necessary to replace private firms where trading interests were not compatible with those of the government, as for example, they were profit making and could not be controlled by the government in the same manner as co-operatives. Similarly, private firms could not be treated as a board's agent and be dictated prices in the same manner as co-operatives. Also, private firms had a well-established marketing network unlike co-operatives which had committee members who did not know external markets.

Since the co-operative was of priority to the Co-operative Department, J.S. Elliott, the co-operative officer, was deployed to Bukoba in 1947 to launch co-operatives in collaboration with the board. But, the board obstructed him in his duties and to meet its commitment. The board was legally positioned and empowered to reject proposals as it had a vast monopoly and control of the coffee industry. Also, the board had power to appoint an agent or contractor to purchase coffee from growers. Owing to

---

[1] TNA 29585, Registrar/Commissioner of Co-operative Development to Chairman, BNCB, Ref. Co-op. 29585/IL/485a, 22 September 1949, BNCB, Bukoba district

such difficulties the Registrar threatened to transfer Elliott to where he could be better utilised.[1]

This led the Registrar of Co-operatives to attempt to influence the appointment of a co-operative officer, A. Horley, to fill the post as Executive officer of the BNCB.[2] This was meant to address his Department's interest in promoting co-operatives as he pointed out that 'here would be more reality in the aiding of co-operative societies'.[3] The Registrar managed to convince government during the 1947 Provincial Commissioners conference that the appointment was an opportunity to stir enthusiasm within the board and manipulate policies in favour of the Registrar and Department.

Consideration to recruit a co-operative officer to be a BNCB executive officer was cautiously made in a Secretariat meeting, and declined on the grounds that the country had a shortage of co-operative officers. However, the Registrar was promised that the board would facilitate promoting co-operative societies. This development illustrated that the intention to have Horley recruited would have a far reaching impact on the Department of Co-operatives and the movement as a whole. Instead, T.M. Revington was recruited,[4] and, the board did not fulfil its promise to foster co-operatives. As a result, the Registrar raised his concern telling the board that 'the good intention and commitment of the Board to foster co-operation have paved the road to nowhere';[5] which was an indication that the board's promise had not implemented.

A new development was unveiled under the African Agricultural Products (Control & Marketing) Ordinance, 1949. This was comprehensive legislation that had to deal with all native or African-produced cash crops. Unlike the 1937 native coffee control and marketing legislation, this Ordinance recognised the existence of co-operatives and compelled the marketing boards to promote co-operatives. This was a significant policy shift with legal backing for promoting co-operatives. The 1949 legislation categorically provided for the appointment of co-operatives as the agents of the boards. Under the Ordinance, the board's functions were extended to include promotion and development of the co-operative movement.[6] Addi-

[1] TNA 29585, Registrar/Commissioner of Co-operative Development to Chairman, BNCB. Ref. Co-op. 29585/IL/485a, 22 September 1949. BNCB, Bukoba district
[2] TNA 11969/9, Registrar of Co-operative Societies recommended the appointment of A. Horley to the DA, Coffee Cultivation in Bukoba, Registrar of Co-operative Societies to DA (Biggs), Ref. Co-op. 1152/76, January 1950; TNA 11969/9, Advertised in *Tanganyika Standard* (weekly edition) on 7 January 1950
[3] TNA 11969/9, Registrar of Co-operative Societies to PC, Lake Province and Chairman BNCB, Ref. Co-op. 1153/8, 11 January 1950
[4] TNA 11969/9, PC, Lake Province to Secretariat Members of Agriculture and Natural Resources, Ref. 29585/304, 3 February 1950
[5] TNA 24545, Registrar to BNCB, 22 September 1949, Report on Bukoba Coffee Marketing
[6] TNA 11969/9, DA to the Secretariat Members of Agriculture and Natural Resources,

tionally, the legislation provided that surpluses accrued by the boards were to be returned to growers through the co-operatives; thus the boards lost power on spending the surpluses as growers had to benefit as co-operative members.

The policy shift was obvious and advantageous to coffee growers in Kagera. Under the legislation, colonial officials and the BNCB were obliged to promote co-operatives to market growers' coffee. However, the establishment of co-operatives experienced some historical challenges from the outset of commercialisation of coffee trade in Bukoba as explained previously. It was through purchasing crops from all races that minimised racial tension, unlike in Kilimanjaro where settlers agitated against Africans growing coffee and in the WCGA where Indian traders cheated growers which led to the emergence of the *mabebete* in the WCGA.

Faced with difficulties, government, through the Co-operative Departments, initiated the formation and registration of societies. The whole exercise was dominated by a government-led top-down approach.[1] Such an approach was necessary and justified owing to lack of enthusiasm by growers. Thus, Eckert's[2] argument that co-operatives in Tanzania were mainly the result of initiatives from the local rural population and can thus be seen as a movement 'from below', were not imposed upon Africans by the British.[3] Eckert's arguments are challenged by this evidence from Kagera region, which also suggests that arguments provided in existing literature do not hold ground as they tend to maintain that co-operatives were established in reaction to Asian traders monopolising cash crop marketing.[4] Similarly, Baldus[5] and Manday[6] posit that co-operatives were set up and charged with combating exploitation by traders.

In setting up co-operatives the colonial authority, mainly the Co-operative Department, did not educate members. There was no clear reason other than that education could delay formation of co-operatives being established. Irrespective, the campaigns would likely have faced difficulties and opposition from traders whose interest in coffee marketing would be

---

Ref. 1369/7561, May 1952

[1] Tanganyika Government, *Annual Report on Co-operative Development* (Dar es Salaam: Government Printer, 1951) paragraph 6

[2] Andreas Eckert, Useful instruments of participation? Local governments and co-operatives in Tanzania, 1940s-1970s, *International Journal of African Historical Sstudies*, vol. 40, no. 1 (2007) pp. 97-118

[3] Ibid.

[4] Göran Hydén, *Efficiency Versus Distribution in East African Co-operatives* (Nairobi, East Africa Literature Bureau, 1973) p. 9

[5] Rolf D. Baldus, The Tanzanian Co-operative Movement at the beginning of the Eighties: A comment, *Internationales Afrikaforum*, vol. 16, issue 1 (1980) pp. 63-64

[6] E.A. Manday, A New Structure for Co-operatives in Tanzania, *Annals of Public and Co-operative Economy*, 48, 2 (June 1977) pp. 239-244

threatened. Government's move towards co-operatives was justified by its commitment or desire to have a single buyer for the region and attain policy consistency, as in Kilimanjaro, and Songea where societies were an integral part of marketing policy. A single buyer in this case implied replacement of agents who were expensive when commission was paid and contracts were under the Ministry of Food; the commission rate as per the contract was 3/- shillings per ton.[1] A single buyer being the main motivation for promoting co-operatives in Kagera challenges Holmén's argument that co-operatives were formed by the colonial authority to facilitate tax collection.[2]

Forty co-operative societies were registered by March 1950 and the figure increased to 49 by the end of the year. Nine registered co-operatives which commenced operations prior to March 1950 handled 3,612 tons of coffee.[3] The newly registered societies were set up in various villages; the criterion for establishing them having been borrowed from the KNCU. The borrowed approach was also reflected in the BCU which was formed and registered on 19 October 1950 with registration number 144. The BCU was renamed Bukoba Native Co-operative Union (BNCU),[4] presumably, since it was hastily formed, there was no time to digest a name. The BNCB initially borrowed its name from the KNCU, thus it changed its name to Bukoba Co-operative Union in 1963.[5] The registration of the BCU was followed by a process to appoint a supervising manager. The process has not been documented in any existing literature; including an autobiography of one of its managers, Sir George Kahama.[6] When the BNCU was registered, A. Horley[7] was appointed by the governor as the first BCU supervising manager up to 1951. The power to make such an appointment was provided for under Section 36 Cap.211 of the African Agricultural Products (Control & Marketing) Ordinance, 1949. Chapman[8] took over from 1952.

The intervention by government in appointing BCU's supervising manager was one of two occasions. In such appointments, colonial officials

---

[1] TNA 37200, Memorandum as agreed at special group on the hard coffee exporters, 14 February 1947

[2] Hans Holmén, State, co-oeratives and development in Africa (Upsalla: Scandinavian Institute of Africa Studies, 1990) p. 23

[3] TNA 29585, Co-operative Department Bukoba to Commissioner of Co-operative Development, BNCB

[4] The BCU Annual Reports, 1959/1961

[5] Kituo cha Elimu ya Ushirika Moshi (CEC), *Jifunze Ushirika* (Moshi, Co-operative Education Centre, 1968) p. 39

[6] Joseph Kulwa Kahama, *Sir George: A Thematic History of Tanzania Thorough His Fifty Years of Public Service* (Beijing: Foreign Language Press, 2010) pp. 23-25

[7] TNA 28585, Co-operative Department to the Secretariat Agriculture and Natural Resources, Ref. Co-op. 144/F/1, 11 October 1951

[8] TNA 28585, Co-operative Department to the Secretariat Agriculture and Natural Resources, with Ref. Co-op. 144/166, 20 March 1952

(co-operative officers) were appointed to the post. The government intervention, however, illustrated a commitment and political will to realise that in Bukoba there was a lack of interest that itself had deliberately fostered co-operation. However, this shows that the BCU was an extended body of government with no grassroot grower foundation.

The formation and registration of co-operatives in Bukoba emerged during the renaissance era prompted and stirred by the Registrar of Co-operatives. He had to do so in line with the mandate of his office. The initiative was based on the fact that growers seemed inactive, less concerned and not motivated. The reason for lack of enthusiasm has been pointed out; that Bukoba presented a unique case in which the indigenous were actively involved in coffee purchase. This was demonstrated by larger numbers of indigenous traders who were granted licences for the purpose in the 1930s.

Changes in the BCU's personnel by government took into consideration credible officers. Both Horley and Chapman had once served as co-operative officers in the Bukoba district before their appointments. In an effort to reinforce the union's personnel, in 1955 it recruited a treasurer, Sir George Kulwa Kahama, who received management training from his superiors. When it was felt that Kahama was capable, he was appointed to a managerial position in 1956, replacing Chapman. Following his appointment, Sir Kahama became the first African manager, serving until 1961 when he took a Ministerial position in the independent government. Kahama's position was covered by G.M. Rugarabamu who was the BCU's Head of Coffee Cultural Section. But he was replaced by G. Ishengoma, following his appointment soon after independence as Assistant Permanent Secretary to the Ministry of Agriculture.[1]

At the time of BCU's registration, there were 31,642 members of whom 200 were women, which was only 31 per cent of entire growers' population.[2] The number of societies increased to 58 in 1954 and 73 in 1964 with 58,765 members.[3] By 1950, membership and delivery of coffee produce to a co-operative society was compulsory. Importantly, it was not the outcome of a popular demand, but was essentially the act of a government anxious to set up co-operatives for growers. Compulsory membership of co-operatives was necessary because growers formed the majority of coffee producers. They needed to deliver coffee to societies to fill a vacuum caused by the expiry of the zonal agents' contract.[4] In understanding that a vacuum

---

[1] The BCU Report for years 1961/62, 1962/63 and 1963/64, p. 7
[2] Tanganyika Government, *Annual Report on Co-operative Development* (Dar es Salaam: Government Printer, 1951) paragraph 6
[3] The BCU Report for years 1961/62, 1962/63 and 1963/64
[4] TNA 37200, Member for Tanzania's Finance, Trade and Economic to Director of East Africa Produce Disposal and Supply Council (Nairobi), Ref. 37200/701, March 1948; Note

would be created, a measure was provided under Clauses 2 and 10 of the agreements with zonal agents which permitted societies to deal with or through the zonal agents at the will of the board. The emphasis at this stage was ensuring coffee marketing was not disrupted.

The formation and registration of societies was a significant development that led to transferring the functions of BCNB to co-operatives. One responsibility was to facilitate and induce growers to improve production by encouraging them to weed their coffee farms, prune coffee trees and spray insecticides. It was obvious that this could effectively be bridged through the co-operatives.[1] The African Agricultural Products (Control & Marketing) Ordinance, 1949, provided for devolution of some of the board's functions and directed such functions to be handled by the co-operatives. In 1956, the BNCB provided BCU a sum of 875,000 shillings as a free loan to purchase the BNCB 51 per cent share from the Bukoba Coffee Curing Plant (BUKOP);[2] in this respect, the BCU was able to buy BNCB shares.

A fund for the purchase of coffee was made available from two main sources. First, from accumulated capital through members' shares; second, a grant was provided to each society for buildings, equipment and working capital for crop finance, at one per cent interest,[3] that enabled them in 1951 to handle 80 per cent of the coffee crop.[4]

In Bukoba, societies were financed by the BNCB from its accumulated surplus from coffee sales amounting to 25,000,000 shillings between 1945 and 1952,[5] in accordance with the 1949 African Agricultural Products (Control & Marketing) Ordinance. The Registrar of Co-operatives was empowered to recommend the board advance a loan for new and existing co-operatives as working capital for purchase of equipment on the understanding that the co-operatives had insufficient funds. Under this relationship the colonial authority employed its funds loaned to the co-operative as the the principal tool for collecting the produce. In this way, the colonial authority took direct responsibility to control and market coffee produced by Africans. The funds accumulated by the BNCB were set aside as a stabilisation fund to buffer against possible falls in coffee prices. The BNCB accumulated 9,328,911.18 shillings and 20,553,267.31 shillings in 1949 and 1950 respectively,[6] so that some funds were made available to

---

on Coffee Licensing, June 1950, Foreign Agriculture, September, vol. XII, no. 9, 1948, p. 102
[1] TNA 11969, vol. II Coffee in Bukoba, Coffee Cultivation Bukoba
[2] The Uganda War destroyed much of Tanzania's coffee output from Kagera; TNA 41011, Secretariat, Agriculture and Natural Resources, Ref. AN. 1/29/09/66, 10 April 1956,
[3] Tanganyika Government, *Annual Report on Co-operative Development*, (Dar es Salaam: Government Printer, 1950) p. 6
[4] TNA 11969/9, Extracts of the 25th meeting of the BNCB held on 25 October 1951
[5] Ibid.; Coulson, *Tanznia: A political economy*, p. 65

newly established societies for purchase of crops and construction of storage facilities. Facilitation of the funds by the board illustrates a cordial business relationship. It also shows that co-operatives were by and large complementary to the work of the agriculture marketing policy.

The practice in Kilimanjaro was that co-operatives were granted a marketing monopoly on the produce produced by natives. This was to maximise profit and protect growers from middlemen. However, this was not the case in Kagera when co-operative societies were registered in 1950. There was a clear reason for not granting them a monopoly as in Kilimanjaro: Kagera had limited capacity and experience; also co-operatives were yet to be established across the region. Traders were operating parallel with zonal agents who had a long term contract with the agents and the Ministry of Food which was in operation until 1954. Under these circumstances, the Commissioner of Co-operatives Development declined a request by the BNCB to compel traders under the African Agriculture Products (Control & Marketing), Cap.211 of 1949 to sell through the BCU.[1]

The existence of the parallel marketing system in Kagera had its effect on the co-operatives. For example, grower and trader responses in support of co-operatives were by and large uncertain and mixed. Firstly, the conditions created by accommodating a parallel marketing system and having all population groups involved in coffee marketing had far reaching impact as stakeholders reacted differently to the establishment of co-operatives. As a result, response towards the co-operatives was largely detrimental for the colonial marketing policies and the co-operative movement in the region as a whole. This was evident when co-operatives were introduced in response to coffee smuggling (*okutwala emwani oumagendo*) which had sprung up from Bukoba to Uganda where Robusta fetched better prices than in Tanzania.[2] This manifested itinerant traders' resistance and struggle to survive and secure better prices and a good profit. Indian and Arab traders exploited their networks to smuggle coffee as far as Mombasa where it was sold at auction with the board and had the Bukoba Native Plantation fair average quantity (FAQ) mark.[3]

Smuggling in Bukoba was facilitated by geographical proximity. The border with Uganda is long and porous, and along the border on both sides, communities share the same ethnic background and family ties that make it possible for people to travel or visit each other. It is believed that during

---

[6] TNA 29585, Co-operative Department Bukoba to Commissioner of Co-operative Development

[1] TNA 41011, BNCB to Members of Agriculture and Natural Resources, Ref. C.13/4, 23 February 1953

[2] Tanganyika Territory, *Annual Reports on Co-operative Development* (Dar es Salaam: Government Printer, 1956) p. 9

[3] TNA 29585, Illegal Traffic in Bukoba Coffee: Confidential Letter 45/46, 13 August 1952

such visits they carried coffee to sell in Uganda to where 25 per cent of the crop was smuggled.[1] An attractive price was the incentive for coffee smuggling to Uganda where the price was bolstered by a price stabilisation fund. Coffee from Kagera had to be sold under contract to the Ministry of Food, with the result that the price was low. At the same time, coffee auctions were held in Kampala which offered better prices. Such conditions prompted smuggling from Kagera. Thus, *okutwala emwani oumagendo* practices emerged as traders paid growers better compared with the co-operatives.

Non-natives were also cultivating coffee in Bukoba but the African Agricultural Products (Control & Marketing) legislation exempted them being subjected to NA regulations and they were not required to sell coffee through the BNCB.[2] The non-native-produced coffee could be sold and exported with no restrictions but was strictly monitored by the colonial authority in an attempt to ensure quality and curb smuggling. The records show that non-native annual coffee production was only 10 tons of Arabica and 50 tons of Robusta which they exported and auctioned in Mombasa.[3] However, in 1951, non-natives exported 315 tons, 450 tons in 1952 and 844 tons in 1953. These records confirmed that most exports were bought from growers.[4] This was also an indication that smuggling was taking place in which non-natives were involved and they exploited their trading network to facilitate such malpractice. Importantly, non-natives exploited decontrol of coffee trade provision to export coffee from the region which was sold at Mombasa, and later Kampala auctions, where they fetched better prices. This led to a considerable quantity, estimated around 3,155 tons between 1959/60 and 1960/61 seasons, which was smuggled into Uganda.[5]

Provision was in place to terminate traders, of whom about 200 were non-natives and 400 Africans,[6] under Section 44 of Cap.211 of the African Agricultural Products (Control & Marketing) Ordinance, 1949, that provided for the compulsory sale of produce through a registered co-operative society, which the BNCB attempted to exploit.[7]

The Commissioner of the Co-operative Department clearly perceived traders had good intentions and any drastic change would lead to problems; but the fact that traders 'advanced credits' to growers was nothing other

---

[1] Tanganyika Territory, *Annual Reports on Co-operative Development* (1956) p. 9
[2] Bukoba Coffee, Bukoba Coffee: Marketing Organisation, TNA 41011
[3] TNA 29585 BNCB to Commissioner of Co-operative Development, Confidential, Ref. 45/46 13 August 1952
[4] Ibid.
[5] Tanganyika Government, *Annual Report on Co-operative Development* (Dar es Salaam: Government Printer, 1960) p. 7
[6] TNA 29585, BNCB to Chairman, Coffee Licensing Board, Conf., C.1/64, 3 August 1951, Conf. Report 45/32 on Illegal Purchase & Smuggling of Coffee Produced in Bukoba district
[7] TNA 41011, BNCB to Members for Agriculture and Natural Resources (conf.) Ref. C.13/4, 23 February 1953

than purchase of the produce before it was harvested on what was popularly referred to as *okuguza obutula* in Kihaya or *kuchumbia kahawa* in Kiswahili which implies mortgaging of coffee produce. The Bukoba DC shared a similar view with the Commissioner of Co-operatives that there should be no abrupt discontinuation of coffee traders even after expiry of the Zone Agent agreement in October 1954. The decision was justified for fear that if co-operatives could not efficiently handle the crop, it would ferment agitation to the detriment of the movement.[1] On the other hand, it was perceived by the BNCB that the Co-operative Department policy partly created a space for traders to escalate coffee smuggling and it was strongly believed that continuation of the traders' activities further fuelled the chaotic situation to the detriment of the industry and the movement.[2]

An exchange of statements illustrates that at this juncture, the BNCB appeared to support the co-operatives basically because the rate of smuggling was on the increase which jeopardised its existence. Moreover, failure to collect levies would lead the BNCB into bankruptcy and embarrass the NA in not meeting its development goals and obligations.[3]

In an attempt to instil a positive sense to stakeholders in the co-operative movement, the BCU launched a strategy to curb smuggling by increasing coffee prices.[4] It also increased awareness and risks of smuggling through the *Buhaya Co-operative News* in 1957; the paper was in two languages, Kiswahili and Haya, and the *Bukoba Monthly* was launched the same year with 3,500 copies. In 1967, the paper was renamed *Bukoba Co-operative News*. However, smuggling persisted until the early 1960s when coffee prices fell drastically in the world markets.

Apart from smuggling, the BCU and its affiliated societies were further challenged by the Buhaya Coffee Planters Association (BCPA). The BCPA was formed in 1954 in Bukoba under the leadership of H. Rugazibwa, who in the 1930s led the NGA. The BCPA was a manifestation against the BCU and its affiliates. Rugazibwa was chairperson of TANU, Bukoba branch from 1954. He utilised TANU to resuscitate NGA interest in the late 1950s against the failure by the BCPA leadership to recall and appreciate difficulties faced by the NGA that obstructed it from registration because of its affiliation with politically motivated organisations.

BCPA's object was to serve 800 non-co-operative individual growers in Bukoba and to help them export and sell their coffee directly to Mombasa so they could benefit from better prices. Presumably, it also meant to

---

[1] TNA 7/4011, PC, Lake Province to Members of Agriculture and Natural Resources Secretariat, Confidential, Ref. CA3/1/1358, 19 November 1953

[2] TNA 7/4011, BNCB to Members for Agriculture and Natural Resources, Ref. C/10/44, 1 August 1953

[3] TNA 7/4011, 'Bukoba Coffee'

[4] Tanganyika Territory, *Annual Reports on Co-operative Development* (1956) p. 9

address the smuggling problem. Generally, the BCPA was a challenge to BNCU as it managed to instil in farmers a sense of being a better alternative for coffee marketing and income. It also posed itself as a non-exploitative organisation in that farmers had to hold their crop for some time. The BNCU launched a successful campaign to convince farmers that it was not exploitative as alleged by the BCPA. It made clear that prices offered by the BNCU were dictated in the world market.[1]

The BCPA's idea was timely and justified on the basis of the amended Section 6 of the 1949 African Agricultural Products (Control & Marketing) Act that repealed the boards' powers to appoint agents and made marketing for co-operatives compulsory from July 1951. The amended Section 6 was an opportunity for the BCPA to be granted a license. The BCPA targeted its members from Kamachumu and Ihangiro where Arabica coffee was produced. Apart from serving non co-operative members the association was meant to challenge both the BCU and BNCB by creating a new and alternative coffee marketing outlet. However, it was refused registration under the Bukoba and Kimwani Native Coffee (Compulsory Marketing) Order, 1954, published as Government Notice 199 of 1954, that empowered the BNCB to control coffee produced by the natives in BCPA targeted villages.[2]

The ultimate goal of the Order was to serve the colonial interest in the supply of coffee, showing that the BCPA was strategically and politically insecure. Moreover, the Order was enforced by the BNCB which declared that all coffee had to be sold by producers to BNCU and in that case the registration of BCPA was null and void.[3] Therefore, BCPA's intention to control the coffee industry could not materialise as the monopolistic marketing regulation embedded in the Order was granted to BCU and BNCB. The legislation was introduced by the colonial authority to protect the BCU, which it created, from facing competition by an organisation formed from below.

Rugazibwa made several appeals within Tanganyika and the UN against his declined registration. He pursued registration of the BCPA with the CS after it was declined at provincial level. In his appeal, he alleged the gross misconduct of the BCU as it was involved in cheating its members and growers, and employed a compulsion approach to non-co-operative members to sell their produce through BCU affiliated societies, which he viewed as violation of human rights.[4] However, the CS rejected his appeal[5] because

---

[1] Tanganyika Government, *Annual Report on Co-operative Development* (1960) p. 5
[2] TNA 7/2348/B, DC Bukoba to TANU Branch Bukoba, Ref. A.6/16/49, 17 July 1956
[3] TNA 7/2348/B, BNCB minute 677 note 8, 1 November 1954
[4] TNA 7/2348/B, TANU Branch Bukoba to CS Lake Province, Ref. TANU/BK/29/6, 18 August 1956

he produced fabricated complaints that the BCU was cheating growers.[1]

The rejected application by the CS kept Rugazibwa determined to exploit other avenues for registration of the BCPA. He took his appeal to UNO arbitration, expecting the case to be heard at its meeting on 12 July 1957 during session 839; but it was not discussed. The matter became more serious when the colonial government decided to deregister the TANU branch in Bukoba on grounds that 'the society was being or was likely to be used for purposes prejudicial to or incompatible with the maintenance of peace, order and good government'.[2]

The closure of TANU, Kiberezo branch in Bukoba displeased its members, which led to intervention by TANU at provincial level. In 1958, TANU discussed Rugazibwa's BCPA and abuse of office in demanding registration of a co-operative society or a company that aimed at marketing coffee with no consensus by TANU members. Rugazibwa was given two options by TANU: to remain in TANU leadership or concentrate on the BCPA. He opted to concentrate on BCPA instead of politics. His aim of using TANU to accelerate the BCPA's popularity was put on hold, and denied him a vehicle to build popular support. The TANU decision culminated in his loss of an anchor that he depended upon, but seemed to suggest that it had been democratic by providing Rugazibwa with a choice. Similarly, TANU's decision demonstrated that a priority was its own political development in Bukoba which was being exposed to a tug of war with the colonial authority by Rugazibwa. It was evident that TANU wished to keep politics away from the co-operative movement.

At this stage Rugazibwa considered a new option for registering BCPA as a company, and presented an application to the Lake Province, PC.[3] Once again, his application was rejected. Also, the Registrar of Co-operative Societies sent a separate letter to the BCPA giving reasons for rejecting its application: 'could not be registered because it contravened the provision of Section 352 of the Companies Ordinance (1921) that requires a company to have not more than 20 members but BCPA had 800 members'.[4]

13.2.3: Development in the WCGA

In the early 1950s, several other organisations were formed in the WCGA with or without support of the colonial government. The evidence from Geita district shows that in 1952,[5] embryonic growers' associations were

---

[5] TNA 7/2348/B, CS to TANU Branch Bukoba, Ref. ANC.17/43/020/198, 11 November 1956

[1] TNA 7/2348/B, TANU Branch Bukoba to CS, Lake Province, Ref. TANU/BK/29/8, 10 October 1956

[2] TNA 7/2348/B, Registrar General to BNCPA, Ref. G.2/28/122, 5 June 1958

[3] TNA 7/2348/B, TANU Branch Bukoba to PC Lake Province, Ref. TANU/BK/29/4, 27 July 1956

[4] TNA 7/2348/B, Registrar General to BNCPA, Ref. G.2/28/122, 5 June 1958

formed in Buchosa and Karumo Chiefdom such as *Wakulima wa Kiafrika*, Wafikiri African Union Association of Sengerema, *Wakulima Stadi*, Sukuma Union and Zinza Union. These societies in Geita went as far as forming a secondary society, the Mweli Co-operative Union. The members of societies formed in Geita were among the cotton growers who emerged from the post-Second World War policy that promoted progressive farmers who enjoyed financial and technical support from the colonial government. This had provided them with access to agricultural credit and high-yield cotton-seed varieties, as well as extension services.[1] Thus, support for formation of co-operatives was partly an economic initiative as well as political, that aimed to accommodate soldiers returning from the Second World War battlefields by defusing or diverting their political interest from engaging in the struggle against colonial rule.

The unregistered societies in Ukerewe were also formed with affiliation to the MATCS (Mwanza African Traders Co-operative Society). The most prominent society was the Ukerewe Farmers Society, which demanded entry into cotton marketing and in some instances, did so illegally. Unlike in Geita district, colonial officials did not provide support to any society in Ukerewe. This was viewed as calamitous as far as cotton marketing was concerned.[2] However, colonial officials supported the continuation of cotton marketing by Indian traders who were believed to be crucial in generating government revenue.[3]

In contrast, growers formed groups, popularly referred to by the colonial authority as independent weighers groups or as the *avapimiva magafu*, in Ukerewe and *mabebete* among Wasukuma. These groups were stationed in every cotton buying post and were formed primarily as a measure to check cheating of cotton growers by Indian traders. The colonial officials, particularly in Ukerewe, viewed them as troublesome and a nuisance to cotton buyers.[4]

The growing number of organisations in the WCGA with varied interests as far as cotton marketing was concerned was a weak point to pressurise the colonial government to promote co-operative movements. This was realised by MATCS's leaders who had to reconsider the approach following rejection of its attempt to market cotton, that led to the formation of the Lake Province Growers Association (LPGA). The primary motivation for the formation of the LPGA was to become a key participant in cotton

[5] TNA 215/1423/C, Geita DC to Sukumaland (Ibanza) Administrative Officer in charge on 6 July 1952
[1] TNA 215/A3/1, South Lake County Council to Chiefs of Mwanza, Ilemera & Bunegeji, Ref. P/LEG, 22 November 1956
[2] TNA 215/1423/C, Ukerewe DC to PC Lake Province, 3 September 1948
[3] Ibid.
[4] TNA 215/1423/C, Geita DC to Sukumaland Administrative Officer in charge, 6 July 1952

marketing in the WCGA.

Since the LPGA intended to cover the entire WCGA, it became necessary to bring grassroots organisations and unregistered societies under its umbrella. Having organised various associations under its auspices, the LPGA provided a pivotal base in pressing for opportunities to be open to native organisations. In its capacity, it began to challenge the existing colonial authority barriers preventing natives from being involved in the cotton trade. The LPGA for example, protested the exclusion of natives in cotton marketing under the war's cotton marketing policies, on one hand, and that reinforced the East African Exporters Group, on the other.

The same war and post-war policies indicated a lack of confidence in natives to be engaged in cotton trading. This was seen in the Co-operative Department's hesitation to register cotton marketing co-operative societies in the WCGA. The Registrar of Co-operative Societies, himself, openly undermined the possibility to have natives in cotton trading in an act viewed as discriminatory by the LPGA leadership. Thus, the LPGA had an agenda to exert pressure on the colonial government as it demanded a review of the colonial officials' attitude. This went hand in hand with a threat by LPGA leaders to mobilise growers to boycott selling their produce in the 1953 season. The threat worked as the colonial government was forced to deploy the co-operative officer, promote co-operatives and register co-operative societies from 1953 to promote cotton marketing in the same year.[1]

The newly registered societies proved their ability to handle cotton from growers, and managed to grasp a substantial share. Government backing as well as financial and logistical support enabled societies to gain ground with effect from their first season in marketing cotton from the LSMB.[2] The sum of £32,500 was made available to registered co-operative societies in 1953, repayable over five to ten years with interest of four per cent, for the purchase of equipment such as cash boxes, safes, and tarpaulins.[3] A total of £3,900 was allocated to purchase trucks for the transportation of cotton.[4] In 1954, the LSMB provided loans to 65 societies to erect cotton stores as well as to purchase capital equipment.[5]

---

[1] TNA 215/1423/C, Commissioner of Co-operative Development to PC, Lake Province, Ref. Co-op. 1038/3/191, 18 February 1952; Registrar of Co-operative Societies to PC, Lake Province, Ref. Co-op. 1058/3/191, 18 February 1952; TNA 215/1423/C, PC, Lake Province to DC, Geita district to, Ref. TNA 215/1423/A/303, 1 March 1952

[2] TNA 215/1423C, Commissioner of Co-operative Development to LSMB, Ref. Co-op. B/9/24 and Co-op. B/9/26, 11 April and 24 April 1953

[3] Ibid.; TNA 215/1423/A, Tanganyika, Annual Report on Co-operative Development, 1954, p. 11; LSMB Annual Report, 30 June 1954

[4] TNA 215/1423C, Ag Regional Assistant Director of Agriculture, Lake Province to Secretary LSMB Ref. 247/35, 1 June 1953

[5] TNA 215/1423/A, LSMB Annual Report, 30 June 1954

Further, in 1957 the LSMB made a loan amounting to 540,000/- shillings to two societies in Maswa district.[1] The support provided by the LSMB and Co-operative Department was to enable societies to market cotton efficiently. In the early 1960s, the Maswa Cotton Co-operative Society business operations were extended to Iramba and Singida because growers in these districts had no outlets through which they could sell their cotton produce. The two districts, Iramba and Singida, as well as Kondoa were in Central Province. No co-operative society was formed in these districts during colonial rule. However, in the early 1960s, Lutheran Missions, particularly in Iramba and Singida, provided support for the formation of cattle marketing; oilseed and groundnut co-operative societies which did not materialise.[2]

Within two seasons, more societies were registered in the WCGA. At the beginning, they too were under the umbrella of the LPGA which was not a co-operative society. This was viewed as a weak point in organising emerging societies. It was also seen as a vacuum that could weaken the spirit which was just gaining momentum, unless secondary societies were formed to oversee the needs of primary societies in, for example, the marketing of their crop. In this regard, the secondary co-operative society (union) had to be formed to serve cotton producing and processing zones. This was geared towards reinforcement of primary societies' capacity. It was also to ensure that primary societies were not susceptible to ginners' influence and competition because they had limited experience in managing and organising marketing for growing cotton .

The decision to form secondary societies was a significant departure for primary societies' reliance on assistance from government institutions, the LSMB and the Co-operative Development Department. In an attempt to move away from depending on government support and cotton traders, and ginners' intimidation, the process of forming unions was co-ordinated by the LPGA. It introduced significant reforms in the creation of the cotton marketing structure in each cotton production zone. Such reforms went hand in hand with recruiting personnel to manage the marketing process.

The unions were charged to supervise the activities of affiliated societies. They became a link between societies and the ginners, and control over the movement of crops from buying post to ginnery. The unions operated within cotton producing zones, some of which were set up in the 1930s. In 1955, seven unions were formed and registered. The setting up of the union created the need for an umbrella organisation to look after the interests of affiliated primary and secondary societies, and to facilitate negotiations on behalf of cotton growers with the government and ginners, which were at that time dominated by Asian traders. This culminated in the LPGA transforming into an apex organisation which was renamed the Victoria

---

[1] TNA 215/1423/C, Maswa District Annual Report, 1957
[2] Central Province Annual Report, 1961, p. 8

Federation of Co-operative Unions (VFCU) on 15 May 1955, which by 1967 had 19 affiliated unions, over 445 primary societies and 174,245 individual members who were cotton growers.

On 15 May 1955, the VFCU had seven affiliated co-operative unions all registered in 1955.[1] Masanja Shija became the first President of the Federation and Paul Bomani its general manager. By the early 1960s, the VFCU was the largest growers' organisation in Sub-Sahara Africa with over 275 primary societies and over 100,000 members. In 1959, the VFCU was granted an exclusive trade monopoly for cotton. The Indian cotton merchants' monopoly on the cotton market was finally broken following VFCU's appointment as the LSMB's agent;[2] a significant blow to the Indian cotton traders.[3]

---

[1] Co-operative Union of Tanganyika, 1962/63 Annual Report, p. 18
[2] Seimu, The Growth and Development of Coffee and Cotton Marketing Co-operatives
[3] NR Fuggles-Couchman, *Agriculture Change in Tanganyika: 1945–1960* (Stanford, California, Food Research Institute, Stanford University, 1964) p. 50

Table 34: Secondary Societies (Unions) Affiliated to the VFCU

No	Union	Translation	Zone	Registered
1	Ikumbo	Broom	Manawa - Kwimba	1956
2	Iyungilo	Filter	Bukumbi - Mwanza	1960
3	Kimisha	Awakening	Nyambiti - Kwimba	
4	Chenge cha Balimi	Torch/firebrand	Uzogole - Shinyanga	1956
5	Kipyena Bayanda	Exorcize children	Bukumbi - Geita	July 1956
6	Kiguna Bahabi	Sponsor of the poor	Nassa - Mwanza	1955
7	Nyamagana	One who give birth to hundreds	Ngasamo - Mwanza	
8	Kishamapanda	Road builder	Mhunze - Shinyanga	1960
9	Tupendane	love each other	Ushashi - Mara	
10	Mweli/Ng'weli farmers	Western Farmers	Geita - Mwanza	1954
11	Mugango	-	Mugango - Musoma	1955
12	Namuzuna	Supporter	Kibara - Ukerewe Mainland	1955
13	Buchililo	A place to recuperate	Nyamililo - Geita	1954
14	Idetenya bageni	Terror to aliens	Kasamwa - Geita	1955
15	Isangijo	Meeting place	Malampaka - Maswa	1955
16	Kilagabageni	Farewell to strangers	Sola - Maswa	1960
17	Lukubanija	Facilitator	Luguru - Maswa	1955
18	Engabo Union[1] (Bukerebe)	-	Murutunguru - Ukerewe Island	1955/1961
19	Kilelamhina	One who cares for the poor	Ihale - Mwanza	1956
20	Gwaging'olo Bageni	Disappointment of strangers	Magu - Kwimba	1960

Source: Annual reports on Co-operative Development 1959–1961

---

[1] Liquidated and Bukerebe was formed

14. Post-colonial Era

The chapter examines three major aspects of the co-operative movement's development in the post-colonial era. First, it gives a background to the post-colonial co-operative development policy. Second, it discusses co-operative development policy continuity, and finally, provides a critical analysis of the development of co-operative movements in relation to the changing political and ideological inclination during the first two decades of independence.

14.1: Co-operative Movement Expansion Policy

The history of the co-operative in Tanzania dates back to 1932, while support by government in promoting marketing co-operatives from the 1950s gave momentum for their growth. The co-operative movement was regarded by both government and the party as a vehicle for rural development. More stimulation was given by the independent government in the early 1960s whereby co-operatives were promoted across the country to include areas and regions that, until then, had no such organisation. However, the Co-operatives Society's Ordinances Cap.211 as amended in 1944 obstructed the initiative.

In order to do away with the situation in which the Registrar could reject an application, it was necessary to amend the Ordinance so that all co-operative societies were registered. The amendments were made in 1963 whereby the Minister responsible for co-operatives was given political powers for registering societies over the Registrar. The Ordinance stripped and undermined the Registrar, whose power was taken over by a politician auhtorised by the legislation to order registration of societies. The key role of the Registrar became record keeper of registered societies and membership.

To achieve this, the government amended Section 50 of the co-operative legislation in November 1962,[1] substituting the responsibilities of the Registrar of Co-operative Societies to the Minister responsible for co-operatives, George Kahama until 1965. Vesting the Registrar's powers and functions in politicians was partly addressing frustrations or red tape

---

[1] Amendments to Co-operative Societies Ordinance (Amendment) Act 72, 1962, Cap.211 were specifically Sections 37, 49, 50, 55. In these sections the word 'Registrar' was substituted for the word 'Minister'. Section 45 of the Ordinance was amended by deleting the words 'Governor in Council' wherever they appeared except where they formed part of the expression 'Governor in Council of Ministers' and substituted therefore in each case the word 'Minister'.

experienced by the Lake Province Growers' Association in the Western Cotton Growing Area. Paul Bomani made efforts to register co-operative societies for cotton marketing in the early 1950s, but was initially disappointed by the Commissioner of Co-operative Development who spearheaded such efforts.[1]

The amendment of law and rules were considered necessary because they were an obstacle to government's intention to register more co-operatives. The law and rules governing registration of societies required a society to be economically viable to be considered for registration. The assessment of viability and decision to register a society was made by the Registrar. This threatened to retard government's commitment; and in a move to facilitate the formation and registration of societies, section 67 was amended in 1967.[2] Following the amendments to Section 67, a room for registering societies was opened. This was basically a political move that hijacked the process for forming a co-operative society.

Alongside government's efforts to promote and register the primary co-operatives societies and some unions it also facilitated the formation of a co-operative apex organisation in 1961, the Co-operative Union of Tanganyika (CUT) – *Muungano wa Vyama vya Ushirika* in Kiswahili.[3] CUT was registered (number 848) on 27 November 1961 and became the ICA member, drawing membership from all Co-operative Unions in the country. The idea to form an apex body had been proposed by Northcote in 1932; it would perform audit and supervision functions.[4] The ideas were further expanded and there were some government indications for the preliminary move towards formation of the apex co-operative organization in the late 1940s. Its envisaged functions were:[5]

a. To promote African co-operative societies;
b. The organization of further societies;
c. Training of staff;
d. Provision of accountancy and audit services;
e. Bulk purchase and sale; and
f. Provision of co-operative education and propaganda.

The drive towards this position was based on the economic achievement attained by co-operatives during the colonial period. This convinced the post-colonial government that the same could be replicated simply by encouraging them. However, they did not take into account contributing

---

[1] Seimu, The Growth and Development of Coffee and Cotton Marketing Co-operatives
[2] Tanganyika Co-operative Societies Act
[3] CUT had affiliated members which were all co-operative unions in the country. One of CUT's functions was to encourage the growth of the movement and ensure the well-being of its members including adherence to co-operative principles and practices.
[4] TNA 19005, Organization of the Co-operative Societies in Tanganyika, paragraph 103
[5] Tanganyika Government, *Annual Report on Co-operative Development* 1947 report paragraph 6

factors for successes in other areas. Expansion did not adhere to certain basic aspects such as training of staff and education of co-operative members. Hence, some newly registered societies failed in the first instance to provide minimum services for their members.

Many societies and unions too small and weak[1] to be economically viable were registered. Hence there were 229 co-operative societies in 1963. Under this Ordinance, all applications for registration of a proposed society were accepted, even if not proven to be economically viable. Additionally, these societies had few or no qualified book-keepers or experienced committee members to efficiently lead and supervise affairs of the society. This led to the closure of several societies as shown in Table 35. However, such efforts did not take into account contributing factors from other areas, and expansion did not adhere to certain basic aspects such as training of staff and education for co-operative members. Hence, some newly registered societies failed in the first instance to provide minimum services for their members.

The expansion of the movement was not associated with an increase in qualified manpower in the Co-operatives Division. The growth and development of most newly promoted societies was a failure from the onset because the programme was rushed and hastily prepared, not adhering to certain basic aspects. The expansion of the co-operative movement overstretched the Co-operative Department in the spheres of supervision, auditing, shareholding, management and regulation as evidence shows that in 1960 there were only 157 co-operative officers employed by the government to provide technical support for 691 societies. Most of these officers were in a few regions/provinces where co-operatives were active; whilst in 1966 there were only 331 serving 1,616 societies that had grown like weeds. Of the 331 co-operative officers, only 137 were fully trained while the rest were apprentices. Consequently, a lack of supervision meant that dishonest persons found it only too easy to steal from new societies.[2]

The politicians exerted pressure for the formation and registration of co-operatives soon after independence. The expansion of the co-operative movement was such that in 1952 there was a total of 172 registered marketing societies. The number of societies increased from 857 in 1961 to 1,533 in 1966 and to 2,299 in 1973. The number of secondary unions or Co-operative Societies decreased from 34 in 1961 to 29 in 1973. At the end of 1974 there were 21 unions, all of them regional unions except two.

Table 35 shows that there were 1,364 active societies in 1964 compared with 857 in 1961 this marked an increase of 597 societies within three years.

---

[1] Report of the Presidential Special Committee into Co-operatives and Marketing Boards. (Dar es Salaam: Government Printer) p.37

[2] J.K. Nyerere, *Tanzania: Ten Years after Independence* (Dar es Salaam: Government Printer, 1971) p. 10

Table 35: Number of Co-operative Societies, 1961 – 1971

Up to 31 December	No of active societies	No of cancelled societies
1961	799	58
1962	974	72
1963	1201	74
1964	1364	90
1965	1508	111
1966	1616	122
1967	1649	169
1968	1694	169
1969	1741	210
1970	1754	224

Source: P Mgeze, Ushirika Tanzania (Dar es Salaam, Tanzania Publishing House) p. 14

Historically, most of the regions in the country had no co-operative societies until a year or so after independence. The formation of the societies was the government's means to ensure that every farmer had access to services. In this regard, the government proposed amalgamation of societies where societies were hoping for more government support.

A drive towards this position was the economic achievement attained by co-operatives during the colonial period which convinced the post-colonial government that more could be replicated simply with encouragement. However, such efforts did not take into account contributing factors from other areas, and expansion did not include certain basic aspects such as training of staff and education for co-operative members. Hence, some newly registered societies failed in the first instance to provide minimum services for their members.

Among government's efforts to promote and register the primary co-operative societies and some unions, it also facilitated the formation of a co-operative apex organisation, the Co-operative Union of Tanganyika (CUT),[1] which was registered on 27 November 1961. Such commitment was incorporated in TANU rural development policies; and was made clear by the Minister of Co-operative and Community Development, Hon. J.S. Kasambala, in his inauguration speech of the CUT first general meeting held on 16 and 17 February 1962. He pointed out that:

> Co-operatives will be called upon to play an increasing part in the building up of the economy of this country. Firstly, co-operatives will be used as a means to achieve our declared policy of creating greater wealth among our peoples and we should not be contented only with the event of distribution of what we now have, nor because

---

[1] The CUT had affiliated members which were all co-operative unions in the country. One of CUT's functions was to encourage the growth of the movement and ensure the well-being of its members in maintaining the co-operative principles and practices.

Table 36: Regional/area Distribution of Co-operatives, 1965

Region/area	Unions	Affiliated	Non aff	Type of produce
Arusha	2	14	6	Coffee (Arabica) pyrethrum, maize
Dodoma	1	53	1	Oil seeds, maize, paddy
Coast	1	10	3	Seed cotton, cashew nut, oil seeds, paddy
Iringa	2	40	3	Coffee (Arabica), maize, pyrethrum
Kilimanjaro	5	84	50	Coffee (Arabica), maize, seed cotton
Kigoma	1	13		Coffee, paddy, seed cotton, mixed produce
Mara	4	85	2	Coffee, maize, millet, Ghee, rice/paddy, sisal, seed cotton
Mbeya	4	59	20	Coffee (Arabica), oil seed, cashew nut, Maize, rice/paddy, mixed
Morogoro	3	37	4	Coffee (Arabica & Robusta), maize, rice/paddy, oil seed, mixed
Mtwara	1	98	7	Cashew nuts, oil seeds, maize, paddy, mixed produce
Mwanza	12	261	1	seed cotton, sisal, rice/paddy
Ruvuma	2	35	4	Coffee (Arabica), tobacco, oil seed, maize, mixed produce
Singida	1	20	1	oil seed, maize, paddy, honey, cotton
Shinyanga	6	161	-	seed cotton, sisal, rice/paddy, cattle, goats
Tanga	2	18	4	Copra, maize, Seed cotton, timber, oil seed wattle park, cashew nut, mixed produce
Tabora	2	73	10	Seed cotton, maize, paddy, mixed
West Lake (Kagera)	2	87	1	Coffee (Arabica & Robusta), mixed

Source: URT, Annual report on co-operative development (Dar es Salaam: Government Printer, 1965) pp. 36-37

we have so little, should we quarrel about this share among ourselves. Secondly, and this is equally important, government feels strongly in many spheres of economic activity such as our local industries, the safest and best road to social security will be achieved through the medium of co-operative movement which will go far to address the unhappy economic balance in which we find ourselves in this country.[1]

---

[1] *Muungano wa Vyama Vya Ushirika*, 1977

Against this backdrop, registration and promotion of co-operatives became a political issue. Politically, a drive to expand the footprint that could easily be achieved by transferring such functions and powers from the Registrar to politicians. The Minister approved societies and the Registrar maintained records. This undermined the ICA procedures that recommend the co-operative movement should remain an economic entity that aimed to serve members' interests.

Generally, the whole exercise was plagued by lack of adequate preparation and this precipitated a weak movement. Government involvement in promotion of the societies meant the members or farmers felt the institutions did not belong to them. Therefore, growth and development of newly promoted societies was a failure from the onset as agricultural production was low, reflected by the volume and real value of produce handled. This was due to the fact that production among farmers remained subsistence while tools for production and farming practices were poor.

As a result of amending legislation, mass co-operatives were formed with no consideration of economic viability. The policy was implemented under the top-down approach because government thought it had an obligation to help growers. It was thought transplanting co-operatives into rural areas were important mainly to mobilise and modernise agricultural development. The government promoted co-operatives and employed them as xenophobic tools aimed to facilitate Africanisation of the economy by displacing foreigners who had controlled the agricultural economy for many years. The government involvement in engaging co-operatives was obvious and necessary, but the challenge was how to carry out the exercise. The best approach was to have pilot areas from which lessons could be learnt for replication in other parts of the country.

Technical judgement in handling mass co-operatives suggests officers were under pressure to serve newly established societies, even to provide assistance to enable them to make sound decisions and manage co-operatives. Financial resources had to be stretched and it is obvious that it was too demanding to produce and develop a healthy new movement; if so, the old societies were affected by a lack of attention. Lack of professional support from the Co-operative Department led to critical inefficiency among newly introduced organisations; the 'old' organisations that comprised the primary and secondary societies were also affected as they experienced decreased efficiency.

At independence, TANU regarded the co-operatives as suitable rural institutions that would facilitate economic independence. It certainly was viewed that in the absence of government intervention, social change and agricultural transformation were unlikely.[1] To achieve this commitment,

---

[1] Seimu, The Growth and Development of Coffee and Cotton Marketing Co-operatives

there had to be a crash programme. The government's rash intervention resulted in the registration of societies. Despite the good intentions of those activities, there was little attempt to explain to the masses, the precise nature of a co-operative, and the principles that govern them; hence, they could not deliver. The exercise lacked sensitisation and co-operative education as well as training that led to members having little or no interest in organisations that were imposed upon them. Therefore, these were, in principle, government co-operatives rather than true membership-based co-operative societies.

In accordance with expansion policy, co-operative unions were also encouraged by government (see Table 37). This was a significant development given it was only four years after independence. These unions and those formed before independence were assigned a number of functions, such as distribution and control of agricultural credit to societies and ultimately to growers.[1]

Table 37: Co-operative Unions Registered after Independence

Union	Region/District	Year
Njombe	Iringa	June 1962
Mbeya	Mbeya	April 1963
Tarime	Mara	June 1963
Ulanga	Morogoro	October 1963
Mtwara	Mtwara	December 1963
Kilosa	Morogoro	February 1964
Singida	Singida	July 1964
Tanga	Tanga	July 1964
Kigoma	Kigoma	February 1965
Nguvumali	Tabora	June 1965
Igokelo	Kagera	1965
Irqobawe	Mbulu district	1965
Tunduru	Ruvuma	June 1965

Source: *Muungano wa Vyama vya Ushirika Tanganyika, Ushirika Wetu* (Dar es Salaam, 1977) p. 51

It is evident from Table 37 that there were no additional unions in Kilimanjaro and WCGA as they were already saturated; but, two primary societies were registered in Kagera, Itongo and Ilemera.[2] Igokelo was formed to handle cotton in Biharamulo, which was one of the districts in Kagera, and the Livestock Union, Wafugaji Co-operative Union, was formed in Tarime district in Mara Region in the WCGA.

Furthermore, the idea behind the promotion of mass co-operative societies across the country served both a political and economic agenda. The

---

[1] URT, *Annual Report on Co-operative Development for Tanganyika* (Dar es Salaam: Government Printer, 1965) p. 1

[2] BCU Reports 1961/62, 1962/63 and 1963/64 (Bukoba: BCU Printing Unit) p. 1

policy aimed to utilise co-operatives as a tool to unify Tanzanians divided as a result of colonial rule but government's intervention did not consider the healthy growth of newly registered societies. Co-operatives were assigned an effective role, particularly for improving the agricultural and rural economy. This was based on the fact that it would be a daunting task for the government to administer projects targeting isolated individuals in need of government assistance and services including credit for raising production and productivity.

The plans stressed co-operative business diversification, for example agricultural credit, input distribution, farming, supply of consumer commodities, and processing. The marketing of crops was a monopoly of the co-operatives and marketing boards, both institutions at this juncture being under the control of government. Thus, government had the upper hand in crop marketing and processing. Such control was deliberate so that private traders did not have access to purchase crops. Government control of crop marketing was necessary so that it could generate revenue, especially foreign exchange which was important not only for balance of payments but also for accumulation of financial capital.

To achieve national unity, the government and ruling party TANU (CCM since 1977) were directly engaged in a policy move appointing some co-operative movement leaders to Ministerial positions. Such leaders included George Kahama from the BCU (Home Affairs Ministry), Paul Bomani from the VFCU (Agriculture and Co-operatives), Asanterabi Zaphaniah Nsilo Swai from Meru Co-operative Union (Commerce and Industries), and Jeremiah Christina Kasambala from Rugwe Co-operative Union (Transport and Buildings, in the 1965 reshuffle he became Minister for Co-operative and Community Development).[1] Some officials, such as Paul Bomani and George Kahama, were among five LEGCO members during the colonial era. Having this number of co-operators was an indication of the importance of co-operatives, not only socially and economically but also of life in the public sector of the country.

The government was committed to Africanise the economy in all sectors. This was evident when it set out to replace 14,000 Asians who controlled retail, and 4,000 wholesale businesses, where the presence of Africans was negligible.[2] Against this backdrop, it was envisaged that the co-operative movement was a platform to engage Tanzanians in attaining economic independence and eventually self-reliance. At this stage, the post-colonial government demonstrated its racial motivation.

---

[1] Seimu, The Growth and Development of Coffee and Cotton Marketing Co-operatives
[2] Gerald Albaum & Gilbert L. Rutman, The Co-operative-Based Marketing System in Tanganyika, *Journal of Marketing*, vol. 31, no. 4, Part 1 (October 1967) pp. 54-58; *Muungano wa Vyama vya Ushirika, Ushirika Wetu* (Dar es Salaam: CUT, 1977) p. 55

The motivation was realised by setting up co-operatives, not in every part of the country but in every sector, including credit and industrial. The Co-operative Supply Association of Tanganyika (COSATA) was formed in 1962 by the government as a wholesaler and supplier of consumer goods to co-operative societies in the urban areas with technical support given by Israeli agency, AMIRAN.[1] COSATA was also entrusted with the responsibility of advancing the formation of consumer co-operatives in the country and to train Africans to manage co-operative shops. It was given distributive rights over consumer goods made and sold locally by industries, and it was envisaged that COSATA would gradually transfer trade, eventually securing 10 per cent of the retail trade, to co-operative societies. However, such commitment was not realised due to a lack of skilled manpower to manage consumer co-operatives, AMCOs were unwilling to become agents and limited capital to cover the whole country.[2]

The objective was not to facilitate training to Africans so they could become private shopkeepers but rather to enable them to work in consumer co-operatives. However, attempts to promote consumer co-operatives in Tanzania had limited achievement due to the lack of capital among the members while support from government was insignificant as more attention was paid to AMCOs.

Transportation co-operatives were encouraged, hence the formation of the Coast Region Transport Co-operative (CORETCO) and COCABS that provided taxi services in the city of Dar es Salaam. All these sectors were traditionally under the control of Asians. This was a step towards replacing the Asian shopkeepers. It was further envisaged that for effective utilisation and profit realisation, co-operative movements had to diversify their businesses to include marketing food crops, processing plants and agriculture production, effectively becoming multi-purpose.[3] This signified a shift of emphasis by having AMCOs undertake new businesses, again as a measure to replace private traders in every economic sector.

14.2. The Presidential Commission

The colonial era's primary co-operative societies and unions managed to render their co-operative services with a good degree of efficiency. However, considerable difficulty was experienced by the newly established societies and unions which had not been able to grow, assume responsibilities and carry out their duties owing to lack of sufficient knowledge and experience.[4] Growing complaints about inefficiency in management, cases

---

[1] *Muungano wa Vyama vya Ushirika, Ushirika Wetu*, p. 23

[2] Ibid.

[3] URT, *The Second Five-Year Plan for Economic and Social Development, 1964-1969* (Dar es Salaam: Government Printer, 1969) pp. 31-32

[4] Annual report on co-operative development for Tanganyika, 1965, p.10

of misuse of funds, and corrupt practices within the co-operatives were used as grounds by government to control agricultural marketing. Generally, the newly established societies were characterised by the failure of co-operative societies to deliver goods and services as expected by government. It was also alleged that co-operative members complained about some discrepancies between the co-operative unions and marketing boards.

Government responded by setting up a commission on 26 January 1966 when the President of the United Republic of Tanzania formed the Presidential Special Committee of Enquiry into the Co-operatives System and Crop Marketing Boards, known as the Mhaville Committee. The committee was given the following terms of reference:

> to review the staffing and, where necessary, the organisational structure of the co-operative movement and Marketing Boards in order to recommend what steps should be taken to strengthen them for the maximum benefit of producers and consumers alike

and to investigate the VFCU.[1]

The Committee published its report in June 1966. It pointed out that the top-down pressure exerted upon the formation of societies was considerable, but there was low enthusiasm, demand or knowledge among potential members.[2] Most co-operatives were put in place under weak economic circumstances; the political pressure that emerged after 1961 was considerable and it was disappointingly revealed that the failure of expansion of co-operatives was specifically in new areas. It was also reported that the sudden increase in the number of co-operatives created a burden for the Co-operative Department in providing reliable services for inspecting the books of account, and training. Such a huge number of societies resulted in challenges for the co-operative officers efficiently to provide professional support. Lack of professional support led to critical inefficiency, not only for newly registered societies but also the 'old' that comprised both primary and secondary societies.

The most important was the Committee of Enquiry into the Co-operatives Movement and Marketing Boards. The Presidential Commission in its findings detected six main defects in the co-operative movement namely:[3]

a. Uninformed membership;
b. Lack of democracy at union level;
c. Shortage of appropriate manpower;
d. Lack of consultants in co-operative venture;

---

[1] Annual report on co-operative development for Tanganyika, 1965, p. 10
[2] URT, The Presidential Commission of Enquiry on Co-operative Movements and Marketing Boards (1966) p. 5
[3] Report of the Presidential Special Committee into Co-operatives and Marketing Boards. (Dar es Salaam: Government Printer) pp. 9-12

e. The susceptibility of co-operative movement to political interference;
f. Low prices paid for farm produce, although later the crop boards sold them at reasonably higher prices; this was due to boards' high operational costs that forced low prices paid to growers so that the boards could meet such costs;
g. Failure of unions to pay growers their second installment payments due to financial losses, which result was viewed by growers as exploitative as the private traders;
h. Numerous deductions from gross proceeds of the produce delivered to co-operatives by growers;
i. Improper and unfair grading of produce.

In its findings the committee made some major recommendations, which were:[1]

a) The creation of a Unified Co-operative Service,[2] which would be responsible for the engagement of, discipline, terms of service and dismissal of all employees of registered societies. The engagement and dismissal of employees would thus be removed from the legal control of the committees of the co-operatives.
b) As a temporary measure, until Unified Co-operative Service could become effective, the Registrar should be given emergency powers to terminate the employment of any person appointed by the committee of a society.
c) In regions where there was more than one co-operative union they should be amalgamated.
d) Provision of co-operative education to the general public so that farmers could understand their rights and obligations in their co-operative societies
e) Setting up new separate boards assigned to handle food and cash crops.

In response to the committee findings and recommendations, government published its reaction later that year in Government Paper 3 of 1966. It accepted two of the recommendations which were incorporated into subsequent legislation. The third finding pointing out a lack of democracy at union level was viewed differently; government opinion being that this was exaggerated and was baseless. More reaction was placed on political interference. It was remarked that:

> ... it must be agreed that by their nature and by the role they play in the economy of the country, the co-operatives cannot be isolated

---

[1] URT, Report on the special presidential committee on reviving, strengthening and developing the co-operatives in Tanzania (2005) p. 8
[2] This was first brought to the Union in 1963 by the Minister of Commerce and Co-operatives but it was rejected.

from political life and must therefore, be subject, from time to time, to political consideration. The term 'political interference' however, requires to be defined as many instances of such 'interference' have proved to be completely beneficial, while others have proved to be equally disastrous ... As it is Government policy to employ the economic arm of co-operation to achieve the political aim of socialism, it is inevitable and also necessary that the two should be met and overlap from time to time.[1]

As from 1968, co-operatives continued to be given responsibilities as recommended by the Presidential Commission which were not part of the original co-operative agenda. One echoed an earlier idea of the Co-operative Department that led to the creation of a Unified Co-operative Service under Act 1968 (Cap.4, 1968), demonstrating active government intervention and control of the management of unions. The Unified Co-operative Service was a centrally directed body with the power to impose standards upon co-operative personnel and to move them from place to place in line with national policy decisions. One main object of this proposal seems to have been to inculcate a spirit of 'professionalism' in the movement and protecting them against the worst pressures of local committee men.

Government Paper 4 of 1967 provided a new policy direction for the co-operative movement. The paper called for the creation of multi-purpose co-operative societies. This was a clear policy shift from single purpose to multi-purpose co-operative organizations envisaged to enhance structural changes by having organised to perform production functions. In this respect, the secondary societies became multi-purpose whereby new business ventures were established in addition to serving affiliated primary societies like wholesale and transport, hotel services, tractor services and agriculture farming projects. Under the ArD more emphasis was placed on the agricultural sector in which co-operatives, apart from cash crops, were charged with marketing of food crops, and production.[2] It was stated that to build and maintain socialism it was essential that all the major means of production and exchange in the nation were controlled and owned by the small-scale growers through the machinery of government and their co-operatives.[3] For effective utilisation and profit realisation, it was recommended by the Presidential Commission that all organisations needed to diversify their business to include marketing food crops, processing plants and agriculture production so that they became multi-purpose co operatives.[4]

---

[1] Westergaard, Co-operatives in Tanzania as Economic and Development Institutions, pp. 131-132
[2] Second Plan, vol. I, p. 43
[3] Nyerere, *Freedom and Socialism, The policy of socialism*, p. 233
[4] URT (1969) pp. 31-32

The reorganisation of co-operative unions forcing them into multi-purpose activities enormously disrupted and restarted their plans, performance and progress. It overburdened their managerial and financial capacity apart from the lack of knowledge in executing some aspects of the business. For example, in an attempt to comply with government policy, unions had to engage in new business ventures that required financial resources; at the same time new ventures required knowledge and experience that a society lacked.

As a result of the enquiry, new co-operative legislation and reorganisation of the co-operative movement followed. Some of the recommended steps by the Special Committee of Enquiry described above were implemented in the second era/phase which began in 1967 which provided for dismanting unions across the country.

14.3. Dismantling agricultural marketing secondary societies

The Presidential Commission of Enquiry recommended strengthening the co-operative unions. As a result, the co-operative unions assumed regional boundaries. All these were carried out without the consent of members. One questions whether there was any forum for the co-operative movement to voice its complaints in a formal way. In implementing this order, government considered regional administrative boundaries a primary factor, and totally neglected considering key aspects such as business risks and prospects, and importantly, members' interest and commitment. This not only portrayed a top-down political idea and decision but also militated against building a self-sustaining and member-controlled co-operative movement. Logically, the policy was meant to ensure that each region had one union. The essence of the policy was the 1966 Presidential Committee recommendation effected under the 1968 co-operative legislation. The amalgamation of unions was viewed by government as cost-effective and helped to some measure to resuscitate poorly performing unions.[1]

The commission recommended that the Registrar be given emergency powers on a temporary basis to resolve the crisis in the movement. However, government took a more critical position by deciding to amend the 1932 legislation in regard to the Registrar's powers under the 1968 Co-operative Societies Act. Under this Act, the Registrar or his/her representative was given the ultimate power to decide on a number of management issues in the movement. Basically the Act provided the Commissioner of Co-operatives with new powers and an expanded department. Under the Act, government intensified direct control over 16 co-operative unions. It had powers to influence the day-to-day activities of co-operatives that included periodic government inspection.

---

[1] Seimu, The Growth and Development of the Coffee and Cotton Marketing; Seimu, Politics and Politicisation of the Tanzania's Agricultural Marketing Co-operatives

Another power provided to the Registrar by the Act was removing power from the leadership of any society when s/he felt necessary. In implementing such power the VFCU was reorganised and the board and senior staff were removed from office to restore legitimacy and governance. Government policy and its extensive intervention in the co-operative movement breached the aim of building democratically member-based controlled organizations.

Table 38: Regional Co-operative Unions

s/n	Union	Registration number	Date of registration
1	Arusha Region Co-operative union	1899	2. 5.1969
2	Coast Co-operative union	1515	2. 6.1965
3	Central Co-operative union	1305	5. 5.1964
4	Iringa Co-operative union	2410	15. 3.1973
5	Kigoma Co-operative union	1468	6. 2.1965
6	Singida Co-operative union	1368	1. 7.1964
7	Kilimanjaro Native Co-operative union	12	29.12.1933
8	VUASU	812	1. 1.1961
9	Mara Co-operative union	1945	8.11.1969
10	Mbeya Co-operative union	1968	1. 9.1970
11	Morogoro Co-operative union	1891	20. 3.1969
12	Mtwara Co-operative union	1272	6.12.1969
13	Lindi Co-operative union	2270	12. 6.1972
14	Nyanza Co-operative union	1818	31.12.1967
15	Ruvuma Co-operative union	2324	7. 9.1972
16	Shinyanga Co-operative union	2130	1. 1.1973
17	Tabora Co-operative union	2187	13. 4.1972
18	West Lake Co-operative union	2500	28. 6.1974
19	Rukwa Co-operative union	2501	1. 7.1974
20	Tanga Co-operative union	1958	11. 6.1970
21	Dar es Salaam Co-operative union	2502	10. 9.1974

Source: *Muungano wa Vyama vya Ushirika Tanganyika* (Dar es Salaam: CUT, 1977) p. 51

The policy was politically motivated. Cost effectiveness was a question to be considered by unions themselves and not to be told or instructed by the government. Amalgamation of societies was carried out by the government without the consent of members. As a result, the co-operative unions that were in existence had to be amalgamated through reorganisation and/or dismantling of those in place. At this juncture, the co-operative principles were marginalised and the political features, structures and objectives slotted in that marked a significant shift from the colonial model of co-operation which was supposedly inappropriate. This generated a complete new organisation: quasi-co-operatives based on regional geographical boundaries designed to serve political interests. This became a common phenomenon in which the movement's interests were marginalised.[1]

The 1966 Presidential Special Committee of Enquiry into the Co-operative Movement and Marketing Boards produced a special and separate interim report regarding the VFCU. The report identified a number of issues. Nepotism was a concern. This ranged from recruitment of staff, embezzlement of funds and corruption, to mention a few.

Some accusations may have had substance. For example, Paul Bomani had family members employed in the VFCU some of whom were in-laws. His own father, Lazaro Bomani, was Kimisha Co-operative Union Manager and his brothers, Jonathan and Emmanuel, were deputy manager at Buyagu ginnery which was in Kipyanabayanda Co-operative Union.

Under good governance criteria the recruitment of relatives on this scale might be seen as nepotism. However, the VFCU recruitment policy had been clear since its inception in 1955. Throughout this period it maintained a tradition of recruiting staff from within its operational area. The idea was to create employment for qualified individuals with an understanding of the culture, and especially of local languages spoken by the people in the province since Kiswahili was not popular in rural areas. It was also considered important to employ staff who were knowledgeable in the cotton industry. Staff were paid as per the VFCU scheme of service. Generally, salary and fringe benefits offered were far better than what was paid to civil servants. All these were a concern of the committee as it led to inequality within the Federation. It was thought that the Federation exploited growers only for the benefit of a small section of staff who were enjoying a luxurious life contrary to *Ujamaa*/socialist policy.

The Federation Manager at the time of investigation was Emanuel Bomani, who was accused of corruption and wealth accumulation. The board members were also accused of nepotism. So, the VFCU was viewed by government as an epicentre of corruption. However, neither investigation persued and there was no prosecution in regard to the allegations. Thus, the entire leadership had to be removed from office. This dramatic development took place in January 1968; the VFCU was dismantled. This recommendation was implemented by government dissolving all twenty unions affiliated to the Federation on 1 January 1968. This was the first tertiary co-operative organisation in Tanzania to be victimised prior to the promulgation of the 1968 Co-operative legislation. The VFCU, the largest co-operative organisation in Tanzania covering three regions, the major cotton producing location in the country, was fragmented into three co-operative unions that served Mara, Mwanza and Shinyanga Regions.

---

[1] Ibid.

Government's position was that the VFCU had divorced itself from the grassroots members, societies and unions.[1] Reorganisation of the VFCU into the Nyanza Co-operative Union (NCU) was followed by government order to form co-operative unions in each region in the country. The policy was backed by Government Notice 3 of 1966 that called for the amalgamation of co-operative unions in each region into one.

The passage of the 1968 co-operative legislation stemmed from the 1966 Presidential Committee recommendation that co-operatives have autonomous status and political interference be minimised, if not eliminated.[2] The legislation justified the government decision to dismantle and split the NCU, which was the predecessor of the VFCU. It was also illogical for a secondary society, the VFCU, to operate in three regions. Moreover, the BCU and KNCU were also affected; logically, policy consistency could be derived by having one union in each region.

Co-operative unions were formed under government influence, especially in regions where co-operatives were not prominent during the colonial era (Table 38). Secondary societies in Morogoro, Singida, Mtwara, Tanga, and Kigoma Regions were considered too small and weak therefore they amalgamated to form a union in each region. The amalgamation process emanating from government faced no resistance due to central pressure and local consent.[3] The formation of regional co-operative unions was completed in 1974 by registration of the then newly formed Dar es Salaam Region.

The post-Arusha Declaration (ArD), especially the Second Five Year Development Plan (1969–1974) supposedly revolved around the ArD policy. At this point, the salient feature of the co-operative policy was that the movement was perceived as a key instrument for the implementation of socialist policy as well as rural development. The overall result was that co-operatives became an instrument of state policy concerned with all round economic development. This was a shift away from having co-operatives serve the interests of its members. Rather, they were to propagate the ideology. Co-operative societies and AMCOs were thus engaged in affairs beyond their establishment. It also suggests their functions were being hijacked, falling under control of the party and government.

The basis for the promotion of co-operatives and development explained above was in practice an integral part of government's socialist policy that aimed to promote the welfare of the poor, mostly growers in rural areas. Since the Tanzanian development policy was anchored upon *Ujamaa*, the involvement of government was justified by ILO's 1966 Recommendation 127 that called for state intervention in the promotion

---
[1] *Muungano wa Vyama vya Ushirika Tanganyika* (1977) p. 36
[2] Seimu, The Growth and Development of Coffee and Cotton Marketing Co-operatives
[3] Hyden, *Co-operatives in Tanzania*, p. 15

of the co-operative movement throughout developing countries. On the other hand, Nyerere asserted that government was active for two reasons: first, because it was strongly held that it was only through co-operatives that growers could defend themselves against exploitation, something echoed by the socialist co-operative school.[1] Second, it was geared towards achieving modernisation of rural communities. This was reinforced by Government Paper 4 of 1967, which stated that:

> There was no other type of organisation (than co-operatives) which was so suited to the problems and concept of rural development. The re-utilisation of the co-operative movement in Tanzania was therefore vital to any programme of rural development. It was also emphasised that a co-operative society was basically a socialist institution and a considerable strength for the growth of socialism. This underlined a push by the government of the co-operatives' core orientation from their original crop marketing purpose to concentration on serving the party's Ujamaa ideological objectives.[2]

This was a significant break from the ICA co-operation model, supposedly to be more appropriate and specific to the national context by enlisting them to suit a country's ideological orientation. The co-operatives were obliged to be production oriented;[3] and were expected to fully participate in building and propagating modern production techniques, based on socialist ideals, in rural areas where they had a strong base among growers. The movement was utilised because it was the only institution with a rural stronghold and had thousands of members to whom socialist or *Ujamaa* ideals could be passed. Government argued that:

> There was no other type of organisation, which was so suited to the problem and concept of rural development; it would be impossible for government's administrative machinery to deal with individuals requiring government assistance and services, including credit for raising production and productivity. Without the use of co-operatives, the number of people wanting government help would make the dissemination of government services and assistance financially very expensive and administratively almost impossible.[4]

A further shift was signalled in a policy document, Socialism and Rural Development (*Ujamaa na Maendeleo Vijijini*) in September 1967 which aimed to address social and economic inequality in rural areas and bring to an end

---

[1] Alex F. Laidlaw, Co-operatives and the Poor: A Review from within the Co-operative Movement, *Co-operatives and the Poor* (London: ICA, 1978) pp. 51-90

[2] Nyerere, *Ujamaa: Essays on Socialism*, pp. 67, 352

[3] URT, Tanzania Second Five-Year Plan for Economic and Social Development, 1 July 1969 to 30 June 1974, vol. I (Dar es Salaam: Government Printer, 1969) p. 31

[4] URT, Paper 4 (Dar es Salaam: Government Printer, 1967)

exploitation of man by man. The policy stressed the importance of rural transformation under which the co-operative had to play its part. Certainly, this suggests that the post-colonial state's commitment to build a socialist state by use of the co-operative system was in jeopardy. It also demonstrates a failure of government to exploit and use the co-operative as a tool to propagate socialist ideology. The resistance heightened friction between government and the movement.

The policy was a framework for rural and national development set out in the Second Five Year Development Plan (1969-74) and Presidential Circular 1 of 1969. This stressed the importance of rural transformation under *Ujamaa* where people in rural areas should live together,[1] own the means of production and work communally. The main reasons for the adoption of a policy of concentrating new developments within existing societies arose from an attempt to prevent the overlapping of services in given areas by multiple societies all of which possessed wide powers under the usual Rules adopted at the time of incorporation. Existing co-operative societies had reserves of capital available which could be used for development in the locality. For example, in 1964, J.S. Kasambala, then Minister for Co-operative and Community Development, stated that co-operatives had an annual surplus of between \$2,500,000 and \$3,000,000 which could be invested, rather than redistributed to native producers.[2] They were usually in a position to borrow money for capital investment based on their business status and often without security demands. These factors along with others made it reasonably easy for them to initiate new developments if they possessed the necessary drive and vision. The very idea of economic development and of direct state intervention meant to safeguard and advance the standard of living of rural communities was a predominant concept in the post-colonial era.

Ujamaa villages were a model that borrowed elements from the colonial era settlements schemes, and echoed Chinese and Israeli rural development programmes as well as Indian community development programmes. In 1962, Israeli experts assisted in the WCGA to develop agriculture, particularly co-operative farming.[3] Powerful unions such as the KNCU, BCU and VFCU resisted implementation of government plans as they believed they would harm members who had accumulated wealth, for example land, through progressive and transformation approaches.[4] This heightened

---

[1] Presidential Circular 1 of 1969, The Development of *Ujamaa* Villages (Dar es Salaam: State House, 20 March 1969, Mimeo) p. 3

[2] *Tanganyika Standard*, 26 March 1964, p. 1

[3] Abel Jacob, Foreign Aid in Agriculture: Introducing Israel's Land Settlement Scheme to Tanzania (Undated), http://afraf.oxfordjournals.org/content/71/283/186.full.pdf, Accessed 22 December 2014

[4] Seimu, The Growth and Development of Coffee and Cotton Marketing Co-operatives

friction between the government and movement. It also indicated the failure of government to subdue or win over co-operatives and the difficulty of drafting them into implementing its policies as well as having them play a role in propagating its ideology.

14.3 Ideological orientation and National Development Plans

The First Five-year Plan[1] marked the beginning of the political shift away from capitalism towards socialism, unveiled in the Arusha Declaration of 5 February 1967.[2] Under the ArD the major means of production and exchange were extensively nationalised and placed under the control of workers and peasants through the government and co-operatives. With the nationalisation of estates and plantations, government could not cope with managing nationalised farms due to lack of staff and funding. Therefore, the plan emphasised strengthening co-operative organisations. For example, the KNCU was given nationalised coffee plantations. Thus, the movement became integral in the control of all major means of production and exchange. It was argued that:

> To build and maintain socialism, it was essential that all the major means of production and exchange in the nation were controlled and owned by peasants through the machinery of their government and their co-operatives.[3]

To this effect, government strengthened the administrative apparatus responsible for co-operation, adjusted co-operative legislation to fit the new strategy, so they became subject to strict political and ideological imperatives under government and the ruling party. Against this backdrop, it was envisaged that the co-operative movement would facilitate moving Tanzanians towards economic independence and self-reliance.

14.4. Illegitimacy of primary marketing co-operatives

In further response to the 1966 Committee of enquiry the marketing boards were transformed into crop authorities. To that effect, the NAPB was split into several crop authorities in 1973 whereby the NMC (National Milling Corporation) was created in 1968 to take over from eight private milling companies that had been nationalised and amalgamated to form the NAPB. Additionally, the NAPB was charged with responsibility to maintain strategic grain reserves and importation of agricultural products. Similarly, the existing marketing boards were transformed and restructured in 1973. For example, the LSMB became the Cotton Authority to handle cotton and the

---

[1] URT, *First Five-Year Plan for Economic and Social Development, 1964-1969*, vol. I (Dar es Salaam: Government Printer, 1964) p. 43

[2] Nyerere, *Ujamaa: Essays on Socialism*, pp. 13-37

[3] Nyerere, *Freedom and Socialism*, pp. 233-234

Coffee Board became the Coffee Authority to handle coffee while GAPEX was established primarily for export of crops. Bsed on an assumption that the crop authorities could perform better than the marketing boards, they were given a much wider mandate that included agricultural input supply (seeds, fertilizer, pesticides, insecticides), credit research and extension services. Such a mandate demonstrated government's desire to monopolise and entirely control agriculture production.

The crop authorities' functions remained the same as during the colonial era. The boards and crop authorities before and after independence provided a guarantee for the purchase of crops from co-operatives. However, co-operatives were restricted by law not to engage in international business, so were not given a chance to access world markets. This limited co-operatives to local markets, where the boards appointed the co-operatives as mere crop collection agents and a price taker for all collected crops.

By the mid 1970s, the commitment to build a socialist state using the inherited co-operative system was in difficulty. The co-operative movement with capitalist-oriented elements could not contribute to building a socialist state. The co-operative societies in place were characterised and guided by accommodation of the principles that encouraged individualism based on voluntary membership. Such features failed to deliver a communal way of life that was enshrined in *Ujamaa*.

To rejuvenate and realise such development, the policy required a new orientation. This was realised under the 1975 Villages and Ujamaa Villages (Registration, Designation and Administration) Act. The legislation was passed to provide legality of all newly established villages. At the same time, it made agricultural marketing co-operatives illegal. The legislation emphasised the inadequacies contained in Co-operative Societies Act 27 of 1968, mainly designed to cater for marketing co-operative societies. Against this backdrop, a new policy and legislation became necessary to accommodate villages as multi-purpose producer-co-operative societies. The Act designated villages as agents and basic crop collection points for crop authorities of coffee and cotton (formerly undertaken by marketing boards). The newly formed institutions, such as the National Milling Corporation (NMC) and General Agricultural Export Company (GAPEX) were all created in 1973 with much wider vertical responsibilities for production and development. Eventually the state itself took on the role of merchant in the form of crop authorities. Under the new marketing arrangement, primary co-operative societies and unions were made redundant.

Under Section 13, the village was deemed to be a co-operative society, and treated as one being assigned other crop handling responsibilities on behalf of the crop authorities. This signified an attempt by government to control the entire economy as it was thought the measure could salvage it from the crisis and eventually improve social and economic conditions, which were in decline. For example, the dissolution of co-operatives was a stepping-stone towards the access and control of levies accrued by co-operatives for every kilogramme sold by every grower in the country.

The Act rendered previous co-operative legislation redundant as primary co-operative societies, a dominant feature in villages, were replaced by villages taking on the function. Against this background, regional co-operative unions would no longer have access to crops. This was also an indication of declining government interest in the traditional model of co-operatives as both agent of social and economic change as well as a political instrument to promote African socialism and nationalism.

Sub-section 14 of the legislation indicated that 'co-operative society is allowed to operate within villages'. The legislation framed and structured village management by borrowing key elements from the co-operative legislation and the ruling party constitution. Practically, the Act eventually made regional co-operative unions redundant. The Act provided the villages opportunity to buy crops from producers and market their produce directly to the statutory crop authorities on the one hand, while denying the primary co-operative societies the opportunity. The village at the lowest level in government's hierarchical structure was unlike co-operatives and more suitable to both political control of the rural community and engaged in supervision of crop production and marketing.

Additionally, each village became a political and ideological unit as provided for under Sub-Section 15 of the Village Act, which maintained that 'functions of Village Assembly and Village Council to be under Party's aegis'. The imposition of village-based co-operative societies was a legal government measure for the exploitation of rural resources. The Village and Ujamaa Village Act stipulated the form of organisation that included the village assembly that elected the chairperson who also chaired the co-operative organisation. The village council was vested with the power to plan and co-ordinate economic activities. Leadership and governance were not a product of democratic practice, but imposed by government.

Membership included all village residents 18 years of age and above. Membership for all adults became compulsory, and was automatic for all who turned 18 years old. This meant a lack of incentive because membership was not free and voluntary. It fell short of the principles that governed the co-operative movement. Politics became part of the daily function of the co-operative movement, which was contrary to co-operative principles.

14.5. The disbandment of co-operative unions

With effect from 1974 crop authorities began purchasing crops directly from primary societies, a function that was still under co-operative unions that marked a new beginning and signaled a new government direction towards surpassing the movement; in ensuring that it grabbed surpluses previously accrued by the unions while ensuring growers reasonable prices for their produce. However, payment of 'good' prices to growers did not materialise owing to the fact that prices for commodities had always been determined in the world market.

The illegitimacy of primary marketing co-operative societies did not go hand in hand with unions or secondary societies. According to the Village Act, 1975, unions were not declared illegal until 1979 when they were disbanded. The dissolution of AMCOs and secondary societies was, however, a shock to growers as the agencies imposed on them were not their choice but dictated by government. This marked the beginning of villages and entire rural communities coming under direct control of government through its parastatals. This political decision culminated in the move towards nationalisation with the agriculture sector finally placed under government's socialist-controlled economy.

Government had installed socialistic co-operatives at village level, socialising the means of production, whereby growers were detached from their assets, and separated from their property at the expense of private household capital accumulation. This pattern of capital accumulation at the local household level created apathy and a low level of commitment to the new village co-operatives. Other factors had prompted and reinforced government to embark upon such moves. For example, in the wake of the 1973 oil crisis and drought of the early 1970s, Tanzania experienced an economic crisis.[1] Declining prices for agricultural products in the international markets and worsened terms of trade,[2] had far-reaching effects on Tanzania's balance of payments.

The policy further disempowered growers who were left without institutional arrangements or fora where they could meet, discuss and decide on the fate of their general welfare. Understandably, such functions were handed over to the village government who were expected to operate like Israel's *kibbutz* and *Moshav*.[3] *Ujamaa* villages were designed to be production co-operatives, ideal for economies of scale by pooling resources such as

---

[1] Seimu, The Growth and Development of Coffee and Cotton Marketing Co-operatives

[2] S. Ponte, Trading Images: Discourse and Statistical Evidence on Agricultural Adjustment in Tanzania (1986-95), in P.G. Forster & S. Maghimbi (eds.), *Agrarian Economy, State and Society in Contemporary Tanzania* (Aldershot: Ashgate, 1999) pp. 3-25; Benno Ndulu, *Stabilisation and Adjustment Policies and Programmes. Country Study 17 Tanzania.* (World Institute for Development Economic Research of the United Nations University, 1988) pp. 1-2

[3] Maxwell Owusu, Agriculture and Rural Development since 1935, in Ali Mzrui (ed.) *Africa Since 1935* (Oxford: James Currey, 1999) p. 323; Seimu, The Growth and Development of Coffee and Cotton Marketing Co-operatives; Jacob, Foreign Aid in Agriculture

land to farm together using modern farming machinery. Ideally, the primary objective was to meet the political need and commitment of the ruling party. In this, the party was committed to eradicate all types of exploitation of man by man But, the village leadership in this respect paid more attention to the ruling party's interests than those of the co-operatives. To this effect, issues regarding co-operatives were neglected by the leadership; thus, the village as a co-operative or *kibbutz* and *moshav* concept failed.

The village co-operative had neither legal mechanisms nor bye-laws that provided for managing village co-operative businesses. The only guidance available was based on the village's party branch powers that had nothing to do with the co-operative. In a critical case, government did not utilise the managerial competence that could be offered by ousted staff and committees if co-opted to village government. The co-operative model was shredded, crippled and became meaningless. It was paid only lip service by the ruling party. Furthermore, the co-operatives were maintained as a draconian political approach in suppressing growers' interests.

This transformation was against the original Rochdale or ICA co-operative philosophy. Under the new model, societies were merely pseudo co-operatives with leaders appointed by government and the political party, TANU. In 1977, TANU and ASP joined to form *Chama Cha Mapinduzi* (CCM) and continued the aims of TANU to establish itself at all levels of society and to push Tanzania's socialist revolution to a higher degree. A move toward having Party Supremacy appeared in 1975 by amending Section 3 of the Interim Constitution. The amendment provided that all political activities be performed under auspices of the ruling party.

At this point, co-operative principles were marginalised and replaced by political features and structures where political objectives became paramount. The co-operative movement was not spared as it was incorporated into ruling party politics on 23 May 1979, Act 9 that provided for the establishment of the UCS or Union of Co-operative Societies (*Jumuiya ya Muungano wa Vyama vya Ushirika* in Kiswahili). UCS became a fully-fledged organ of the ruling party along with other civil societies and organizations representing women, trade unions, youths and parents. *Jumuiya ya Washirika* officially became the arm of the ruling party responsible for mobilising, providing guidance and supervision of growers and villages as well propagating all types of co-operatives.[1]

CUT was dissolved leaving UCS the only institution representing the movement which nonetheless was not in existence; so it represented villages and villagers though not democratically since its leaders were appointed by the party. Ideally, it was envisaged to make all these organisations,

---

[1] Owusu, Agriculture and rural development, p. 323; Seimu, The Growth and Development of Coffee and Cotton Marketing Co-operatives; Jacob, Foreign Aid in Agriculture

including the co-operatives, more directly subordinate to the ideological agenda of CCM which implied nothing other than wiping out the movement as an economic entity altogether.

Moreover, looking at the structure and function prescribed, one sees that this was not a co-operative organisation, but a political and government entity. These pseudo co-operatives were established and legally entrenched in rural areas. Government forcefully installed a completely new structure that villagers did not demand. The installed co-operatives were politically motivated to meet the interests of political leadership in which member control did not exist. Consequently, a different structure was developed and operated from co-operatives in the West. The ICA principle of the centrality of democracy in member-based organisations was clearly subverted, as the secretary of a society was a government appointee and village executive officer.

Villages became an administrative and political unit of the party and government. Elected representatives at lower levels of the party hierarchy were imposed on growers – serving political interests rather than economies. One change brought in by this Act was the direct and immediate takeover of the crop marketing function by villages on the grounds that regional unions were too bureaucratic, and expensive middlemen had to be replaced by direct transactions between villages and crop authorities. Villages were appointed agents of the crop authorities and boards. The newly established multi-purpose producer co-operative societies (villages) sold crops to crop authorities and boards, as directed by legislation and policies. Under this new arrangement, co-operative societies and unions were not only side stepped but also made redundant.

While the former regional unions were deemed too bureaucratic and expensive, due to a lack of facilities and experienced staff in the majority of villages, the parastatals had to extend their own arrangements. On occasion where villages were producing varied crops, it called for arrangements with a number of parastatals. The actual result seemed to be that villages, instead of being masters, became more subservient to crop marketing parastatals. Subservience extended to obedient acceptance of pricing and internal marketing cost budgeting policies of the parastatals.

The 1975/1976 changes did not affect urban-based co-operatives on the side-lines. Although they numbered over 1,600, the initial concern of the Union of Co-operative Societies concentrated on *Ujamaa* villages. The urban-based co-operatives had no representation on the UCS National Implementation Committee. The situation created by the sudden changes caused a noticeable slowdown in technical assistance delivery activities by Nordic and other donors.

This was an unfortunate moment for co-operatives, which were the biggest and most advanced in Africa, and the oldest in East Africa. This was nothing other than a nationalisation exercise propagated under the 1967 Arusha Declaration that aimed at control of the agricultural economy by the state. It was primarily an attempt by government to distance itself from its 1967 Arusha Declaration policy that maintained control of the economy by workers through trade unions and co-operatives. It also demonstrated the failure of government to exploit and use the co-operative as its tool to propagate socialist ideology. Again, this was an obvious use of power by government against an element that posed an obstacle to its policies. It is significant that government's decision to dissolve agricultural marketing co-operatives did not affect consumer, industrial, savings or credit co-operatives; it was vengeance against agricultural marketing co-operatives.

The dissolution of the unions left farmers without organisations to which they could turn for credit, agricultural input, extension services and marketing. As previously mentioned, the co-operative apex body, the Co-operative Union of Tanganyika (CUT), had been formed in 1962 by government. In 1979 under the *Jumuiya ya Washirika* Act, the CUT was renamed the Union of Co-operative Societies (UCS), *Jumuiya ya Washirika*, and officially became the arm of the ruling party responsible for mobilising, providing guidance and supervision of growers and villages as well propagating all types of co-operatives.[1] The post-colonial era witnessed two major constitutional changes. The first was in 1965 that provided for a single party democratic state under TANU; this came after a Union between Tanganyika and Zanzibar in 26 April 1964. In 1975, the year in which the party became supreme it concentrated immense powers in the President.

For a couple of years, co-operatives were accused by the post-colonial authority of fostering corruption and inefficiency in delivering its responsibilities. However, these accusations were generalised, as the performance of many societies was incredible. A witch-hunt was evident. In addition, government was displeased at seeing societies run and dominated by wealthy peasants who used them to exploit producers; thus, they were converted from service provision to exploiting institutions contrary to socialist ideals. Others were of opinion that co-operative unions, under the rural petty bourgeoisie, posed a political threat to post-Arusha Declaration Tanzania.

In 1975, government appointed a commission of enquiry, the Masomo Commission, to investigate the co-operative movement following the accusations of corruption and inefficiency. The commission comprised representatives from the prime minister's office, the CUT, COASCO (the Audit and Supervision Fund), Unified Co-operative Service Commission and Moshi Co-operative College. This commission proposed that RCUs should

---

[1] Seimu, The Growth and Development of Coffee and Cotton Marketing Co-operatives

be maintained with the exception of VUASU (whose affiliated societies were North Pare Native Co-operative, South Pare Native Co-operative, Gombero Copra Co-operative, Usambara Native Coffee Co-operative and Kihurio Co-operative Societies). The commission recommended that regional co-operative unions should not be abolished but be replaced by distinct co-operative unions.

Government shelved the Masomo recommendations. Instead, it passed the Villages and Ujamaa Act of 1975. The terms of this Act stipulated that each village co-operative would be multi-purpose and handle all the crops produced in that village, and that the village had to function as a consumer co-operative as well, making the regional co-operative unions redundant.

Between February and April 1976, the TANU national executive committee met. On the agenda, was the dissolution of all RCUs. The movement representatives in the meeting were asked to present their case. This agenda was challenged by co-operative movement delegates represented by CUT as well as party delegates who were co-operators like K.K. Nangale from SHIRECU. It was finally agreed that the delegates from CUT and from the movement should vote. When the vote was cast, members from Kagera, Kilimanjaro, Arusha, Shinyanga, Mwanza and Mbeya Regions lost. Nevertheless, RCUs were not dissolved until 15 June 1976, when Prime Minister Rashidi Mfaume Kawawa issued a government decree to dissolve them.

Finally, on 14 May 1976 the unions were dissolved. The assets of primary co-operative societies were handed over to the village government designated as basic collection points for specialised crop authorities. The government decision to dissolve the producer co-operative organisation did not affect other types of co-operative which were allowed to continue operating under the 1968 Co-operative Act. This generates an assumption that this was a deliberate action by government to suppress marketing co-operatives. Some critics of the 1975 Act are of the view that the act was vague and hastily approved without much study of possible precedents. Moreover, it is silent on matters related to possibile joint ventures between neighbouring villages or on the relationship between villages and marketing authorities. It also placed more emphasis on agricultural production and marketing with less on other businesses such as handcraft, artisanship, savings and credit co-operatives.

The measure culminated in employing villages as an integral part of the ruling party. This was further reinforced in the 1982 Co-operative and Societies Act whereby all villages in the country became members, marking the climax in integrating the co-operative movement into the ruling party structure. It also provided for considerable government interference in the affairs of co-operatives, for example, the relevant Minister or Registrar of Co-operative Societies could appoint party members in key co-operative positions. The 1982 co-operative legislation thereby created no room for growth or development of independent movements free from government interference.

Tanzania experienced reasonable economic prosperity with an average real GDP annual growth rate of 5.0 per cent during the first decade of independence. However, prosperity lasted only a few years. A crisis began in the 1970s that resulted in a decline of per capita GDP growth to an average of 0.2 per cent between 1976 and 1978 and an average real decline of -2.5 per cent per annum between 1979 and 1984.[1] A number of contributing internal and external factors caused the economic crisis. Internal factors included serious drought in 1974, and war with Uganda, 1978-9, in which US$500 million was spent in an effort to remove Idi Amin from power. Other factors were inefficiency in managing public parastatals.[2] External factors were the break up of the East Africa Community in 1977, and an increase in global oil prices in 1978/9 that necessitated doubling defence expenditure. In response to the economic crisis confronting Tanzania in 1979, government approached the World Bank and IMF.

The World Bank and IMF imposed conditions designed to decrease the role of government in the economy while increasing the role of the free market, to reschedule its debts and to qualify for continued foreign aid. Tanzania rejected the offer, only to embark on home grown SAPs referred to as the National Economic Survival Programme (NESP), instead of embarking on reforms prescribed by the Bretton Wood institutions, that is, the International Monetary Fund (IMF) and World Bank. However, NESP proved a failure by 1982.[3] The rejection of IMF and World Bank recommendations had been based on the contention that privatisation of the economy would sway the country towards capitalism.[4] In so doing, *ujamaa* policy was compromised. Refusal by government to accept and adopt the World Bank and IMF conditions suggests rigidity of government to ease its grip upon the economy.

Failure of NESP and pressure from Nordic countries forced Tanzania once again to approach the World Bank and the IMF for support to guide it through economic reforms in the country. The intensity of the crisis had been evident in the 1980s, when there was a severe deterioration of social

---

[1] B. Ndulu, Stabilisation and Adjustment Policies and Programmes: Country Study – Tanzania (World Institute for Development Economics Research of the United Nations University, 1987) p. 1

[2] D.B. Kamala, The Voices of the Poor and Poverty Eradication Strategies in Tanzania. *an open lecture delivered at the University of Hull Business School on 14 January 2004* http://www2.hull.ac.uk/hubs/pdf/memorandum45.pdf . Accessed 15 February 2013

[3] P. Gibbon, 'Mechanisation of Production and Privatisation of Development in Post-Ujamaa Tanzania: An Introduction; in P. Gibbons (ed.), *Liberalised Development in Tanzania: Studies on Accumulated Pricesses and Local Industry* (Upssala: Nordic African Institute, 1995) p. 12

[4] Seimu, The Growth and Development of Coffee and Cotton Marketing Co-operatives

services. Shop shelves were empty as industries could not produce commodities for lack of raw materials, most of which were imported, and government's parastatals responsible for importing consumer goods were short of foreign exchange to pay for goods. Worse, the country was in acute balance of payment deficit. These problems generated a political rift in how to resolve the crisis. The first group, the die-hards, led by President Nyerere and some party ideologists and cadres such as Kingunge Ngombale-Mwiru, ex-Prime Minister Rashidi Kawawa and economist Kighoma Malima, maintained that the crisis was primarily due to factors such as rising oil prices, the Ugandan war, and unfavourable commodity prices in the world market, which for them were all temporary, thus promoting a 'wait and see' policy. For them, the status quo dominated their position; self-reliance as embedded in the ArD policy. By 1980, the problems relating to crop authorities had become so serious that government decided to resuscitate the co-operative movement.[1] Importantly, since government relied on agricultural export for servicing and repayment of debts, it found itself in crisis following the crop authorities' poor performance. Therefore, the government of Tanzania decided to reinstate AMCOs in 1982 as part of an economy-wide reform and due to its parastatals' inefficiency and failure in accomplishing their basic functions of crop collection and payment of farmers.

The need for reform was accelerated by internal factors, particularly by appointing Ali Hassan Mwinyi as President. He was pro-reform following the retirement of Julius Nyerere, a staunch socialist. Other prominent individuals who accelerated reforms were Paul Bomani, a co-operative pioneer in the WCGA and government minister, and Cleopa Msuya, previously Minister of Finance who led the pro-economic reform group.[2] This group was in favour of the market-oriented approach. For them, socialist policy had failed and was unworkable. This group had support from donor countries that pressurised the government which eventually gave in to implement the Structural Adjustment Programmes (SAPs) from 1986. The SAPs had conditions attached. The most significant was trade liberalisation. Consequently, it became necessary that government loosen its noose on agricultural marketing policy and the economy in general.[3] The implementation of SAPs paved the way for the reinstatement of the co-operative movement provided for under the 1982 Co-operative Societies Act. However, the Act's objectives stated that 'the co-operative movement should

---

[1] E.H. Moshi, The Dilemma of Agricultural Marketing Co-Operatives in Tanzania in Liberalised Economy, *Paper presented to the Co-operative College Annual Symposium*, September 1997, p. 4
[2] Seimu, The Growth and Development of Coffee and Cotton Marketing Co-operatives
[3] Kjell J. Havnevik, Tanznaia: The limits to development from above (Upsalla: Nordiska Afrikainstutet, 1993) p. 61; Andrew Salehe Zuakuu Kiondo, The Politics of Economic Reforms in Tanzania 1977-1988 (Ph.D. Thesis, University of Toronto, 1989) pp. 199-200

strive in accordance with its democratic socialist and co-operative outlook', which implied they remained under ruling party influence and control.

In an attempt to keep up with the economic adjustment pace, it became necessary to enact new legislation, the Co-operative Societies Act of 1991. The reinstatement of AMCOs came at a time when government was embarking upon economic reforms when deregulation and globalisation were central global economic agenda items. In this regard, the agricultural marketing reforms affected AMCOs for the first time since 1937 following the passage of the Agricultural Industry (Marketing & Control) Ordinance. Under the legislation, AMCOs' commercial status was reduced to an agency role, mainly to facilitate handling of crops from growers on behalf of the marketing boards. Similarly, the crop authorities authorised villages to handle crops from growers. Though co-operatives were undermined by agricultural marketing legislation, they were given a monopoly over crop handling to enforce effectiveness. However, the legislation exposed a potentially weak organisation as far as business competition was concerned.

In line with reinstating the co-operative movement, crop marketing legislation was amended providing for the re-establishment of marketing boards. In 1984, government promulgated a new Act referred to as the Coffee Marketing Act that transformed the crop authorities back into marketing boards and re-established the three-tier marketing system.[1] Under this legislation, the Tanzania Coffee Marketing Board (TCMB) was established. The Act repealed the 1977 Coffee Industry Act that led to the creation of the Coffee Authority of Tanzania. What differentiated the Coffee Authority and Coffee Marketing Board was extension services to farmers, which was one of the functions of the CAT; the extension services under the 1984 Act were transferred to the Ministry of Agriculture and Livestock Development and Ministry of Local Government, Co-operative and Marketing as well as co-operative unions.[2]

In a further development, in 1992 Tanzania embraced a multi-party politically oriented constitution. This development provided room for AMCOs to be dislodged or disentangled from the ideologies and control by *Chama Cha Mapinduzi* (CCM). Hence, the political reforms, *Jumuiya ya Washirika*, ceased to be an arm of the ruling party; hence it was renamed the Tanzania Federation of Co-operatives (TFC), registered on 8 December 1994. As such, internal political reforms and economic liberalisation prompted endorsement of the autonomous status of the co-operative movement in Tanzania for the first time since independence, embedded in

---

[1] W. Ngirwa, 'Agriculture Transformation Issues in Tanzania, *Paper presented in Agricultural Transformation Workshop* (1995) http://aec.msu.edu/%5C/fs2/ag_transformation/ngirwa.pdf. Accessed 14/02/2013

[2] A. Carlsson, *Co-operative and the State: parties in development? A human resource perspective* (Stockholm & Oxford: Institute of International Education & Clarendon Press, 1992)

the 1991 co-operative legislation.

Despite the adoption of multi-party politics in Tanzania, ruling party elements and influences were retained. Understandably, tens of hundreds of co-operative members maintained membership of the party and many others joined newly formed political parties. Some were voted to society positions as no regulation or legislation barred them from doing so. Obviously, this resulted in some cases of party politics in co-operative societies. In a move to end the practice, the 2013 Co-operative Act addressed the matter under Section 132 that maintains that:

> a member of a co-operative society who holds an appointed or elected political or public office shall be deemed to have conflict of interest and shall not be eligible for being elected as a leader of a co-operative society or appointed a member of the Board or any committee to the co-operative society.

The liberalisation of agricultural marketing attracted tens of private traders and companies to the country. For example, in Karagwe there are over 15 companies currently operating in the district. Under such circumstances, AMCOs' monopoly market share dwindled as growers had additional marketing avenues that in some instances presented attractive alternatives and enjoyed freedom to sell their produce to whomever. This forced some AMCOs to the verge of collapse and some into bankruptcy. The crisis prompted government to investigate the problem and come up with measures to resolve the challenges as addressed in the 2000 Presidential Special Committee on the Revival, Strengthening and Development of Co-operatives. The Presidential Committee report culminated in the 2002 Co-operative Development Policy that reaffirmed government's commitment to International Co-operative Principles and Values.

Liberalisation of the agricultural marketing policy was disastrous to AMCOs. Under the policy, government had to withdraw its support of co-operatives, particularly financing. The AMCOs were high-risk with regard to credit for agricultural activities. As a result, AMCOs were exposed to critical financial challenge in purchasing crops from its members. To fill the gap through an opportunity that exploited liberalisation of the banking sector, the Kilimanjaro Co-operative Bank (KCBL) was the first to be registered under the Co-operative Societies Act 15 of 1991, followed by Kagera Farmers' Co-operative Bank. The KCBL was established to mobilise savings from the public and co-operative societies and lend money to AMCOs to facilitate them purchasing crop marketing.

Understandably, the agricultural marketing reforms brought in new skills and knowledge in managing international businesses. But the co-operative movements' marketing practices remained the same. There were no self-initiatives from co-operatives to learn entrepreneurship skills and gain knowledge. There was also no attempt made by the governments of donor countries to pressurise for reform by imparting new practices among co-operative members and staff in marketing to help them survive competition. However, for most AMCOs, the reforms crippled and disoriented their facilitative agency status as they managed business only within villages and transportation of the produce to neighbouring towns, and in some instances to the exporting ports of Dar es Salaam and Tanga. The AMCOs lost decades of monopoly and protection provided by government through agricultural marketing legislation.

In response to global deregulation and globalisation, in 1995 the ICA stressed, and granted, Tanzania co-operative entrepreneur status. Recognition of the co-operative as an enterprise echoed in the 1997 Co-operative Development policy. In addition to their loss of monopoly and protection, co-operatives faced difficulties operating in a liberalised economy because agricultural marketing and financial reforms brought capital, new skill and knowledge to businesses from private traders that led to increased competition. In addition, it allowed the union to establish and decide where and to whom to sell or export its produce. The growth of a number of co-operative societies was in line with in the early 1960's commitment by government. In contrast to why co-operative societies were compelled to become multi-purpose, the trend in the post-liberalisation era is that they produce or deal with specific enterprises as shown in Table 39; all co-operatives are recognised under Section 27 of the 2013 Co-operative legislation.

Table 39: Co-operative Societies in Tanzania as at June 2011

Type of co-operative society	Number of societies	Membership
Agricultural Marketing	2,819	845,700
SACCOS	5,314	1,552,242
Industrial	161	3,220
Consumer	107	10,700
Livestock	211	21,000
Fishery	122	6,100
Service	213	21,300
Housing	29	1,450
Mining	72	3,600
Irrigation	114	5,700
Others	361	36,100
Total primary Co-operatives	9,523	2,506,412
Co-operative Unions	40	
Apex	1	
Federation	1	
Total	9,565	2,506,412

Source: Ministry of Agriculture, Food Security and Co-operatives, 2011

15. Conclusion

Following the 1884/5 Berlin Conference, Tanganyika came under German colonial rule with the name German East Africa including the current Rwanda and Burundi, but excluding Zanzibar. During the First World War, German colonial rule began to disintegrate as British and Belgian forces occupied northern parts of the country. At the same time, the British installed civil administration in its occupied parts of the country where economic and infrastructure restoration was initiated.

When the war ended, the country was divided into three countries, Tanganyika, Rwanda and Burundi. These countries were handed over to two European powers, Britain took most of Tanganyika whereas Burundi and Rwanda went to Belgium, all governed under the League of Nations Mandate System which was instituted in 1919. In 1920 the office of Governor as Commander in Chief was set up in Tanganyika. The office was made answerable to the Secretary of State for Colonies in London. The western parts of the country that comprised Ngara and Kigoma which were under Belgian occupation were handed to Britain in March 1921.

British rule in Tanganyika was provided for under Article 22 of the League of Nations Charter that called upon the new power to administer the country, promoting the inhabitants' material and moral well-being, with social progress as a key agenda. This signified a departure from legitimisation of colonialism and exploitation of the colonised to one of protection under the League of Nations. The British embarked on political reconstruction of the administration by setting up departments and installing administrators, drawing the administrative boundaries for districts and provinces, and appointing provincial and district administrators.

The Indirect Rule policy which was put in place by the British was meant to serve the interest of the colonial authority. Local chiefs were appointed as part and parcel of Indirect Rule. The appointed chiefs were supposed to be good colonial authority collaborators. Under Indirect Rule, the colonial authority dismissed chiefs who failed to meet colonial authority expectations in facilitating colonial agendas. Basically, the appointed chiefs were figureheads and tools to rubber stamp colonial policies. As per Indirect Rule, NAs were responsible for enacting bye-laws, supervising agricultural development and marketing. They were also responsible for tax collection.

The agriculture development policy among small-scale producers was important for three major reasons. First, the sector was the largest economic activity that comprised both plantation and small-scale growers. Second, it was envisaged to facilitate economic recovery and economic development of the country. Third, it was a source of raw materials and food crops that had to generate revenue through exports to cover administrative costs, and was a means for the colonised to generate revenue to pay taxes. To achieve this, in the 1920s, the colonial authority created crop marketing channels which were the Native Authority Treasury, particularly No. 2 and Suspense Accounts, as well as merchants and local growers' marketing associations and organisations.

The colonial authority accommodated the colonised in the cash crop agricultural sector through production of small-scale cash growers. As a result of implementation of both the League of Nation's commitment and the need to generate revenue, there arose a predominance of small-scale growers in the production of coffee and cotton. Generally, small-scale growers proved a success through colonial authority intervention to ensure its sustainability. The colonial authority aided growers in every way to increase agricultural output, distributing seeds in the case of tobacco and cotton and seedlings for coffee.

The colonial authority exploited the NAs to introduce and cement cash crop production among small-scale growers. A series of legislation and regulations were enacted by the NAs geared towards, not only, compulsorily engaging small-scale growers in cash crop production, but also to ensure increased volume to maintain export supply commitments which was evident during economic depressions and throughout the 1940s and 1950s. For example, cotton farming among small-scale growers in the WCGA was guided by policies that compelled growers to produce the crop without consulting them, in response to demand in Britain. The policies were meant to confine small-scale growers to cotton farming. Such policies were primarily exploitative and marginalised growers, by preventing them from access to the most profitable portions of the cotton value chain. Such a lucrative portion of the cotton value chain was handed over to Indian cotton merchants who through various policies had an exclusive monopoly in buying, processing (ginning) and exporting the crop. The small-scale growers were excluded from cotton ginning and export, which was yet another example of marginalization.

Crop marketing for crops produced by small-scale growers was through three main channels: the NAs' No. 2 and Suspense Accounts, merchants mainly Indians, and growers' marketing associations or organisations. These channels evolved over time to become agricultural co-operative marketing societies depending on the surrounding forces. The history of agricultural marketing co-operatives in Tanganyika dates back to 1932 when the Co-operative Societies Ordinance was passed, followed by registration of several small-scale growers' co-operatives; the first in Kilimanjaro, followed by Ngara, Ruvuma, Southern Highlands, Kagera and WCGA. Evidence shows that the emergence of agricultural marketing co-operatives in the WCGA was bottom-up which was a unique feature given that the country was under colonial rule. This was not the case in other parts of the country, such as Kilimanjaro, Ruvuma, Southern Highlands and Kagera Regions, where it happened at the behest of the colonial authority. The same applied in many other areas where the post-colonial authority championed for the formation and registration of co-operative societies. The necessity for co-operative legislation in Tanganyika was prompted by the popularity of the KNPA among growers, which caused the colonial authority and the chiefs in Kilimanjaro to see it as a trespass into political spheres, hence a threat to the establishment.

The co-operative legislation was drafted with the colonial authority's interests being a priority and neither the growers, native authorities nor chiefs were consulted. In this regard, the legislation was biased in favour of colonial interests through the overseeing and execution of control of growers and what they produced. The legislation was not meant to facilitate promotion of the co-operative movement in Tanganyika, but was a move to replace the KNPA by KNCU and its affiliated societies: KNPA grew out of growers' demand whereas KNCU was imposed on growers.

The KNCU and its affiliated societies enjoyed a monopoly in handling coffee, grown not only by its members but also non-members. Such compulsions were facilitated by the legislation provisions such as Section 36 of the Co-operative Societies Ordinance, the Chagga Rule and Native Coffee (Control & Marketing) Ordinance of 1937. The legislation reinforced KNCU's position in particular, by having it appointed by the board to handle coffee grown by Africans on the slopes of Mount Kilimanjaro. This gave it the power to emerge as a dominant and unchallenged organization.

Legislation created a monopoly that side-lined private traders, mainly Indians, in Kilimanjaro, jeopardizing the competitive business environment. Traders' complaints were disregarded in Kilimanjaro on the basis that it was essential to exercise control over the native coffee industry. However, Indian traders were not affected in other regions of the country where they were given exclusive monopoly of coffee as in Kagera Region and cotton in the WCGA. Yet, the agricultural marketing policies were controversial and inconsistent, characterised by double standards.

Unlike Kilimanjaro, co-operative promotion in other districts across the country was almost impossible and remained alien to growers until the late 1940s and 1950s. This was because the colonial authority viewed co-operatives through a political lens, rather than realisation of economic development of the members as understood by the League of Nations and later

UNO. Moreover, the colonial authority set out conditions for a society to be registered which was only if they emerged spontaneously. This was almost impossible, when the condition to be met required a level of exposure to such modern institutions which was a challenge given the majority of growers were illiterate. Additionally, government did not set out any strategy to identify such societies. It also did not put in place mechanisms like sensitization, taking into consideration that the majority of the rural population had no idea or concept of modern co-operation.

Attempts to register organisations that emerged spontaneously were declined. The NGA and one by the Bukwimba Chief are two cases where the colonial authority openly indicated that having them registered would lead to political instability. The colonial authority discarded these early co-operative impulses by the NGA, and later BPCA in Kagera region, due to internal and external factors: Coffee growers were not subject to a serious threat that would prompt forming an organisation to challenge government and small-scale coffee growers did not engage in farm labour. Farmers utilised labourers from Ngara, Burundi and Rwanda, which generated some degree of complacency and inhibited the rise of groups with a desire for a co-operative movement.

Unlike any other product in this study, Africans were licensed to purchase coffee. This was an important factor that inhibited the rise of interest in co-operatives. This was also an indication that preference was for free trade in which family members were involved either as traders themselves or as employees. Against this backdrop, co-operatives emerged not only as a threat to traders' livelihoods but resulted in increased coffee smuggling from the mid-1950s.

Since coffee trade in Kagera was operated under free trade policy, hundreds of Africans traded the produce just the same as Arab and Indian traders. The trading scheme was throughout a challenge to the emergence of co-operatives, as growers seemed inactive, less concerned and not motivated. It was therefore decided by the colonial authority that interest for co-operatives had to be imposed, and an obstruction by the BNCB was dismantled through legislation that weakened the board's powers paving the way for the formation and registration of co-operatives by the colonial authority without any attempt to persuade the members. It has been noted in this study that the BCU was prescribed to growers under external pressure, first the instruction from the Colonial Office and pressure exerted through the Registrar of Co-operative Societies, then resort to applying the African Agricultural Products (Control & Marketing) Ordinance, 1949 which provided for marketing boards to support the formation of co-operatives.

The post-war era coupled with pressure for agricultural policy reforms to align with colonial powers' demand for raw materials, caused agricultural marketing co-operatives to be encouraged; amendments to Ordinance were part of policy reforms. This signified a major post-war policy shift in favour of co-operative development, unlike during the Northcote era when such policies were primarily rejected by the colonial authority. In addition, a combination of external and colonial powers' supportive policies unveiled a co-operative renaissance in Tanganyika. All these provided for expansion of the movement, so the footprint covered more geographical areas, though some places such as WCGA and Kagera experienced difficulties. Expansion of the co-operative footprint was noticeable in new locations such as in the Southern Highlands.

Co-operatives were hastily formed in Kagera. And there was no patience on the part of government to simulate or wait for the enthusiasm. Understandably, at this stage government was under pressure to have a single buyer as dictated by the Colonial Office, and incorporated in the African Agricultural Products (Control & Marketing) Ordinance, 1949. This manifested in the emergence of the BPCA in Kimwani Chiefdom of Biharamulo and escalation of coffee smuggling. The emergence of mentioned 'problems' demonstrated what was desired by the growers as they willingly supported them regardless of membership numbers. Again, traders who opted for smuggling suggest they were not ready to offer their trading skills and knowledge to co-operatives but to resist. It also illustrated that the problem was not lack of enthusiasm for co-operatives, but that growers were comfortable with the system in operation.

In the WCGA, merchants utilised their status to undermine and exploit growers. The exploitation frustrated growers who hardly reaped a profit from farming the crop, as they could not access the cotton ginning and export value chain. Growers aired their concerns about exploitation, but the colonial authority ignored their demands for fair trading. This prompted growers to look for a solution through grassroots associations. Such associations formed a formidable army against marginalization whose winds of change blew across the WCGA in the late 1940s and early 1950s.

The grassroots movement was supported by embryonic organizations and local chiefs, who managed to exert pressure that forced the colonial government to register cotton marketing co-operative societies. This marked a significant step in the control of the cotton value chain by growers in the WCGA. Such success was possible due to a combination of factors. The growers brought together two elements: the produce (that is, cotton), and a new genuine non-exploitative structure to market their produce (that is, co-operatives). Having a strong sense of unity, they succeeded in overcoming decades of marginalization by both the colonial authority and cotton merchants. Such victory was achieved by having growers through co-operatives from 1953 that led to a cotton business power shift away from Indian traders.

Moreover, the alliance created between traders, grassroots groups and growers, demonstrated a unique development related to the emergence of co-operatives in the WCGA. It provided a platform or foundation for bottom-up growth of the movement that was also reflected in two other levels or structures, secondary societies and an apex body. Secondary societies were necessary as support units for primary societies reinforceing the movement's penetration and capturing cotton marketing. Moreover, important secondary society solidarity links eventually facilitated the growth of the VFCU as the hub of the entire co-operative movement in the WCGA. In this way, the movement in the WCGA was able to create a unique identity.

Co-operatives provided the machinery through which control of the board could be effective at the level of the grower. Importantly, both the boards and co-operatives had a common purpose, providing services to growers and quality control of the produce. Both aimed to achieve the economic goal of both institutions and the country as a whole. Private enterprise's ultimate goal was profit generation, so they could not deliver a satisfactory medium for the board, similarly the board could not satisfy private enterprise. Moreover, since co-operatives were represented on the board, the feeling was engendered that they were in control of the board and had an opportunity to present their views and frustrations, all of which were resolved through discussion. This brought the board closer to growers and co-operative members, unlike private enterprises or middlemen.

Co-operatives were further bolstered by complex marketing schemes by the post-colonial government designed to protect producers. In this regard, in 1962, the Colonial African Agricultural Products (Control & Marketing) Ordinance 5, 1949 was amended. Hence, the NAPB was set up as provided for under the National Products (Control & Marketing) Act, 1962 (56 of 1962) which came into force to control agricultural produce, both cash and food crops. The policy was implemented by the post-colonial government, which established several marketing boards envisaged to eliminate private firms and consolidate crop marketing under state control because it was anticipated it would increase production and enhance efficient tax collection. Just as in the colonial era the post-colonial marketing boards became the sole buyers and the co-operatives collectors of crops. The creation of the NAPB was designed to achieve several objectives, namely:

- Increase the tax revenue of Tanganyika so that unavoidable government and development expenditures could be more satisfactorily covered by the state itself;
- Create additional possibilities for industrial processing of agricultural products;
- Increase the market possibilities for the consumer industry by strength-

ening the buying power of the producer, i.e. of rural families.

The National Products (Control & Marketing) Act, 1962 (56 of 1962) replaced previous legislation which was viewed by the post-colonial authority as discriminatory as it targeted only crops produced by Africans but not so those produced by non-Africans mainly Europeans and Indians, and led to setting up of a three-tier marketing structure.

The policy was implemented by the post-colonial government, which established several marketing boards that were envisaged to eliminate private firms and consolidate crop marketing under state control. This, it was anticipated, would increase production, and enhance efficient tax collection. Just as in the colonial era, the post-colonial marketing boards became the sole buyers and co-operatives the collectors of crops. Under the National Agricultural Products (Control & Marketing) Boards Act, 1962 the Minister responsible for agricultural affairs was empowered to establish marketing boards with exclusive rights to market scheduled crops and appoint agents. The legislation was a move towards Africanisation of the country's economy and extended its interest to cover all crops, both cash and food crops. For example, the union and its affiliates were in 1964 appointed as agent of the NAPB for marketing maize in the district as well as a sole supply of sugar. This gave it a monopoly over grain. The NAPB appointed co-operative unions as marketing agents which, directly or through their co-operative societies, purchased maize and other food products from farmers and sold the produce to the NAPB for resale to grain millers. Similarly, cashewnuts were purchased by NAPB through co-operative societies and unions. This was maintained until 1974 when the Cashew Nut Authority of Tanzania (CATA) was established and took over from the NAPB in marketing cashewnuts while the co-operative maintained its status until it was abolished in 1976.

The NAPB had been designed to increase post-colonial government's control in crop marketing and increase the number of producers participating in the production and marketing of cash crops, ultimately to improve the income and livelihoods of growers previously neglected and undermined by the colonial economic system. The policy theoretically sounded a departure from colonial extraction of resources in favour of the growers. However, the post-colonial policy was practically the same as during the colonial era when co-operatives were stripped of their bargaining power element. Moreover, the establishment of the NAPB led to centralisation and coordination of crop marketing and pricing. The National Agricultural Products Board (NAPB) under (cap.486) Section 3 of the Agricultural Products (Control & Marketing) Act, 1962 gave the board a monopoly over prices and marketing of all important agricultural products. As per the legislation, the boards dictated the price of produce to growers without consideration of production costs.

In the 1970s, policy shifted to the establishment of crop authorities which had peculiar authoritative features in crop marketing at every level following abolition of the co-operatives. The crop authorities' monopoly over crop buying from growers and exporting them in the world market accrued foreign revenues. However, they were inefficient in marketing operations, failed to pay growers, cheated them and were unable to supply input to growers, which eventually contributed to a decline in agricultural production.

Until 1972, the National Agricultural Product Board (NAPB) controlled staple food grains (maize, rice, and wheat) marketing. In 1973 several parastatal agricultural crop authorities were established. These took over functions that were under the NAPB. The agricultural crop authorities were given a wider mandate to include input distribution, credit, research and extension. In 1974 the agricultural crop authorities took over marketing functions from the co-operatives. In the 1970s, policy shifted to the establishment of crop authorities which had peculiar authoritative features in crop marketing at every level following abolition of the co-operatives. These crop authorities had monopolies over crops from buying from growers to exporting to the world market to earn foreign revenues.

Under the 1970's reorganization the National Milling Corporation (NMC) took over functions of the NAPB in handling food crops including maize, wheat, rice, cassava, beans, sorghum and millets that were bought by co-operatives from growers. The NMC continued to use the co-operative unions as purchasing agents. When the co-operative unions were abolished in 1976, NMC took over direct purchasing of grain from small-scale growers as well as transportation, milling, thus becoming a wholesale entity including processed maize and wheat flour. Rice was allocated to yet another parastatal, the National Distributors Limited (NDL) and Regional Trading Companies (RTCs). At this stage, the lucrative value chain was under government-owned enterprises. This depicted government as merchant operating business through crop authorities.

The post-colonial authority-inherited co-operative movement footprint was limited to some regions and non-existent in most of them. Unlike the colonial era, the post-colonial government viewed agriculture marketing co-operatives as the vehicle to achieve the government's rural development objectives. This would be by promotion of mass co-operative societies across the country, but was nothing other than a continuation of colonial policies that employed co-operatives to facilitate agricultural policies as well as realisation of both political and ideological agendas.

Against this backdrop, the salient feature of the post-colonial authority, especially in the 1970s, was that co-operatives were perceived as a key instrument for the implementation of socialist policy as well as rural development. Such orientation generated a completely new organisation designed to serve political interest and national objectives while disregarding members' interests. It was backed by the Village and Ujamaa Villages Act of 1975, which reconstituted the village into political and economic entities linked mainly to the upper levels of government, favouring district and regional party and government structures rather than people at grassroots level.

In 1976 agricultural marketing unions operating in each region in the country were dissolved. Between 1977 and 1979 the ruling party, *Chama Cha Mapinduzi* (CCM) and the government maintained efforts to consolidate control over agricultural marketing co-operatives. In 1979, the Co-operative Union of Tanganyika (CUT) was renamed by government and CCM as *Washirika* and taken over as a fully-fledged organ of the party along with other organizations representing women, trade unions, youths and parents. The idea was to make all organisations directly subordinate to the ideological agenda of the CCM. Against this backdrop, the co-operative movement became a political wing for control of the entire rural population in Tanzania. The co-operative model became meaningless, and was paid lip service by the ruling party. At its worst, the co-operative was used in a draconian manner to suppress growers' interests in contrast to co-operative principles.

In 1982, agricultural marketing co-operatives were reinstated under the 1982 Co-operative Act, which clearly stipulated that the movement was charged with constructing a socialist state. The legislation was cosmetic in the sense that all features of the Village Act of 1975 prevailed. Importantly, the 1982 Co-operative Act culminated in employing co-operative societies as an integral part of the ruling party. The intensity of Tanzania's economic crisis took the government to the negotiating table to discuss recovery measures with the World Bank and International Monetary Fund (IMF). These institutions set out conditions, one of which was liberalisation of agricultural marketing. In an attempt to keep with the economic adjustment pace, it became necessary to enact new legislation, the Co-operative Societies Act of 1991. In a further development, in 1992 Tanzania embraced a multi-party politically oriented constitution. This provided room for AMCOs to be free from control by *Chama Cha Mapinduzi* (CCM).

Internal political reforms and economic liberalisation prompted endorsement of the autonomous status of the co-operative movement in Tanzania. Despite the adoption of multi-party politics in Tanzania, ruling party elements and influences were retained. Understandably, tens of hundreds of co-operative members maintained membership of the party and many others joined newly formed political parties. In a move to end the practice of party politics influencing societies, the 2013 Co-operative Act addressed the matter in Section 132. It is yet too soon to say how effective these measures have been.

REFERENCES

Primary Sources from Tanzania National Archive (TNA)
district and Provincial Books
Bukoba District Book
Lake Province Districts' Reports Book I
Shinyanga District Book
Rungwe District Book, 1935
Biharamulo District Book
Southern Highland Province Book
Central Province Annual Report

Accession Files
TNA 5/234, KNCU Financial Position and Policy
TNA 5/243, Report to the League of Nations on Tanganyika Territory, 1937
TNA 5/375 C 24/13, KNCU School Lyamungo
TNA 7/71/A.3/18 vol. II, Secretariat, Agriculture and Natural Resources
TNA 7/4011, Bukoba Coffee
TNA 7/2348/B, TANU Branch Bukoba
TNA 215/A3/2 & 3, Agriculture: Cotton Policy & Cotton Marketing
TNA 215/655, Agricultural: Cotton General
TNA 215/772, Cotton Ginneries
TNA 215/967/823, Mwanza Rural districts Annual Reports 1959
TNA 215/1423/A, Tanganyika LSMB end of the year Reports
TNA 215/2825/5, Agriculture Produce Cotton Lint Disposal
TNA 237, KNCU
TNA 1423/C, Co-operative Buying and Ginning in the Lake Province
TNA 23556, Bugufi Coffee Society: Question Connected with.

Secretariat Files
TNA 11828 Tobacco Industry, Tanganyika Territory, 1947 vol. VII
TNA 11969 vol. II, Coffee Cultivation in Bukoba & Annual Reports
TNA 12809, KNPA – Proposal to Abolish
TNA 13060, Coffee Ordinance and Regulations Attitude of the KNPA
TNA 13698, Application of Co-operative Methods in Economic Development of the Territory
TNA 19005, Co-operative Movement in the Colonies
TNA 19126, Minutes of the KNPA
TNA 19496 Improvement of Cotton Cultivation
TNA 20378, Reorganisation of the KNPA
TNA 20999, Economic Development: Agriculture Production in the Colonies
TNA 21032 vol. I, Proposal to Purchase Ginneries of the BCGA in Kwimba and Biharamulo district
TNA 21032, Lake Province Council on Agricultural and Natural Resources Committee
TNA 22813, Licensing of produce buyers

TNA 2283, Volume II Improvement of cotton roads
TNA 22929, Report on Co-operation
TNA 22983, Co-operative Societies in the Southern Highland Province
TNA 23218, Joint Cotton and Produce Markets, Lake Province
TNA 23556 Bugufi Coffee Society: Question Connected with.
TNA 23752, Native Association Bukoba
TNA 24545, Bukoba Coffee Industry in Report on Bukoba Coffee Marketing
TNA 24870, International Labour Organisation, Co-operative Information, 1-12, 1936
TNA 25038, Legislation on Control of Native Agriculture Industry
TNA 25066, Co-operative Marketing in the Lake Province
TNA 25147, Marketing of Colonial Produce in the United Kingdom and Overseas
TNA 25400, Disturbances at Moshi in Connection to KNCU
TNA 25442, Native Coffee Board: Moshi district
TNA 25777, Native Coffee Industry Enquiry into Reorganisation
TNA 25828, KNCU: Bye-Laws
TNA 26038, KNPA and KNCU Annual Reports
TNA 26054 Agriculture Policies
TNA 26207, KNCU – Application to Raise Loan
TNA 26298/8, Native Agriculture Production Campaign: Lake Province
TNA 27317, Colonial Agricultural Policy/Agricultural policies in the colonial empire
TNA 28259, Agriculture Policy in the Colonial Empire
TNA 28585, Native Coffee Board: Bukoba district
TNA 29121, Cotton Cultivation Orders under Section 8 (r) of Native Authority
TNA 29585 Native Coffee Board Bukoba district
TNA 33017, Development and Reconstruction Establishment of co-operative societies
TNA 34953, Cotton Control and Marketing during Wartime, vol. I & II
TNA 357883, Marketing Primary Products: Price Stabilisation
TNA 37192, Co-operative Development Annual Reports (1946-1950)
TNA 37200, Purchase of Coffee Crop by Ministry of Food
TNA 37443, Overseas Food Corporation
TNA 41011 Bukoba Coffee: Marketing Organisation
TNA 5/243 *Report to the League of Nations on Tanganyika Territory*, 1939

Reports
Agriculture Policy, Increase Cotton Production Programme, Appendix M, A3/1
Annual Report of British Cotton Growing Association, General Items and Reports Manchester Association Of Importers And Exporters, In *The Journal of the Textile Institute*, vol. XIII, 1922
Annual Report to Trusteeship Council for 1947
Bulletin of the Imperial Institute, A Quarterly Record of Progress in Tropical Agriculture and Industries and the Commercial Utilisation of the Natural Resources of the Dominions, Colonies and India, VOL. XX. 1922 (London: Casell, Watson and Viney, Ltd., 1922)
Government of Tanganyika, Annual Report, Northern Province (Dar es Salaam: Government Printer, 1937)
Government of Tanganyika, Annual Territorial Report (London: HMSO, 1925, 1928)
Horne, H., The extension of cotton cultivation in Tanganyika Territory: Report to

the Committee on tour in Tanganyika territory Nov 1920 – July 1921 (London: the Empire Cotton Growing Corporation) The Empire Cotton Growing Review, *Journal of The Empire Cotton Growing Corporation*, vol. XXVIII, No 1, January 1951

Horace Plunkettt Foundation, *A Year Book of Agricultural Co-operation* (London: Routledge, 1930)

Horace Plunkettt Foundation, *Year Book of Agricultural Co-operative* (London: Basil Blackwell, 1949, 1954, 1958, 1961)

IBRD, *The Economic Development of Tanganyika*, (Baltimore: Johns Hopkins University Press, 1961)

Kenya Colony and Protectorate, Colonial Annual Report on the Social and Economic Progress of the People, 1659 (London: HMSO, 1932)

League of Nations, Reports of Mandatory Powers, on the Administration Under Mandate of Tanganyika Territory, 1925

LEGCO Proceedings, February 1932

Report by His Britannic Majesty's Government on the Administration Under Mandate of Tanganyika Territory for the Year 1924 League of Nations Geneva, 1925

Report on Tanganyika Territory Armistice, 1920 (London: HMSO, 1921)

Report to the Board of Trade of the Empire Cotton Growing Committee Presented to the Parliament by Command of His Majesty in 1920 (London: HMSO)

Report to the League of Nations on Tanganyika Territory, 1939

T.S Jervis, Bukoba Coffee: Inspection and Grading in Bukoba District Book

Tanganyika Government Circular 50, 1925

Tanganyika Government Report on Co-operative Development (Dar es Salaam: Government Printer, 1949-61)

Tanganyika Government, Annual Report on Co-operative Development (Dar es Salaam: Government Printer, 1951)

Tanganyika Legislative Council Debates, Hansard, 1950, 29th Session, para. 241

Tanganyika Report by His Majesty's Government to the Council of the League of Nations on the administration of Tanganyika Territory (London: HMSO, 1931)

Tanganyika Territory Report on the Armistice to the end of 1920, Cmd. 1428 (1921)

Tanganyika Territory, Annual Report for the Year, 1931, Colonial 71 (London: HMSO, 1932)

Tanganyika Territory, Annual Report, (Dar es Salaam: Government Printer, 1959)

Tanganyika Territory, *Annual Reports on Co-operative Development* (Dar es Salaam: Government Printer, 1955, 1956)

Tanganyika Territory, Department of Agriculture, Annual Report, 1945, and Twelfth Annual Report of the Coffee Experimental Station, Lyamungo, Moshi, 1945

Tanganyika Territory, LEGCO, A report on the Kilimanjaro Native Co-operative Union (Dar es Salaam: Government Printer, 1937)

Tanganyika Territory, *Report of the Co-operative Development* (Dar es Salaam: Government Printer, 1948)

Tanganyika Territory: Proceedings of the LEGCO, First Session, 1926-1927 (Dar es Salaam:. Government Printer).

The BCU Annual Report for the Year 1959/60 – 1968/69

The Co-operative Union of Tanganyika, Annual and Balance Sheet 1963/64 Report

The KNCU; Annual Report, 1946/47; 1951/52 (Moshi: KNCU)

The Tanganyika Coffee Board, Annual Report for 1957-1958 (Moshi: The Tanganyika Coffee Board, 1958)

The United Nations Trusteeship Council, United Nations Visiting Mission to the Trust Territories in East Africa, Report on Tanganyika Together with Related Documents, 4 Volumes for 1948, 1951, 1954 and 1960

The World Bank, *Tanganyika Agriculture and Rural Development Sector Study*, vol. II, 10 December 1974 (Baltimore: Johns Hopkins University Press, 1974)

United States Department of Agriculture, *United Kingdom Market for United States Agricultural Products Agriculture Information Bulletin 104* (Washington, DC: The USA Government Printing Office, 1953)

URT, *A Study on Integration of Employment Issues on Development Frameworks*. (Dar es Salaam, Ministry of Labour, Employment And Youth Development and ILO 2010)

URT, *Annual Report on Co-operative Development* (Dar es Salaam: Government Printer, 1964, 1965)

URT, National Human Settlement Development Policy (Dar es Salaam: Government Printer, 2000)

URT, Report on the Special Presidential Committee on Reviving, Strengthening and Developing the Co-operatives in Tanzania (Dar es Salaam: Government Printer, 2005)

URT, Tanzania Second Five-Year Plan for Economic and Social Development, 1 July 1969 to 30 June 1974, vol. I (Dar es Salaam: Government Printer, 1969)

URT, The Presidential Special Committee of Enquiry into Co-operatives Movement and Marketing Boards (Dar es Salaam: Government Printer, 1966)

Government Orders, Memorandums, Notices

1930 Memorandum on Native Policy in East Africa

Colonial Office, Circular Dispatch 199, 20 March 1946

TNA 19595 vol. I. Co-operative Societies Ordinance, Note on the Draft Ordinance, General Government Notice 697 (Cotton), July 1946

Presidential Circular 1 of 1969, The Development of Ujamaa Villages, State House, Dar es Salaam, March 20th 1969 (Mimeo)

Tanganyika Territory Report on Arusha – Moshi Land Commission (Dar es Salaam: Government Printer, 1947)

TNA 13698, Colonial Office Memorandum: Co-operation in the Colonies, Protectorates and Mandated Territories, (HMSO, 21 May 1930)

TNA 19005, Co-operative Movement in the Colonies (London: HMSO, 1946), Col. 199

TNA 19595, Co-operative Societies Ordinance

TNA 34953, The Defence Regulation (Control of Cotton) Order, 1943, Cotton Control Marketing in Wartime vol. I

TNA 37192, The Colonial Office (1947): Confidential memorandum on General Price and Marketing Policy for Colonial Primary Products, the Colonial Office: London, February 1947

Policy Documents

B. King, *International Bank for Reconstruction and Development: Survey of British Colonial Development Policy* (IBRD- Economic Department, 9 November 1949)

H.M. Stationery Office 1956 Report of the Conference on Land Tenure in East and Central Africa held in Arusha, Tanganyika, February 1956. London: HMSO

Presidential Circular 1 of 1969, The Development of Ujamaa Villages, State House, Dar es Salaam, 20 March 1969 (Mimeo)

Session a Paper 4, 1937
Tanganyika Territory, Review of Land Tenure Policy (Dar es Salaam: Government Printer, 1958)
TNA 22929, Marketing of Colonial Produce in the United Kingdom and Overseas
TNA 25147, Marketing of Colonial Produce in the United Kingdom and Overseas
TNA 26054, Agriculture General Policy, Tanganyika Territory: Memorandum on Proposals for agricultural Investigation, Policy and Development
URT, Paper 4 (Dar es Salaam: Government Printer, 1967)

Newspapers and Newsletters
Daily News, 1974
Dar es Salaam Times, 1921, 1922
Standard Newspaper, 1948
Tanganyika Standard, 1942, 1964
The Tanganyika Herald, 1947
Uremi, 1932-35

Speeches
Speeches at Banquet given to Winston Churchill, 7 June 1921, BCGA 74
Speech by Lord Winster in the House of Lords March 1, 2 or 3 1944, TNA 33017
J.K. Nyerere, *Tanzania: Ten Years after Independence* (Dar es Salaam: Government Printer, 1971)
J.K.Nyerere, 'Mali ya Taifa' in J.K Nyerere, *Fredom and Unity* (Dar es Salaam: Oxford University Press, 1967)
J.K. Nyerere, *Ujamaa: Essays on Socialism* (Dar es Salaam: Oxford University Press, 1968)
J.K. Nyerere, *Freedom and Socialism* (Dar es Salaam, DUP, 1968)

Secondary Sources
Agere, S., Towards Public Enterprise: The Role of Community Development in the Promotion of Co-operatives, (Harare, Ministry of Community Development and Women Affairs) *Zambesia* XI (ii) (1983).
Albaum, Gerald and Rutman, Gilbert L., 'The Co-operative-Based Marketing System in Tanganyika', in *Journal of Marketing*, vol. 31, No 4, Part 1 (October 1967).
Anderson, R., *The Battle for Tanga 1914* (Stroud: Tempus, 2002).
Anderson, Ross, Norforce: Major General Edward Northey and the Nyasaland and North Eastern Rhodesia Frontier Force, January 1916 to June 1918, *Scientia Militaria* vol. 44, no. 1, 2016, pp. 47-80. doi:10.5787/44-1-1162
Anderson, Ross, World War I in East Africa 1916-1918 (University of Glasgow, 2001) pp. 21-40, https://www.academia.edu/17269264/World_War_I_in_East_Africa_1916-1918.
Baldus, Rolf D., *The Tanzanian co-operative movement at the beginning of the eighties: a comment* (Internationales Afrikaforum, 1980).
Bienien, Henry, *Tanzania: Party Transformation and Economic Development* (Princeton: Princeton University Press, 1970).
Bonner, Arnold, *British Co-operation*, (Manchester: Co-operative Union, 1970).
Borzaga, Carlo, and Galera, Giulia, The Concept and Practice of Social Enterprise. Lessons from the Italian Experience, in *International Review of Social Research*, Volume 2, Issue 2 (June 2012) pp. 85-102.
Brode, Heinrich, *British and German East Africa, Their Economic and Commercial Relations* (London: Edward and Arnold, 1911).

Brown, James Ambrose, *They Fought for King and Kaiser: South Africans in German East Africa 1916* (Johannesburg: Ashanti Publishing. 1991).
Buell, Raymond Leslie, *The Native Problem in Africa* (New York: Macmillan, 1928).
Byatt, Sir Horace, In *Journal of the Royal African Society*, XXIV (1924) pp. 1-5.
Callahan, Michael D., Nomansland: The British Colonial Office and the League of Nations Mandate for German East Africa, 1916-1920, *Albion: A Quarterly Journal Concerned with British Studies* vol. 25, no. 3 (Autumn, 1993) pp. 443-464.
Calvert, Albert F., German East Africa (London: T. Werner Laurie, 1917).
Campbell, W.K.H., Practical Co-operation in Asia and Africa (Cambridge: W. Heffer and Sons, 1951).
Cana, Frank R., Frontiers of German East Africa. *The Geographical Journal* vol. 47, no. 4 (Apr. 1916) pp. 297-303, https://doi.org/10.2307/1779697.
Chambo, Suleman Adam, Agricultural Co-operatives: Role in Food Security and Rural Development, Paper Presented to the United Nations Organisation's Expert Group Meeting on Co-operatives, 28–30 April 2009, New York, http://www.un.org/esa/socdev/egms/docs/2009/co-operatives/Chambo.pdf, Accessed on 12/5/2021.
Chidzero, B.G., *Tanganyika and the International Trusteeship* (London: Oxford University Press, 1961).
Church, Archibald, *East Africa: A New Dominion a Crucial Experiment in Tropical Development and its Significance to the British Empire* (London: H.F. & G. Witherby, 1927).
Coulson, Andrew, Agricultural Policies in Mainland Tanzania, in *Review of African Political Economy*, 10 (1977).
Coulson, Andrew, *Tanzania: A Political Economy* (Oxford: Oxford University Press, 1982).
Crowder, Michael, *The First World War and its consequences* (Paris: UNESCO, 1985).
Curtin, Philip, The Colonial Economy, in Philip Curtin, Steven Feierman, Leonard Thompson, Jan Vansina, *African History: From Earliest Times to Independence* (London: Longman, 1995).
Curtis, Kenneth R., 'Cooperation and Cooptation: The Struggle for Market Control in the Bukoba district of Colonial Tanganyika', *The International Journal of African Historical Studies*, vol. 25, no. 3 (1992).
Develtere, Co-operatives and Development Towards a Social Movement Perspective, Occasional Paper Series, #92-03 (Centre for the Study of Co-operatives University of Saskatchewan).
Develtere, Patrick, Co-operative Movements in the Developing Countries: Old and New Orientations, *Annals of Public and Co-operative Economics*, vol. 64, Issue 2 (April 1993) pp. 179-208.
Develtere, Patrick, Co-operatives and Development: Towards a Social Movement Perspective, *Occasional Paper Series, #92-03, (2003)*, http://www.usaskstudies.coop/pdf-files/publications/1992/Co-ops%20%26%20Development.pdf accessed on 18/11/2011.
Downes, W.D., *With the Nigerians in German East Africa* (London: Methuen & Co, 1919).
Dundas, C.F., *Africa at Crossroad* (London: Macmillan, 1955).
Dundas, Charles, *Africa at Crossroads* (London: Greenwood Press, 1955).
East Africa Railways and Habours Magazine, June 1956, vols. 2–9.
Editorial Notes, *Journal of African Affairs*, vol. 16 (1916-1917).
Edmonds, James, *A Short History of World War I* (New York: Greenwood, 1968).

Emor, Ben, Problems Facing the Co-operative Movement in Uganda, in *The Role of Co-operative Movement in Uganda* (Kampala: Uganda Press Trust, 1966).

Evans, L., *The British Tropical Africa: A History Outline* (Cambridge: Cambridge University Press, 1929).

Farwell, Byron, *The Great War in Africa* (New York: W.W. Norton & Co, 1986).

Fecitt, Harry, The Fighting in Northern Rhodesia in November 1918, *The Society of Malawi Journal*, vol. 71, no. 2 (2018) pp. 15-23.

Fiala, Robert Dennis, The Anglo-German agreement over Portugal's African colonies, 1898 (Master of Arts Dissertation, University of Nebraska at Omaha, 1963) Student Work, 437.

Fischer, Fritz, *Germany's Aims in the First World War* (New York: W. W. Norton, 1967).

Foreign Agriculture, September, vol. XII, no. 9 (1948).

Forster, Kent, The Quest for East African Neutrality in 1915, African Studies Review vol. 22, no. 1 (Apr. 1979).

Frank, Billy, The formation of British Colonial Development Policy in the Trans World Wars Two Period, 1942-1953: With special reference to central and southern Africa, unpublished PhD thesis (Edge Hill Lancaster University, 2002)

French, David, *British Strategy & War Aims 1914-1916* (London: Allen & Unwin, 1986).

Fuggles-Couchman, N.R., *Agriculture Change in Tanganyika: 1945–1960* (Stanford, California: Food Research Institute, Stanford University, 1964).

Gewald, Jan-Bart, Colonial Warfare: Hehe and World War One, the wars besides Maji Maji in south-western Tanzania, ASC Working Paper 63/2005, African Studies Centre Leiden, The Netherlands.

Gibbon, P., Mechanisation of Production and Privatisation of Development in Post-Ujamaa Tanzania: An Introduction; in P Gibbons (ed.), *Liberalised Development in Tanzania: Studies on Accumulated Princesses and Local Industry* (Upssala: Nordic African Institute, 1995).

Glenk, Helmut; Blaich, Horst and Gatter, Peer, *Shattered Dreams at Kilimanjaro* (Trafford Publishing, 2011).

Gottfried, O. and Lag, M.B., Problems of Social and Economic Change in Sukumaland, Tanganyika, *Anthropological Quarterly*, vol. 35, no. 2 (April 1962) pp. 86-101.

Hadden-Guest, L., *The Labour Party and the Empire* (London: 1926).

Hailey, Lord, *An African Survey: A study of Problems Arising in Africa South of Sahara* (London: Oxford University Press, 1938).

Havinden, Michael and Meredith, David, *Colonialism and Development: Britain and Its Tropical Colonies, 1950-1960* (London: Routledge, 1996).

Havnevik, Kjell J., *Tanzania: The Limits of Development from Above*, (Uppsala: Nordik Africa Insitute, 1993).

Herskovits, Melville J., *The Human Factor in Changing Africa* (New York: Alfred A. Knopf, 1952).

Hobson, John Atkinson, *Imperialist parallels then and now Part I New Imperialism 1884-1913* (CAEF, 2014).

Holmén, Hans, *State, Co-operatives and Development in Africa* (Uppsala: Scandinavian Institute of African Studies, 1990).

http://afraf.oxfordjournals.org/content/XXXVI/CXLV/461.full.pdf

Horden, Charles and H. Fitz M. Stacks (eds), *Military Operations in East Africa Volume 1, August 1914 – September 1916* (London: HMSO, 1941)

Huxley, J., *Africa View* (London: Chatto and Windus, 1932).

Hyam, R., *The Failure of South African Expansion 1908–1948* (London: Macmillan, 1972).
Hydén, Göran, *Beyond Ujamaa in Tanzania. Underdevelopment and an Uncaptured Peasantry* (London: Heinemann, 1980).
Hydén, Göran, *Efficiency Versus Distribution in East African Co-operatives: A Study in Organizational Conflicts* (East African Literature Bureau, Nairobi, 1973).
Hydén, Göran, The Politics of Co-operatives in Tanzania, in Göran Hydén (et al), *Co-operatives in Tanzania: problems of organisation building*, (Dar es Salaam: Tanzania Publishing House, 1976).
Iliffe, John, *A Modern History of Tanganyika* (Cambridge: Cambridge University Press, 1979).
Iliffe, John, *Tanganyika under German rule, 1905–1912* (Cambridge: Cambridge University Press, 1979).
Iliffe, John, The German Administration in Tanganyika, 1906-1911: The Governorship of Freiherr von Rechenberg (Ph.D. dissertation, Cambridge University, 1965).
Jacob, Abel, Foreign Aid in Agriculture: Introducing Israel's Land Settlement Scheme to Tanzania (Undated) http://afraf.oxfordjournals.org/content/71/283/186.full.pdf, Accessed 22 December 2014.
James, R.W., *Land Tenure and Policy in Tanzania* (Toronto: Toronto University Press, 1971).
Jervis, T.S., Marketing of Coffee in *East Africa Agricultural Journal* (May 1957) pp. 459- 464.
Joelson, F.S., *The Tanganyika Territory (Formerly German East Africa): Characteristics and Potentialities* (New York D. Appleton and Company, 1921).
Kahama, Joseph Kulwa, *Sir George: A Thematic History of Tanzania Thorough His Fifty Years of Public Service*, (Beijing: Foreign Language Press, 2010).
Kamala, D.B., The Voices of the Poor and Poverty Eradication Strategies in Tanzania. an open lecture delivered at the University of Hull Business School on 14 January 2004 http://www2.hull.ac.uk/hubs/pdf/memorandum45.pdf Accessed 15/2/2013.
Kareem, R.O.; Arigbabu, Y.D.; Akintaro, J.A. and M.A.Badmus, The Impact of Co-operative Society on Capital Formation: A Case Study of Temidere Co–operative and Thrift- Society, Ijebu- Ode, Ogun State, Nigeria, *Global Journal of Science Frontier Research Agriculture and Veterinary Sciences*, vol. 12, no. 11 (2012).
Kelemen, Paul, 'Planning for Africa: The British Labour Party's Colonial Development Policy, 1920-1964', in *Journal of Agrarian Change*, vol. 1, no. 7 (January 2007).
Kelemen, Paul, Modernising Colonialism: The British Labour movement and Africa, *The Journal of Imperial and Commonwealth History* (October 2011).
Kieran, J.A., The Origins of Commercial Arabica Coffee Production in East Africa, *African Historical Studies*, vol. 2, no. 1 (1969) pp. 51-67.
Kimario, Ally M., *Marketing Co-operatives in Tanzania: Problems and Prospects*, (Dar es Salaam: Dar es Salaam University Press, 1992).
Kiondo, Andrew Salehe Zuakuu, *The Politics of Economic Reforms in Tanzania 1977-1988*, Ph.D. Thesis, University of Toronto (1989).
Kituo cha Elimu ya Ushirika Moshi (CEC), *Jifunze Ushirika* (Moshi: Co-operative Education Centre, 1968).
Kobia, S.K., *The Co-operative Movement in Kenya: Challenges and Opportunities* (Nairobi: Lukiko Consulting Trust, 2011).

Laidlaw, Alex F., Co-operatives and the Poor: A Review from within the Co-operative Movement, in *Co-operatives and the Poor* (London: ICA, 1978).
Leggett, Edward Humphrey Manisty, The Tanganyika Territory, *Journal of the Royal Society of Arts*, vol. 70, no. 3643 (September 15, 1922) pp. 737-752.
Lettow-Vorbeck, Paul von, *My Reminiscences of East Africa* (Nashville Battery Classics, 1989).
Leubuscher, Charlotte, *Bulk Buying from the Colonies: A study of the Bulk Purchase of Colonial Commodities by the United Kingdom Government* (London: Oxford University Press, 1956).
Leubuscher, Charlotte, Marketing Scheme for Native-Grown Produce in African Territories, *Journal of the International Institute of African Languages and Cultures*, vol. XII, Number 2 (April 1939) pp. 163-188.
Leubuscher, Charlotte, *Tanganyika Territory: A Study of Economic Policy under Mandate* (Oxford: Oxford University Press, 1944).
Listowel, Judith, *The Making of Tanganyika* (London: Chato and Lindus, 1965).
Little, M., Colonial Policy and Subsistence in Tanganyika 1925-1945, Geographical Review, vol. 81, no. 4 (Oct. 1991) pp. 375-388.
Luanda, N.N., European Commercial Farming and Its Impact on the Meru and Arusha Peoples of Tanzania, 1920-1955, University of Cambridge (unpublished PhD thesis, 1986).
Ludwig, Frieder, *Church and State in Tanzania: Aspects of Changing Relationship*, 1961–1964 (Leiden: Brill, 1999).
Lugard, F.J.D., *The Dual Mandate in British Tropical Africa* (London: Frank Cass and Co, 1965).
Lyimo, Francis Fanuel, *Rural Cooperation: In the Co-operative Movement in Tanzania* (Dar es Salaam: Mkuki na Nyota, 2012).
Lyimo, Francis, Peasants Production and Co-operative Experiences in Tanzania: Case Studies of Villages in Moshi Rural and Urambo districts (PhD Thesis, University of Wisconsin-Madison, 1984).
MacDonald, Alexander, *Tanzania: Young Nation in a Hurry* (New York: Hawthorn Books, 1966).
Maguire, G. Andrew, *Towards 'Uhuru' in Tanzania: The Politics of Participation* (Cambridge: Cambridge University Press, 1969).
Mair, L.P., *Welfare in the Colonies* (Bombay: Oxford University Press, 1944).
Mambo, Robert M., Mittleafrika: The German Dream of An Empire Across Africa in the Late 19th and Early 20th Centuries: An Overview, *Transafrican Journal of History* vol. 20 (1991) pp. 161-180.
Manday, E.A. A New Structure for Co-operatives in Tanzania, in *Annals of Public and Co-operative Economy*, 48, 2 (June 1977) pp. 239-244.
Marsh, Zoe and Kingsnorth, K.W., *An introduction to the History of East Africa* (London: Cambridge University Press, 1957).
Mattias, Tagseth, The Expansion of Traditional Irrigation in Kilimanjaro, Tanzania, *The International Journal of African Historical Studies*, vol. 41, no. 3, pp. 461-490.
Mazrui, Ali A., and Tidy, Michael, *Nationalism and New States in Africa: from about 1935 to present* (Nairobi: Heinemann, 1984).
McHenry, Dean, The Ujamaa Village in Tanzania: A comparison with Chinese, Soviet and Mexican Experiences in Cultivation, in *Comparative Studies in Society and History*, vol. 18, no. 3 (Jul. 1976) pp. 347-370.
Metzler, Lloyd Appleton, *Collected Papers* (Cambridge Massachusetts: Harvard University Press, 1973).

Miller, Steven E. (ed), *Military Strategy and the Origins of the First World War: An International Security Reader* (Princeton, 1980).

Moshi Co-operative College, A Paper to the Government on the Revival of Co-operative Unions, Moshi, (31 December 1980).

Moshi, E.H., The Dilemma of Agricultural Marketing Co-Operatives in Tanzania, in *Liberalised Economy*, Paper presented to the Co-operative College Annual Symposium (September 1997).

Moyd, Michelle, Making the Household, Making the State: Colonial Military Communities and Labor in German East Africa, *International Labor and Working-Class* History, no. 80 (Fall 2011) pp. 53-76, doi:10.1017/S014754791100007X.

Moyd, Michelle, Ordeal and Opportunity: Ending the First World War in Africa, The Fletcher Forum of World Affairs, vol. 43, no. 1, *Global Transformations: A Century Since the Great War* (Winter 2019) pp. 145-153.

Muungano wa Vyama vya Ushirika Tanganyika, *Ushirika Wetu*, (Dar es Salaam: CUT, 1977).

Ndomba, Herbert Harald, A History of Peasant Tobacco Production in Ruvuma Region, Southern Tanzania, c.1930-2016 (Unpublished PhD thesis, Stellenbosch University of 2018).

Ndulu, Benno, *Stabilization and Adjustment Policies and Programmes: Country Study 17 Tanzania*. World Institute for Development Economics Research (WIDER, 1987).

Ngirwa, W., Agriculture Transformation Issues in Tanzania, Paper presented in Agricultural Transformation Workshop. (1995) http://aec.msu.edu/%5C/fs2/ag_transformation/ngirwa.pdf. Accessed on 14/02/2019.

Nilsson, David, Sweden-Norway at Berlin Conference, 1884-85: History, National Identity-Making and Sweden's Relations with Africa, *Current African Issues* 53 (Nordica Africa Institute Uppsala, 2013).

Nyerere, J.K., *Freedom and Socialism* (Dar es Salaam, Oxford University Press, 1968).

Nyerere, J.K., *Ujamaa: Essays on Socialism* (Dar es Salaam: Oxford University Press, 1968).

Okereke, Okoro, *The Economic Impact of Uganda Co-operatives* (East Africa Literature Bureau, 1974).

Owusu, Maxwell, Agriculture and Rural Development since 1935, in Ali Mzrui (ed.) *Africa Since 1935*, (Oxford: James Currey Ltd., 1999).

Parsons, Timothy H., Mobilising Britain's African Empire for War: Pragmatism vs Trusteeship, *Journal of Modern European History / Zeitschrift für moderne europäische Geschichte / Revue d'histoire européenne contemporaine*, vol. 13, no. 2, The Crisis of Empire after 1918 (2015) pp. 183-202.

Pim, Alan, *Colonial Agricultural Production: The Contribution Made by Native Peasants and by Foreign Enterprise* (London: Oxford University Press, 1946).

Pires, Ana Paula, The First World War in Portuguese East Africa: Civilian and Military Encounters in the Indian Ocean, *e-JPH*, vol. 15, no 1, June 2017.

Pius Ngeze, *Ushirika Tanzania*, (Dar es Salaam: Tanzania Publishing House Ltd., 1975).

Ponte, S., Trading Images: Discourse and Statistical Evidence on Agricultural Adjustment in Tanzania (1986-95), in P.G. Forster and S. Maghimbi (eds.), *Agrarian Economy, State and Society in Contemporary Tanzania* (Aldershot: Ashgate, 1999).

Potter, Beatrice (Mrs Sidney Webb), *The Co-operative Movement in Great Britain* (London: George Allen and Unwin Ltd., 1930).

Potter, Pitman B., Origin of the System of Mandates under the League of Nations, *The American Political Science Review*, Nov 1922, vol. 16, no. 4 (November 1922) pp. 563-583, accessed from 197.221.218.100 on 12/2/2021.

Rhodes, Rita, *Empire and Co-operation: How the British Empire used Co-operatives in its Development Strategies 1900–1990* (Edinburgh: John Donald, 2012).

Rodney, Walter, *How Europe Underdeveloped Africa* (Dar es Salaam: Tanzania Publishing House, 1973).

Samson, Anne, *War I in Africa: The Forgotten Conflict among the European Powers* (London: IB Tauris, 2013).

Schmitt, Bernadotte E., The First World War, 1914-1918, *Proceedings of the American Philosophical Society*, vol. 103, no. 3 (15 Jun. 1959).

Schneppen, Heinz, *Why Tanzania is where it is: Tanzania's Colonial Boundaries from Berlin Conference 1984-1885 until its independence* (Dar es Salaam: National Museums of Tanzania Occasional paper 11, 1998).

Schoenbrun, David L., A Past Whose Time Has Come: Historical Context and History in Eastern Africa's Great Lakes, History and Theory, vol. 32, no. 4, Beiheft 32: *History Making in Africa* (Dec. 1993) pp. 32-56.

Seimu, S.M.L., The Growth and Development of Coffee and Cotton Marketing Co-operatives in Tanzania, PhD Thesis, University of Central Lancashire (2015).

Smith, Charles David, *Did Colonialism Capture the Peasantry: A case of the Kagera district, Tanzania* (Upsala: Scandinavian Institute of African Studies Uppsala, Research Report 83, 1989) pp.21-24.

Smith, S., Zimbabwean Women in Co-operatives: Participation and Sexual Equality in Four Producer Co-operatives, in *Journal of Social Development in Africa*, 2:1 (1987) pp. 29-47.

Soni, A.K., and Saluja, H.P.S., A Study on Development of Co-operative Movement in Planned Economy, *International Journal of Economics, Commerce and Research* (IJECR), vol. 3, issue 1 (Mar 2013) pp. 39-48.

Spear, T., *Mountain Farmers* (Dar es Salaam: Mkuki na Nyota, 1997)

Stahl, K.M., *History of the Chagga People of Kilimanjaro* (London: Mouton and Company, 1964).

Stahl, Kathleen M., The Chagga, in P.H. Gullier (ed); *Tradition and Transition in East Africa: Studies of the Tribal Factor* (London: Routledge, 1969).

Stapleton, Timothy, *Africa: War and Conflict in the Twentieth Century* (New York: 2018).

Strachan, Hew, *The First World War* (Oxford, University Press, 2001).

Strickland, C.F., Co-operation for Africa, in *Journal of the International Africa Institute*, vol. 6, no. 1 (January 1933).

Strickland, C.F., *Co-operation in the Colonies* (George Allen and Unwin, 1945).

Strickland, C.F., *The Co--operative movement in South Africa* (nd) pp. 461-8.

Swynnerton, R.J.M.; Bennett, A.L.B. and Stent, H.B., *All About KNCU Coffee* (Moshi: KNCU, 1948).

van Velzen, H.V.É. Thoden, Staff; Kulaks and Peasants: A Study of a Political Field, Rural Development Paper 8, Rural Development Research Committee (Dar-es-Salaam: University of Dar-es-Salaam, 1971).

Wakefield, A.J., *Native Production of Coffee on Kilimanjaro, the Empire Journal of Experimental Agriculture, Volume IV* (Oxford: Oxford University Press, 1936)

Wanyama, F.O., Some Positive Aspects of Neo-Liberalism for African Development: The Revival of Solidarity in Co-operatives, *International Journal of Arts and Commerce*, vol. 2, no. 1 (January 2013) pp.126-148.

Webb, H.R., *Cotton in Tanzania* (United States of America: Department of Agriculture, 1970).

Westergaard, P.W., Co-operatives in Tanzania as Economic and Democratic Institutions in CG Widstrand (ed.), *Co-operatives and Rural Development in East Africa* (New York: African Publishing Corporation, 1970).

White, P., *A Century of Spain and Portugal. 1788-1898* (London: Methuen & Co., 1909).

Williamson, Jr, Samuel R., The Origins of World War I, The Journal of Interdisciplinary History, vol. 18, no. 4, *The Origin and Prevention of Major Wars* (spring, 1988) pp. 795-818, doi.org/10.2307/204825.

World Bank, *Tanzania at the Turn of the Century: from Reforms to Sustained Growth and Poverty Reduction: A World Bank Country Study*, (Washington D.C: World Bank, 2001).

Wrigley, G.M., The Military Campaigns against Germany's African Colonies, *Geographical Review*, vol. 5, no. 1 (Jan. 1918) pp. 44-65.

Yoshida, Masao, 'Agricultural Marketing Reorganisation in Post War East Africa, In Agricultural Marketing Intervention in East Africa: A Study in the Colonial Origins of Marketing Policies 1900–1965', *The Developing Economies,* vol.11, Issue 3 (September 1973).

Yoshida, Masao, *Agricultural Marketing Intervention in East Africa*, (Tokyo: Institute of Developing Economies, 1984).

Index

African Agriculture Products (Control & Marketing) Ordinance, 1949 106-7, 175, 188-9, 207, 209, 211, 213, 215, 256-7
African Chief (Repeal) Act 13 of 1963 46
African National Congress (ANC) 8, 37, 41-2
Afro-Shirazi Party (ASP) 8, 43-4, 244
Aga Khan 36, 125
Agents 13-14, 99, 101, 103-5, 107, 152-3, 155, 161, 167, 173, 175, 200, 206-7, 209-12, 215, 230, 241, 245, 259-60
Agricultural marketing co-operatives (AMCOs) 37, 126, 128, 140-1, 230, 237, 243, 249-52, 261
Agriculture Officer 57, 69, 73, 79, 81-3, 99
Akida 11, 28-30
All-Muslim National Union of Tanganyika (AMNUT) 8, 41, 45
Amir, Sheikh Hassan bin 35
Arusha 19, 22, 29, 30, 39, 49, 64, 86, 130, 192-3, 226, 247
Arusha Co-operative Stores Limited 193
Arusha Declaration/*Azimio la Arusha* (ArD) 14, 95-6, 233, 237, 240, 246, 249
Asia 20, 58, 116-7, 122, 173, 181, 185
Asians (Indians & Arabs) 12-3, 16-7, 23-4, 29, 34, 37-8, 40-2, 62, 69, 85, 89, 98-9, 101, 103-4, 108, 111, 114, 117, 124-5, 128, 130-2, 134, 137, 144, 146, 151, 154, 163-4, 166-7, 169, 173, 176, 179, 185, 193, 199-200, 204, 208, 212, 217, 219-20, 229-30, 239, 254-7, 259
Attorney General 34, 117
Australia 21, 117, 176
Bagamoyo 19, 29, 94
Baghwaji Sundweji & Company 109
Baines, Denis Lynch 166
Bananas 58, 70, 72, 78, 81-4, 86
Beer / *rubisi* 78, 84
Bennett, Arthur Leslie Brice 118, 136-7, 140
Biharamulo 13, 29, 62-3, 79, 112-3, 120, 155-6, 167, 228, 257
Biologisch–Landwirtschaftliches Institut/Research station 58
Bismarck, Otto von 16
Bomani, Paul 33, 40, 220, 223, 229, 236, 249

Brett, F.H. 156
Bretton Wood 248
Briggs, P.W. 62
British American Tobacco (BAT) 92
British Cotton Growing Association (BCGA) 60, 62, 109, 163
British Prime Minister 50, 246-7, 249
Buchosa 112, 217
Bugabo 77, 105, 168
Bugufi in Biharamulo district (Ngara district) 13, 102, 156-8, 167, 192
Buhaya Coffee Planters Association (BCPA) 214-6
Buhaya Co-operative News 214
Bujumbura 22
Bukoba (Native) Co-operative Union (BCU/BNCU) 40, 105, 191, 198, 209-12, 214-6, 229, 237, 239, 256
Bukoba 26, 28-9, 33, 46, 54-5, 59, 76, 78-80, 84-5, 99-107, 152-4, 156, 167, 169-70, 177, 191-2, 198-200, 205-6, 208, 210-6
Bukoba Coffee (Compulsory Marketing) Order, 1954 154, 215
Bukoba Coffee Control Board (BCCB) 103, 153-4, 205
Bukoba Coffee Curing Plant (BUKOP) 211
Bukoba Co-operative News 214
Bukoba District Coffee Board (BDCB) 102-3, 106, 153
Bukoba Monthly 201
Bukoba Native Coffee Board (BNCB) 8, 13, 103-5, 153-5, 174, 176, 185, 188-9, 206-9, 211-5, 256
Bukoba Produce Export (Coffee) Rules and the Export Inspection 1929 85
Bukoba-Buhaya Union 33
Bukwaya 109
Burundi 11, 18, 27-8, 49, 157, 253, 256
Busegwe 109
Bushiri ibn Salim al Harth 18
Buyagu 236
Byatt, Horace Archer 26-8, 47, 52, 75
Cameron, Donald 30, 32, 118, 134
Campbell, W.K.H. 127, 145, 178-9, 181-3, 186, 192, 205
Carnegie 121, 124
Cashew Nut 226, 259
Cattle Dipping Scheme 91
Central Province 126, 219
Ceylon (Sri Lanka) 58, 100, 115, 127, 187
Chagga (WaChagga) 30, 45, 54, 70-1, 75-6, 100, 107, 126, 129, 132, 136, 142-150, 161, 171, 193, 255

275

Chama Cha Mapinduzi (CCM) 8, 15, 229, 244-5, 250, 261
Chamber of Commerce 52, 85, 104, 130-1, 154, 170
Chapman 209-10
Chaurembo, Said 35
Chibitoke 22
Chiefs (Abolition of Office: Consequential Provisions) Act, 1963 46
Cinchona (quinine) 58
Clark, Lt. Commander A.M. 133
Clove/cloves 150
COASCO (the Audit and Supervision Fund) 246
Coast Region Transport Co-operative (CORETCO) / COCABS 230
Cocoa 33, 101, 205
Coconuts 58
Coffee (Control & Marketing) Ordinance, 1937 101, 147, 153-4, 185, 205-6, 255
Coffee Authority 241, 250
Coffee Export Rules, 1929 85
Coffee Industry (Registration and Improvement) Ordinance, 1928 73, 85, 133
Coffee Industry Act, 1977 250
Coffee Marketing Act, 1984 250
Colonial Development Act, 1929 32, 66
Colonial Development and Welfare Act, 1945 179, 187
Colonial Development Corporation (CDC) 91
Colonial Development Fund 50, 75, 157, 160, 165-6
Colonial Office 8, 13, 27, 56, 90-1, 115-8, 120, 178, 181, 183-6, 188, 194, 205, 256-7
Colonial Research Committee 58
Colonial Standing Finance Committee 198
Commissioner for Co-operative Development 105
Companies Ordinance, 1921 & 1931 118, 216
Congo (Belgian, Democratic Republic of, River, Basin) 16-21, 25
Constitution 14-5, 40, 43-4, 242, 244, 246, 250, 261
Co-operative Acts 116, 180, 247, 251, 261
Co-operative and Societies Act, 1982 247
Co-operative College 180, 246
Co-operative Ordinances 13, 100, 117, 127, 129-31, 139, 164, 186-7, 190-1, 202
Co-operative Societies Acts 187, 234, 241, 249-51, 261

Co-operative Supply Association of Tanganyika (COSATA) 230
Co-operative Union of Tanganyika (CUT) 8, 14-5, 37, 223, 225, 244, 246-7, 261
Cotton Authority 240
Cotton Ordinance 64, 109-11
Creech Jones, Arthur 186
Cripps, Stafford 90
Cunliffe-Lister, Phillip (later Lord Swinton) 119
Cyprus 127, 185, 190
de L. Crore, Italian settler 67
Defence and Emergency Orders 49
Delamere, Lord 55
Department of Agriculture 56-7, 59, 64, 74, 82, 156, 159-60, 174
Department of Co-operative Development 155
Devani, M.M. 37
Development and Welfare Fund 59
Diamond Jubilee Trusts 125
Dockworkers and Stevedore's Union 38
Dundas, Charles Cecil Farquharson 69-70, 73, 75, 98, 117, 132-3
East Africa Community 248
East Africa Royal Commission 91
East African Co-operative Trading Society 193
East African Exporters Group 164, 218
East African School of Co-operation at Kabete, near Nairobi 180
Eastern Cotton Growing Areas (ECGA) 60-1, 63-4
Elder bin Sudi 33
Elections 14, 37, 40-2, 44-5, 73, 90, 118, 138, 185
Elliott, J.S. 206-7
Emergency Power (Defence) Act, 1939 65
Empire Cotton Board 108
Empire Cotton Growing Corporation (ECGC) 56, 59
Engare Nanyuki 39
Ethiopia 17, 181
Experimental stations 58, 60, 63
Fabian Colonial Bureau 13, 101, 183-4, 186, 188, 192, 205
Federation of Free Trade Unions (TFTU) 8, 45
Fela Malampaka 112
Finance and Economics Committee 176
First World War (WW1) 11, 21, 68, 100, 126, 253

Five Year Social and Economic Development Plan 94
Flynn, Major O.A. 84, 119, 135-6, 139-40
Förster, Dr 67-8
Fort Ikoma 22
Geita 29, 58, 112, 217, 221
General Agreement on Trade and Tariffs (GATT) 176
General Agricultural Export Company (GAPEX) 241
General Notice 329, 8 April 1941 103, 153
General Notice 503, 1942 153
Geneva Convention 65
Ghana (Gold Coast) 115
Gibbons, Conon 34
Gifumbiro 22
Ginneries: Luguru, Uzinza, Mugango 62, 65, 68, 108-12, 219-20, 236
Gisenyi 22
Gladstone, William Ewart 50
Government Notice 50, 65, 103, 113, 119, 155, 176, 186, 215, 237
Government Paper 232-3, 238
Greek settlers 19, 51, 69, 71, 98, 146
Groundnuts 91-3, 126, 186, 219
H Bueb (company) 144
Hai 34
Hailey, Lord 180
Hall, George H. 179, 184, 186, 277
Hallier, C.F. 134, 149
Hamis, Ibrahim 33
Hansing & Company 62
Hehe Democratic Party 45
Hitler 146
Holland 78
Horley, A. 207, 209-10
Horne, Major Hastings 56, 61-2, 66, 111
Hulling 84-8, 103, 154, 167-71, 200-1, 204
Hunt, Bruce 146
Ihangiro 77, 83, 105, 168-9, 199, 215
Ikizu 109
Ilonga 58
IMF (International Monetary Fund) 248, 261
Increase Production Campaign 51, 64, 81
India 21, 25, 58, 118, 121, 151, 173, 185, 187
Indian Companies Act 1913 132
Indian Federal Chamber of Commerce 131
Indirect Rule 12, 14, 27, 30-2, 46, 54, 129, 142, 251
International Institute of African Languages and Culture 121
International Labour Organization (ILO) 13, 181, 183

Iramba 29, 219
Iringa 18, 22, 28-9, 45, 48, 91, 145, 192, 226, 228, 235
Ishengoma, G. 210
Ismailia Credit Co-operative Society Ltd 125
Isoko 85
Israel (AMIRAN) 230, 239, 243
Itete 85, 196
Jamaica 117
Jamal, A.H. 37, 42
Japan 21, 49, 102, 173
Jardine, Douglas James 118-9
Jhaveri, K.L. 37
Joint Action Committee 154
Jumbe 11, 28-30
Jumuiya ya Washirika Act of 1979 15, 244, 246, 250
Kabuku, Handeni 94
Kagera Farmers' Co-operative 30, 51, 76-9, 83, 152, 154, 166-9, 172, 175, 185, 191-2, 198-200, 203-5, 208-9, 212-3, 226, 228, 247, 251, 255-7
Kahama 29
Kahama, George Kulwa 40, 209-10, 222, 229
Kamachumu 105, 168, 202, 215
Kamaliza, Michael 44-5
Kampala, Uganda 166, 177, 213
Kandoro, A.S. 33
Karimjee, A.Y.A. 37
Karumo 217
Kasambala, J.S. 225, 229, 239
Kasanga (then Bismarckburg) 22, 45
Kaselabantu, Joseph 33
Kawawa, Rashidi Mfaume 95, 247, 249
Kenya 18, 23-4, 52-3, 58, 92, 98, 122, 127, 134, 150, 166, 173, 176, 193, 199
Kerege, Bagamoyo 94
Kew Gardens 58
Kiamtwara 83, 168, 199
Kianja 45-6, 77, 83, 168, 199
Kiberege 22
Kibondo Division 29, 112-3, 155
Kibong'oto Co-operative Society Limited 140
Kibosho 69, 73, 76, 132-3, 140
Kidasi, Zibe 33
Kiiza, Clemens 33, 168-70, 202-3
Kilimanjaro Co-operative Bank (KCBL) 251
Kilimanjaro Native Co-operative Society (KNCS) 8, 136-7, 139-40
Kilimanjaro Native Co-operative Union (KNCU) 8, 13, 75, 96, 100-2, 106-8, 119,

126-9, 132, 138-50, 165, 171, 175, 177, 191, 200, 202, 204-5, 209, 237-40, 255
Kilimanjaro Native Planters Association (KNPA) 8, 13, 73-6, 98, 114, 117-9, 127-9, 132-41, 148, 162-3, 168, 171, 181, 200, 202-3, 255
Kilimatinde 19, 22
Kilwa 29, 60, 196
Kimisha Co-operative Union Manager 221, 236
Kimwani Native Coffee (Compulsory Marketing) Order, 1954 215
King's African Rifles (KAR) 11, 24-5, 49
Kingolwira 58
Kinyangereko 168
Kipyanabayanda Co-operative Union 236
Kirilo, Japhet 39-40
Kirua Vunjo Co-operative Society 69, 76, 107
Kisumu 111, 166
Kitete 94
Kivu 23
Kiwira 87-8, 165, 196
Kiziba 77, 83, 105, 168, 199
Kondoa 22, 29, 219
Kongwa 93, 126
Koonialwirtschaftliches Komitee (KWK) 60
Korean War 176
Korogwe 19, 60
Kusi, Raikes 33
Kwamtoro 22
Kwimba 29, 62-3, 112, 126, 162-3, 221, 256
Kyela 88-9, 166, 194-6, 198
Kyimbila 85
Lake Province Growers Association (LPGA) 218-20
Lake Tanganyika 19, 26, 28
Lake Victoria Nyanza 19
Land Development and Soil Conservation Schemes 91
League of Nations 11-2, 26, 33-4, 53-4, 75, 127, 134, 146, 151, 180, 253-5
Legislative Council (LEGCO) 8, 34-5, 37, 39-40, 101, 107, 117-8, 136-7, 151-2, 154, 163, 167, 175, 190, 229
Leguruki 39
Lema, Stefano 73, 76, 133, 140
Lettow-Vorbeck, Paul Emil von 11, 22-3, 25-6
Lindi 22, 29, 48, 58, 64, 235
Lint and Seed Marketing Board (LSMB) 8, 107

Livestock (cattle, sheep, goats) 38-9, 93, 121, 228, 250, 252
Liwale 22
Lubaga, Shinyanga 58
Luguru 68, 94, 109, 221
Lyamungo 76, 145
MacGregor, C.J. 113, 155
Machame 69, 71, 76, 140, 144-5
Mackenzie-Kennedy, Henry Charles Donald Cleveland 122
MacMahon, C. 171
Madibira 22
Mahenge 18, 22, 25, 28, 48, 114, 161
Maji-maji 18, 60
Majisu, Suleiman 33
Maktano, Abel bin 147
Makwai, Chief 34
Malawi (Nyasaland) 17, 20, 23-4, 49, 88-9, 127
Malaysia (Malaya) 100, 115-7, 120
Malcolm, Robin Sydney Wyld 113, 155, 180
Maliti, Joseph 135, 137
Manamba / Migrant labour 49
Mandate 11, 26-8, 32-4, 52, 77, 98, 102, 114, 129, 142, 146, 163, 185, 199, 210, 241, 253, 260,
Manow 85, 87-8, 165
Manufactured goods 16, 50, 184
Marealle, Chief of Marangu 67
Marlborough House Constitution 40
Marua bin Kishimbo 147
Masama 76, 145
Masebe 87-8, 165, 196
Masoko 87-8, 165
Masuwa, Gideon 69, 71
Maswa 29, 94, 219, 221
Matola, Cecil 33
Mawala, Sawaya 67
Mbatama, Klemence Kiiza 105, 169
Mbeya 29-30, 85-9, 130, 195, 197, 226, 228, 235, 247
Mbozi 85, 87-8, 130, 165, 194-7
Mbulu 22, 29, 39-40, 91, 228
Meghji, Ladha 109
Merinyo, Joseph 67, 70-1, 73, 132-3
Meru 30, 39, 51-2, 55, 130, 192, 229
Mgemela, Chief of Bakwimba 162-2
Mhando, Stephen 35
Mhaville Committee, 1966 (Committee of Enquiry into the Co-operatives Movement and Marketing Boards) 231
Ministry of Food 91, 102-3, 106-7, 127, 153, 155, 173-4, 176-7, 206, 209, 212-3

Missionaries (White Fathers, Moravian) 11, 17, 29, 47, 52, 55-6, 60, 85-6, 88,98, 144, 146
Mitchell, Philip E. 55, 117, 120, 122
Mkalama 22
Mkwawa, Chief 18
Mlale, Songea 94
Mombasa, Kenya 19, 99, 111, 153, 166, 167, 172, 177, 199, 200, 212-3, 215
Mombo 19
Morogoro 19, 29, 56, 58, 60-1, 64, 138, 180, 226, 228, 235, 237
Moshi Native Coffee Board (MNCB) 8, 13, 101, 147-8, 152
Mozambique 16, 20, 23, 25, 49
Mpanganya 56,58
Mpima, Ali Said 33
Mpuguso 86
Mpwapwa 19, 29, 126, 138
Msuya, Cleopa 249
Mtemvu, Zuberi M. 37, 40, 42
Mukigoye 156
Munanka, Bokhe 33
Musoma 29, 33, 112, 221
Mwakaleli 85, 87-8, 165, 196
Mwakilima (headman) 88
Mwanza 19, 29, 57-8, 62-4, 68, 111-2, 125, 192, 221, 226, 236, 247
Mwanza African Traders Consumer Cooperative Society (MATCS) 193, 217
Mwanza Credit Co-operative Society Ltd 125
Mwapachu, Hamza Master 35
Mwaya (Mbeya) 89, 196
Mweli Co-operative Union 217
Mwinyi, Ali Hassan 249
Mwivuza 156
Myanmar (Burma) 117-8, 121
Nachingwea 29, 93
Nangale, K.K. 247
Nansio 112
Nasa 33
National Distributors Limited (NDL) 8, 260
National Economic Survival Programme (NESP) 248
National Milling Corporation (NMC) 8, 240-1, 260
National Products (Control & Marketing) Act, 1962 258-9
National Union of Post Office and Telecommunications' Employees 38
National Union of Tanganyika Workers (Establishment) Act 1964 45

National Union of Tanganyika Workers (NUTA) 8, 45
Native Agriculture Control Bill 150
Native Authorities 12, 29, 31, 47, 53, 62, 77, 79, 111, 129, 134, 194, 255
Native Authority (Extension of Powers) Cultivation of Cotton Order, 1935 65
Native Coffee (Compulsory Marketing) Order, 1937 & 1947 103, 153-4, 215
Native Coffee Ordinance, 1937 101, 148, 150
Native Credit Ordinance 55
Native Growers Association (NGA) 8, 168-71, 202-4, 214, 256
Native Produce Board 152
Native Treasury No. 2 Account 12, 162, 194-5, 197, 254
Ndetanyo, Charles 107
Ngara 13, 78-9, 88, 113, 155-7, 253, 255-6
Ngombale-Mwiru, Kingunge 249
Ngoni Matengo Co-operative Union (NGOMAT) 9, 156, 158-61, 174-5, 191
Nigeria 12, 20, 27, 30, 52
Njombe 29, 49, 228
North Africa 78
Northcote, Ronald Cecil 100, 120-4, 138, 146, 161, 167-70, 174, 179, 185-7, 200-4, 223, 257
Northern Province 39, 134, 136
Nyamihanga 79, 156
Nyamirembe Native Tobacco Board 113, 155, 174
Nyerere, Julius Kambarage 35-6, 42-3, 95, 238, 249
Nzega 29, 64
Oldham, J.H. 171
Organisation of Tanzania Trade Unions (OTTU) 8, 45
Ormsby-Gore, W. 34, 100, 102
Overseas Food Corporation (OFC) 91, 126
Overseas Resource Development Bill 90
Pangani 19, 29
Paris / Versailles Peace talks 1919 11, 26-7, 52
Pasha, Emin 76
Patel, D.K. 37
Patterson, G.D. 133
Pennington, A.L. 135-6
People's Convention Party (PCP) 41, 45
People's Democratic Party (PDP) 8, 41, 44-45
Perkins, Major 136
Plant Pest and Disease Regulation, 1928 73-4, 133

Plunkett Foundation 115, 185
Portugal/Portuguese colonies 16-7, 20-1, 23, 27
Post Office 38, 125-6
President/Presidential 14-5, 35, 41-3, 45, 73, 95-6, 133, 135, 151, 168, 170, 202, 220, 230-1, 233-4, 236-7, 239, 246, 249, 251
Preventative Detention Act, 1962 42
Provincial Commissioner 8, 28, 123, 134, 152, 164, 194
Pyrethrum 127, 226
Railway 13, 19, 23, 26, 38, 99, 111-2
Rajan, Habibu 169
Rattansey, M.N. 37
Regional Trading Companies (RTCs) 8, 260
Registrar of Co-operative Societies 100, 106, 113, 119-20, 127, 138, 146, 161, 174-5, 179-80, 186, 188, 190, 195-6, 203, 216, 218, 222, 247, 256
Registration of Plantation Act, 1929 86
Registration of Societies Ordinance, 1954 35
Revington, T.M. 207
Rice 88-9, 114, 165-6, 194-8, 226, 260
Riots 84, 101, 144-50, 169, 172, 181, 205
Rochdale and Raiffesein co-operative principles 125, 143, 189, 244
Rombo 69, 76
Rubber 58
Rufiji 24-5, 29, 60, 64, 88
Rugarabamu, G.M. 210
Rugazibwa, Herbert 168, 170, 202-3, 214-6
Ruhinda, Chief 169
Rukwa 49, 235
Rungwe 29, 51, 55, 85-8, 165, 191-2, 194-8
Rupia, John 35
Rutenganio 85
Ruvu 93
Ruvuma 13, 25, 55, 161, 167, 192, 226, 228, 235, 255
Rwanda 11, 18, 27-8, 49, 157, 253, 256
Sanjo 22
Savile, A.H. 156
Sayers, Gerald Fleming 122
Schnee, Dr Heinrich 18, 21-3, 25
Scupham, W.E. 122
Selya 87-8, 165
Shangali, Abdiel 149
Shangali, Abdiel 34, 149
Sheridan, Joseph Alfred 117
Sheriff Jiwa 105, 144, 200
Shija, Masanja 220

Shinyanga 19, 29, 34, 58, 63-4, 109, 112, 192, 221, 226, 235-6, 247
Shipman, E.L. 89, 195, 197
SHIRECU 247
Simon, John 146
Singida 29, 145, 219, 226, 228, 235, 237
Sisal 8, 12, 49, 51, 64, 77, 152, 226
Smith, H.P. 136
Smuggling 104, 212-5, 256-7
Smuts, General Jan 26-7
Socialism and Rural Development (*Ujamaa na Maendeleo Vijijini*) 95, 238
Solomon, Addiel 146
Somaliland 158
Songea 13, 22, 29-30, 48-9, 94, 102, 158-61, 174, 209
South Africa 21, 27, 89, 121-2
South West Highlands Province 164
Southern Highlands 48-9, 51, 85, 145, 164, 191-2, 194, 255, 257
Stenhouse, A.S. 159
Strachey, John 90
Strickland, C.F. 117, 125, 128-9, 141-2
Structural Adjustment Programmes (SAPs) 248-9
Suez Canal 16, 173
Sugar 58, 259
Sukuma (also Wasukuma) 24, 30, 38-9, 91, 217
Sukumaland 38, 100, 200
Sultan Koroso 88
Sumbawanga 145
Supplies and Services (Transitional) Power Act, 1945 65
Surridge, B.J. 185
Suspension Accounts 12
Swai, Asanterabi Zaphaniah Nsilo 229
Swynnerton, C.F.M. 66
Sykes, Abdulwahid 35
Sykes, Kleist 33
Tabora 19, 22, 26, 29, 37, 49, 64, 111, 120, 130, 138, 171, 226, 228, 235
Tanga 19, 29, 33, 48-9, 54-5, 64, 125, 166, 192-3, 226, 228, 235, 237, 252
Tanga Co-operative Trading 193
Tanganyika African Association (TAA) 8, 13, 33, 35, 39-40, 170, 202-3
Tanganyika African Custom Union 38
Tanganyika African Local Government Workers Union 38
Tanganyika African National Union (TANU) 8, 13-4, 35-46, 214, 216, 225, 227, 229, 244, 246-7
Tanganyika African Union (TRAU) 9, 44

Tanganyika Agricultural Corporation (TAC) 93
Tanganyika Asian Civil Servants' Association 38
Tanganyika Civil Servants' Association 38
Tanganyika Coffee Growers Association (TCGA) 130
Tanganyika Co-operative Trading 193
Tanganyika Domestic and Hotel Workers Union 38
Tanganyika Federation of Labour (TFL) 8, 37-8, 44-5
Tanganyika Indian Association 151
Tanganyika Mine Workers' Union 38
Tanganyika Opinion 151
Tanganyika Plantation Workers' Union 38
Tanganyika Railway African Union (TRAU) 38
Tanganyika Territory African Civil Service Association (TTACSA) 33
Tanganyika Union of Public Employees 38
Tanzania Coffee Marketing Board (TCMB) 250
Tarime 33, 228
Taxes (Poll, Hut) 11-2, 28, 30-2, 47-8, 50, 53, 70, 107, 157, 254
Tea 51, 58
Tengeru 57
Tobacco (Control & Marketing) Ordinance, 1940 112, 155, 161, 175
Tobacco 11-2, 27, 51, 53, 56, 59, 77, 92-4, 112-3, 152, 155, 158-61, 167, 174-5, 192, 226, 254
Trade Disputes (Settlement) (Arbitration & Settlement) Act **43, 1962** 45
Trade Union Ordinance (Amendment) Act, 1962 44
Training school 38
Transport and General Workers' Union 38
Trusteeship Council 34, 39
Tukuyu 86, 102
Tumbo, C.S.Kasanga 42, 44-5
Twining, Edward 35
Ubinza 64
Uganda 19, 23-4, 58, 60, 62-3, 78, 84, 98-9, 107-8, 122, 127, 156, 163-4, 166-167, 173, 176-7, 182, 190, 199, 205, 212-3, 248-9
Ujamaa 95, 236-9, 241-3, 247-8, 261
Ujiji (Kigoma) 19, 22
Ukerewe 29, 33, 60-1, 109, 112, 217, 221

Ukiriguru in Mwanza 57-8
Ukwega 22
Uluguru 39
Umero 22
Undali 87-8, 165
Unified Cooperative Service & Commission 232-3, 246
Union of Co-operative Societies (UCS; *Jumuiya ya Muungano wa Vyama vya Ushirika*) 9, 244-6
United Kingdom Treasury 50, 77, 156, 166
United Nations Organisation (UNO) 9, 13, 34, 36, 39, 181, 183, 192, 205, 216, 255
United States of America (USA) 16, 20-1, 60, 90
United Tanganyika Party (UTP) 9, 36-7, 42
Unyakyusa Co-operative Union 192, 198
Upper Kitete, Karatu 94
Urambo 92-3
Uremi 143, 149
Usa 130, 140, 173
Usambara 19, 39, 91, 130, 192, 247
Ushahi 109
Ushirika 138, 223, 244
Usiha-Samuye 34
Usmao 94
Usogore 68, 109
Uzinza in Geita 58, 109
Victoria Federation of Co-operative Unions (VFCUs) 9, 40, 220-1, 229, 231, 235-7, 239, 258
Village and Ujamaa Village Act, 1975 242, 261
Village Development Committees 95
Wafikiri African Union Association of Sengerema 217
WaHaya 30, 54, 78, 84, 171
WaHehe 18, 45
Wakulima Stadi 217
Wakulima wa Kiafrika 217
WaNyambo 78, 84
Wanyamwezi 24
War Emergency Orders Ordinance, 1939 & 1940 153
Watts, Rawson 33
Webb, Sidney (Lord Passfield) 115, 118-9
West Africa 13, 16, 20, 25, 101, 205
West Indies 100
Western Cotton Growing Area (WCGA) (Sukumaland) 9, 37-9, 49, 57, 60-4, 94, 107-9, 111-2, 162-4, 192-3, 200, 208, 216-9, 228, 239, 249, 254-5, 257-8

Western Province (Kigoma Region) 49, 112-3, 155
Wheat 94, 127, 260
White settlers 36, 55, 132
Winster, Lord 146
Wood, RC 56
World Bank 94, 248, 261
Young, Archibald 156
Zambia (North Rhodesia) 23, 25-6, 49
Zanzibar 12, 16, 20, 24, 43-4, 89, 117, 121, 150, 245, 253
Zimbabwe (Southern Rhodesia) 52-3, 127
Zinza Union (see also Uzinza) 217

www.ingramcontent.com/pod-product-compliance
Lightning Source LLC
Chambersburg PA
CBHW031802220426
43662CB00007B/503